CHAOS THEORY
IN PSYCHOLOGY

Edited by
Frederick David Abraham
and
Albert R. Gilgen

PRAEGER

Westport, Connecticut
London

The Library of Congress has cataloged the hardcover edition as follows:

Chaos theory in psychology / edited by Frederick David Abraham and
    Albert R. Gilgen.
        p. cm.—(Contributions in psychology, ISSN 0736–2714 ; no.
    27)
       Includes bibliographical references and index.
       ISBN 0–313–28961–1 (alk. paper)
       1. Philosophy and psychology. 2. Science and psychology.
       3. Chaotic behavior in systems. I. Abraham, Frederick David.
       II. Gilgen, Albert R. III. Series.
       BF44.C48   1995
       150'.1—dc20   94–29848

British Library Cataloguing in Publication Data is available.

A hardcover edition of *Chaos Theory in Psychology* is available from Greenwood
Press, an imprint of Greenwood Publishing Group, Inc. (Contributions in
Psychology, Number 27; ISBN 0–313–28961–1).

Library of Congress Catalog Card Number: 94–29848
ISBN: 0–275–95140–5

First published in 1995

Praeger Publishers, 88 Post Road West, Westport, CT 06881
An imprint of Greenwood Publishing Group, Inc.

Printed in the United States of America

The paper used in this book complies with the
Permanent Paper Standard issued by the National
Information Standards Organization (Z39.48–1984).

10 9 8 7 6 5 4 3 2 1

Chaos refers to the complex patterns formed by interactive convergent and divergent forces in dynamical systems. We dedicate this book to the spirit of diversity and the spirit of cooperativity that make for the beautiful chaos that is the human enterprise, and to the hope that more fulfillment of the human potential, more joy, and less suffering may be realized as we bifurcate to even better attractors.

We also dedicate this book to the pioneering students who are beginning to explore the potentialities of dynamics for the improvement of our science and its application to the improvement of the human condition. We hope their confidence and enthusiasm in the approach will find some reinforcement or succor from the tentative offerings in this modest volume.

Chaoharmonically
Fred & Al

Contents

Illustrations

FIGURES

TABLES

Prefatory Comments

Albert R. Gilgen

As Program Chair of Division 24, Theoretical and Philosophical Psychology, for the 1992 Bicentennial Convention of the American Psychological Association, I became interested in organizing a program based on a single theme. Because I have a strong interest in the causes underlying conceptual fragmentation and strategies for reducing it, I decided the presentations would focus on models used by psychologists to depict the complexities of the psychological and behavioral domains. I was thinking about stimulus-response conceptions, Lewin's life space, mathematical learning models, cybernetic schemes, computer-inspired architectures, recent connectionist formulations, and so forth. Putting such a program together turned out to be too ambitious an undertaking, but as I discussed my idea with Karl Pribram, whom I invited to update the status of his holographic model of brain functioning, he suggested it would be interesting and timely to have some presentations dealing with the relevance of chaos theory for psychology. I agreed, and called Fred Abraham, one of the founders of the Society for Chaos Theory in Psychology. As a consequence, the program included an invited address on chaos theory by Fred and two symposia. The positive response of those who attended the presentations was the inspiration for this book.

Articles in *Science* and *Nature* on chaos theory, nonlinear dynamics, fractals, and self-organizing systems first caught my attention in the late 1980s. All these interrelated conceptions have to do with ordering processes and complexity and they clearly appeared relevant to psychology. The ability to depict the structure of complex systems, even when short-term prediction is not usually possible, was especially intriguing. This seemed to imply that rather than reducing the intricacies of a complex situation via experimental restrictions or statistical manipulations, one could design research projects that revealed the patterns of change that define the system. The thought occurred to me that psychologists could now study the whole elephant rather than mere bits and pieces. Such an approach to psychological inquiry is, of course, intrinsically integrative and may offer strategies for generating a truly comprehensive body of psychological knowledge.

However, if we want to harness the full potential of chaos theory, there is some homework that we need to do. First, we should examine the ways that we typically deal with complexity; next, we must derive formal procedures for identifying ecologically valid variables and units of analysis; then, we should make more sustained efforts to identify the commonalities among major psychological theories; and, finally, we have to familiarize ourselves with the work of those who have made systematic efforts to determine the relationships among major psychological states and processes. Let me briefly elaborate.

Except when we construct theories or engage in explicitly integrative research, we generally deal with complexity by restricting the options of our subjects and taking out of play things we cannot control via experimental designs. Descriptive statistics reduce the inherent complexities of group data via means, standard deviations, or other summarizing values; and inferential statistics give us information about the likelihood that the variables singled out for study had the predicted effect. In other words, we deal mostly with complexity by trying to reduce, or neutralize, aspects of it.

The determination of ecologically valid, or representative, units of analysis and variables is necessary in order to identify the systems with the most integrative potential. If this time-consuming and challenging work is not done, there is danger that efforts to apply chaos theory to psychological inquiry will be superficial and constitute a passing fad. To a considerable extent, the work called for here involves examining existing classificatory schemes, determining their interrelationships, and, perhaps, deriving new organizational formats. More specifically, this requires inventorying and integrating typologies of people, stages-of-psychological-development conceptions, and taxonomies of psychological states, actions, tasks, routines, plan-structured segments of life, typical situations and environments, and essential contexts.

A good starting point is to read Egon Brunswik's short but insightful book, *Systematic and Representative Design of Psychological Experiments* (1947), which provides guidelines for designing ecologically valid studies. Brunswik points out that just as psychometricians attempt to select subjects who are representative of the populations they investigate, so experimentalists should select environmental features and responses representative of the surrounds and actions, respectively, of the individuals they study. If a research project is representative in the Brunswikian sense, one may reasonably argue that it deals with a natural system worthy of investigation and modeling (we may even get a glimpse of the whole elephant).

Given the comparative analyses of models of mind and consciousness, personality theories, and theories of human psychological development, we need to encourage efforts to identify the dynamic structural features common to all viewpoints or, if not common, at least compatible. This will help us identify the primary dimensions of the psychological domain and assist in selecting the temporal and spatial units of analysis that, when measured, define that domain. To begin with, examination of the work of such integrationists as Arthur Staats, Robert Zajonc, Stanley Schacter, Silvan Tomkins, Richard Lazarus, and James Gibson, who have examined the commonalities or relationships among particular concepts or psychological states, will surely provide useful insights.

Among the practical benefits eventually deriving from the aforementioned scholarly initiatives, would be, first, a reduction in the number of articles published annually in psychological journals (narrowly-focused research reports would be replaced by comprehensive project analyses), thereby facilitating information retrieval; second, an impetus to do collaborative research because of the need for extensive data acquisition; and third, the provision of an incentive to identify large databases that might benefit from nonlinear metamodeling. For example, it might be worth reanalyzing some of the extensive information on military personnel gathered during World War II. For me, the most rewarding aspect of this foray into the dynamics of fascinating complexities has been to meet and interact with American psychologists already deeply involved in pursuing the insights provided by chaos theory. I have especially enjoyed working with Fred Abraham whose agile mind, dynamic personality, giving spirit, and enthusiasm have energized me. The horizons of psychological science are expanding rapidly, and psychologists who fail to inform themselves about the techniques available for representing and analyzing complex systems will be left behind. Furthermore, those who share my interest in devising strategies for constructing a more integrated body of psychological knowledge cannot ignore the potentialities of nonlinear metamodeling.

REFERENCE

Brunswik, E. (1947). *Systematic and representative design of psychological experiments.* Berkeley: University of California Press.

The Leibniz-Abraham Correspondence

Gottfried Wilhelm Freiherr von Leibniz and Frederick David Abraham

The following letter from Leibniz was received at the First Annual Conference of the Society for Chaos Theory in Psychology, August 1991. It was delivered and read to Fred by Allan "Hermes" Combs; it was prepared by Fred, who Hermes-trickestered Allan into playing Hermes-the-messenger because Allan had written on Hermes in his great book *Synchronicity* (Combs & Holland, 1990); Fred's ad lib reply is herein reconstructed for your amusement or disgust, as the case might be.

Gottfried Wilhelm Freiherr von Leibniz
Hanover

15 August 1991

Kind Sir, and the Honorable Assemblage,

Greetings to all the enthusiastic and wonderful scholars gathered at this auspicious inaugural conference of the Society for Chaos Theory in Psychology. Fred, I thought you might need a little help expressing the importance of the theme of the unified language potential for Psychology in the geometry of the nonlinear dynamical systems approach that has evolved from my work.

> Perhaps no mortal has yet seen into the true basis upon which everything can be assigned its characteristic number. . . . And although learned men have long since thought of some kind of language or universal characteristic by which all concepts and things can be put into beautiful order, . . . yet no one has attempted a language or characteristic. . . . A far greater secret lies hidden in our understanding, of which these are but the shadows.

> I said that . . . we ought also to have a new class of categories in which propositions or complex terms themselves may be arranged in their natural order . . . at that time [I] did not know that the geometricians do exactly what I was seeking when they arrange propositions in an order such that one is demonstrated from the other. . . . I necessarily arrived at this remarkable thought, namely that a kind of alphabet of human thoughts can be worked out and that everything can be discovered and judged by a comparison of the letters of this alphabet and an analysis of the words made from them. GC, pp. 221-222

> But when the tables or categories of our art of complication have been formed, something greater will emerge. For let the first terms, of the combination of which all others consist, be designated by signs; these signs will be a kind of alphabet. It will be convenient for the signs to be as natural as possible—e.g. for one, a point; for numbers, point; for the relations of one entity to another, lines; for the variation of angles or of extremities in line, kinds of relations. AC, p. 11

And for motion and temporal change in complex interactions, my "conatus" and "trace," which you call vector and trajectory, have developed into attractors and phase portraits, thus extending my geometry of motion.

> If these are correctly and ingeniously established, this universal writing will be as easy as it is common, and will be capable of being read without any dictionary; at the same time, a fundamental knowledge of all things will be obtained. The whole of such a writing will be made of geometrical figures, as it were, and of a kind of pictures —just as the ancient Egyptians did, and the Chinese do today. AC, p. 11

I thus developed a "science of sciences"[AC/T] as a scientific metaparadigm, which you and your friends are attempting to further develop at your conference. S. S.

Stevens picked up on that, appropriately calling Psychology "propaedeutic." It is to the credit of the Society that you have seen the importance of my work and are now carrying it into its next stage of fruition, a paradigm shift percolating since the unity of science movement of the 1930s and made possible by your fancy toys. The IRIS and other supreme graphics computers are wonderful extensions of my "Stepped Reckoner" and especially important because "further complications and difficulties are necessary to return from the equation[s] to the construction[s], from [algebraic calculus] back to geometry." [GS, p. 254]

In *Dissertation on the Art of Combinations* (1666) I developed these ideas as the *lingua universalis, ars combinatoria, scientia universalis, calculus philosophicus, calculus universalis, character, and characteristica generalis*, and then more fully in the *Dialogue on the Connection Between Things and Words* (1677), *Studies in a Geometry of Situation* (1679), *On the General Characteristic* (1679), and finally in my summary of dynamics which is in *Specimen Dynamicum* (1695). Thus "this more adequate and simple science of geometrical figures, independent of algebra, is due to the invention of the universal character for 'objects of imagination.'" [T, p. 26]

These geometric universal characteristics, as developed largely since Poincaré, and especially in the last three decades, and which constitute, of course, the principle language of your conference and your science, are dynamical systems (vectorfields), phase portraits (including point, cyclic, and chaotic attractors; repellors; saddles; basins; separatices, etc), response diagrams (especially when revealing subtle, catastrophic, and explosive bifurcations), and network diagrams of complex systems and self-organization. Please summarize these in your *Introduction to Dynamics*; I would be enormously grateful as these now constitute the universal language and metaparadigm of science and knowledge, including, thanks largely to all of your efforts, psychology. While your field has had some converts over the past fifteen years, it will be largely due to the efforts of those here assembled, my disciples, to entirely transform your science, such that within five years, virtually every theory in psychology will be dynamical. Either your society will wither away from success or the other societies will be absorbed by you. The choice will be yours.

A caveat is in order. When I wrote "once the characteristic numbers for most concepts have been set up, however, the human race will have a new kind of instrument which will increase the power of the mind . . . which will be as far superior to microscopes or telescopes as reason is superior to sight," [GC, p. 224] I perhaps overstated the case. Characteristic exponents, multipliers, and fractal dimensionality do not an attractor make, they simply represent some of its important properties. My differential equations and my geometrical dynamics are necessary for a full representation of the attractor. As I have also stressed, motion creates form, dimensionality is not limited to integer values. It is to be remembered that universal characteristics are not arbitrary, as "there is some relation or order in the characters which is also in things, . . . there is in them a kind of complex mutual relation or order which fits things; [but] whether we apply one set of characters or another, the products will be the same." [DC, p. 184] In short, different models or equation sets may produce similar attractors which may adequately model the same reality.

Thank you for your kind indulgence, I hope this has provided some support for your efforts to establish my work as the universal scientific metaparadigm.

Yours,

Gottfried

8/15/91

Gottfried Wilhelm Freiherr von Leibniz
Hanover, Germany

Dear Gottfried:

Thank you for your kind assistance. Indeed, without it I would certainly have great difficulty articulating such ideas or convincing this August and spirited group of the universality of the visual language and scientific metaparadigm of dynamical systems in vectorfields, phase portraits, self-organization, and complex systems. As you also know, modern science and philosophy of science have inherited many other of your insights, taking over 200 years for many of your ideas to receive the major influence they deserve. Although your own thinking transcended operationism, you provided its basis, not fully appreciated until Bridgman (1927). You laid the foundations for logical positivism, and for hypotheticodeductive formalism in scientific modeling. You especially saw that all forms of knowledge come up against boundaries (thick fractal separatrices) beyond which one cannot see. Although technological advances may push these frontiers back (sometimes with major bifurcations or paradigm shifts, one of which is now being provided by your dynamical systems approach itself), few individuals have your clarity of reasoning or vision or motivation to see beyond these fractal barriers.

Your paradoxically individualized ecumenicism in all things gave you the vision to seek communalities. Your quest for synthesis in Chinese philosophy (Mungello, 1977), which in general was incomplete due to the neo-Confucist provincialism of the Seventeenth-century Jesuits in the Ch'ing dynasty courts following the long chaotic bifurcation from the Ming dynasty, nonetheless revealed this capacity. Your interest in Fu Hsi's diagrams, the hexagrams of the Book of Changes, because of their correspondence to your interest in binary mathematics has come full circle also in providing the foundation of information theory, itself of universal appeal, and which, in turn, has been applied to dynamical systems and iterative maps following the lead of Rob Shaw and which shares the paradoxical feature of throwing out informational infancy with the mathematical bathwater, as you mentioned in your letter with respect to attractor dimensionality. Also, the complementariness of *li* and *ch'i* as it relates to your own principles of universal pattern and fixed essences as with the monads, anticipated modern physical concepts of energy and matter enunciated by Albert Einstein and also the quantum physicists. Your speculations make the New Age discussions of such matters seem like childish exercises. But I must leave these matters to the Leibniz scholars, for my own knowledge of your work is most rudimentary. Rather, I should mention some implications of the dynamical systems approach for benefits to the field of psychology today.

First is its minimal role in providing a better modeling and research and design strategy that emphasizes temporal patterns of change among interactive variables. Models emphasize deterministic trajectories summarized in phase portraits, dynamical systems, and dynamical schemes. Research recovers information in the form of trajectories and associated measures such as fractal dimension. Much of such recovered information has hitherto been discarded as error in the linear (causally and mathematically) strategies of the past. As a metamodeling strategy, it is still no cleverer than the explanatory concepts conjured up by the scientist. You still have to be imaginative. In this minimal sense, it should satisfy the most operationally bound enthusiasts. I'll call this the Level 1 Benefit. It provides Abraham's First Posiplatitude: *Dynamics is essential to progress in science, but you still have to think.*

Second, your concepts of encyclopedia and universal language, were restated by Neurath in the lead-off article in the International Encyclopedia of Unified Science (1938), as goals of communicating better in science, holding to communalities despite diversifying trends in science, minimizing the isolation due to proliferating, shrinking idiosyncratic scientific island domains, and reducing any estrangement of science from personal and social problems. Within psychology, there is a principal schism between the analytical, operational, or reductionistic approach, with the subject as "it," versus the holistic approach, stressing complexity and process, with the subject of study more enveloped in the "I-Thou" intimacy of Martin Buber. From the Platonic ideals to the Bridgman operationism, the ecstasy of order has been characterized by what Eisler (1987) might call the dominator model of science, while from the pre-Socratic-Taoist to Lewinian Gestaltism, the ecstasy of chaos is better characterized by what Eisler might call the cooperative (she used the term *gylanic*, combining the greek roots *gyne* for woman and *an* for man) model of science. Analytic and holistic, order and chaos, like yin/yang or *li/ch'i*, are but complementary perspectives of the same reality, according to the views of dynamics, Heraclitus, Lao-Tzu, and yourself, our dear Leibniz. In giving an analytic tool to the holist camp of psychology and a holistic tool to the analytic camp of psychology, dynamics may provide the control parameter leading to a bifurcation uniting these two camps. Or at least, as their differences are not likely to be wholly eliminated, it may allow them to more easily see the legitimate claims of the other, to borrow from each other, and to reduce their occassional animosities. Besides breaking asunder this fundamental schism—and we must remember that this schism is deeply rooted in the personalities of the participants, so that this view implies bifurcations in the personalities of the participants—dynamics also allows easy communication and theoretical fusion among many disciplines, especially vertically across many levels of scale of size and time. I'll call this the Level 2 Benefit: the encyclopedia of unified psychology. It is characterized by Abraham's

First Gylaniplatitude: *You can set all the psychologists on the same mountain, and although they may not ski the same line through the bumps, they can each show off in the assurance they will be appreciated by a larger audience.* Their coupling constants will be greater, though not as tight as my friends Didi and "Smitty" Stevens, who skied with their arms about each other. DynamSKI, the universal language, unites skiers from the diverse disciplines of cross country, telemarking, alpine skiing, jumping, and freestyle skiing, not only with each other, but with equestrians, artists, and corporate managers.

René Thom (1972/1975) and Christopher Zeeman (1977) are recent pioneers of the revitalization of your thought, in versions they called *morphogenesis* and *catastrophe theory.* Their approach gave prominance to bifurcations in modeling for science and psychology. Both of them stressed Level 1 and Level 2 ideas, though René followed the lead of your geometry of motion in stressing the primacy of visual intuition in modeling and communication in mathematics and science. Christopher pushed beyond René's acceptance of face validity in modeling to stress the need for scientific verification. These are views to which my mathematician brother Ralph and I are dedicated.

Third, we now get religious. The dynamical systems approach provides visions about what psychology should be, not only about its strategies, just discussed as a Level 1 Benefit, but about its subject matter. It motivates especially strong convictions about the chaotic and complex nature of psychological phenomena. Although we imagine, and the history of our science is replete with examples, that many psychological phenomena may be modeled by homeostatic point attractors or chronobiopsychological periodic attractors, we believe that these can be found in only the most constrained experimental conditions, and that these usually bifurcate to chaotic attractors. We believe that chaos represents the true nature of most psychological phenomena, and that disorderly features of behavior are not merely due to the vicissitudes of the impact of a disorderly environment, but are inherent within the processes under investigation. It can provide the alphabet of thought as you said because it represents the complexity of mind, brain, and behavior (or, rather, it has the potential to do so). We believe that chaos is the archetype that drives the universe, is its deep structure. Behavioral and cognitive processes are chaotic.

When you peer down the highest-powered electron microscope, at the output of the most potent accelerators, through the most probing telescopes, into the most rigorous behavioral apparatus studying inductive phenomena, or into the deepest cognitive event, neural net, or cellular molecular substrate, you run into that limit to knowledge, that imposing fractal separatrix that you and I have mentioned before. The operationist says, here is the limit of what science can do. And it is good to define the limits of the scientific enterprise, as you have emphasized. But you have also demonstrated that the thinking scientist hill-climbs into the next basin, becoming a mystic, drawn into the ultimate chaotic attractors, imagining what lies beyond the limits. The dynamics viewpoint stimulates the imagination for making this climb.

This awareness and conviction of the chaotic "nature of things," to borrow your phrase, is a benefit of dynamics to psychology that represents a deeper level, what I'll call the Level 3 Benefit: faith in the myth of the chaos/dynamical archetype and the ubiquity of chaos in psychological phenomena.

The Level 4 Benefit, the deepest level, Gottfried, is the importance of self-organization in all psychological processes. Self-organization (self-control) mainly refers to control of a system from within the system by acting upon its control parameters. It may be immediate or intermediated by interaction with other systems. It may also include even the creation and modification of bifurcation possibilities and of use of dimensions of control and state spaces, and the very dynamical systems being parametrically controlled. It is especially important because it is the vehicle by which a system may cause its own transformations, its own bifurcations. Another aspect of this conviction focuses on the belief that most complex psychological and social systems undergo irreversible bifurcations, are hierarchically organized, evolve progressively toward greater complexification (you and Teihard believed also toward a greater perfection; many of us worry about the rate of progress), are self-organizing, self-directed, and are not doomed by thermodynamic entropy. This benefit has led to Abraham's First Prognostiplatitude, *that self-organization will be the most exciting area of development of the dynamical systems' metamodeling strategy within the field of psychology.*

I will leave it to my much more accomplished colleagues over the remainder of this conference to show you that while we are still struggling to get these ideas clear, we are among the disciples who will bring this vision to play in the fore in psychology. As you conjectured in your letter, *within five years, the dynamical vision will be the hegemonical view in psychology, awaiting bifurcation to a new, yet unforseen, version of describing complexity and process* (Abraham's Second Prognostiplatitude).

Well, Gottfried, that's it for now. Thank you for your inspiration and assistance in this effort.

Chaoharmonically, your humble servant,
Fred

ACKNOWLEDGMENTS

Thanks to Larry Vandervert for sharing his passion for Leibniz and for a copy of Leibniz's *On the General Characteristic*. Conversations with other Leibniz aficionados have also been a pleasure; they include Karl Pribram and Al Gilgen. Other ideas have benefited from pleasant interactions with virtually all of the authors in this volume, especially Ralph Abraham, Allan Combs, Tom Gentry, Steve Guastello, Hector Sabelli, and Sally Goerner, as well as with many other friends including Norm Wienberger, Ted Melnechuk, Steve Bernstein, Rik Paar, Bob Artigiani, Lucio Geronazzo, S. S. "Smitty" Stevens, Virginia Voeks, David Loye, John McCrary, Ed Green, Igor Gamov, and Riane Eisler.

REFERENCES

Bridgman, P.W. (1927). *The logic of modern physics*. New York: Macmillan.
Combs, A., and Holland, M. (1990). *Synchronicity*. New York: Paragon House.
Eisler, R. (1987). *The chalice and the blade*. San Francisco: Harper & Row.
Loemker, L. E. (Trans. & Ed.). (1956/1969). *Gottfried Wilhelm Leibniz philosophical papers and letters*. Chicago: Chicago University Press/Dordrecht: Reidel.
See especially essays:
   1. Dissertation on the art of combinations, 1966
   17. Dialogue, 1677
   24. On the general characteristic, ca. 1679
   27. Studies in a geometry of situation, 1679
   46. Speciment Dynamicum, 1695
Mungello, D. E. (1977). *Leibniz and Confucianism: The search for accord*. Honolulu: University of Hawaii Press.
Neurath, O. (1938). Unified science as encyclopedic integration. In O. Neurath, R. Carnap, & C. Morris (Eds.), *International encyclopedia of unified science*, vol. 1, pp. 1–27. Chicago: Chicago University Press.
Parkinson, G. H. R. (Trans. & Ed.). (1966). *Leibniz logical papers*. Oxford: Clarendon.
Stevens, S. S. (1936). Psychology: The propaedeutic science. *Philosophy of Science, 3*, 90–103.
Thom, R. (1972/1975). *Stabilité structurelle et morphogenèse. (Structural stability and morphogenesis*, H. Fowler, Trans.). Reading: Benjamin.
Tymieniecka, A. T. (1964). *Leibniz' cosmological synthesis*. Assen, Netherlands: Van Gorcum. Especially chap. 1.
Zeeman, E. C. (1977). *Catastrophe theory and its applications*. Reading: Addison-Wesley.

Quotations noted by superscripts:
   AC = *Dissertation on the art of combinations,* from Parkinson.
   DC = *Dialogue on the connection between things and words;*
   GC = *On the general characteristic;* and
   GS = *Studies in a geometry of situation,* from Loemker, 2nd Ed.
   T = from Tymieniecka.

Part I

BASIC ORIENTATIONS AND CONCEPTS

1

Chaos and Deep Ecology

Sally J. Goerner

This chapter summarizes the broader scientific revolution of which Chaos is the most visible tip. This broader revolution is discovering the importance of interdependence in shaping the world at all levels from the molecular to the societal. The hard science arm of the revolution is creating a physical understanding of how organization arises, why change is inevitable, and what factors underlie transformations. The unexpected result is a radically transformed understanding of evolution and a radically deepened understanding of ecology. This new physical view has profound empirical, philosophical, and metaphysical implications for psychology. Empirically a physical/mathematical science of interdependence fits much more reasonably with psychological phenomena; thus, it provides tools and concepts. Philosophically, it shows the connections between traditionally irreconcilable views of the world from mechanism, to organism, to contextualism, to ecologism. Metaphysically, it changes our sense of how humankind fits in the universe and where we are going. We are faced with a vision of an evolving, deeply ecological universe—and this vision is not just metaphor. This chapter brings the lessons of various physical science branches of the revolution together into a single easily understood thread and draws out its implications for psychology (Goerner, 1994).

A strange thing is happening with the new scientific approach of Chaos. It is being embraced by psychologists of radically different and even traditionally oppositional schools of thought. For example, existing work argues that this new science supports a renewal of Freudian psychology (Goldstein, 1990; Langs, 1989), behaviorism (Koerner, 1992), Jungian psychology (Rossi, 1989; May & Groder, 1989), and cognitive psychology (Abraham, Abraham, & Shaw, 1990). In this book it will be used in neurophysiology, discussions of art, conceptualizations of intelligence, learning theory, family therapy, neural nets, feminist psychology, and perception. How can this be? What is this thing? So, first the 30-second tour of Chaos.

First, what is Chaos? Chaos is used in this chapter as an umbrella term for various approaches to and explorations of nonlinear interdependent systems (explained below). It implies tools, methods, and models that do not use assumptions of independence and/or that are restricted to the linear range. It also refers to a set of theories/observations that come out of using these tools. Common examples include dynamical systems theory, neural nets, self-organization theory, and fractals.

Why is Chaos important? The answer is surprisingly simple. Before the advent of computers, science was effectively restricted to simpler models, ones that use assumptions of linearity and independence. It is not that earlier workers had not known about interdependence or nonlinearity, it is that they could not deal with these things effectively because of the computational difficulty. Thus, Chaos represents the first real scientific explorations of the nonlinear interdependent world—and this exploration produces two startling results. First, retrospectively it becomes quite obvious that the earlier models allowed us to see only the smallest corner of the real world. "Linear" and "independent" are limited idealized cases of "nonlinear" and "interdependent." Thus, as Ulam quipped, "calling Chaos the study of nonlinear systems is like calling zoology the study of nonelephant animals." The second result is that these first baby steps into the larger world show us just how profoundly early models shaped the scientific sense of how "things" worked. Those "things" include the motion of planets, the weather, economies, the human brain, and dripping faucets precisely because the concepts of interdependence and "more-than-a-line" apply to models of anything. It is shocking just how "nontraditionally" an interdependent world works. Scientific wisdoms—such as Laplace's idea that given equations and initial conditions, all things are predictable—drop like flies. Chaos is the story of how science's sense of the world changes as the broader-case systems (i.e., nonlinear interdependent ones) are explored.

Chaos's most important finding relates to one thing—structuring. Classical science saw interdependence as messy, a block to scientific understanding. Chaos's most important realization is that interdependence produces such things as patterns, coherence, self-organization, coordination, networks, and synchronization. Understanding nonlinear interdependence is key to understanding how and why systems structure themselves. From the mundane (why does water boil?) to the cosmic (why did life evolve?), Chaos helps explain how and why the physical universe produces intricately interwoven structures. Chaos is important because it changes our vision of interdependence (interaction) and opens the door to seeing the order-producing side of the physical world.

It is this order-production that ties to ecology and evolution. Before Chaos, ecology was a metaphor drawn from biological ecologies. Chaos suggests a broader understanding. Mutual-effect dynamics—nonlinear interdependent ecological dynamics—generate ecologies everywhere from the molecular to the economic; a biological ecology is just another example. Chaos finds that the world at large is ecological. When Chaos is tied to energy flow, these ecological dynamics lead to new images of when, how, and why structures arise and change. There are also energy reasons why the world's structuring is interconnected and hence why evolution might be one worldwide coevolutionary process. The result is an integration of physical, biological, and human evolution. In short, Chaos produces an altogether more profound form of ecological thinking—a physical, nonmetaphoric, deep ecology tied to evolution.

As this brief overview suggests, Chaos is part of a much bigger and more important revolution in human understanding than can be explained with technical terms like nonlinear and interdependent. Ecology (interconnection/interdependence) and evolution (rapid, unpredictable, structure-shaking change) have become the metaphors of our time. Global economy, world order, world environmental summits—ours is the age when the world's complexity has finally tied us all together in a way we can no longer ignore. Chaos represents a physical science branch of a deeper evolving ecological vision. This deeper vision radically transforms our sense of how humankind got here, where we are going, and how we fit in the larger scheme. It is this integrated vision that has profound philosophical and metaphysical implications for psychology. To understand why Chaos speaks to so many people across so many different discourses, one needs to see this bigger picture.

MODELS AND MYOPIA

To understand why Chaos might have far reaching implications, one must understand how utterly simple and completely common nonlinearity and interdependence are. Popular Chaos literature tends to hype nonlinearity as something exotic, but it is neither new nor exotic. Technically, nonlinearity means that the relationship between two things is not always proportional (for example, an increase in X does not necessarily mean a proportional increase or decrease in Y). The "headache" system gives you a simple example: Taking ten aspirin does not decrease a headache ten times as much as taking one aspirin. Nor is the second critical concept, interdependence, news. Interdependence has to do with whether two things mutually affect each other. For example, a conversation is an interdependent (or interactive) communication between two people; both people are affected and the exchange becomes a reciprocating mutual effect system. Interdependence can be (1) instantaneous, as in X and Y affect each other; (2) circular, as in X affects Y, which affects Z, which affects X; (3) self-reflexive, as in X affects itself; or 4) networked, where X, Y, and Z have complex interrelationships. Interdependence ties to concepts such as feedback, circular causality, recursion, and self-reflexivity. (Interdependence and nonlinearity are not necessarily related.)

Now obviously both concepts are straightforward and well known. So why does more fully incorporating them produce a scientific shift? The answer is actually simple: All real systems have some degree of nonlinear interdependence, but the bulk of current science is built on models that either use assumptions of linearity and/or independence or focus on them. Including nonlinear interdependence reveals hidden behaviors. A long list of subjects taught in disciplines from physics to psychology focus on linear aspects, for example, linear algebra, linear regression, or linear correlation (usually just called correlation). In many cases the models have highly nonlinear aspects, but as is the case with "linear" statistical models, the primary focus of investigation is on linear aspects. Heretofore science has largely avoided the nonlinear interdependent aspects of systems and as a result has tended to discount those effects. In psychology, for example, most nonlinear interaction effects are tossed away in the error term.

In addition, linear approximation techniques lie behind many traditional scientific images, and these too do not fit the broader-case world. For example, calculus is at the heart of many traditional beliefs about what science should do and how systems should work and calculus is basically a way of approximating complex shapes with little pieces of straight lines. Thus, if a model can be solved via calculus (that is, if it can be integrated), then the following images hold: (1) unlimited ability to predict and control, (2) the ability to dissect and isolate things with impunity, (3) the ability to trace effects through the system, and (4) the assumption of smooth gradual change. It comes as a surprise to most people that (for theoretical reasons, not just practical ones) the vast majority of nonlinear interdependent systems cannot be integrated and hence do not fit the images listed above. Nevertheless, as Prigogine and Stengers (1984) note, physical science's agenda had been set:

> Any integrable system may be represented as a set of units, each changing in isolation, quite independently of all the others. . . . Indeed [classical science hoped that] through a clever change in variables, all interaction could be made to disappear. . . . Generations of physicists and mathematicians tried hard to find for each kind of system the 'right' variables that would eliminate the interactions. (p. 71)

In short, the reason there is a revolution is that science's image of how the world should work was heavily shaped by the first tools it developed and the first systems it could unravel. The advent of the computer allows us to handle the computations required for new tools, better models, and more complex systems. With this broader perspective comes a very different picture of the world.

Chaos's new models reveal new aspects of the world, features that are both radical and familiar. The elegant twist of this revolution is that while it up-ends traditional physical science expectations, it reveals a world that is remarkably consonant with "soft" discourse observations from psychology to Eastern religions. Hence its ability to integrate traditionally irreconcilable schools of thought (more on this later). What is beautiful about this revolution is that it both expands science and recasts its character. Many of the harsher, antiholistic, anticonnectionistic, and essentially arrogant scientific images melt away.

Classical science emphasized linear, independent, closed, and equilibrium models, and these created a particular image of the world—one that did not include the emergence of order. Classical science's machine world is regular, predictable, controllable, completely knowable (in principle), passive, directionless, and incapable of spontaneously producing order. This image of a dead, order-hostile universe makes it difficult to explain where coordination comes from. To avoid being labeled a mystic, classical scientists had to invoke accident, anomaly, or at a minimum some "mysterious" a priori order maker as the source of the directedness and order they observe. For example, classically life started from mysterious accidental origins, evolution requires mysterious selfish genes, and psychology starts with the mystery of the brain and behavior as inexplicable starting points. The sad thing about all this is that the emergence of order becomes a mystery apart from the physical world, and this creates a schism between hard science and life-centered discourses of all types. The message of Chaos is that this schism is artificial. This schism turns out to be an illusion of the tools and models used by beginning science. C. P. Snow's two cultures stand a chance of being reconciled because the new science sees farther than the old.

CHAOS: THE GEOMETRY OF BEHAVIOR

Now on to the story of what the new science sees. Chaos represents the expansion of mechanics, the branch of physics that studies motion. It provides the foundations of an ecological sense of how things work with a few rather simple lessons, as follows. (This is a selected, not exhaustive, list of findings.)

Order is hidden in Chaos. There is order in nonlinear interdependent complexity. The order is geometric. Mutually affecting variables tend to coeffect themselves into ordered patterns—and even patterns of patterns. These patterns can be uncovered, modeled, quantified, and used in prediction, explanation, and verification of theory. We did not tend to see these patterns before because we were looking at data with linear, calculus-shaped, analytic mind-set tools. Figure 1.1 gives a quick impression of both the geometry and the difference from previous views. Note: The stable pattern shown in Figure 1.1, B is called an attractor.

The holistic order in chaos is a result of interdependent variables co-effecting each other—push-me pull-you fashion—in chains, circles, networks, and in the immediate moment. The result is a hidden pattern of the whole. It does not come from any one element having a regular pattern or effect, and you cannot see it if you look at the system one piece at a time. A whirlpool provides a simple example. What we call a "whirlpool" is actually a dynamic pattern; it is the result of a bunch of water molecules mutually affecting themselves into a stable global form. In order to see this form, you have to step back and see the whole, you cannot see it from the level of a single water molecule.

The holistic order in Chaos provides a mechanical explanation for "mysterious" hidden global ordering observed throughout the ages. For example, Adam Smith spoke of an invisible hand at work behind the operation of economies. Hegel

Figure 1.1: Time Series (A) Versus a Geometric View (B) of the Same Data (Sacks, Oliver, *The man who mistook his wife for a hat and other clinical tales*, 1989, p. 357; courtesy HarperCollins. Based on the work of Edward Lorenz.)

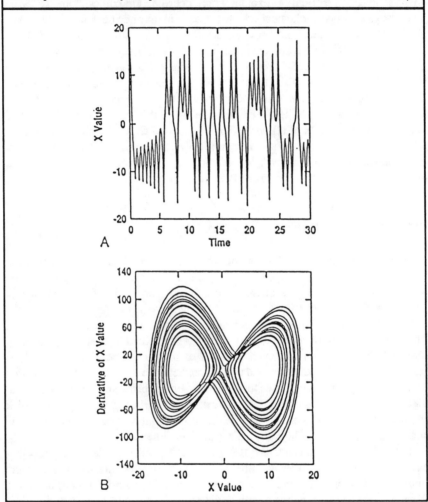

described the world evolving through dialectics and order hidden beneath surface vicissitudes. Mutual-effect systems that weave order throughout the whole provide a mechanical basis for this type of observation. The corollary to this understanding is that the context in which a phenomenon exists is much more ordered than a Newtonian view leads us to expect. In fact, the concept of randomness itself becomes questionable; as in random-number generators, nature's processes may be at best pseudo-random (Feigenbaum, 1980).

The order in Chaos is caused both from the top down and from the bottom up. The elements of a mutual-effect system create global order, but this mutually created global order creates a pressure on individual elements toward conformity to the global pattern. The easiest way to think of this is as a momentum effect, for example, like in a treadmill. Walking on the treadmill causes it to move but its motion creates a pressure to keep walking and even to walk faster. In a complex mutual-effect system this you-caused-it/it-causes-you phenomenon tends to be subtle, omnipresent, and quite potent. The types of phenomena noted in family systems therapy are not only supported but can be extrapolated to many other types of systems. The very pleasant upshot is that holistic and reductionistic views need not be oppositional. The world is created from the top down and the bottom up; it must be thought of as coming from both.

Interactive dynamics create networks and wholes out of parts. Not only do mutual-effect systems create holistic order, they literally create wholes. Previously separate things become coupled together into a larger whole. The classic example of coupling (also called entrainment) is the phenomenon of self-synchronizing cuckoo clocks. If you hang a number of cuckoo clocks on a wall with their pendulums moving in different directions, after a while their pendulums will become synchronized. As the pendulums swing they send small perturbations through the wall that push each other toward a common mutually maximizing rhythm. The many independent cuckoo clock systems couple into a larger integrated clock system; they act as one. The point here is that the spontaneous self-organization of assemblies (or unities), is quite natural even in completely mechanical systems. In an interactive world, coupling is common.

A dynamic may have many different patterns and changes between patterns appear as sudden transformations of behavior. One dynamic may have multiple competing forms of behavior, each representing a stable mutual-effect organization. A single parameter often controls whether you get one organization or another. When the control parameter crosses a critical point, a sudden reorganization (called a bifurcation) of behavior occurs. The classic example here are a horse's gaits: walking, trotting, and galloping. Each gait represents a completely different organization of leg motion. The transition between gaits occurs as a sudden reorganization. In the case of gaits, bifurcations occur as the speed parameter increases. The horse goes faster and faster within one gait and then suddenly shifts to a new type of organization that allows a faster speed—walk to trot, trot to gallop.

Bifurcations are notable because linear calculus-shaped science tended to imagine change as smooth and gradual. Chaos suggests that a great deal of change involves punctuated equilibrium, periods of stable sameness broken by sudden rapid reorganizations into a new form. Biological evolution (Gould, 1980), scientific knowledge (Kuhn, 1972), and growth in children (Lampl, Veldhuis, & Johnson, 1992) all exhibit punctuated equilibrium; classical science portrayed them all as changing smoothly. Figure 1.2 shows the bifurcations between patterns (attractors) in stirring as the speed of the stirrer is increased.

   Chaos provides a completely mechanical understanding of ecological dynamics.
The next branch of the revolution, self-organization theory adds the dimension of
energy flow.

SELF-ORGANIZATION AND ENERGY FLOW

   Thermodynamics is the science of energy flow. Self-organization theory, which
comes out of thermodynamics (Prigogine, 1980; Prigogine & Stengers 1984),
suggests that coherent identifiable self-maintaining organizations (living and nonliving)
occur only in particular conditions, the "far-from-equilibrium" condition. "Far-
from-equilibrium" means that there is a large energy concentration or buildup in
the field; that is, the energy is not evenly distributed. Energy buildups create a
pressure to flow (just think of what happens when you release a balloon full of air).
Self-organization theory teaches us that energy's pressure to flow plays a
fundamental role in the creation of structure. A tornado, for example, is an
identifiable "entity" with self-maintaining dynamics that is driven into being by a
large energy buildup.
   Self-organization theory also describes common patterns and processes that hold
across types of self-organization systems. Foremost among these is the concept of
order-through-fluctuation. In the jargon of the field, new organizations are usually
a result of "a small fluctuation being amplified into a new form." Roughly this
means that new dynamical organizations emerge when a small novel configuration
becomes a conduit for an energy buildup, which triggers a positive feedback cycle

Figure 1.2: Bifurcation Points in a Stirred Fluid
(Abraham & Shaw, 1988; courtesy Aerial Press.)

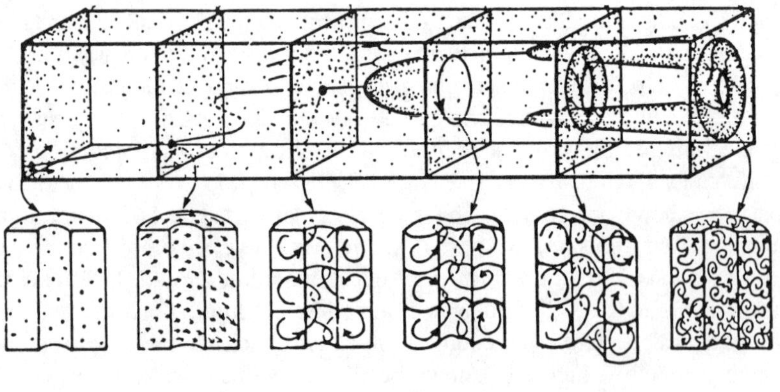

creating a stable self-maintaining system. A simple fluid experiment called the Benard cell gives a concrete example of what this means. The Benard cell is a box with fluid to which heat is added. At low temperatures the heat is spread by random molecular collisions. The fluid appears homogeneous; there is no coordinated motion. Little collections of relatively hot or cold molecules randomly occur and move apart all the time, but as the temperature rises a new context, one set for change, emerges. Hot collections are lighter and more buoyant than their cooler surrounds, so at some critical gradient randomly occurring collections of hot molecules begin to move some distance upward as a whole. Eventually some random collection rises all the way to the top, pulling other molecules up in its wake, loses its heat to cooler regions at the top, and sinks back down. Suddenly the entire region erupts into a coherent coordinated circular motion. In a context ripe for change, a small randomly occurring difference has seeded a new form of organization.

Prigogine shows that this same type of order-through-fluctuation process occurs in all sorts of systems from heat, to chemical, to living. It is easily seen at least metaphorically in human situations such as the recent upheavals in Russia: energy buildup, a random new configuration becomes a conduit and seeds transformation.

Self-organization theory is quite radical in its social implications. Contrary to the mechanistic image, it suggests that systems will structure themselves given the right conditions. Social systems shaped by the mechanistic view tend to suppress the system's creative tendencies; they are oriented toward external control. Organizational consultants are using self-organization's message to help businesses unleash the self-organizing tendencies in their own system, often just by structuring the system to let change happen.

THE BROADER STORY OF EVOLUTION

The next phase of the story has even deeper social implications. Just as Chaos is expanding and recasting physical science, Chaos plus the "new biology" is expanding and recasting our vision of evolution. Biological evolution is seen as a specific example of a much broader, more encompassing evolutionary process. Here again, energy flow is key. This general evolutionary process involves the "growth of complexity" (i.e., increasingly intricate and interdependent systems) and runs from plasma and molecules to life and civilizations. Tying together work from physics and biology to psychology and anthropology, general evolutionary theorists build a picture of this process as physical, inexorable, happening in the here-and-now, and more than just a matter of genes.

The full story of general evolution is beyond our scope, but we will deal with it briefly as an energy-flow story. The basic idea is that "increasing levels of ordered complexity" come about because energy always seeks to flow as fast as possible and structured flow moves energy faster. When there are very large ongoing energy

Table 1.1: Accelerating Energy Flow in Increasingly Intricate Organizations
If order is driven into being as a product of dissipative efficiency then in
Chaisson's words "what is important is the rate at which free energy enters a
system of some given size. . . . The operative quantity used to specify the order
and organization in any system is the flux of free energy density, denoted here
by the symbol F."
(Adapted from Chaisson, 1987, p. 254.)

Structure	F (ergs s^{-1} gm^{-1})
Milky Way	1
Sun	2
Earth's climasphere	80
Earth's biosphere (plants)	500
Human body	17,000
Human brain	150,000

buildups, the system creates higher and higher levels of increasingly interwoven
structure in the process of going faster and faster.

The patterns by which such ordered complexity grows are easy to explain and
fit with long-observed patterns in social and psychological evolution. A buildup of
energy creates a pressure to flow, a force. Resistance in its many forms (inertia,
barriers, etc.) blocks this pressure. If the pressure is greater than the resistance,
energy begins to cycle faster and faster within its current form. However, there is
a limit to how fast any particular type of flow can go. If the pressure to flow is still
greater than resistance when that limit is reached, a crisis (bifurcation) occurs and
the context restructures itself into a new, more efficient configuration—this may
include the emergence of new forms, the splitting of large forms into smaller ones,
or the coupling of previously independent systems. Massive pressure creates a cycle
of evolution. New forms come into being, accelerate, reach their limits, and are
succeeded by yet more efficient forms. In the Benard cell, first you get large rolls;
these split into smaller more efficient rolls, which split into more intricate
interweavings, and so on. Such driven systems exhibit a type of developmental
process wherein each stage serves as a foundation for the next. They exhibit
punctuated equilibrium, that is, periods of relative sameness followed by sudden
change. They also exhibit an accelerating pace of change, increasing energy-flow
efficiency, and increasing complexity. The earth being between the sun and the cold
sink of space is in such a massively "far-from-equilibrium" system. The evolution
of the earth-field exhibits all these qualities.

The connection between increasingly intricate structuring and increasing energy
flow rates has been observed over the succession of ecosystems (grass plains to oak

forests), the evolution of life on earth, and the evolution of the universe (atoms to galaxies) (Chaisson, 1987; Odum, 1988; Morowitz, 1968). Table 1.1 shows the increasing energy flow rates for increasingly complex organizations. And, as Figure 1.3 shows, the succession of dominant life forms on earth has been a succession of higher-rate metabolizers, which essentially means higher-rate energy processors. Carniero (1987) even provides evidence that restructuring of aboriginal villages fits a typical energy- flow pattern (in this case a 2/3 power surface-to-volume ratio).

This energy vision of evolution also links up with themes in the new biology. For example, because all energy flows in a region are deeply interdependent, evolution is primarily a phenomenon of a whole energy-flow ecosystem, not of individual elements. The Gaia hypothesis (Lovelock, 1979) has also provided ample evidence that the biosphere functions as an intricately interwoven, co-evolving whole. Material cycles go up through the atmosphere, down through the oceans, in through plant and animal life both simple and complex—all coordinated and

Figure 1.3: Accelerating Energy Flow in the Evolution of Life
This figure is notable because it also shows that the different forms co-evolved with the level of atmospheric oxygen. %PAL stands for percent of present atmospheric oxygen levels. Oxygen allows higher rates of metabolism. As higher-rate species evolved, they also contributed to higher levels of oxygen which allowed even higher rate species to evolve.
(Swenson, 1989, p. 51; courtesy ISSS.)

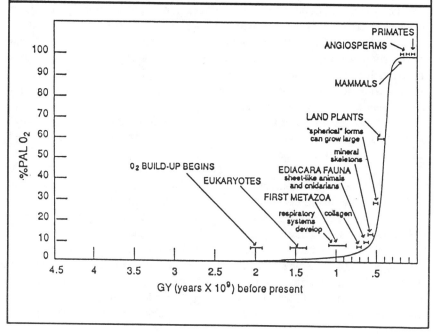

interconnected, in a massive self-reinforcing, self-generating way. Thus in energy-based evolution, as in the Gaia hypothesis, the whole is a self-organizing interdependent web, which means that the evolution of any particular system, be it science or species, is part of a much larger process.

Like the new biology, energy-based evolution also describes the main thrust of evolution as involving the coupling of previously independent forms into larger coordinated systems. Thus, Maturana and Varela (1987) describe biology via coupling: single cells to multicellular animals to families to herds to civilizations. Margulis (1981) has strengthened this basic notion with her theory of serial endosymbiosis. She shows that the major path of biological evolution is through the coupling of independent forms into more efficient and more creatively adapted cooperatives. She notes that the main internal structures of cells such as mitochondria did not originate inside the cell but reflect a long-standing coupling. Similarly land plants emerged through symbiotic coupling between lichens and photosynthetic algae. Thus, in biological evolution, as in fluid dynamics, increasing levels of coupling (coordination) produce increasing structure, increasing efficiency, and increasing ability to persist (i.e., survive).

Finally, Chaos clarifies the dynamics underlying this biology. Thus, Eigen and Schuster's (1979) notion of hypercycles describes how self-sustaining cycles develop, increase in coherence, and spread their interconnections. Chemical hypercycles can be seen in living systems (the Krebs cycle) and nonliving systems (the carbon cycle) and at scales from the microscopic to the interplanetary. Like smaller forms of self-organization, such cycles have many behaviors that mirror life. For example, Csanyi (1989) describes how cycles begin to reproduce themselves, creating widespread replicative networks. The spontaneous emergence of replicating cycles, self-maintained boundaries, self-maintained internal coordination, and internal/external exchanges in nonliving systems makes life seem like a much more natural thing. Even work on the origin of life is beginning to be recast as a coupling of independent forms into a cooperative with qualitatively new survival-enhancing properties (Dyson, 1985).

To sum up, the image of an intricately interwoven ecological universe—self-ordering, driven by energy flow, and built by nonlinear dynamics—is already well supported. Notably, this expanded view of evolution has a distinctly different character than the traditional view. Where the traditional view sees life adapting to a relatively fixed environment, here life and environment co-evolve. Where traditionally competition is the creator of fitness, here competition has to do with short-term survival but cooperation (coupling, coordinating, etc.) is the source of the largest leaps in efficiency and hence the key to long-term survival. Where traditionally evolution is of species, here evolution is of the whole interwoven earth ecosystem. Finally, where traditionally chance dominates descriptions, here evolution is a strange blend of chance and inexorability. When there is enough pressure, more efficient forms are inexorably driven into being, but what actually emerges is influenced by random elements and would never happen the same way twice. Thus, evolution is lawful and inexorable, but history is idiosyncratic, not inevitable, and, of course, largely unpredictable. The emerging motto is that everything affects everything—eventually. The field's pressure to flow bringsus and all other things into being in co-evolving ecological interconnectedness.

ECOLOGICAL PHILOSOPHY AND METAPHYSICS

The philosophical implications of Chaos are exceedingly broad, so I shall restrict myself to an area of particular interest to modern psychology: How to integrate psychology's many diverse approaches into a more unified field. Chaos counters fragmentation: It has a penchant for speaking to psychologists of radically different persuasions. We will use Stephen Pepper's (1946) theory of world hypotheses to explain this appeal as a result of Chaos's ability to connect different metaphors for how the world works.

Pepper notes that various traditions of human thought usually house a root metaphor for "how the world works." Thus some traditions see the world as a machine and others as a developing organism. He describes how six basic metaphors, or world hypotheses, underlie six major threads in intellectual thought. The six hypotheses are: (1) mechanism, (2) organicism, (3) contextualism, (4) formism, (5) mysticism, and (6) animism (see Berry, 1984, for a discussion of these hypotheses in psychology; see also Table 1.2). Pepper also notes that each hypothesis tends to assume both its own completeness and universal scope. Unfortunately, in their traditional forms, none of these ways of looking at the world adequately explains the major focus of any of the others. For example, traditional mechanism does not explain the directedness of organismic development, and traditional organicism does not explain how parts can generate a developmental flow. The common results of assuming one's own view to be complete and seeing no way to another's view is insularity; each view stands alone and may either ignore or throw stones at the others.

Now, the point of Table 1.2 is not that everything that has been said in the name of the various world hypotheses is true but, rather, that the main premises of each is expanded and shown to be consonant with the main observations of its fellows. A mechanist should no longer laugh at the formist notion that matter is attracted toward a form nor a mystic decry mechanism's inability to fathom humankind's embeddedness in the large mystery. Well-meaning individuals from all quarters can reach each other's perspective.

The idea of mystery brings me to my last point, the metaphysics of Chaos and deep ecology. It is said that Copernicus caused a major shift in human self-image by showing that the earth was not the center of the solar system. Our cherished illusion of being the center of the universe and the apple of God's eye went up in smoke. If that is what came of discovering the sun did not revolve around the earth,

Table 1.2: Summary of World Hypotheses in Psychology

Hypothesis-Metaphor	Philosopher/Time	Primary Observation	Seen in Psychology in
Mysticism & Animism The mystical experience; inanimate things are seen as having human characteristics.	Predates Western philosophy.	Connectedness or relatedness of all things; humanity is part of a larger Being; direct intuitive knowledge is possible.	Transpersonal psychology, shamanism, Eastern religions, and some types of consciousness studies.
Formism The similarity between two things.	Plato, Aristotle (400 B.C.).	Similarity results from being pulled toward similar forms.	Diagnostic categories. Typologies.
Mechanism The machine.	Descartes, Bacon, Kant (A.D. 1600).	Describes how parts create the event and hence supports prediction; adds the precision and clarity of mathematics.	Skinnerian behaviorism, early learning theory, Pavlov, Hull's behavior system, many schools of cognitive psychology.
Organicism The biological organism.	Hegel (A.D. 1800).	Describes underlying dynamics sustaining the system and developing toward an end.	Rogerian therapy, family therapy, some Jungian therapy.
Contextualism The complex historic event in context.	James, Dewey, Peirce, Mead (A.D. 1900).	Recognizes that all events are unique and therefore must be related to the specific context in which they occur.	Transactional analysis, phenomenology, gestalt therapy.

just think about the implications of discovering that life, intelligence, and civilization are all part of a profoundly embracing physical process.

The difference in view is multifaceted. On the one hand, general evolution reduces our status as the apple of God's eye. In a deep ecological universe all aspects are equally co-creating and created partners. We (our intelligence, complex civilization, etc.) are inexorable products of the great process and also historical accidents that may end in termination or as merely a platform for the next round of evolution. Yet, we also find ourselves embraced. Here we are members of a community of Being and partners in a mysterious evolutionary process. We are not just accidents. We are co-creators, but not Gods, since absolute prediction and control are not possible. Creation is not an ancient surrealistic event but a process that is going on now. Athough all of this is radical scientifically, it is familiar to the perennial philosophy and esoteric disciplines of many lineages.

This very spiritual sense of the world also ties to the pragmatic world as well. Chaos has been successfully applied to many problems in the physical sciences, medicine, engineering, and psychology. Yet this pragmatic knowledge also ties directly and pragmatically to more noble visions. For example, where mechanism pushed control, homogeneity, and competition as the road to efficiency, Chaos suggests that diversity, cooperation, and open-endedness are the keys to efficiency in the broader-case world and hence the most efficient route to survival. Chaos suggests that noble truths may also have been pragmatic truths all along.

CONCLUSION

Countless words have been spent on the rocky relationship between classical physics and psychology. Another countless set has been spent on paradigm shifts and the soullessness of modern science. It has been difficult to imagine a type of science (physics, mathematics, biology, chemistry . . . psychology) that allows us to do science and is nevertheless at home with the human aspects of humanity from meaning and morality to connectedness and spirituality. Yet that is what Chaos is about. At its core, Chaos is about reconciling the two cultures—without suppressing either to the images of the other.

Science is still science; all of the old facts and techniques remain. These facts, however, are framed in a very different context. The world is the same, yet very different. The oddest thing about the whole situation—the new scientific approach and deep ecology in its many guises—is that science, pragmatism, and spirituality are in fact becoming intertwined. This is one of those reconciliations devoutly wished, long-deemed impossible, and apparently coming true.

REFERENCES

Abraham, F. D., Abraham, R. H., & Shaw, C. D. (1990). *A visual introduction to dynamical systems theory for psychology*. Santa Cruz: Aerial Press.

Abraham, R., & Shaw, C. (1988). *Dynamics the geometry of behavior: Part four: Bifurcation behavior*. Santa Cruz: Aerial Press.

Berry, S. M. (1984). An introduction to Stephen C. Pepper's philosophical system via world hypotheses: A study in evidence. *Bulletin of the Psychonomic Society, 22*, 446–448.

Carniero, R. (1987). The evolution of complexity in human societies and its mathematical expression. *International Journal of Comparative Sociology, 28*, 111–128.

Chaisson, E. (1987). *The life era*. New York: Atlantic Monthly Press.

Csanyi, V. (1989). *Evolutionary systems and society: A general theory of life, mind and culture*. Durham: Duke University Press.

Dyson, F. (1985). *Origins of life*. Cambridge: Cambridge University Press.

Eigen, M., & Schuster, P. (1979). The hypercycle: A principle of natural self-organization. Berlin: Springer-Verlag.

Feigenbaum, M. J. (1980). Universal behavior in nonlinear systems. *Los Alamos Science, 1*, 4–27.

Goerner, S. (1994). *Chaos and the evolving ecological universe: A study in the science and human implications of a new world hypothesis*. New York: Gordon & Breach.

Goldstein, J. (1990). Freud's theories in light of far-from-equilibrium research. *Social Research, 52(3)*, 9–45.

Gould, S. (1980). *Ever since Darwin*. New York: W. W. Norton.

Koerner, J. (1992). *Nonlinear dynamic systems in behavioral psychology*. Unpublished doctoral dissertation, University of Minnesota.

Kuhn, T. (1972). *The structure of scientific revolutions*. New York: Houghton Mifflin.

Lampl, M., Veldhuis, J. D., & Johnson, M. L. (1992). Saltation and stasis: A model of human growth. *Science, 258*, 801–803.

Langs, R. (1989, March). Psychotherapy and psychoanalysis defined by mathematical models. *Psychiatric Times*.

Lovelock, J. (1979). *Gaia: A new look at life on earth*. Oxford: Oxford University Press.

Margulis, L. (1981). *Symbiosis in cell evolution*. San Francisco: W. H. Freeman.

Maturana, H., & Varela, F. (1987). *The tree of knowledge*. Boston: Shambhala.

May, J., & Groder, M. (1989). Jungian thought and dynamical systems. *Psychological Perspectives, 20(1)*, 143–156.

Morowitz, H. J. (1968). *Energy flow in biology: Biological organization as a problem in thermal physics*. New York: Academic Press.

Odum, H. T. (1988). Self-organization, transformity, and information. *Science, 242*, 1132.

Pepper, S. (1946). *World hypotheses: Prolegomena to systematic philosophy and a complete survey of metaphysics*. Berkeley: University of California Press.

Prigogine, I. (1980). *From being to becoming*. San Francisco: W. H. Freeman.

Prigogine, I., & Stengers, E. (1984). *Order out of chaos*. New York: Bantam Books.

Rossi, E. (1989). Archetypes as strange attractors. *Psychological Perspectives, 20(1)*, 143–156.

Swenson, R. (1989). Emergent evolution and the global attractor: The evolutionary epistemology of entropy production. *Proceedings of the 33rd Annual Meeting of the International Society for the Systems Sciences, 3*, 46–53.

2

The Kiss of Chaos and the Sleeping Beauty of Psychology

Walter J. Freeman

ABSTRACT

Neuropsychology has been dominated for the past century by some pervasive doctrines, which have been crucial for its growth in the past, but which now tend more to impede than facilitate its further development. Three of these are the neuron doctrine, the reflex doctrine, and the doctrine of the sufficiency of forward action, by which feedback interactions among neurons are downplayed or omitted altogether. The constraints imposed by these fundamental concepts have encouraged deterministic views and models of brain function, including the primacy of sensory input for specifying motor output, the notion of information processing, storage and retrieval as the mechanism for memory, the positivistic idea that each memory can be assigned to one neuron or to a specific synapse or protein, and the idea that the basal so-called spontaneous activity of the brain is epiphenomenal and should be removed as "noise" in the search for signal.

Recent developments in nonlinear dynamics have made possible a new view of neurons, which is that they form interactive ensembles by virtue of their feedback relations through collateral axons and synapses. The mathematical techniques for analysis of feedback in dynamical systems are essential to define, characterize, and measure the activity of these neural populations. The solutions of these equations include not only the traditional steady state and periodic firing of nerve cells but also the aperiodic and seemingly "noisy" activity that constitutes chaos. The hallmark of systems operating in chaotic domains is that they create information, which takes the form of novel spatiotemporal patterns of neural activity in sensory cortex. These are essential for the adaptive processes of the brain to deal with the ceaselessly changing and unpredictable environment. The theory of chaos in the very near future will greatly change the way in which brain function is conceived by psychologists.

INTRODUCTION

Some philosophical questions are like museum pieces or family heirlooms. Each new generation takes them out of storage, polishes, displays, and debates them, and then puts them back to go on to other more productive enquiries. Two age groups seem to be particularly attracted to them: the adolescent embarking on a life of the mind, and the inveterate researcher awakening in an obsolescent, technological cul-de-sac but still able to dream. For the neuroscientist these questions are often encapsulated in the antinomies of consciousness versus automatism, monism versus dualism, free will versus determinism, localism versus holism, reflex versus instinct, reductionism versus globalism, and so on. Yet when literate laypersons ask the brain researcher what he or she is doing, he or she often retreats into specialized obscurities, turning away nonscientific colleagues. Their eyes glaze over, or they glance sideways for the exit, and we find ourselves in mutual embarrassment. The neuroscientist asked to share his or her work with philosophers confronts the dilemma of either polishing antique silver or displaying expertise that may serve to impress, but certainly not to inform, the literate nontechnical community. Rarely does a brain scientist have the opportunity to contribute to the development of new disciplines. Yet it does happen occasionally. My intent here is to inform the interests of the literate nonscientific community by sharing some of my observations and findings about the biological processes that take place in brains during behavior, not to polish silver nor to flaunt technological intricacies, but to invite other disciplines to share in the development of the meaning that modern neuroscience has opened. It is well worth the effort to pursue the dialectic between brain science and other disciplines, for our dreams can only find new direction and expression if each is able to inform the other in an open cooperative effort.

Over the centuries, understanding of what we know, who we are, and what our purposes are, has been largely defined by well- or misconceived understanding that has been developed from what we know about our brains and how they work. What can modern brain science contribute to contemporary thought? To psychology? To contemporary philosophy? To its epistemology and metaphysics? Looking back, stretching as far as history, we can see the litter of uninformed philosophical views derived from mistaken science, necessitating caution in our response to the question, How much of what we hold to is wrong and needs to be replaced? Many brain scientists are attempting to think through the implications of the rapidly changing field of brain science in detail. What little we do know suggests that these are astonishing and likely will precipitate a revolutionary shift first in neuroscience, then in psychology and philosophy, and consequently in our culture. In order to resume the discussion, I intend to demonstrate that the foundations of modern brain science, psychology, and other biological disciplines are grounded in fallacy; then I will outline a new conceptual structure that is emerging from our research. Along the way, the philosophical problem of free will versus determinism will get another generation's spin before being returned to storage.

My comments revolve around three foundational concepts of most contemporary research on the nervous system, which I used to hold and use in company with the majority of my colleagues, but which I now see as mistaken not in themselves but in their applications. Further, I have come to regard the misleading use of these doctrines as a source of mischief in attempts to comprehend the brain. They are (1) the *neuron doctrine*, which posits that the function of the single nerve cell or neuron is the elementary "particle" of the brain; (2) the doctrine of *forward action*, which holds that the brain can be understood in terms of forward actions without need for consideration of the recursive and recurrent actions of neurons, indirectly, but still inevitably, back onto themselves; and (3) the doctrine of the *reflex* and the consequent structuring of behavior as a hierarchy of reflex actions. In order to get a truly fresh start at understanding perception, it is essential that we consider the fundamental limitations of each of these doctrines as well as the formulation of their corrective replacements.

None of these doctrines of the neuron, the sufficiency of forward action, and the reflex was initially accepted without controversy, and all have been criticized and condemned repeatedly in the past century. They are still under vigorous attack and may soon crumble, taking with them the greater part of the structure of traditional neurobiology and cognitive science. But it is not my responsibility as a working scientist to document that historical process, which is a proper activity for philosophers and historians of science. My intent here is to describe what I see through the splitting seams of the chrysalis of modern neuroscience. Nor do I claim authorship for the changes that are taking place, only for my perspective on the process developed from and peculiar to my own research experience. The roots of these new ideas lie in new technologies and experimental mathematical tools that are permeating and revitalizing many heretofore stable, and even stale, areas of science.

These pages may appear to have more the cast of catalecta than that of an integrated philosophy because my integrated body of work is largely technical, even though it reflects some variety in its selection of metaphysical tools and positions, dependent on particular research goals. However, I admit to a certain steadfastness of purpose over the past forty years, so observers may see a degree of coherence in my story, one that I might judge, perhaps prematurely, to be illusory. I would like that.

THE NEURON DOCTRINE

The nineteenth century saw two main revolutions in biology. The better known was the Darwinian doctrine of evolution. The other was the cellular doctrine of Rudolf Virchow, who came to understand that the functional basis for life is the cell, the protoplasmic sac that seems to float in an extracellular sea of salt water, enclosed completely by its own limiting membrane. There are said to be 100 billion of them in the human nervous system, but that is probably a substantial underestimate.

The teaching and practice of physiology and medicine are entirely based on this cellular doctrine, just as they had been previously based on the ancient doctrine of humors. Within the cellular doctrine, it is undoubtedly correct to say that the great majority of the neuron's janitorial functions take place in, and are best understood at, the cellular level, processes such as replication, differentiation, growth, repair, general chemical maintenance, metabolic fueling, disposal of wastes, and the modification of connections in the molecular and membrane processes that underlie memory and learning.

However, the basic assumption of the neuron doctrine can and should be questioned. Is the information that is used in the elaboration of goal-directed behavior, as well as in the control of interactions by the brain with the environment, expressed in, or operated on, by neurons acting as individual summing and switching elements? The common answer for nearly a century has been, of course it is! One of the principal reasons for believing that the neuron acts individually has been an assumption that the most prominent "signal" generated by neurons, the action potential, is primary to the activity of a neuron. The neuron is commonly observed to generate long sequences of these action potential impulses. Such a cell is called a "unit" with a "spike train," and it is commonly thought that the "message" of the cell resides in the temporal patterns of the spikes, in the manner that a message resides on a telegraph wire in a pattern of dots and dashes.

One problem with this view is that the great bulk of physiological studies cited in its support came from anesthetized or paralyzed animals under conditions in which goal-directed behavior was deliberately suppressed. When studies were undertaken in normally behaving animals, the variability of the observed unit activity was so great that the data were uninterpretable. Researchers then resorted to averaging their data in such a way that the extracted information appeared to be locked to a stimulus or response selected by the observer, not to the endogenous brain activity itself. This procedure culled from the data that very small fraction of the activity that was locked to an external event, and then discarded the overwhelming bulk of the activity as "noise." A common phrase to describe this procedure is "throwing out the baby with the bath water."

Our studies of the behavior of single neurons in waking animals in relation to the tens and hundreds of thousands of their neighbors have shown that even though the activity of a single cell appears to be largely unpredictable and therefore seemingly "noisy," great masses of cells cooperate in ways that produce coherent patterns of activity in the whole. This cooperative ensemble activity is sometimes pejoratively referred to as "the roar of a football crowd," but a more apt analogy would be the intentional action of a collection of celebrants to organize a cocktail party, or the intentional behavior of a collection of ants to organize a colony.

In studies of the olfactory systems of small mammals by my colleagues and myself (Freeman, 1975, 1987, 1991), the results are unequivocal. The neural information that correlates with the behavior of animals exists in the cooperative activity of many millions of neurons and not in the favored few. In the first stage of the olfactory system, discrimination of odors first takes place in the olfactory bulb where there is little convincing evidence that the bulb signals to the rest of the brain by any small number of neurons unique for each odor. On the contrary, our data indicate that, for every discriminable odor, every neuron in the bulb participates. We have shown that perceptual information cannot be observed in uniquely individual neurons, leading us to conclude that it is incorrect to say that perceptual information exists in the activity of individual neurons. It exists in patterns of activity that are distributed concomitantly and continuously over tens and hundreds of millions of neurons. Therefore, I conclude that the interpretation of the neuron doctrine, holding that the neuron acts individually, is fallacious in the neural system for olfactory perception.

THE DOCTRINE OF FORWARD ACTION

By analogy to the neural process, one might say that information in a photograph does not exist in single particles of silver in gelatin but in the pattern of the whole. This analogous understanding, however, would miss a crucial aspect of the genesis of information-bearing patterns of neural activity. Silver particles do not interact with each other; neurons do, and it is by intentionally directed individual actions and reactions that they cooperate to generate global patterns. Photographic plates can imprint only patterns that are projected onto them, whereas neural masses act to create their own patterns out of raw sensory inputs that are delivered to them.

The main reason that the cellular doctrine fails for neurons but holds so well for most other cells is that nerve cells are uniquely different from all other types of cells. Neurons project long protoplasmic filaments, many thousands of times greater in length than in diameter, with exceedingly large numbers of branches outwardly from their centers. The filaments that transmit information away from the cell to other cells are called axons. It is these axonal filaments that generate action potentials. The axons end in small swellings at their tips that abut onto the filaments of other neurons. These receiving filaments are called dendrites. The dendrites seldom generate action potentials. Instead, they generate continuously varying wavelike currents.

In fact, the real work of each neuron is, first, to receive the action potentials and change them to brief flows of current at the abutments, called synapses and, second, to sum the currents over time and along the lengths of the dendrites. The resulting sum is delivered to its axon (each cell has only one, though it may branch extensively), where the amplitude is expressed as a rate of action potentials on the axon. The higher the sum of current, the faster the axon fires. In this way, since each pulse of action potential is carried reliably to the end of every branch, the sum is delivered rapidly and without loss to many other cells.

Local masses of neurons, such as the olfactory bulb and the olfactory cortex (about the size of a large pea or a lima bean) tend, when left to themselves, to lapse into a low energy state of activity that has all the appearance of "noise," since it has no discernible spatial or temporal pattern. Neurons generate this activity because they interact with each other, but they are not obsessed with each other and are receptive to activity imposed from other neurons outside. When they do receive a burst of input, not only are they activated, but the amount of internal cross-talk goes up. When a certain threshold is reached, the entire mass goes into a spasm of cross-talk, and they are too busy to accept input from outside. This spasm lasts only a tenth of a second or so, but the neurons in the bulb are now highly active and thereby impose their activity onto other masses of nerve cells with which they are interconnected. Such bursts of transmitted activity, often taking place several times a second, serve to destabilize those other masses and cause them to go into local spasms of cross-talk, too, and engender yet other masses to cross their thresholds. And so life goes on in the self-stimulated brain like a gaggle of geese or the gossip in a village when a stranger arrives.

Notably, the train of action potentials of a neuron is actually an "analog" signal in which the firing rate is proportional to the strength of dendritic current at the starting end of one axon, and to the strength of current that is induced in the dendrites of the next receiving neuron. The train of action potentials is not "digital" in the sense that is meant for rates of identical strengths of pulses in computers. The digital computer was initially modeled on a mistaken idea of how nerve cells operate. This shows that scientists do not have to be correct to be successful in unexpected ways.

Each neuron transmits to thousands of others in its vicinity, and also in some cases for astonishingly great distances, often thousands of times greater than the diameter of its axon, equivalent to a highway six meters in width and sixteen kilometers in length. It also receives from as many neurons in its surround, on the order of 1,000 to 10,000, although no one really knows exactly how many. But herein lies the key to interaction. Each neuron, because of its membrane, has a relatively high degree of local autonomy, and yet everything that it does is felt by many others that provide an environment to which in turn it responds. It is these widespread actions and reactions that lead to the emergence of a constant, ceaseless, ever-fluctuating activity of masses of nerve cells. In great numbers they start talking and never stop. In fact, if they do stop because they are cut off from commerce with their neighbors, they soon atrophy and die.

Interconnections among neurons are of two main types. Local connections within areas of cortex and within subcortical nuclei form the basis for interactive masses, which create and maintain fluctuating patterns of activity over the entire spatial extent of each mass. Distant connections serve to transmit patterns from one local mass to another and back again, almost always in reciprocal paths, again subserving interaction and not merely action. These reciprocal connections form the basis for feedback loops. The entire brain at all levels has distributed feedback as its hallmark of structure and function. Yet the overwhelming majority of results from past and contemporary studies of the physiology of the brain that are expressed in the form of flow diagrams show the inferred connections as all forward. Feedback pathways are omitted. Why? The reason is that the dynamics of feedback, especially in nonlinear, distributed, multineuronal systems is very complicated, and most physiologists are not trained to handle it. The mathematicians and engineers who have been properly trained either do not know the necessary anatomy and physiology or already know the complications and prefer not to get involved.

This is the point at which the new experimental mathematics and nonlinear dynamics come into play, along with the new technology afforded by digital computers, which makes it possible to set up and solve the differential equations that simulate the dynamics of neural masses in the brain, and to display the solutions in graphic patterns. Experimental work in the olfactory system demonstrates that the brain cannot be understood in terms of forward action without need for consideration of the recursive and recurrent actions of neurons, indirectly, but still inevitably, back onto themselves. Therefore, contemporary neuroscience loses yet another of its foundational concepts, for the argument for the sufficiency of forward action is also seen to be fallacious.

THE REFLEX DOCTRINE

Physiologists and psychologists who work with animals often have the illusion that they control the behavior of their subjects by manipulation of schedules of reinforcement. This belief is based on the feed forward models that the observers carry in their heads to explain to themselves how it is that a conditioned stimulus (CS) that is paired with an unconditioned stimulus (US) will elicit the conditioned response (CR) preceding the unconditioned response (UR). They presume that all behavior can be expressed as the sum of responses to stimuli, which can be seen to include and ultimately to be derived from such fundamentals as the slaking of thirst, the assuaging of hunger, the titillation of sex, and the placation or subjugation of other animals.

In their chauvinistic arrogance they fail to note that in the typical experiment it is the animal that is controlling their behaviors, in that they spend (or should have spent) many thousands of dollars on the care, feeding, and housing of their subject, tailor the equipment and tasks to the capabilities of the species, familiarize and train it, and then sit waiting for it to deign to stop eating, licking, grooming, or just looking around long enough for them to give it a CS. There is little question that schedules of reinforcement work best in dealing with animals and small children if one has neither the time, patience, nor inclination to make friends with them or has to employ sufficient numbers of subjects to construct statistical norms and cannot get to know them as individuals. What is lost is the fact that animals like to play. This is not the response to a stimulus.This is the emergence of bodily activity as an expression of the internally generated activity of the nervous system. And where does that come from? That is from the cross-talk in the village, whether or not a stranger comes to town, which is the local and largely autonomous reexcitation among neurons interconnected by the thousands.

This is the point at which a strange kind of word comes into effect; we say that the activity of the brain is *self-organizing*. This may raise the ire of those philosophers who adhere to the notion that nothing can cause itself. Yet in its simpler and inanimate forms, the behavior that the word denotes is commonly experienced. We see it, for example, in the emergence of cloud patterns in a previously clear blue sky, in the bubbles that form at the bottom of a heated pan of water, and in the formation of differing patterns of drops of water from a leaky faucet, rather than the tap-tap-tap of periodic drops. Self-organization appears in the earliest stages of the development of the brain from the fertilized ovum on into the embryo, because its structure and function come not simply from genes. The expression of genetic information leads to the formation of a fluid-filled cylinder of cells, the neural tube, that invaginates, folds, bends, buds, and creates temporal patterns of flow, which in turn support the growth of spatial patterns of cell migration and the growth of axons and dendrites. The genetic code provides basic instructions that lead to self-organization of form. This is the case with memory as well, which is a process of construction and not of retrieval (Bartlett, 1932), in which synaptic connections provide small sets of instructions that are essential for the construction of recollections.

In principle, then, it is possible to see how neural structure in the form of interconnected neurons, having the capacity to be connected to their histories, can lead to the emergence of spatial and temporal patterns of activity, which are expressed in the discharges of motor neurons in concordance with such patterns. That is, behavior can arise from within by self-organizing patterns of neural activity in the interconnected masses of the brain, and it is not simply the sum of conditioned or unconditioned responses to stimuli. Psychologists have gotten it backwards. Some philosophers, including Dewey (1896, 1912), Sherrington (1906), and Merleau-Ponty (1964), have recognized this, but for nearly a century there has been no widely accepted alternative, and in science even a bad theory is preferable to none at all. Scientific experimental evidence of self-organization requires us to rescind a fundamental tenet of current neuroscience, the reflex action and the consequent structuring of behavior as a hierarchy of reflex actions, for that argument is unsuccessful.

Having established on the basis of our research what we consider to be fundamental fallacies in the dominant foundational concepts of most contemporary research on the nervous system, we find perceptual neuroscience to appear bereft of adequate foundations and its dependent ally, psychology, to exist in a Morphean mist. Chaos and the theory of nonlinear dynamics with the journeyman tools of the computer emerge to waken the sleeping beauty of behavioral neuroscience and psychology. Awakened, the sights beheld by them are both fresh and amazing!

CHAOS IN SELF-ORGANIZING BRAINS

Chaos in the traditional meaning refers to the formless void from which order arose. The new technical meaning is rather close to the old one. It refers to a state of matter or neurons or populations in which order is not present but is latent and can emerge in the twinkling of an eye. To invoke another oxymoron, it is controlled disorder. By definition, a self-organizing system cannot be made, only facilitated. We have a good recipe for encouraging the emergence of a self-organizing system: (a) Assemble together a large number of distinct elements such as molecules, ants, people, or neurons, and allow each to transmit to many others in the group, and to receive from many others matter, energy, information, or all three. (b) Specify that the relationship between input and output for each element be nonlinear. This means that if the input is increased in small steps from a low level to a high level, the output will change, but it will not change in direct proportion to the level of input. For example, if molecules in a pan of water are heated, they will move faster in the pan, but above some threshold they will turn to steam and leave the pan. If someone steps lightly on your toe you may move it; more strongly, you may demand an apology; yet more strongly, you may seek medical and legal aid. If a neuron is stimulated weakly it may release current but not action potentials. Above a certain threshold it will fire. This distinctly different kind of output from the same kind of input at different levels is the essence of nonlinear behavior. (c) Make certain that the system is open; that is, that it has a ready supply of energy, food, money, blood, or other resources, and that there is a good disposal system for heat and other wastes. (d) Turn up the energy level; that is, apply some heat uniformly, or step on the ant hill, or spread rumors of a gold strike, or inject an excitatory chemical into the bloodstream. Something interesting is likely to happen, and it is likely to be unpredicted. With some initial conditions and boundaries there will emerge new and sometimes fascinating patterns. They may congeal and by their fixity terminate the experiment. Or they may move, rotate, and reform endlessly. Or they may dissolve into ceaseless activity without a discernible spatial and temporal structure that looks like noise. In a way, it is noise, but of a special kind. It is chaos.

Mathematicians and engineers refer to degrees of freedom, which mean the number of variables, the number of different kinds of things that comprise the system, and therefore the number of dimensions or coordinate axes that are needed to describe the dynamics of a system. The noise of city traffic is high dimensional (has a great number of things in it producing noise), therefore making it very difficult to control. The noise of an orchestra that is tuning up is low dimensional (whatever the number of instruments tuning up) because it can be stopped with a rap of the baton. Numerous methods have been devised to generate noise, for it can be used to study many natural systems. Traditionally, engineers did it by applying heat, and psychologists did it by reading numbers from telephone directories. Computer programmers meet their needs by solving equations that generate random numbers, that is, "artificial" noise. The quality of randomly generated noise is very high. Very new and often very difficult techniques are needed to distinguish it from "real" noise, but those techniques confirm that "artificial" noise is low-dimensional, has a relatively low number of variables, and therefore is chaotic. Most surprising to everyone is the fact that the equations for artificial noise are deterministic. That is, they have the same basic form as Newton's Laws that so precisely serve to predict eclipses hundreds of years into the future. Given the initial conditions and the stable structure of the system of equations with set parameters, the solutions grind out answers that have definite forms, and if the system is backed up and re-started, it will pursue precisely the same course all over again. This is the basis for the determinism of Laplace, the hubris that says, given the present state of the world in sufficient detail, we can predict the future to the end of time. Yet studies of coupled nonlinear systems have shown that we cannot always predict what they will do. For one set of conditions they may go to rest; for another, into sustained regular, periodic oscillation; for yet another, into aperiodic oscillation, which is the hallmark of chaos. Exceedingly small changes in the initial conditions that are below our abilities to observe can and do result in divergences from predicted time courses of system evolution. The divergence increases exponentially with time. Thereby what was initially unobservable becomes observable, and new information is created regarding the system and its initial conditions.

Nonlinearity is familiar to us in terms of the nursery rhyme "For want of a nail the battle was lost," but the intrusion of chaos theory into the orderly citadels of physics has been accompanied by varying degrees of denial and demoralization. We cannot know the present state of the world sufficiently to predict its future with any accuracy, and even if we could write the correct predictive equations, we could not solve them in time before the future arrived. This results in a peculiar and very human state of affairs, for determinism and its meaning for humankind become enigmatic. Some philosophers claim that all is chaos, and that noise and randomness are illusory. God in Her omniscience knows the initial conditions for our fully deterministic universe, and in Her omnipotence can reach back in time to tweak the initial conditions and work miracles. Some seriously claim that Laplacian determinism, and therefore all other forms of universal determinism, are illusory, and that each self-organizing system has the capacity to determine itself and shape its own future. Let us have a symposium and drink together!

In order to reformulate this generation's response to the philosophical problem of determining how brains work, we need to take seriously the recent finding in neuroscience that shows that the activity of neurons in masses in the brain is chaotic and that what has been looked upon as "noise" and an undesirable and epiphenomenal by-product of brain function is instead a necessary and controlled activity of the brain. If brain chaos is the deliberately disordered state from which order springs, and thereby from which our behavior emerges, then it is the necessary condition that must precede any act of creation. If we wish to account for and explain our behavior in any terms other than those of stimulus-response determinism, we must come to terms with the existence and fundamental roles of chaos in our own brains and see it as the basis for flexibility, adaptiveness, trial-and-error coping, and for the use of imagination to invent new actions with which to sustain our commerce with an unpredictable and ever-changing environment. Without it, we would find ourselves trapped in stagnation or in perseverative periodic oscillations. This understanding is the contribution that modern brain science can make to our generation's discussion of brain function, which is the basis for our understanding of our organ of the episteme. We await a responsive contribution to it from psychology and philosophy with anticipation and interest.

ACKNOWLEDGMENT

Supported by grant MH 06686 from the National Institute of Mental Health.

REFERENCES

Bartlett, F. C. (1932). *Remembering*. Cambridge: Cambridge University Press.
Dewey, J. (1896). The reflex arc concept in psychology. *Psychological Review, 3*, 357–370.
Dewey, J. (1912). Perception and organic action. *Journal of Philosophy, 9*, 645–668.
Freeman, W. J. (1975). *Mass action in the nervous system*. New York: Academic Press.
Freeman, W. J. (1987). Techniques used in the search for the physiological basis of the EEG. In A. Gevins & A. Remond (Eds.), *Handbook of electroencephalography & clinical neurophysiology Vol. 3A, Part 2* (chap. 18, pp. 583–664). Amsterdam: Elsevier.
Freeman, W. J. (1991). The physiology of perception. *Scientific American, 264*, 78–85.
Merleau-Ponty, M. (1964). *The primacy of perception*. Chicago: Northwestern University Press.
Sherrington, C. S. (1906). *The integrative action of the nervous system*. New Haven: Yale University Press.

3

Introduction to Dynamics: A Basic Language; A Basic Metamodeling Strategy

Frederick David Abraham

Vox Clamantis In Deserto Deutero Isaiah 40:3

The search for truth should be the goal of our activities; it is the sole end worthy of them.
But sometimes the truth frightens us. And in fact we know that it is sometimes deceptive, that it is a phantom never showing itself for a moment except to ceaselessly flee, that it must be pursued further and even further without ever being attained. Poincaré, 1905

My basic assumptions and contentions are these: (1) Science and Psychology are in the midst of a great bifurcation. Goerner has shown that as with many great bifurcations, they are epochs in history; they are periods of ferment and hope and innovation during a long evolutionary process. We are in an embryonic phase of this bifurcation and know not yet where this trajectory leads us, but we know it liberates and empowers us greatly. The remaining chapters of this book represent many (and by no means all) of the directions, as tentative, diverse, and elementary as they may yet be, of this search to represent the temporal, spatial, behavioral, and cognitive complexity of the interactive processes we study in our discipline. (2) Dynamical systems theory, or dynamics for short, a basic mathematical discipline, stands at the center of this revolution, and provides the basic language and metamodeling strategy for science at this juncture. Although in its present form it may not yet be adequate to represent the full complexity of our phenomena, it does provide the starting place from which most explorations must stem. Furthermore, interactive animated computer-graphics for model simulation and data analysis makes it more highly communicable and easier to master than other previously existent forms of complexity language, such as stochastic and markov processes, general systems theory, neural nets, and stochastic resonance. Most of the features of other recent techniques of studying complexity share the basic features of dynamics and can often be understood in terms of them, and many of the multiple usages of terms in energy and equilibrium theory can be resolved by recourse to principles of dynamics. Thus dynamics is key because of its ability to provide a core unifying language, broadly applicable, and easily masterable, and to provide a metamodeling strategy that will empower an evolution of our science in subject, experimental design and analysis, and theory.

This chapter will provide a minimalist tour of this linguistic landscape, covering the four most elementary concepts: dynamical system, dynamical scheme, complex dynamical system, and self-organization. Their corresponding graphical (geometric) representations are the phase portrait, the response diagram, and the network diagram. The prey-predator model will be used to illustrate these, along with a few applications of that model to psychology. Other examples, such as a nonlinear version of the famous fifty-six-year-old approach-avoidance conflict, can be found in Abraham, Abraham, and Shaw (1990) along with a more complete visual presentation of dynamics. Even more complete treatment of the visual approach to dynamics can be found in the original works by Abraham and Shaw (1992) and of the mathematical approach in Thompson and Stewart (1986).

DYNAMICAL SYSTEMS

A *dynamical system* in practice involves a set of interacting variables (the mathematical theory requires that their behavior meets certain conditions of smoothness and continuity, and of infinite resolution and duration). For example, consider two variables that interact with each other, such as the firing rate of two neurons that talk to each other via a pair of synapses, or two competing responses such as pressing a lever versus eating the pellet, or a mother's tension and a son's anger.

State Space, Vectorfield, Trajectory, and Phase Portrait

The *state space* is the graphic representation of all the possible states the two variables may take on. It is not quite the same as the cartesian space, as not all of a cartesian space may be occupied by the system, and also because some of the manifolds (occupiable space) may be curved rather than straight or flat. Because a dynamical system is one that changes with time, each point in the state space when occupied by the system, has a tendency associated with it for the system to change, which can be represented by a vector. Graphically, this vector appears as an arrow indicating how much each variable will change over the next instant in time. The collection of all such vectors for each point in the state space is called the *vectorfield* (Fig. 3.1, A). If this vectorfield can be summarized by a set of differential equations (one for each variable of the state space, two in these examples), then this vectorfield defines the *dynamical system*. If the system is started at some initial

Figure 3.1: Prey-predator Model for a Neural Net, a Family Interaction, or a Response Competition A. Vectorfield (Lotka-Volterra Model). B. Phase portrait (Lotka-Volterra Model), a center. (A is from Abraham & Shaw, 1982; both A and B are in Abraham, Abraham, & Shaw, 1990; courtesy Aerial Press.)

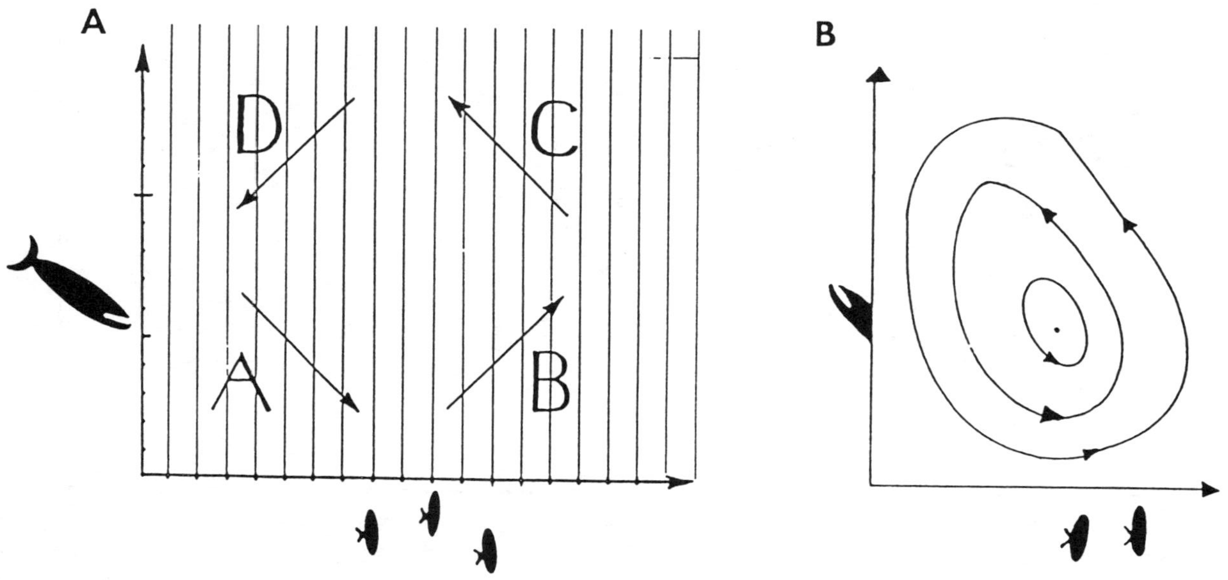

Figure 3.1, continued
C. Phase portrait, fixed-point attractor. D. Phase portrait, periodic attractor. E. Poincaré Section, chaotic trajectory. (C and D are from Abraham & Shaw, 1982 and also appear in Abraham, Abraham, & Shaw, 1990; courtesy Aerial Press; E is from Sprott & Rowlands, 1990; courtesy American Institute of Physics and Sprott.)

state, the forces creating the vector push the system to a new state, and a succession of states and their vectors creates a path, called a *trajectory*. The graph of the collection of all possible trajectories for all different initial conditions is a *phase portrait*, another graphic representation of the dynamical system (Fig. 3.1, B).

Attractors, Basins, Separatrices, Saddles, and Repellors

There may be some trajectories to which all nearby trajectories tend. Such trajectories are called *attractors*. Attractors are usually classified into 3 categories, fixed point, periodic, and chaotic (Fig. 3.1, C-E; see also Goerner, this volume, Fig. 1.1, B, for a chaotic attractor). Sometimes the chaotic attractors are subdivided informally between those that are more nearly periodic (low-dimensional attractors), and those that are more complex (high-dimensional).

The space occupied by the trajectories going to an attractor is called a *basin*. If there is more than one attractor, a trajectory separating basins and tending to neither is called a *separatrix*. A trajectory to which some trajectories tend and others depart is called a *saddle*, and may be a saddle point or a periodic saddle. Separatrices frequently go toward saddles; from the saddles some trajectories may tend to one attractor, some to another. Trajectories that emit other trajectories and attract none are *repellors*. Examples of each of these are shown in Fig. 3.2.

The state spaces and trajectories may be generated by theory or by measurement of observable variables or from some combination of theoretical and observable variables with the usual constraints of theory construction (MacCorquodale & Meehl, 1948). Theory hosts an equation for each variable of the state space. These equations are rules of change of how each variable changes over time. They represent the vectors for each point in the state space.

For Figure 3.1, the prey-predator model, the vectors show that the change in each variable depends on itself and upon the other variable. When x is the firing rate of a spontaneously active cell (S, the prey) with an excitatory synapse "feeding" the normally quiet cell (Q, the predator), and y is the firing rate of the normally quiet cell, Q, with an inhibitory synapse back on the normally active cell, S, the vectorfield says that when both rates are high (upper right quadrant), the active excitatory synapse makes x, the firing rate of Q, go up, and the increased activity at the inhibitory synapse makes x, the firing rate of S, go down. As x goes down, the excitatory input to Q goes down; without that driving input, the normally silent cell slows down (upper left quadrant). As y of Q diminishes, x of S can recover (lower left quadrant); as S recovers, it again activates Q and both rates go up (lower right quadrant). In this overidealized model (the equations are given in the appendix to this chapter), the periodic trajectories (Fig. 3.1, B) are not attractors but, rather, constitute what is called a center; nearby trajectories do not tend to it; any starting point within that basin cycles back through the starting point. More realistic models are also shown (Fig. 3.1, C-E).

Figure 3.2: Basic Features of Phase Portraits
A. Point repellors (open circles); point attractors (filled circles); separatrices (vertical trajectories) going to a saddle (half-filled circle) with basins of trajectories to the right and left attractors. B. Model for Tomkins' conservative-liberal ideology (I). The state space is I', rate of change of I, versus. I. The shaded basin contains trajectories going to the right-hand (conservative) attractor, the trajectories of the unshaded basin go to the left-hand attractor (liberal), the separatrices are the trajectories on the border of the basins going to the repellor between them. The unshaded basin is larger, showing a liberal bias.
(A. © Fred Abraham; B. from Abraham et al., 1990; courtesy Aerial Press.)

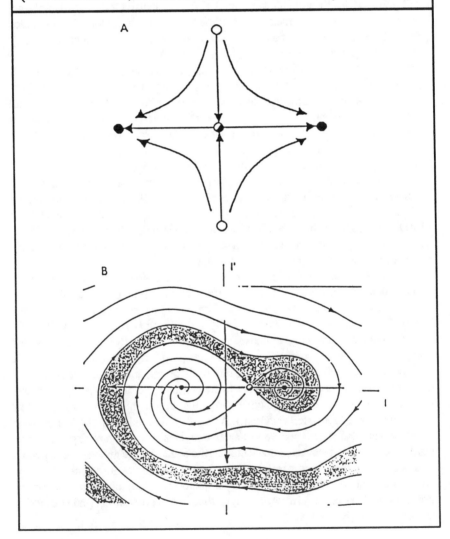

In family systems therapy, a similar model has been proposed (Elkaïm, Goldbeter, & Goldbeter-Merinfeld, 1987) where a mother's 'tension' replaces Q and y, and a son's 'anger' replaces S and x. They interpreted the son's anger synergystically, not as aggressive so much as motivated to relieve the mother's tension (heavily driven by a cyclically drunk father, which was not formally included in their model but could easily be incorporated). A third psychological example that could be represented by this same model is that of competing responses such as lever pressing and eating when the two are incompatible, for example, at any given instant as might result from a food bin separated from an operant lever (Hanson & Timberlake, 1983). Eating and hunger could also be modeled this way. This model is overly simple and in fact quite unstable, and in its present form, it is incapable of very complex behavior, even though it is nonlinear (the equations describing change over time have nonlinear components, especially in the terms in each equation that mutually couple the change to the other variable; Sprott & Rowlands, 1990). Such nonlinearity is required to allow bifurcations, that is, major changes in the behavior of the system (as seen in the phase portraits), and for chaotic attractors to exist. These are found in dynamical schemes, to which we now turn.

DYNAMICAL SCHEMES

In the dynamical system each variable is a dimension of the state space, and other factors remain constant (and appear as constants in the equations). However, when the constants are modified, the behavior of the dynamical system changes. The behavior of the system as a function of changes in the constants (parameters) constitutes a *dynamical scheme*. The graphical representation of the dynamical scheme is called the *response diagram* (Fig. 3.3).

Bifurcations

For example, change in a factor that might represent the strength of influence of the excitatory synapse, the strength of influence of the son's anger, or the ease of performing one of the competing responses might cause a phase portrait of a dynamical system to shift from a fixed point to a periodic attractor. Were the system a bit more complex, that is, of a higher dimension, it might also change to a chaotic attractor, say, if a third neuron, another family member, or another response or drive condition were involved. A bifurcation is when the system changes in a major way rather than just in a small quantitative way, remember. When the bifurcation occurs, the value of a *control parameter*, that is, a parameter responsible for bifurcations, is called the *bifurcation point*. Bifurcations are classified as *subtle, catastrophic,* or *explosive. Bifurcations* are *subtle,* like those just mentioned, when an attractor changes type (e.g., fixed point to periodic, which is known as a Hopf bifurcation). A

Figure 3.3: Response Diagram for Mood

The three-dimensional state space is for the variables of mood, self-image, and their rate of change. The control parameter is dependency à la Freud. Attractor types and bifurcations are indicated. (Abraham, Abraham, & Shaw, 1990; courtesy Aerial Press.)

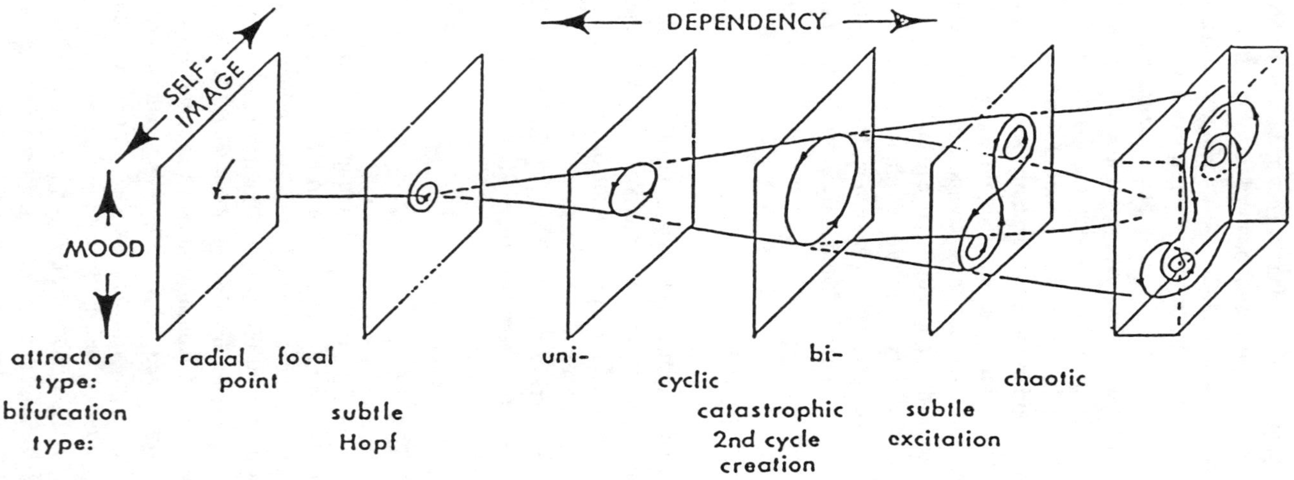

Table 3.1: Subtle Bifurcations

Type of Attractor before Bifurcation	Type of Attractor after Bifurcation		
	Fixed-point	Periodic	Chaotic
Fixed-point		Hopf	Ueda
Peroidic	Reverse Hopf	Octave Jump Neimark	Excitation of Chaos
Chaotic	Reverse Ueda	Relaxation of Chaos	

classification of subtle bifurcations is shown in the Table 3.1. A *catastrophic bifurcation* is when an attractor is created or annihilated along with its basin. That is, an attractor appears where none existed before, or it disappears. A bifurcation is *explosive* (or *implosive*) when it gets suddenly larger (or smaller); it may be accompanied by changes in other features and also include characteristics of one of the other types of bifurcations.

Stability

When not near a bifurcation point, a system is most likely occupying some state in one of its potential attractors (if it has run long enough to get past start up transient trajectories), and these are quite stable conditions. Small perturbations or changes in the parameters often make for only small changes in the system behavior. But the system becomes less stable as control parameters approach bifurcation points, and it is very unstable at bifurcation points and at saddle points. The concepts of homeostasis (fixed-point attractor) and equilibrium may thus often be better thought of in terms of stability; and all types of attractors, fixed point, periodic, and even chaotic, can be considered quite stable, that is, behaving with dynamic equilibrium. Think of two people just sitting on a teeter-totter and the ratio of their masses as a control parameter. If the ratio is far from 1:1, one of the two fixed-point attractors dominates in a very stable way, with one person on the ground; if the ratio is 1:1, the two are balanced very unstably on the now horizontal board, probably with some chaotic swaying for each subtle shift in position or wind current.

Hysteresis and the Static Cusp Catastrophe

Bifurcation theory underwent major development by René Thom (1972/1975) and was brought into psychology, social science, and neurophysiology by Christopher Zeeman (1977). The initial development was with elementary catastrophe theory, where the bifurcation of a fixed point occurs. The most famous of these elementary catastrophes was the cusp catastrophe (Fig. 3.4), used heavily in psychology (Callahan & Sashin, 1987; Frey & Sears, 1978; Guastello, 1985; Guastello et al., this volume; Zeeman, 1977). For the cusp catastrophe, the response diagram shows a phase portrait for each point in the control space. The control space is the two-dimensional horizontal plane (two control parameters), and the state space is one-dimensional (a single-variable system, represented by the vertical axis in this typical figure). The phase portrait consists of two fixed-point attractors, a saddle point between them within the area of the cusp, and their associated trajectories; outside the area of the cusp there exists only one fixed point for each point in the control space. The unshaded part of the folded-blanket-like manifold shows the loci of the fixed-point attractors; the shaded surface shows the loci of the saddle

Figure 3.4: Static Cusp Catastrophe
The state space is one-dimensional (vertical). The horizontal control plane is two-dimensional. Within the cusp there are two point attractors (their loci are on the unshaded surface) separated by a point repellor at each point in the control space (their loci are on the shaded surface). Outside the cusp is only one attractor at each point in the control space (its loci are on the unshaded surface). The double-fold catastrophe is similar but with only one control parameter.
(From Abraham & Shaw, 1987; courtesy Plenum.)

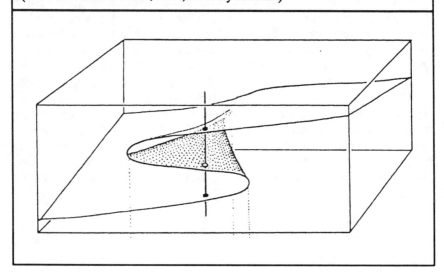

points. Thus if the control parameter of the front horizontal axis were continuously decreased from the right to the left, the fixed point would disappear at the extreme left of the fold in a catastrophic bifurcation because the value of the trajectory at that time would be above the saddle. At that bifurcation point, when the upper fixed-point attractor disappears, a new fixed-point attractor appears on the lower part of the fold. If the value of the parameter is increased from the far left to the right, a similar bifurcation occurs when the right most extreme of the fold is reached, with the lower fixed-point attractor disappearing catastrophically and a new fixed-point attractor appearing at the upper surface, again because the trajectory was below the saddle until that point. Thus there is a hysteresis effect for repeated sliding up and down of the control parameter.

Bifurcation Sequences

Many dynamical schemes involve a system evolving through a whole sequence of bifurcations as control parameters are changing. The famous Ruelle-Takens sequence is point–cycle–braid–chaos. Others include octave jumping and period doubling, also often ending in chaos (see Goerner, this volume, Fig. 1.2). Sometimes some of these bifurcations are reversible, with or without hysteresis effects, although for many systems they are not; this is a subject of considerable interest and made popular by Prigogine and Stengers (1984), who highlighted energy considerations affecting dynamics and bifurcations. The reader should be cautioned about the multiplicity of meanings by different authors concerning the language of equilibrium and far-from-equilibrium conditions in such discussions (see Guastello et al., this volume; Rosen, 1970; my epilogue, this volume). Another cautionary note: although this chapter attempts to establish a basic vocabulary, most of the terms herein have had synonyms abounding in the literature; but the context should make their meanings, that is, their equivalency to the definitions here, fairly clear (again, see my epilogue).

The concepts of bifurcation and bifurcation sequences are especially important to psychology, as, for example, in describing the sudden changes (a) in motivational states, (b) in learning, (c) in brain activity and neuroendocrine function, (d) in developmental stages and their associated increasing complexity, (e) in personality and family organization, both spontaneous and managed as within therapy and self-help programs, and (f) in social, economic, and organizational systems (for a more complete list, see Gilgen, Chap. 9, this volume). For example, many therapists and teachers consider pushing people to bifurcation points, even though the process of occupying a bifurcation point may be uncomfortable, in order for growth to occur from worn-out, uncomfortable, or maladaptive albeit stable (and safe) attractors to new ones with their greater potential for a satisfying and productive life. Kugler suggests that intentional systems may like to be near bifurcation points in order to make choices among attractors more readily.

Dynamical Mechanisms of Change

There are several mechanisms of making a change or facilitating a change in dynamical systems and schemes. These focus on changing the likelihood of realizing one of several potential attractors. The simplest is specifying a new initial condition, as, say, in a different basin, thus pushing its likelihood to 1. Another is to build features into the system that enable it to jump basins (hill-climbing). Adding chaos, whether low-dimensional (Hubler, 1992) or high-dimensional, is an example. The latter is exemplified by stochastic resonance where noise within a sensory system enables a fast sequence of bifurcations for more accurate and efficient response to an oscillating signal (Chialvo & Apkarian, 1993). Another similar example would be simulated annealing in learning where control parameters are moved away from nonoptimal fixed points using probabalistic principles (Szu et al., 1993).

Some dynamical systems may have fractal separatrices that are complex and involuted; the basins interdigitate in a convoluted fashion such that trajectories passing quite near each other are in different basins and end up in different attractors (for a novel use in psychology, as in Lewin's life spaces, see the chapter by Ralph Abraham). Such fractal separatrices may be more easily jumped by the stochastic processes just outlined.

The final mechanism of changing the likelihood of realizing one of several attractors is in making bifurcations to change the pattern of available attractors by using self-organization to maneuver or navigate the control space of the response diagram. The strategy may attempt to time itself to favor the locus of a trajectory at the moment of bifurcation, or it may simply stack the deck by changing the relative size of basins, which are proportional to the probability of realizing an attractor. These will be again mentioned in connection with dynamical aspects of cognition (Part III).

CHARACTERISTICS OF CHAOS

Chaotic attractors have several important properties. Although these are well known, there are some interesting misinterpretations and overstatements about some of these characteristics, such as those concerning predictability/ unpredictability and determinism/indeterminism. These stem from the famous "sensitivity to initial conditions," also known as "sensitive dependence on initial conditions" and "the butterfly effect."

Convergence and Divergence

A chaotic attractor exists because there are a mixture of forces being resolved, some of which are convergent (i.e., move trajectories toward the attractor) and some of which are divergent (i.e., tend to repel trajectories away from each other along the attractive surface or area). Obviously the attractive forces must be greater for the attractor to live. For states more central in the attractor, the stronger become the divergent forces; for states more peripheral in the attractor, the stronger become the convergent forces. Thus the trajectory wanders closer and farther, folding back on to itself when it gets too far away, making a thick layered surface much like bread dough or taffy being repeatedly pulled and folded—a metaphor popularized by Rössler for low-dimensional, well-behaved attractors like Rössler's and Lorenz's.

Sensitivity and Insensitivity to Initial Conditions

One consequence is that any two trajectories once on the attractive surface will tend to diverge from each other for a while, no matter how close they may be without being perfectly identical (Fig. 3.5). Figure 3.5 shows that any set of trajectories in some arbitrarily small area, if followed for a short while, comes to occupy a larger area, thus showing divergence or expansion. This has been called "sensitivity to initial conditions." But one should note a few things before trying to conclude that this implies unpredictability. First is that if ordinary calculus applies and the equations are deterministic, exactly specifying the initial conditions always results in placing the trajectory in the same place after a given amount of time. The unpredictability comes only when you leave the idealized world of infinite duration and resolution of deterministic calculus for the real world of imprecision of measurement and finite time duration and resolution. Thus in the real world, there is an area of uncertainty (as in Fig. 3.5). A set of nearby trajectories is all that is known from this error of observation, and this error or dispersion increases with time after the initial condition or observation.

Another way of introducing unpredictability is for the equations of change to have a stochastic or probabalistic component, as in the cases of stochastic resonance and simulated annealing, just mentioned, which is tantamount to saying that a small jitter or noise or resetting of initial conditions is constantly occurring. Unpredictability in this context does not mean absolutely no predictability or total independence, however. The trajectory remains in the attractor, always obeying the same smooth vectorfield. Therefore very strong conditional probability statements can be made. Also, a trajectory from any given initial condition always pierces every region of the attractor given enough time, and thus it samples the vectorfield everywhere, revealing its basic nature. Any trajectory is as good as any other; only one trajectory is needed to represent the attractor. Furthermore, in practical terms, usually an exact prediction is of little interest, although Lorenz, as a meteorologist,

Figure 3.5: Rössler's Chaotic Attractor
Rössler's attractor showing expansion of the area occupied by a set of trajectories due to divergence of trajectories within the attractor. The area, x, within a Poincaré section, shows the trajectories contained within have expanded to the area, R(x), the first return map, after one trip around the attractor.
(From Abraham & Shaw, Part 2, 1983; and Abraham et al., 1990; courtesy Aerial Press.)

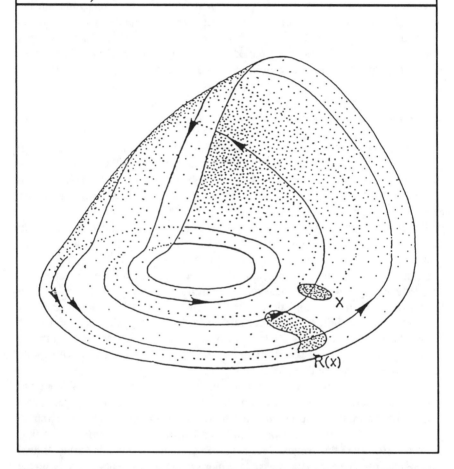

of course was so interested, and anyone planning an outdoor concert or picnic may also be. But the tree doesn't care, and neither do you if you keep an umbrella in the car; you simply want the attractor to behave as it usually does so you have enough drinking water and the garden continues to grow. I shall call this unconcern with exact predictability and initial conditions *"insensitivity to initial conditions."* Sensitivity/ insensitivity to initial conditions is important not for exact prediction but for reminding us of the nature of a chaotic attractor and the forces that shape it.

Fractal Properties

Trajectories as they evolve tend to fill up the thick attractive surface in an orderly process that is simpler the lower the dimensionality of the state space. The *Poincaré section*, a slice through the attractor that is one dimension less than the state space, reveals a pattern in its development. A *Lorenz section*, perpendicular to the Poincaré section, reveals how the layering of the thick attractive surface builds up. When the process is very low-dimensional, the process looks like a simple fractal, an iterative Cantor-like, self-similar process. The higher-dimensional the process, the more complex it appears, although the complexity depends not only on the number of interactive variables but on the strength of their mutual influence, the coupling (control) constants. The complexity can be estimated by numerical algorithms such as fractal dimension and Liapounov exponents. When applied to data gathered from research rather than that generated by models (models are the sets of differential equations or sometimes, more informally, sketches of phase portraits), their complexity, their fractal dimension, may be greater than the number of observable variables and may crudely reflect the number and strength of the theoretical variables influencing the observable ones. The modeling skill comes in guessing those variables and their relationships, as with any modeling enterprise. Usually comparing empirical trajectories, fractal dimension, and other measures of time series such as recurrence plots and measures of power spectra, cospectra, coherence spectra, and phase spectra (despite their linearity) can combine to give better clues to the process involved. The chapters by Combs (Chap. 8, this volume) and Sabelli et al. (Chap. 7, this volume) show some of these comparisons. And the trajectory by Burlingame, Fuhriman, and Barnum (Chap. 6, this volume) shows a novel result, where the fractal dimension becomes a variable in the state space for the trajectory.

SELF-ORGANIZATION AND COMPLEX DYNAMICAL SYSTEMS

Dynamical systems may be distinguished arbitrarily as simple or complex. A *complex dynamical system* is one that can be subdivided into simpler components for easier analysis. Conceptually, mathematically, the component systems are coupled together by having the control parameters of some under the influence of the state of other components of the complex system, which are usually depicted by network diagrams. Neural net modelers are masters of depicting the relationship among variables in a system by diagrams (Part IV, this volume), though their diagrams are not limited to complex systems connected by influences upon control parameters but include the variable-to-variable interactions as well.

In a complex network, very likely, a control parameter of a component subsystem will be under the influence of another component subsystem that was itself influenced by the first, perhaps not directly, but through a chain of other component subsystems. Thus there is a feedback loop. This concept of feedback is more restrictive than the earlier concepts of feedback by the general systems theorists, who also included the interaction of variables in the concept of feedback. The lineage (Poincaré, 1905; Thom, 1972/1975) represented here assumes such interaction as a matter of course not requiring the term *feedback*. Feedback here means that a system influences its own control parameters. It may do so directly without the intervention of communication with other systems (Fig. 3.6, A) or via a communication network among systems comprising a complex dynamical system (Fig. 3.6, B). The distinction is somewhat arbitrary, as the complex system could be collapsed conceptually into a single simple dynamical system if one chose to do so.

Self-organization is the most important subject of dynamics for psychology (remember *Abraham's First Prognostiplatitude* in the Leibniz correspondence in the Preface, this volume; Abraham et al., 1990) for obvious reasons. All living and psychological systems are *self-organizational*. That is, they can control their own

Figure 3.6: Self-organization and Network of Complex Dynamical System
A. Direct self-control of the state of a system back onto its own control parameter shown for the response diagram of a single dynamical scheme for one individual, you. B. A complex dynamical system shown by a network of dynamical schemes with the control parameters of some influenced by the states of others; self-organization is expressed by the feedback chain of a system influencing itself mediated by other schemes in the network. A social system for three individuals (for description of the social situation see Genesis or Miller (1959) on approach-avoidance conflict). Variables of the state space: IRS is instrumental response strength, a function of positive and negative conditioned emotional responses; DG is physical or psychological distance from a goal. The control parameter, F, is sensitivity to fear or some similar factor.
(© Fred Abraham)

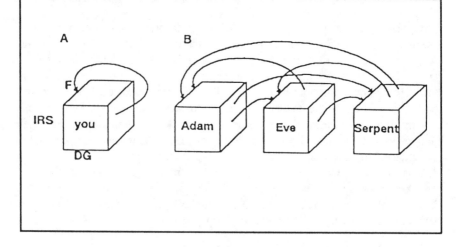

control parameters, giving them the capability to make bifurcations within their own dynamical schemes and complex dynamical systems. Sentient beings can thus learn their own response diagrams, so to speak, can learn to navigate them, and can imagine extrapolations of those diagrams and test a new universe of self (chapters by Combs, Prueitt, Torre, and others focus on this cognitive navigation).

CONCLUSION

The field of psychology is like a chaotic attractor, with forces of convergence and divergence. Overly convergent periods of its history have seen too great attention paid to a few hegemonical theories that grew too large and rigid to adapt to the complexity of the field. Similarly there have been overly divergent periods where the mulitiversity and idiosyncrasy have been so great that communication of communalities become impossible (Bevan, 1991; Gilgen, 1987; Staats, 1991). Despite its inadequacies and its embryonic and transitional nature, the common language summarized here is seen as a basis for communication and strategy that will enable a healthy balance of the evolution of unification and diversity within our field (also emphasized in chapters by F. Abraham, Gilgen, Goerner, and Tryon, this volume). It is easily mastered, it is clear and simple, it can be pursued to more sophisticated levels or remain as a metaphoric clarification of ideas. It will empower us to pursue complexity, wean us from some of the linear design and analysis and modeling restrictions of the past, get us focused again on the complexities of interacting aspects of behavior over time, and recover much that is there that has been lost to the error terms and static snapshots of behavior in time. We will be able to heal some of the schisms between analytic and holistic approaches (Tryon, Chap. 18, this volume), and do so with respect for the continuity in our historical development (Leahey, 1992), but with an appreciation of the excitement of periods of ferment, this time metamodeled by the very process that is playing a central role in the metamodeling revolution. We are developing the tools to study complexity and to model and communicate it more clearly. We are becoming enchanted with our new vision of the complexity of the universe.

APPENDIX:
ORIGINAL LOTKA-VOLTERRA PREY-PREDATOR EQUATIONS

$dx/dt = ax - bxy$
$dy/dt = cxy - dy,$ where x and y are the prey and predator variables,
                        and a, b, c, and d are constants.

DEDICATION

To Ralph Abraham, Lover To The Universe And To All Its Creatures, And Superb Navigator Of Its Complexities, Traveling In Awe And Serenity, With Humor And Creativity. Inspirator Supreme.

REFERENCES

Abraham, F. D., Abraham, R. H., & Shaw, C. D. (1990). *A visual introduction to dynamical systems theory for psychology*. Santa Cruz: Aerial.

Abraham, R. H., & Shaw, C. D. (1982–1988/1992). *Dynamics, the geometry of behavior Vols. (Parts) 1–4*. Santa Cruz CA USA: Aerial. (2nd ed.). Reading: Addison-Wesley.

Abraham, R. H., & Shaw, C. D. (1987). Dynamics, a visual introduction. In F. E. Yates (Ed.), *Self-organizing systems*. New York: Plenum.

Bevan, W. (1991). A tour inside the onion. *American Psychologist, 46*, 475–483.

Callahan, J., & Sashin, J. (1987). Models of affect response and anorexia nervosa. In S. H. Koslow, A. J. Mandell, & M. F. Shlesinger (Eds.), *Perspectives in biological dynamics and theoretical medicine. Annals of the New York Academy of Science* (Vol. 504, pp. 241–259). New York: New York Academy of Sciences.

Chialvo, D. R., & Apkarian, A. V. (1993). Modulated noisy biological dynamics: Three examples. *Journal of Statistical Physics, 70*, 375–391.

Elkaïm, M., Goldbeter, A., & Goldbeter-Merinfeld, E. (1987). Analysis of the dynamics of a family system in terms of bifurcations. *Journal of Social and Biological Structures, 10*, 21–36.

Frey, P. W., & Sears, R. J. (1978). Model of conditioning incorporating the Rescorla-Wagner associative axiom, a dynamic attention process, and a catastrophe rule. *Psychological Review, 85*, 321–340.

Gilgen, A. R. (1987). The psychological level of organization in nature and interdependencies among major psychological concepts. In A. W. Staats & L. P. Mos (Eds.), *Annals of theoretical psychology* (Vol. 5). New York: Plenum Press.

Guastello, S. J. (1985). Euler buckling in a wheelbarrow obstacle course: A catastrophe with complex lag. *Behavioral Science, 30*, 204–212.

Hanson, S. J., & Timberlake, W. (1983). Regulation during challenge: A general model of learned performance under schedule constraint. *Psychological Review, 90*, 261–282.

Hubler, A. (1992). Modeling and control of complex systems: Paradigms and applications. In L. Lam (Ed.). *Modeling complex phenomena*. New York: Springer.

Leahey, T. H. (1992). The mythical revolutions of American psychology. *American Psychologist, 47*, 308–318.

MacCorquodale, K., & Meehl, P. E. (1948). On a distinction between hypothetical constructs and intervening variables. *Psychological Review, 55*, 95–107.

Miller, N. E. (1959). Liberalization of basic s–r concepts: Extensions to conflict behavior, motivation, and social learning. In Koch, S. (Ed.), *Psychology: A study of a science, Vol. 2, General systematic formulations, learning, and special processs*. New York: McGraw-Hill.

Poincaré, H. (1905/1913). *Valeur de science* (The value of science). (In G. B. Halstead, Trans., *Foundations of science*). New York: Science Press.

Prigogine, I. & Stengers, I. (1984). *Order out of chaos*. New York: Bantam Books.

Rosen, R. (1970). *Dynamical system theory in biology*. New York: Wiley Interscience.

Sprott, J. C., & Rowlands, G. (1990). *Chaos demonstrations*. Raleigh: Academic Software Library.

Staats, A.W. (1991). Unified positivism and unification psychology. *American Psychologist, 46*, 899–912.

Szu, H., Telfer, B., Rogers, G., Lee, K., Moon, G., Zaghloul, M., & Loew, M. (1993). Collective chaos and neural network learning. In K. H. Pribram (Ed.), *Rethinking neural networks: Quantum fields and biological data* (pp. 475–482). Hillsdale: Erlbaum.

Thom, R. (1972/1975). *Stabilité structurelle et morphogenèse/Structural stability and morphogenesis*, 1975 (H. Fowler, Trans.). Reading: Benjamin.

Thompson, J. M. T., & Stewart, H. B. (1986). *Nonlinear dynamics and chaos*. Chichester: Wiley.

Zeeman, E. C. (1977). *Catastrophe theory and its applications*. Reading: Addison-Wesley.

Part II
DYNAMICAL ANALYSIS OF BEHAVIOR

4

Stability and Variability: The Geometry of Children's Novel-Word Interpretations

Linda B. Smith

Dynamical systems theory is gaining ground in developmental psychology, obviously fertile territory for dynamical changes over time, as witnessed by the recent number of new books and major articles on the topic (Fogel, 1993; Freyd, 1992; Smith & Thelen, 1993; Thelen & Smith, 1994). The growing excitement stems directly from the potential of dynamical systems theory to solve fundamental problems. In this chapter I consider one such problem: the relation between the global structure of a behavior and its local variability.

Each time we perform some act, for example, each time we understand the word *cat*, we do the same sort of thing. There is a stability to the idea of cat across its individual occurrences. Yet each time we perform this mental act, there are also differences. How we understand *cat* varies with whether we are thinking about barns or Africa, whether the objects before us are kittens or Garfield, and whether we are anxious or happy. Each understanding is locally unique. The question I consider in this chapter is the relation between the global stability and the local variability of cognition. How are individual mental acts at one and the same time globally similar to each other but locally unique and adapted to the idiosyncrasies of the moment? Dynamical systems theory offers new answers to these questions, answers that change the kinds of experiments we do, the phenomena we think important, and the kinds of explanations we entertain.

THE TRADITIONAL VIEW

The central goal in traditional cognitive theories has been to explain the stability of cognition. How is it that each time we hear the word *cat*, we think about the same kind of object? How is it that when we hear the sentence *That is an odd cat* and when we hear *That is a fat cat*, we understand both as referring to a common kind

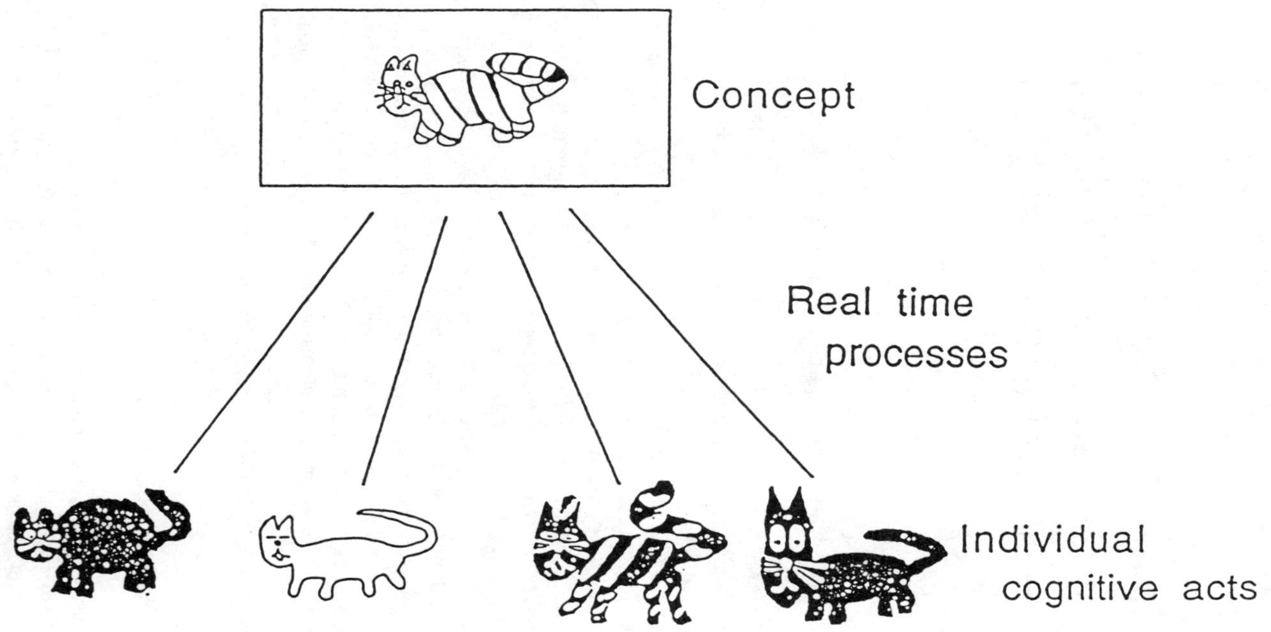

Figure 4.1: A Cartoon Illustration of the Traditional Explanation of Stability and Variability

of animal? According to the traditional view, we do so because we possess an underlying structure that specifies what *cat* means. This structure, commonly called our concept of cat, sits in our head until it is needed, that is, until it is activated by occurrences of the word *cat*. In this view, the activation of the concept is understanding. Thus, the reason we understand the same thing each time we understand the word *cat* is because we engage the very same structure each time—the very same concept of cat. According to this view, the reason there is stability in cognition is because we have static representations that are repeatedly activated in different contexts.

Stability, however, is only one fact about cognition. In the two cases of the *fat cat* and the *odd cat*, we do not really understand *exactly* the same thing. We have different ideas in the two contexts about the cats to which we refer. In the traditional view, this local variability is not caused by our concept of cat, which is a constant, but rather by the real-time processes that activate the concept and somehow modify it to fit the local task. Critically, then, stability and variability are seen as having separate causes. This prevailing view of global order and local variability is summarized in Figure 4.1: There is a constant stable concept of cat that causes the stability across different instances of thinking about cats, and there are the real-time processes that access, select from, and adjust that constant structure to make adaptively variable outcomes.

This partition of cognition into stability (structure) and variability (process) has played a major role in how research is done. The strategy has been to discover cognitive structures by abstracting what is the same across multiple occurrences of the "same" cognitive act. Thus as scientists we try to discover people's concept of cat by determining what is the same about each and every understanding of cat: What is the core invariant that is there both in the odd cat and the fat cat? Answering this question requires discarding variability. It is what is constant across individual cognitive acts that is important because, in this view, knowledge is a constant. Indeed, the highest, most advanced, most mature forms of intelligence are the most stable—the most general and most context insensitive. Being smart about cats in the traditional view means an abstract constant concept of cat that can be applied in many diverse and locally variable contexts.

THE DYNAMICAL VIEW

The traditional approach to cognition is being questioned because it means at best an incomplete understanding of the very stability it seeks to explain (Smith & Thelen, 1993). There is an increasing realization that there can be no understanding of the global order without an understanding of the variability. We need to explain not just *that cognition is stable* but *how it is stable in the midst of adaptive, context-specific, variability*. What are the processes that make what we think about kittens and barn cats similar yet at the same time appropriately different? There is no real understanding of intelligence without an understanding of variability. Intelligence is not doing the same thing over and over. Intelligence is doing something new that perfectly fits the needs of the moment.

The dynamical systems view offers an alternative to the traditional view, and here variability rather than constancy is the key. In dynamical systems, the global order and local variability have a single cause; *the local details of real-time processes* make both variable individual acts and the global structure that transcends the individual acts. In this view, cognition is caused by complex (high-dimensional) interactions in which stability is emergent and adaptively variable because the order is always made anew, in real time, in context.

The bifurcation sequence of the increasing number of cells on the route to turbulence in a fluid as heat is applied or stirring speed is increased (see Goerner, this volume, Fig. 1.2) shows many patterns. The patterns of movement are stable, but there are no structures. The global orders are made in real time in the collective action of individual molecules, and these global orders have no permanent reality outside their real-time occurrence. In brief, those cells are *events* in time. Are concepts like the cells? Are our concepts of barn cat and fat cat assembled in real time through the interaction of many forces and not by accessing a constant represented structure? How do we investigate such a possibility? Several lessons are to be learned from thinking about stability and variability from the example of fluid cells and turbulence, to be recalled from earlier chapters. The system is nonlinear; all the patterns result from the same system; the global patterns are products of the local processes, not the cause of them; and the system exhibits several patterns of a dynamical scheme that could be shown in a response diagram, which can include the creation of novel patterns not previously encountered as the control parameter is pushed to new values.

If cognition is similarly dynamical, then we can understand it only by looking for change, not just constancies. We need to study variability. Dynamical systems theory offers several useful tools for describing how systems change, as described in earlier chapters (those of Abraham, Goerner). In the remainder of this chapter I show how cognition is dynamical.

I specifically consider the problem of assembling word meanings in context. I don't ask, however, how we modify cat to arrive at *fat cats* and *barn cats*. I ask how people, indeed very young people, can figure out the intended meaning of words they never heard before. The specific phenomenon is children's novel-word interpretations. This phenomenon challenges the traditional view of cognition precisely because it is about creative cognition, about doing something that one has never done before—understanding a novel word from the context in which it is heard.

NOVEL-WORD INTERPRETATION IN CHILDREN

Between the ages of eighteen months and five years, children acquire, on average, nine new words a day (Templin, 1957). In order to acquire so many words so fast, children must figure out the meaning of many words from hearing them used just once in context. Explaining how children understand novel words in context means explaining how they do something new that fits the situation. One way to study this phenomenon is to ask young children to do in the laboratory what they do in the world: that is, to present them with a novel object, name it with a novel word, and then ask the children what other objects have the same name.

A large number of studies using this technique have found that two- and three-three-year old children attend to the shapes of objects and maintain that objects have the same name that have the same shape (Jones & Smith, 1993; Markman, 1989; for reviews). Attending to shape when naming objects is smart behavior; many basic categories of the kind that children learn first (e.g., dog, cat, table, cup) appear to be organized by shape (Biederman, 1985; Rosch, 1973).

Importantly, however, young children only attend to shape when interpreting a novel word; they do *not* attend to shape when making other kinds of judgments. In one experiment, Landau, Smith, and Jones (1988) used the stimuli shown in Figure 4.2. They presented two- and three-year-old children with one of two tasks. In the novel-word interpretation task, the child was shown the exemplar object and told, for example, "This is a dax"; then the child was asked what other objects were also a dax. The children judged test objects that were the same shape as the exemplar (test objects A, B, and C in Fig. 4.2) to have the same name and consistently judged objects that were different in shape (test objects D, E, and F in Fig. 4.2) to not have the same name. In a second task, a different group of children were asked to make similarity judgments about the same stimuli. They were shown the exemplar and then asked for each test object, "Is this one like that one?" In this task the children did not attend to shape but, rather, to amount of differences regardless of dimension of difference (test objects A, E, and F were said to be like the exemplar and test objects B, C, and D in Fig. 4.2 were said not to be like the exemplar). Thus the global order to be explained is children's attention to shape when interpreting novel words.

Where does children's global order come from, and how is it realized in the particulars of a specific real-time task of naming? One possibility is that this stable behavior is caused by a stable cognitive structure. That is, children might possess an abstract rule that directs them to attend to shape whenever they are confronted with a rigid object and a novel name. Many theorists of cognitive development have proposed that children possess just such rules; indeed, some have speculated that they might be innate (Markman, 1989; Soja, Carey, & Spelke, 1991). Evidence indicates that this account is wrong; children's novel-word interpretations are too exquisitely creative and intelligently context-sensitive to be explained by a word-learning rule. I present this evidence in the next two sections.

Figure 4.2: Sample Stimuli
(Landau et al., 1988)

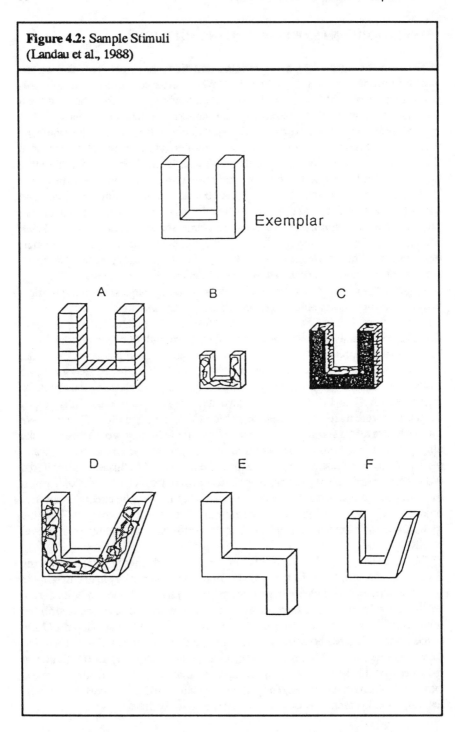

PERFORMANCE REGIONS

The old approach of looking for constant cognitive structures encourages the use of group means as a summary statistic and the relegation of variability to error terms. A dynamical systems approach requires different measures, measures that emphasize variability as well as global order. To this end I invented *performance regions* (see also Smith, 1991; Smith & Sera, 1992) to derive dynamical properties of children's attention in novel-word interpretation and similarity-judgment tasks.

The idea of a performance region began with scatterplots of individual children's performances in state spaces. Figure 4.3 shows the scatterplots of individual children's performances in the Landau et al. (1988) experiments described earlier. Children's performances are depicted in terms of locations in a state space defined by response to two kinds of test objects: those the same shape as the exemplar and those different in shape from the exemplar (Fig. 4.2). In the state spaces (Fig. 4.3), then, the location of each dot indicates one child's performances on both kinds of test items. The region in the upper right of the space thus corresponds to a performance in which all test objects are judged to have the same name as (or to be like) the exemplar. The region in the lower left corresponds to a performance in which none of the test objects was judged to have the same name as (or to be like) the exemplar. The region in the bottom right corresponds to attention to shape, a performance in which test objects were judged to have the same name as (or to be like) the exemplar if they were the same shape as the exemplar. The upper left region corresponds to attention to the other dimension, a pattern of performance in which test objects are judged to have the same name as (or to be like) the exemplar that match it in color or size but not shape.

The location of an individual subject in the state space provides a measure of that subject's performance. The general location of most subjects in the space provides a measure of the global order, the pattern of performance generally observed in this context. One can easily see that in the task of interpreting a novel noun, all the children attended to shape, but in the task of making similarity judgments there is not obvious global order in the behavior across individuals. Thus, the spread of individual performances in the space shows the magnitude of between-subject variability. This index of variability provides a measure of the strength of contextual forces on the system. If the contextual forces play a strong role in organizing attention, then all children should find the same solution and fall close together in the state space. As is apparent (Fig. 4.3), children *do* find the same solution in the novel-word interpretation task but *do not* in the similarity judgment task. From the location and spread of the performances in the state space, then, we may conclude that in the task of interpreting a novel word, the attentional system is attracted to shape but that in the similarity judgment task there is at best a shallow behavioral attractor.

Performance regions highlight these two key properties of the location and spread of individual performances in a state space. A performance region is the

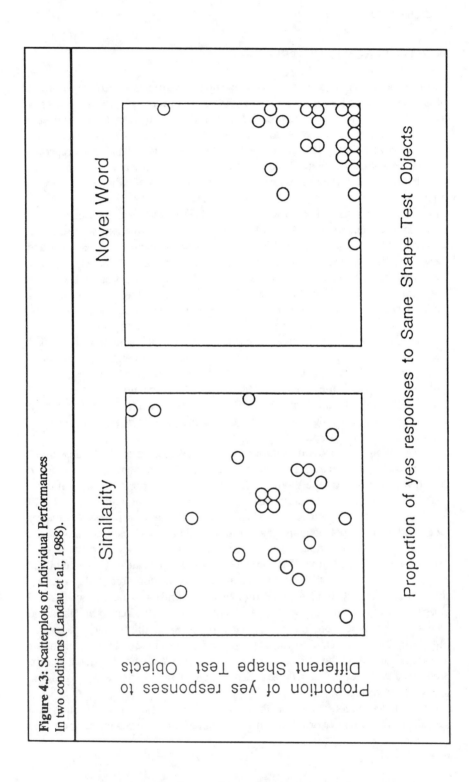

Figure 4.3: Scatterplots of Individual Performances
In two conditions (Landau et al., 1988).

region in the state space under which 80 percent of the individual subjects' performances fall. The shaded regions in Figure 4.4 show the performance regions for the data in Figure 4.3. The performance region is determined by an algorithm that locates the mode (the middle of a smaller region where more children's performances fall than any other equivalent region) and then moves out from that point in the most dense direction until it reaches a gap (10 percent of the possible range of scores). This procedure is repeated until a boundary is found that includes 80 percent of all the individual subjects' performances. This boundary defines a performance region—the region in the state space under which 80 percent of the subjects' performances fall. These performance regions provide a unitary picture of the global structure and variability of behavior under a particular set of contextual forces. In so doing they provide information about children's attentional systems. The two performance regions in Figure 4.4 provide clear information about one force on children's attention: the *task of interpreting a novel word* organizes and directs children's attention to shape. The next question is whether there are other forces that cause other global orders.

MULTIPLE GLOBAL ORDERS

Jones, Smith, and Landau (1991) reasoned that there should be contextual forces with different behavioral outcomes than attention to shape. An intelligent cognitive system would not rigidly attend to shape in all naming contexts; rather it would attend to other properties when prudent to do so. They reasoned that one context in which it might be prudent to attend to more than shape is when naming objects with eyes. Eyes are an attribute of objects that might be expected to be particularly salient to children. Moreover, in naming things with eyes, shape is not the only important property. Texture is also important because it provides information about what the object is made of, which is quite relevant to, for example, the naming of dolls, people, toy cats, and real cats. Do young children "know" to attend to texture as well as shape in the context of eyes?

Jones et al. (1991) showed that children did just that in an experiment using two stimulus sets (Fig. 4.5) that were identical, except that in one set all the objects have eyes and in the other they do not. Jones et al. presented the eyed stimuli to one group of three-year-olds and the eyeless stimuli to another group of three-year-olds in either a similarity judgment task or a novel-word interpretation task. Figure 4.6 shows the performance regions in state spaces defined by children's responses to just two kinds of test objects: those that differed from the exemplar in shape but matched it in everything else and those that differed from the exemplar in texture but matched it in shape and everything else.

As Figure 4.6 shows, the performance regions in the similarity judgment task for both the eyeless and eyed stimuli are wide and sit in the center of state space. Again, children's attention to specific object properties is not well organized when

Figure 4.4: Performance Regions
From the data of Figure 4.3. The shaded area covers 80 percent of the individual performances.

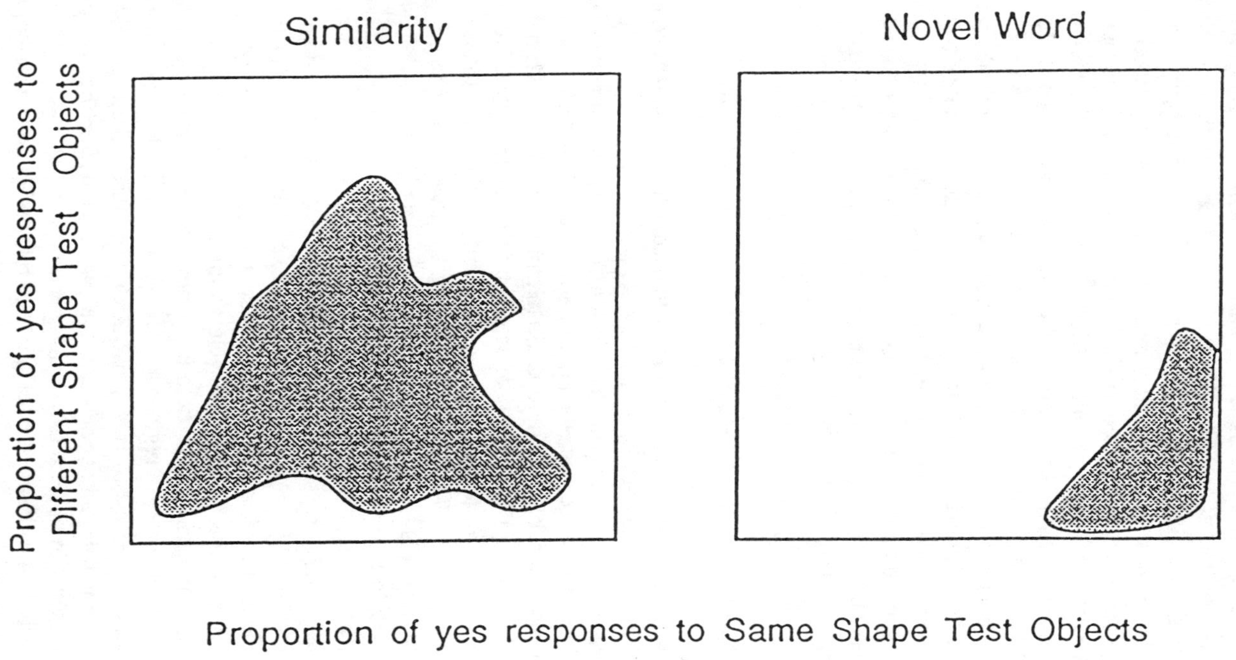

Similarity

Novel Word

Proportion of yes responses to
Different Shape Test Objects

Proportion of yes responses to Same Shape Test Objects

all they asked is whether one object is like another. Eyes alone do not shift attention to shape or away from it.

In contrast, the performance regions in the two novel-word interpretation tasks are small and tightly circumscribed, but they are in different locations depending on whether the objects have eyes or not. When the objects did not have eyes, the children attended to shape; they said an object had the same name as the exemplar if and only if it had the same shape. When the objects had eyes, however, children attended to both shape and texture; they said an object had the same name as the exemplar only if it matched in both shape and texture. Thus, in the eye condition, the children rejected the two kinds of test object used to define the state space, objects that matched the exemplar in either texture or shape but not both. Children in this condition did consistently extend the exemplar's name to test objects that matched the exemplar in both shape and texture (Fig. 4.6).

The total pattern of results clearly shows that there is more than one global order in children's novel-word interpretations: Sometimes children attend to shape and sometimes they attend to shape and texture. The results also show that more than one force organizes children's attention. The presence of a novel word organizes children's attention, and the properties of the objects themselves recruit attention to other properties. Moreover, these two forces work together to collectively determine the properties children attend to. A novel word alone and eyes alone do not yield the same pattern of attending as do the presence of eyes when interpreting a novel word. This last fact shows that what children "know" about attending isn't simply some set knowledge about how words name categories nor some set knowledge about the relevance of certain properties. Rather what children know may be in the moment, in interacting pulls on attention.

Multiple pulls on attention that interact nonlinearly have the potential to create multiple organized patterns and creative new solutions. In a series of subsequent experiments, Smith, Jones, and Landau (1992) showed that this description fits children's attention well as it organizes and reorganizes itself in the task of interpreting a novel word. These experiments examined three-year-olds' performances in three tasks: (1) similarity judgment, (2) novel-word interpretation when the novel word was a noun, as in the previous studies, and (3) novel-word interpretation when the novel word was an adjective. In this third new task the exemplar was presented, the child was told "this is a dax one," and then the child was asked whether each test object was also "a dax one."

The experiments also employed two different stimulus sets. One set was designed to challenge the potency of shape. In both stimulus sets, test objects matched the exemplar in either color or shape. But in one set, the colors were realized with ordinary matte paint, whereas in the other the colors were realized with glitter. Further, in the glitter condition the stimuli were presented in a darkened chamber with a spotlight such that the objects glowed and twinkled. In other words, one stimulus set pit shape against dull colors and the other pit shape against glitter.

Figure 4.5: Sample Stimuli
(Jones et al., 1991)

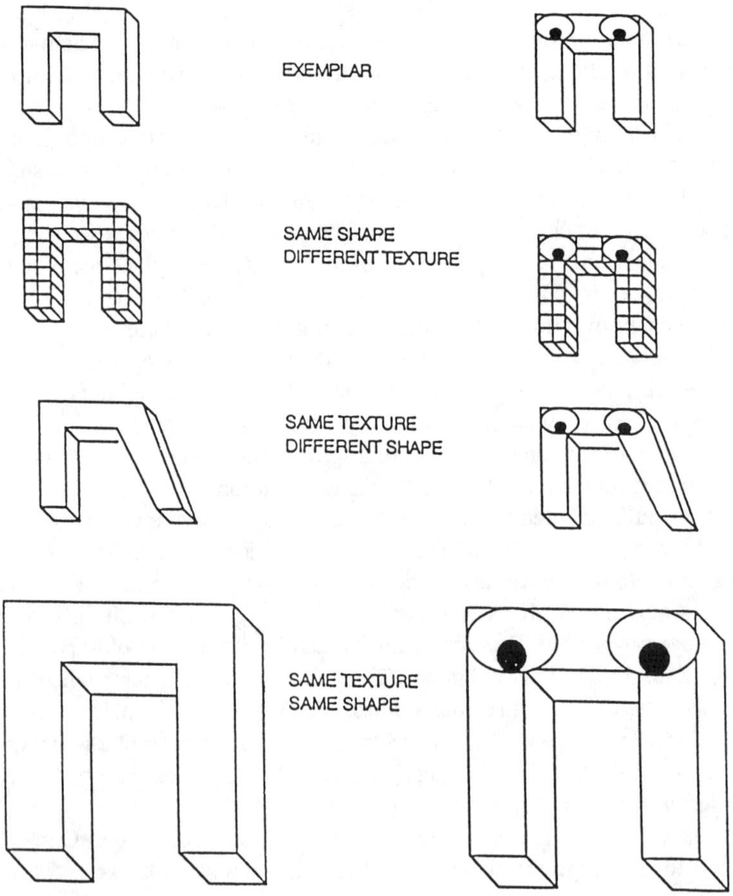

EXEMPLAR

SAME SHAPE
DIFFERENT TEXTURE

SAME TEXTURE
DIFFERENT SHAPE

SAME TEXTURE
SAME SHAPE

Figure 4.6: Performance Regions
(Jones et al., 1991)

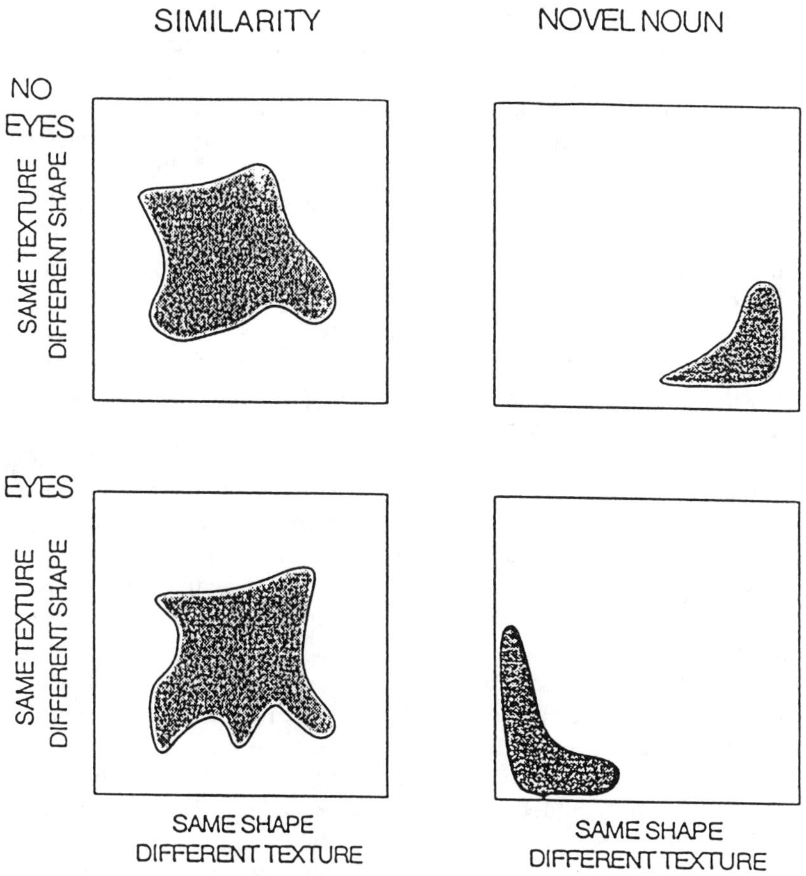

Figure 4.7 shows the performance regions in state spaces defined by the frequency of saying "is like," "is a dax," or "is a dax one" to same color, different shape test objects and to same shape, different color test objects. In the similarity judgment task, both with the dull colors and glitter the performance regions are large. The performance region for the glittery stimuli is shifted a bit to the upper left relative to the performance region for ordinary colors. This shift in location indicates greater attention to glittery colors than painted ones. Apparently glitter is a force, albeit a weak force in the similarity judgment task on attention.

The two performance regions in the task of interpreting a novel noun are compact and located in the region of the state space that corresponds to attention to shape. Both when the stimuli vary in ordinary colors and when they vary in glittery colors, young children judge objects to have the same name as another object when they are the same shape. Glitter did not alter the global order in this task. Interestingly, though, in the noun-glitter condition there is the beginning of a small performance region corresponding to attention to both shape and color. Perhaps if color were made even more dazzling, all individuals would shift to that new location. Still, the results in this experiment strongly suggest that in the context of a novel noun, attention to shape is not easily perturbed. Put another way, attention to shape in the context of a novel noun is a very deep attractor.

The performance regions in the adjective conditions present a quite different picture of the system. The two performance regions differ dramatically depending on whether there are dull colors versus exciting ones. In the ordinary color condition, children principally attended to shape. In the glittery color condition, however, children attended to the glittery colors. There is in the adjective condition a bifurcation. The behavior of the system jumped from one region of the state space to another with a change in one force, the attention-grabbing properties of glitter, in the context of another force, the task of interpreting a novel adjective.

This experiment thus shows three forces on the system: the task, the syntactic frame of the novel word, and the attention-grabbing nature of particular properties. Moreover, these forces interact nonlinearly. Glitter is a weak force in controlling children's attention in a similarity judgment task, has almost no influence on performance when children are trying to understand the meaning of a novel noun, and leads to qualitatively different interpretations of a novel adjective. These different interpretations of a novel adjective in the two contexts appear adaptive. "A dax one" said by a child about an object with twinkling colors seems more likely to be about the colors than "a dax one" said about an object with ordinary colors. The system appears to put together an organized and sensible attentional response across disparate forces.

That novel-word interpretations jump around and that they are influenced by such heterogeneous forces as syntax, eyes, and glitter implicate a nonlinear complex system. I believe no other interpretation of the results is possible. Certainly, the stability and variability of children's novel-word interpretations are not easily explained by a rule, by some constant structure in the head that is invoked when

Figure 4.7: Performance Regions
(From data reported by Smith et al., 1992.)

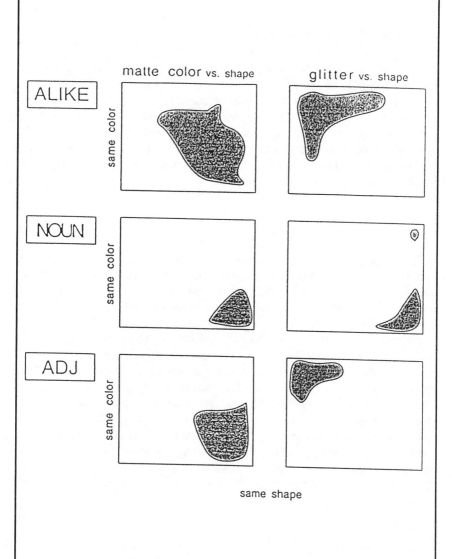

children are faced with a novel word. Were there such a rule, it would have to be a complicated one, such as "Attend to shape if there is a novel noun unless the objects have eyes and then attend to shape and texture. If there is a novel adjective attend to shape unless there is some other property that is very salient, then attend to that." Young children's novel-word interpretations seem too systematic and intelligent to be noise but too fluid to be caused by some constant cognitive structure.

A DYNAMICAL SYSTEM ACCOUNT

The context-sensitivity of children's novel-word interpretations suggests that children assemble the meaning of a just-heard word in context, from multiple interacting forces. What is this system of interacting forces like? How does it organize attention to the different properties of objects? How does it work? The performance regions in the state space—what I call a state-space-portrait—tell a great deal about the system that gives rise to it. We know that various kinds of forces matter, that forces interact nonlinearly, and that some global orders are more stable than others.

Various Kinds of Forces Matter

The experiments show that a novel noun has different effects than a novel adjective, that object properties like eyes matter, and that attention-grabbing and idiosyncratic properties like glitter under lights also influence attention. These various forces seem likely to have different developmental origins. The relation between nouns and shape is most likely learned. Jones, Smith, Landau, and Gershkoff-Stowe (1992) have supporting evidence for this idea. They found that attention to shape when naming objects does not emerge in individual children until they have fifty nouns in their productive vocabulary, a fact that suggests children must learn a number of prior words before their systems "know" to attend to shape. The relevance of texture for objects with eyes is probably also learned. Attending to glitter, however, seems unlikely to depend on prior learning nor to reflect any general truths about lexical categories or kinds of things in the world. Rather, twinkling glitter seems specific to the moment and to grab attention in context. The system that enables children to figure out the meaning of a word in context is a system that organizes both learned and unlearned forces into a single behavioral outcome.

Forces Interact Nonlinearly

One way these various forces could interact is additively. The various pulls and pushes on attention could simply be combined with attending determined by the average of them all. This is not the case: The presence of a novel noun pulls for shape; glitter pulls for glitter. But a novel noun in the context of glitter does not yield attention between shape and glitter. We know that the forces interact nonlinearly in the case of novel-word interpretation because performance regions jump about in the state space—sameness in shape either matters or it does not. The nonlinear shifts that we see in performance in novel-word interpretation, however, are not there in similarity judgments. Apparently, naming an object recruits processes that alter the intrinsic dynamics of attending. The specific nonlinearity involved may be a threshold for attending such that an individual dimension is either attended to or not, with no intermediate degrees of attending, no partial attention to an individual dimension, possible (see Smith, 1989, for an earlier discussion of this possibility).

Some Global Orders Are More Stable Than Others

The state-space-portraits present a clear picture of multiple stable attractors but also suggest that some attractors are more stable than others. This is illustrated in Figure 4.8 which shows a response diagram implied from the state-space-portraits; specifically, small performance regions were taken as indicating deep attractors and wide performance areas were taken as indicating shallow attractors. This response diagram for the similarity judgment task portrays a flat terrain; similarity judgments can fall anywhere. The response diagram for the novel-noun task shows a deep strong attractor that is difficult for the system to resist. Attending to shape is a state that the system is highly likely to reach. There is, however, an additional nearby attractor of attending to shape and texture in the context of eyes. Moreover, a third deep attractor is shown because it seems likely that as we explore the system further we will find other attractors, other sites the system "likes" in other contexts. Finally, the response diagram of the novel-adjective task shows there are multiple and shallower attractors—adjectives can be about lots of different properties. The relative strength of different states provides further important clues to the nature of the system and the developmental history that gave rise to it. For example, the stronger organization of attending to shape in the context of a novel noun than in the context of a novel adjective suggests that there is a more regular relation between nouns and attending to shape than between adjectives and attending to any one property.

Clearly these ideas constitute a beginning understanding of the system that enables children to so sensibly and creatively make sense of novel words and the kinds of objects those words refer to. But from this beginning the value of studying

Figure 4.8: Response Diagram
Size of attractor (indicated by performance region) is a theoretical indicator of attractor strength and stability, and attentional features (stimulus properties) constitute a control parameter.

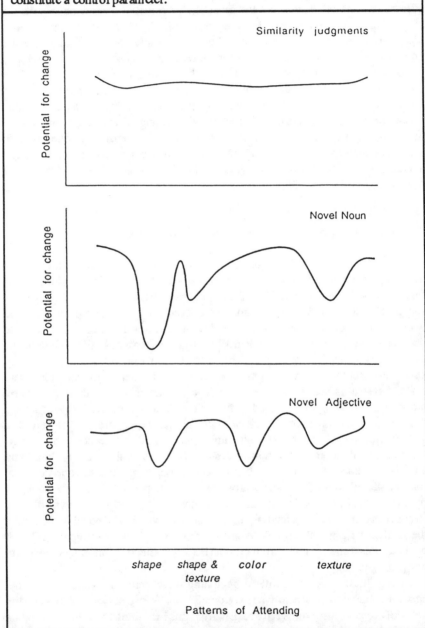

variability should also be clear. By studying variability, instead of throwing it away as noise, we may ultimately learn how children understand words they have never heard before and in so doing how they do something adaptive and new.

STABILITY, VARIABILITY, AND INTELLIGENCE

In traditional cognitive psychology stability is explained by knowledge structures. Knowledge is like an encyclopedia on the shelf. When faced with a task, one pulls the appropriate volume off the shelf to solve the task at hand. The fundamental problem with this solution to cognition is that the entry in the encyclopedia—the "canned" solution—is never enough. Each real-time problem has its own special properties, its own special needs. Thus it is not enough to know what a cat is; we also have to know what a barn cat is, what a show cat is. This is the importance of the phenomena of children's novel-word interpretations. Novel words have no structure already waiting in the head, but children nonetheless assemble sensible and regularly patterned meanings in context—in the moment. If such flexible order can emerge in real-time processes in novel-word interpretation, might they not do the same in the flexible interpretations of known words? If so, do we need the theoretical idea of knowledge structures at all?

Dynamical systems theory offers a new solution to the old dilemma of stability and variability. In this new solution there are no knowledge structures, just process. Thus, children's novel-word interpretations exhibit both a global structure and a local adaptability because these interpretations emerge in context as the result of a nonlinear attentional system that creates new solutions from past experiences and the particular properties of the perceptually present. Stability and variability emerge as joint products of real-time process.

In solving the problems of stability and variability, the dynamical systems approach also provides a new perspective on cognition itself. Intelligence is *not* abstract transcendent thought. Intelligence is *not* doing the same thing over and over. Intelligence means adaptively fitting cognition to changing contexts. A smart system seems unlikely to ever do the exact same thing twice and thus has no need for invariant cognitive structures. A smart system shifts its behavior subtly or dramatically to fit the task. Novel-word interpretation in children is smart like a dynamical system.

REFERENCES

Biederman, I. (1985). Human image understanding. *Computer Vision, Graphics, & Image Processing, 32*, 29–73.

Fogel, A. (1993). *Developing through relationships: Origins of communication, self, and culture*. New York: Harvester Wheatsheaf.

Freyd, J. J. (1992). Five hunches about perceptual processes and dynamic representations. In D. Meyer & S. Kornblum (Eds.), *Attention & performance XIV: A silver jubilee.* Hillsdale: Earlbaum.

Jones, S. S., & Smith, L. B. (1993). The place of perceptions in children's concepts. *Cognitive Development,* in press.

Jones, S., Smith, L., & Landau, B. (1991). Object properties and knowledge in early lexical learning. *Child Development, 62,* 449–516.

Jones, S., Smith, L., Landau, B., & Gershkoff-Stowe, L. (1992, October). *The developmental origins of the shape bias.* Paper presented at the Boston Child Language Conference.

Landau, B., Smith, L., & Jones, S. (1988). The importance of shape in early lexical learning. *Cognitive Development, 3,* 299–321.

Markman, E. M. (1989). *Categorization and naming in children.* Cambridge: MIT Press.

Rosch, E. (1973). Natural categories. *Cognitive Psychology, 4,* 328–350.

Smith, L. B. (1989). A model of perceptual classification in children and adults. *Psychological Review, 96,* 125–144.

Smith, L. B. (1991). Perceptual structure and developmental processes. In G. Lockhead & J. Pomerantz (Eds.), *The perception of structure.* Washington, DC: American Psychological Association.

Smith, L. B., Jones, S. S., & Landau, B. (1992). Count nouns, adjectives, and perceptual properties in children's novel word interpretations. *Developmental Psychology, 28,* 273–289.

Smith, L. B., & Sera, M. (1992). A developmental analysis of the polar structure of dimensions. *Cognitive Psychology, 24,* 99–142.

Smith, L. B., & Thelen, E. (1993). *A dynamic systems approach to development: Applications.* Cambridge: MIT Press.

Soja, N., Carey, S., & Spelke, E. (1991). Ontological categories guide young children's inductions of word meanings: Object terms and substance terms. *Cognition, 38,* 179–211.

Templin, M. C. (1957). *Certain language skills in children.* Minneapolis: University of Minnesota Press.

Thelen, E., & Smith, L. B. (1994). *A dynamic systems account of the development of action and cognition.* Cambridge: MIT Press.

5

In Search of Chaos in Schedule-Induced Polydipsia

Brian R. Metcalf and Joseph D. Allen

One basic theme of chaos is that even simple deterministic systems can produce random-looking behavior. For example, simple pendulums have been used to demonstrate routes to chaos within a completely deterministic system (see Tritton, 1986). The usual motion of a pendulum can be best described as very orderly and predictable. Indeed, pendulums have been used for years as mechanisms in clocks. Under certain, still deterministic conditions, however, the clockwork flow of a pendulum can break down to a motion best described as random looking. Pendulums serve here as an analogy for the study of a more complicated deterministic system. Our purpose is to demonstrate how the analytical tools from chaos theory can be used to reveal the chaos and order that emerge within an operant approach to behavior analysis.

When rats reduced from their free-feeding weights by limiting food intake are exposed to certain fixed or variable food delivery schedules and water is freely available, a curious behavior occurs. Though never deprived of water, and apparently not "thirsty," the rats exhibit a pattern of copious water consumption immediately following each pellet delivery. Falk (1961) first demonstrated this phenomenon with rats earning food by lever-pressing on a variable-interval 1-min schedule. The water intake during these daily lever pressing sessions (3.17 hours) amounted to nearly one-half their body weights. The occurrence of excessive drinking has been repeatedly confirmed and has been labeled schedule-induced polydipsia (SIP). SIP is one of a class of schedule-induced or adjunctive behaviors that appear in a wide variety of species including humans (Fallon, Allen, & Butler 1979; Allen & Butler, 1990).

WHAT HAS SCHEDULE-INDUCED POLYDIPSIA
TO DO WITH CHAOS?

Chaos has offered procedures to identify the underlying order in random looking phenomena. SIP is quite an orderly and robust phenomenon, and under the right contingencies, almost no rat will fail to develop it (Falk, 1961). Furthermore, there is a stereotypical pattern of drinking seen during intervals of polydipsia sessions. During fixed-interval (FI) or fixed-time (FT) schedule sessions, a burst of drinking immediately follows almost every pellet delivery. However, being the product of a complex biological system (such as a rat), the drinking patterns seen in SIP sessions inevitably include variability. The overall orderliness of this behavior pattern, in addition to the inherent variability contained within a system driven by deterministic mechanisms, makes SIP an excellent candidate for analysis using the tools of chaos theory. Additionally, SIP and many other operant behaviors have traditionally been best understood and analyzed in visual, graphical terms. The computerized graphical nature of chaos theory lends itself well to the study of such systems.

A particularly salient control variable in the production of SIP is the rate that pellets are delivered to the animal, or, inversely, the size of the interpellet interval. As the interpellet interval increases over a range of values from approximately 4 sec to 120 sec, total session water intake steadily increases above baseline intakes obtained where the animal has ad lib access to an equal number of food pellets. At interpellet intervals longer than 120 sec, session water intake typically declines again, describing a bitonic, or ∩-shaped relationship between interpellet interval and water intake. The bitonic function has been reported for a variety of species (rats: Falk, 1966; Flory, 1971; monkeys: Allen & Kenshalo, 1976).

The bitonic function of drinking discussed above is interesting from the perspective of chaos. We find it instructive to make an analogy between this function and the motion of the simple, driven pendulum. It has been shown that even a system as completely deterministic as a simple driven pendulum can exhibit chaos. Such a pendulum, driven "too quickly" by its motor, will produce a chaotic, random-looking motion. The production of SIP, too, is quite deterministic. We therefore propose that drinking is "driven" by the intermittent delivery of pellets in a manner analogous to that of a driven pendulum. Just as the swing of a pendulum can transform from complete order to chaos and back, dependent entirely upon its rate of driven oscillation, so too might these drinking patterns. We predicted that bifurcation points between order and chaos should be observable when this system is driven too quickly by reinforcer deliveries. To test this proposition we systematically varied the interpellet interval between medium (64 sec) and short (3 sec) values, sampling mainly from the shorter range of values.

GRAPHICAL METHODS USED

The traditional analysis of schedule-induced behavior has relied heavily on graphical rather than statistical techniques. Figure 5.1(a) depicts a time series, with the number of licks per bout (bout size) plotted for each of the 128 pellets delivered in a session by a FT 48-sec schedule. A graphical representation of this time series provides a snapshot of the entire session and provides information about the structure of the behavior. However, a simple depiction of the time series of the data can obscure order within it.

In an effort to portray the order or patterns hidden in disorderly looking data, chaos theory has relied heavily on several mathematical constructs and data-plotting techniques. These include phase portraits of the state space with their attractors, and Poincaré sections with their first return maps. Plots are produced here to examine the trajectory of drinking behavior and to allow for a process known as *reconstruction of the attractor* (Peitgen, Jürgens, & Saupe, 1992). An example of a phase plot can be seen in Figure 5.1(c). The abscissa of the phase plot consists of the bout size at interval number X_n. The ordinate consists of the first derivative, $X_n - (X_{n+1})$. In other words, this plots how the change in bout size from one interval to the next is related to the size of the present bout. This derivative coordinate pair is plotted, and the sequential pairs are connected by straight lines. We call this a phase trajectory.

Reconstructing the attractor begins with the construction of the phase plot. The next step is to produce what we call a Poincaré section, a plane that bisects the phase trajectory. Poincaré sections were created here by slicing the phase trajectory along the abscissa through the zero point of the ordinate. When an interpolated line segment of the phase trajectory crosses this section, the location along the abscissa is noted.

Once a Poincaré section is taken, a first return map can be produced. Figure 5.1(d) displays the graph of the first return map generated from the Poincaré section of the phase plot in Figure 5.1(c). The first return map is helpful because it can display the properties of the underlying attractor. If the system is being drawn toward a single value by a point attractor, the first return map will display points converging on a single value. If a periodic attractor is driving the system, a circular or elliptical series of points will be produced. When a chaotic attractor is controlling the behavior of the system, an irregular but describable shape or pattern will appear in the first return map. Lastly, when the system is truly random or turbulent, the first return map will produce a correspondingly erratic, random scattering of points.

The next graphical technique demonstrated in Figure 5.1(b) we call the next-period (NP) plot, after Schimz and Hildebrand (1992). The NP plot consists simply of graphing the bout size at one time period sample versus the bout size at the next period sample, and repeating this for all successive interpellet intervals. In this case, the bout size at each interval X_{n+1} is correlated with the bout size at interval X_n. Although the trajectory of the system is not reconstructed by the NP plot, the

Figure 5.1: A Sample of Each of the Graphical Techniques Employed
The time series plot (a) depicts the number of licks on the drinking tube during
each consecutive interval. The next-period plot (b) correlates each consecutive
bout size (X_n) with the bout size of the next interval (X_{n+1}). The phase portrait
(c) depicts how the change in bout size for one interval (X_n) to the next (X_{n+1})
is related to the present bout. The first return map (d) is created by passing a
plane parallel to the abscissa through the zero point of the ordinate and plotting
each successive bout size that transects that plane with the next bout size. The
spectral density function (e) plots the relative density of each frequency possible
in the time series.

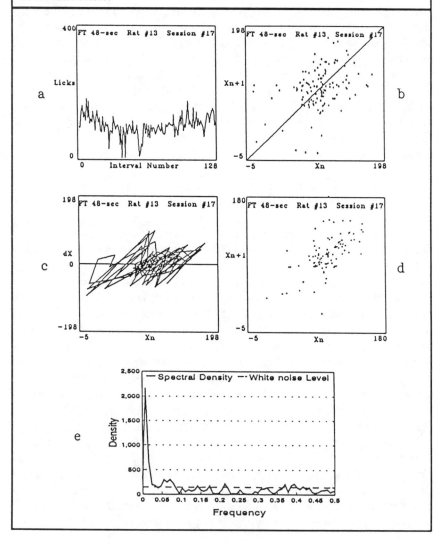

structure or patterns developed reveal information about the underlying dynamics of the system in question. Systems driven by low-dimensional periodic attractors will result in a rather well defined point or elliptical clustering of coordinates. A system subject to true turbulence will result in a scattering of points in random fashion. Any other well-defined curve or complex structure points to the possibility of the presence of a chaotic attractor and suggests deterministic chaos.

Lastly, spectral density (SD) plots are provided here to reveal the presence of any periodicities that might lie in the time series (Gottman, 1981). Periodic attractors would show as sharp peaks in the spectral density functions, noise as broad band power, and chaos as intermediate between these two extremes. Distinguishing between the presence of noise and chaos may require some modeling and testing.

CRITERIA FOR CHAOS

Mathematicians have provided clear criteria describing chaotic attractors. However, although completely deterministic models can be developed that exhibit random-looking behavior, determining whether or not real systems are displaying chaos is not always simple. Marr (1992) states three criteria that are tautological repetitions of the nature of chaotic attractors (they should look like chaotic attractors, be sensitive to initial conditions, and have broad-power spectral density functions).

A clear and concise description of what visual characteristics define the structure of chaotic attractors is lacking. Schimz and Hildebrand's (1992) criterion for deterministic chaos was "a well defined curve or any structure of higher complexity in the next-period plot" (p. 459). Peitgen et al. (1992) point out that chaotic attractors should include "trapping regions" for all iterations, a sensitivity to initial conditions, a fractal structure, and a singular structure (not two attractors mixing). They continue by stating, "The discussion about what should be the most appropriate definition mathematically is still going on, and it seems that we will have to wait for the final clarification until some kind of breakthrough in understanding strange attractors has been achieved" (p. 671). The term *chaotic attractor* will be used here to describe structure in the first return maps that is more complicated than that seen by fixed-point or periodic attractors but that shows more organization than would be expected from truly random processes.

METHODS

Eight male albino rats, 179 days of age at the onset of testing, were housed individually, always provided with water, and maintained at 85 percent free-feeding body weight with daily food supplements. Polydipsia sessions were conducted in four standard operant conditioning chambers. Forty-five-mg food pellets were delivered by a pellet dispenser to a food cup located in the center of the control panel. Water was always available through a drinking tube recessed behind an opening in the control panel to the right of the food cup. A computerized lickometer circuit recorded licks on the drinking tube. Lickometer data acquisition, and all session parameters and chamber controls were accomplished through programming a personal computer interfaced with each operant box. The data collected for each session consisted of the total milliliters of water consumed, the number of drinking bouts, and the number of licks per bout.

Over eighty-four consecutive days, a series of fixed-time schedules, each delivering 128 pellets, was employed. An FT schedule delivers a food pellet after a set interval of time regardless of the behavior of the organism. The following sequence of FT schedules was implemented: 64, 48, 32, 16, 8, 6, 4, 3, 4, 6, 8, 16, 32, 16, 8, and 4 sec. These FT intervals were selected in order to investigate the drinking patterns produced by "driving" this system to its limits.

RESULTS AND DISCUSSION

Sample graphical analyses for six of the FT schedules presented to rat 18 are shown below. This rat, these intervals, and these sessions were selected on the basis of their being either representative or interesting in the patterns of drinking displayed. Although all animals were run in the alternating descending and ascending FT sequences outlined in the procedure, there were no noticeable differences in the drinking patterns that were displayed for each FT value as it was repeated throughout the sequence. That is, the drinking patterns produced by a given FT schedule appeared to be similar whether it was during a descending or an ascending leg of the sequence.

Figure 5.2 displays time series of consecutive bout sizes for six different FT values. Although session water intakes for most animals appeared quite stable at each FT schedule, the time series of individual bout sizes during any session displayed a high degree of variability. Generally speaking, during most FT sessions, the drinking bout sizes were confined to a restricted range. Drinking tended to fall within a range of bout sizes specific to that FT value, or it did not occur at all. The range in bout size variation decreases as the FT interval decreases. Indeed, the drinking patterns seen in the FT 64-, 32-, and 16-sec schedules appear from a time series perspective to be fairly random.

Somewhat different and more periodic drinking patterns emerged, however, at the shorter FT values (8, 6, and 4 sec). It is interesting to note that the time series plots at FT 8- and 6-sec display an alternating sawtooth pattern of drinking, indicating that bout size alternated between two discrete values. The FT 4-sec time series depicts a pattern of drinking very similar to the pattern that would be seen if a sine wave function were generating the data.

Figure 5.2: Sample Time Series Plots
For rat 18 at six FT schedules (FT 64-, 32-, 16-, 8-, 6-, and 4-sec).

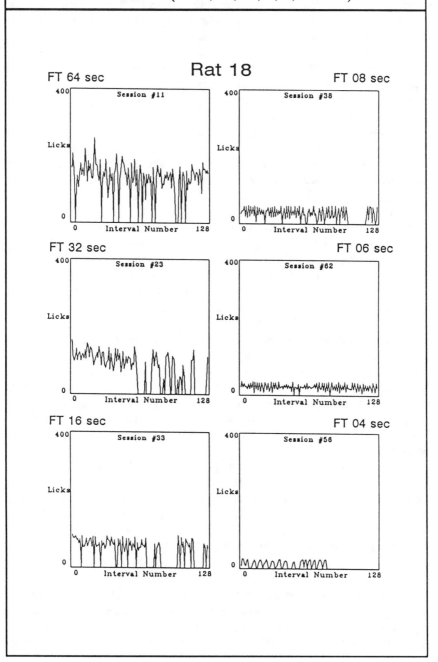

Figure 5.3 depicts the phase trajectories for these sessions. The FT 64-, 32-, and 16-sec sessions are suggestive of chaotic processes at work in producing the patterns of drinking observed. The portraits for the FT 8- and 6-sec intervals, however, display a rather strikingly periodic drinking sequence, alternately tracing from a lower-left basin attractor area to an upper-right basin attractor. Finally, the trajectory produced by the FT 4-sec schedule very nearly describes a periodic pattern. The emergence of these more simplistic, orderly attractor patterns produced by this rat at the shorter FT schedules from the more complicated, chaotic attractors produced at the longer FT schedules are suggestive of a bifurcation or emergence of order from a chaotic system.

The first return maps seen in Figure 5.4 for the FT 64-, 32-, and 16-sec schedules yield distinct, complicated structuring, suggestive of chaos. Had the bout sizes actually been randomly determined, these maps would have displayed a scattering of points with no particular density or structure. Conversely, if a simpler order were driving the system, something resembling a fixed point or periodic attractor would have been apparent.

The NP plots in Figure 5.5 for the three longest intervals are quite similar to their first return maps. The NP plots for FT 8-, 6-, and 4-sec schedules, however, demonstrate the presence of less complex attractors. As suggestive in the time series plots for the FT 8- and 6-sec schedules, the bout sizes appear to alternate between two relatively discrete values. This has resulted in NP plots showing the attractions of these two basins. The FT 4-sec schedule data, on the other hand, produced NP plots displaying a rather clear periodic attractor.

The spectral density functions in Figure 5.6 for the three longer schedules show the lack of periodicity expected with chaotic behavior. The FT 8- and particularly the 6-sec sessions, however, reveal a periodicity of approximately two intervals, evidenced by the prominent spikes near a frequency of 0.5. The double spike seen in the FT 6-sec SD plot suggests the presence of two overlapping cycles near a frequency of 0.5. The FT 4-sec SD plot reveals a periodicity of approximately six intervals. This can be confirmed by comparison with the time series plot for this same data.

The first return maps and NP plots presented here show more structure and organization than would be expected to occur from purely random processes. Three findings in these results imply the presence of chaos in the drinking behavior of these animals: (1) the presence of complicated, nonrandom, distinct structures in most of the first return maps and NP plots; (2) the corresponding lack of a discernable periodicity present during the longer FT intervals; and (3) the transformation (bifurcation) at shorter FT intervals from complicated behavior patterns to quite simple, orderly structures.

The rates of food delivery used in this study provided extremely orderly, periodic driving forces. These periodic perturbations to the system resemble the periodic perturbations given to a simple pendulum driven by a mechanical oscillator. It would be reasonable to predict that such a system, driven by gentle and regular

Figure 5.3: Sample Phase Trajectories
For rat 18 at six FT schedules (FT 64-, 32-, 16-, 8-, 6-, and 4-sec).

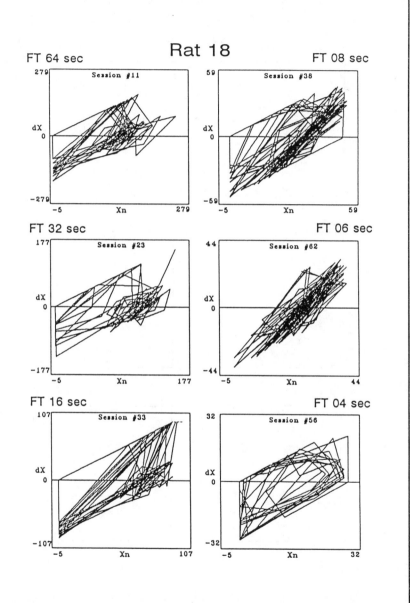

Figure 5.4: Sample First Return Maps
For rat 18 at six FT schedules (FT 64-, 32-, 16-, 8-, 6-, and 4-sec).

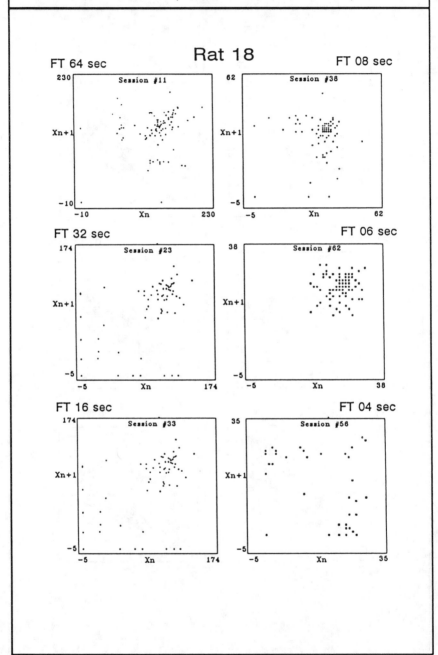

Figure 5.5: Sample Next-period Plots
For rat 18 at six FT schedules (FT 64-, 32-, 16-, 8-, 6-, and 4-sec).

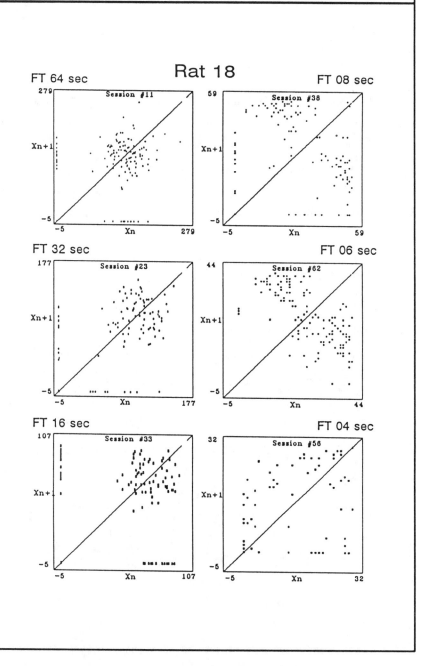

Figure 5.6: Sample Spectral Density Plots
Plots for rat 18 at six FT schedules (FT 64-, 32-, 16-, 8-, 6-, and 4-sec).

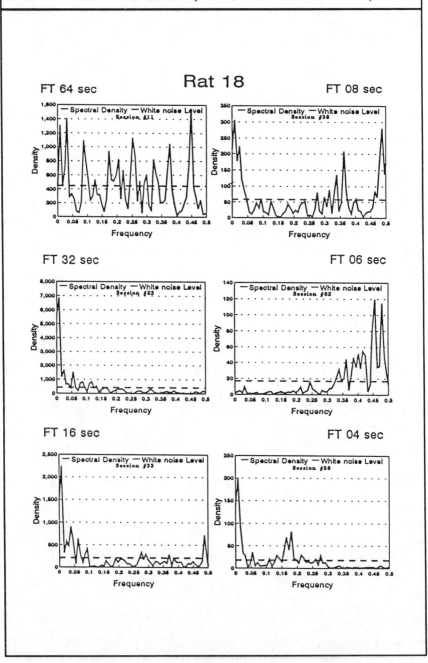

input would produce equally regular and periodic behavior. Under the right conditions, this is precisely what happens in pendulums and other simple deterministic systems. However, just as such simple systems under certain conditions can exhibit wild, erratic behavior, so too might a more complicated system. This is what may have been observed here. The very same system could show both behavior patterns when only the periodic rate of food delivery differed. Amidst the rather chaotic patterns produced as this drinking system was driven by briefer interreinforcement intervals were "islands" of more orderly looking patterns (i.e., the alternating and sinusoidal patterns of drinking observed at FT 8-, 6-, and 4-sec). Such islands of order are seen, for example, in the bifurcation maps of the logistic map model of biological populations (Peitgen et al., 1992). By making gradual increases to the control parameter in this equation, bifurcation points are crossed, taking the system through transitions from order to chaos and back. The results of our research suggest to us that SIP is sensitive to a similar dependence on control parameters, and that perhaps there exists bifurcation points at which the drinking patterns transform from periodic to chaotic and back.

NOTE

Portions of this study were presented August, 1993 at the Third Annual Conference of the Society for Chaos Theory in Psychology and the Social and Life Sciences held at Geneva Park, Orillia, Ontario. This work was part of Brian Metcalf's research in partial fulfillment of the requirements for the Master of Science Degree. Address correspondence to Brian Metcalf (CMSPSY64@ UGA.CC.UGA.EDU) or Joseph D. Allen (JALLEN@UGA.CC.UGA.EDU), Department of Psychology, University of Georgia, Athens GA 30602.

REFERENCES

Allen, J. D., & Kenshalo, D. R. (1976). Schedule-induced drinking as a function of interreinforcement interval in the rhesus monkey. *Journal of the Experimental Analysis of Behavior, 26*, 257–267.

Allen, J. D. & Butler, J. A. (1990). The effect of interplay interval on adjunctive behavior in humans in a game playing situation. *Physiology and Behavior, 47*, 719–725.

Falk, J. L. (1961). Production of polydipsia in normal rats by an intermittent food schedule. *Science, 133*, 195–196.

Falk, J. L. (1966). Schedule-induced polydipsia as a function of fixed interval length. *Journal of the Experimental Analysis of Behavior, 9*, 37–39.

Fallon, J. H., Allen, J. D., & Butler, J. A. (1979). Assessment of adjunctive behaviors in humans using a stringent control procedure. *Physiology and Behavior, 22*, 1089–1092.

Flory, R. K. (1971). The control of schedule-induced polydipsia: frequency and magnitude of reinforcement. *Learning & Motivation, 2*, 215–227.

Gottman, J. M. (1981). *Time series analysis: A comprehensive introduction for social scientists*. New York: Cambridge University Press.

Marr, M. J. (1992). Behavior dynamics: One perspective. *Journal of the Experimental Analysis of Behavior, 57,* 249–266.

Peitgen, H. O., Jürgens, H., & Saupe, D. (1992). *Chaos and fractals: New frontiers of science*. New York: Springer-Verlag.

Schimz, A., & Hildebrand, E. (1992). Nonrandom structures in the locomotor behavior of *Halobacterium*: A bifurcation route to chaos? *Proceedings of the National Academy of Sciences, USA, 89,* 457–460.

Tritton, D. (1986, July 24). Chaos in the swing of a pendulum. *New Scientist,* pp. 37–40.

6

Group Therapy as a Nonlinear Dynamical System: Analysis of Therapeutic Communication for Chaotic Patterns

Gary M. Burlingame, Addie Fuhriman, and Karl R. Barnum

For the history that I require and design,
special care is to be taken that it be at wide
range and made to the measure of the universe.
For the world is not to be narrowed till it
will go into the understanding (which has been
done hitherto), but the understanding is to
be expanded and opened till it can take in
the image of the world.

Francis Bacon, *The Parasceve*

RESEARCH ON THE PSYCHOTHERAPEUTIC PROCESS

Psychotherapy is a vital specialty that is making a significant impact on health care costs in the United States. With the growing acceptance of psychotherapy as a treatment for mental disorders comes an increasing level of scrutiny regarding its effectiveness. Although ample empirical evidence exists to substantiate the overall efficacy of psychotherapy in successfully treating a wide variety of mental disorders and populations (cf. Garfield & Bergin, 1986), establishing the effectiveness of a treatment is not sufficient. Thus, in recent years investigators have moved to examining and articulating the events within therapy sessions that are critical to facilitating patient improvement. This, then, is the domain of research on the psychotherapeutic process.

Nearly all investigations of the psychotherapeutic process conducted over the past few decades can be placed within one of two broad definitional categories: either process as phenomenon or process as interaction. *Process as phenomenon* studies typically investigate some aspect or characteristic of client or therapist behavior by selecting static samples of the variable of interest (representing a macro approach) (Fuhriman, Drescher, & Burlingame, 1984). If tracking change in psychotherapeutic process is of interest, repeated static samples are taken in order to plot shifts over time. For example, a typical study of the emotional climate in a psychotherapeutic group will select a client and/or therapist self-report measure (e.g., cohesion) that is composed of several statements that describe one's experience within the group. These statements are then rated by the client or therapist on an evaluative scale, resulting in a summative score that is used to describe the level of cohesion in the group at the time of measurement. Process as phenomenon studies essentially use these snap shots or fixed points in time to capture the dynamical properties of the psychotherapeutic enterprise.

In contrast, *process as interaction* studies detail the reciprocal transactions of participants in a therapeutic endeavor (Fuhriman et al., 1984) by measuring a variable of interest on a moment-to-moment basis (micro approach). For the most part, measures used in these investigations are constructed to identify the content or related meaning within each utterance of therapy by participants. For example, a typical study in group treatment might examine patient and therapist utterances drawn from random segments of three or four group therapy sessions. Each utterance is then rated using an instrument that defines a value contained within the specific statement or utterance, namely, the Hill Interaction Matrix (HIM) (Hill, 1965). In the case of the HIM, statements are classified as to the content and style of interaction, permitting inferences to be made regarding the interactional climate of the entire group. If stratified samples of early, middle, and later sessions are used, inferences can be made regarding the developmental changes of interaction across the life of a group.

Problematic to the process research described above is the random selection of interaction, the aggregate of frequency data, the assumption of homogeneity, the acceptance of linearity, and the meaning of time. Not only do these issues and assumptions create problems in the conduct of process research, but they raise conceptual problems regarding the definition of process.

Researchers have recently begun to address these concerns and in doing so have offered increased definitional refinement to process analysis. Reinforcing the definition of process as "interaction," they further specify focusing on process transactions, "activity over time," and "directional change" (Greenberg & Pinsof, 1986); more precisely, the suggestion is to focus on change and discover the mechanisms of change (Greenberg & Pinsof, 1986; Rice & Greenberg, 1984). Additionally, they stress the importance of observing natural behavior in naturalistic contexts (Bakeman & Gottman, 1989) and considering interaction as "temporal form" (Gottman & Roy, 1990). These foci require directed attention on the *interactive* context and the reality of multiple influences. Thus, investigators of psychotherapeutic process are now faced with understanding human change in context, a context involving a complexity born of multiple levels, interactive influence, and competing values.

In response to this tripartite call to focus on change, define it in context, and describe multiple, concomitant influences, recent studies have utilized measurement and statistical tools of sequential and contextual analyses. Although fairly long chains of events can be addressed by lag sequential analysis, and the initiation of randomness determined, it is nonetheless necessary to understand the patterns of processes that are occurring in specific contexts (Greenberg & Pinsof, 1986), as well as the patterns emerging in global contexts. If we are ever to comprehend the nuances of psychotherapeutic process and the particulars of dynamical human change, we will best be served by conceptualizing and measuring process as fluid and continuous.

Although extremely limited, examples of measuring and analyzing the continuity of therapeutic process exist. For the most part, they are found in the marital and family literature and tend to measure the entire interaction of a single session. A number of investigators have detailed approaches to the measurement of continuous flow, but the reason for doing so has been to determine the appropriateness of sampling, computer assessment, and computer data collection rather than to understand the process.

It appears that what is required at this point in the evolution of research on the psychotherapeutic process is a thoughtful exploration of the nuances of complexity over time (the missing links, the vacant fields, and the interactional dynamic). Specifically, this analysis of complexity requires a number of considerations, which regrettably have received only modest attention in the past. These considerations include the *system as a whole* and an understanding of its evolution, the *interaction* of the parts and the *relationship* of said interaction to the "evolution" of the system, *time* in relationship to space or context, individual *points of choice and selection*, and *embedded patterns* of order and disorder.

LINKING CHAOS THEORY AND THE PSYCHOTHERAPEUTIC PROCESS

As a science of change, chaos theory may hold promise for conceptualizing and, ultimately, understanding the complexity of a human, interactive process. Three qualities characterizing the therapeutic process lend themselves to an application of chaos theory: nonlinearity, multiple interactive parts, and system evolution.

Nonlinearity

Psychotherapy is a process involving human systems, and as such, there are many contributors to the nonlinear nature of the process. Human systems are active and reactive and operate in far-from-equilibrium conditions. The individuals and the systems they create are self-reproducing information systems and contain various types of self-organization; their behavior can be both periodic and aperiodic. Initial conditions surrounding the unit and the subsequently occurring dynamics are not independent of each other. In addition, each individual action has the potential for a collective effect that can impact the system, contributing to increased complexity. Uncertainty resides; there is never either "a definite set of interacting units, or a definite set of transformations" (Prigogine & Stengers, 1984) that can be taken as a given. Change and movement are ever present. Given this interactive, responsive nature, the striking aspect of nonlinearity is that the system is irreversible. The bedrock of therapeutic process is human exchange, which is perhaps the most irreversible process accessible to our understanding (Prigogine & Stengers, 1984); it is a progressive increase of information and knowledge.

Multiply Interactive Parts

It is readily apparent that a psychotherapeutic process is not only characterized but influenced by multiple levels. These levels exist within the intrapersonal sphere (i.e., emotional, physiological, cognitive), the interpersonal sphere (i.e., responsiveness, attraction), and the global sphere (i.e., micro, subgroup, and macro levels). Although no one level may be individually preeminent, each could potentially be connected to or influence another, thus contributing to process change and evolution. Growth and change of any one component has the potential to influence and be influenced by the other components with which it interacts and relates. If we understand the history of one component, we are more likely to gain information about relevant, interacting components (Crutchfield, Farmer, Packard, & Shaw, 1986). In a sense the presence of interactive multiples suggests that ultimately it is impossible to analyze a single part in isolation, and we must seek to discover and describe the embeddedness present among the various levels. Combined with the concept of nonlinearity, the presence of multiple parts and levels suggests an interconnectedness and a subsequent supposition that a subtle order is present within the system (Briggs & Peat, 1989).

System Evolution

The "therapeutic relationship" construct in the individual therapy literature and, to some degree, "development" in group literature presumes the presence and influence of unit and system properties. Whether unique parts within the system change or the system as a whole changes (or both), some change and movement appears attributable to the *collective* body. Such interaction and connectedness invites the application of a creative science of change and circumstance, one capable of describing the conditions emerging from previous evolution that have been "transformed into states of the same class through subsequent evolution" (Prigogine

& Stengers, 1984, p. 310). Typically, psychotherapeutic research does not record all the facts or the flow of a system, but only a few, thus making the data vulnerable to misunderstanding. Given the characteristic sensitivity to fluctuations and feedback that occurs in psychotherapy, any effect has the potential to reach macroscopic, or systemic proportions rather quickly (Crutchfield et al., 1986). Such rapidity of change necessitates an examination of a continuous data set, one that enlarges both the microscopic and macroscopic view. The constant uncertainty of the system demands depiction by a method capable of tracking fleeting bits of periodic behavior, points of choice and change (iteration and bifurcation), and embeddedness (variables nested within time). In complex human systems (i.e., psychotherapeutic formats), the system's initial definition or description is not likely to be perpetuated in latter stages of its evolution, due to unpredictable change, thus creating a situation wherein the definition of the entities and their concomitant interaction must continually be modified by evolutionary parameters (Prigogine & Stengers, 1984). In the evolving effort to measure the "universe" of therapeutic process, perhaps now is the time to be willing to expand our understanding until it takes in the whole image of growth and change.

CHAOS IN GROUP PSYCHOTHERAPY: AN ILLUSTRATION

A psychotherapeutic group is a social microcosm and by nature is complex and disorderly, thus making an accurate representation very difficult (Weick, 1982). Few successful attempts have been made to describe the ongoing and changing processes of psychotherapeutic groups in a generalized fashion (Fuhriman & Burlingame, 1990). As a result, the literature on group psychotherapy is bereft of data necessary to describe core principles *or* models that could systematically guide clinicians and process researchers to an understanding of the dynamical properties of group therapy. However, the dynamic, interactive properties of a therapy group in many respects parallel those of the physical and biological systems that have been successfully modeled with deterministic chaos methodology. Thus, an application of chaos methodology seemed a promising endeavor in which to examine the question: Does nonlinear order exist in apparently random interactions of group members?

Testing the viability of chaos methods to explore the dynamical properties of a psychotherapeutic group requires the observation and measurement of as much of the social system as possible. The fact that psychotherapeutic groups may continue for months or years in an open-ended fashion creates an insurmountable methodological obstacle; that is, one cannot garner the requisite resources to observe and measure a social system for that length of time. However, the advent of time-limited group psychotherapy attenuates this constraint in that the imposition of a time limit essentially creates a "closed" system in which to study the dynamical properties (Burlingame & Fuhriman, 1990). Hence, the data used in the following illustration of deterministic chaos is drawn from a single, thirty-hour, time-limited psychotherapeutic group that spanned fifteen weeks.

Interaction as a Dynamical Dependent Variable

When attempting to model a complex system, the dependent variables that one selects are crucial. If one assumes that a system has an underlying nonlinear order, but the selected variables do not accurately tap the dynamical properties inherent in this order, one could erroneously conclude that the best description of the system is that it is random. Thus, caution and care should be exercised in selecting dependent variables.

One of the more recognizable and observable dynamical properties of psychotherapeutic groups is the ongoing and changing interaction among the participants of the group, including both therapist and clients. The HIM (Hill, 1965) enjoys one of the longest and most productive histories in the group literature (cf. Fuhriman & Burlingame, 1994) as a measure of the changing interactional patterns of group participants. The HIM classifies verbal interaction according to two dimensions: content (what is being discussed) and style (how it is being discussed). The crossing of these two dimensions results in a weighted scoring matrix that orders the therapeutic quality of verbal interaction on a continuum that ranges in value from one to sixteen (least to most therapeutic).

The HIM is one of the few group process instruments where a systematic attempt has been made to tabulate reliability (Rho coefficients .85-.96), validity, and normative data. Over the past two decades, more than ninety articles and papers and 120 dissertations and theses have relied on the HIM. An additional advantage of the instrument is that it can be used to quantify the moment-to-moment, interactive properties of the group by using either a real time or interactive time scheme to unitize the dialogue.

However, the HIM is not a flawless measure of group interaction. An exhaustive literature review on the HIM concluded that while the HIM could "be reliably used to discriminate variations in group process . . . further research is needed to test its ability to measure how these varying processes are related to therapeutic growth or improvement in groups having different goals" (cf. Fuhriman and Burlingame, 1994). The caution stems from the sparse literature in support of the HIM as a reliable interval scale, particularly as a weighted scoring system where higher scores invariably denote higher therapeutic quality of interaction. Nevertheless, ample literature supports the nominal viability of the instrument, and there is a clear precedent, albeit in other disciplines, for examining changing patterns in system properties rated on a nominal level of measurement (e.g., Berthelsen, Glazier, & Skolnick, 1992; Richards, 1990).

To summarize, the selected dynamical system consisted of a single, thirty hour time-limited psychotherapeutic group. The dependent variable was the therapeutic quality of group participants' verbal interactions as measured by the HIM. Every verbal utterance of the participants in every session was rated using typed transcripts, resulting in a time series of HIM ratings containing 14,453 data points (intrarater reliability r=.93). Each data point in this array represents a unique member or therapist utterance and essentially portrays the complete interactive life of a single psychotherapeutic group.

Fractal Estimates of a Psychotherapeutic Group's Interaction

The entire array of HIM codes from a single group is depicted in Figure 6.1. This evolving time series has an X axis representing consecutive interactions of group participants and a Y axis reflecting the therapeutic quality of each interaction. To determine whether this time series has a nonlinear but ordered pattern of change first requires that it be transformed. The transformation involves creating a new distribution of points or trajectories by embedding each value of the time series within a theoretical environment called state space. In this illustration a state space was generated by transforming the original array (Figure 6.1) up through embedding dimension 10.

Analysis of this series of new data points essentially enables one to understand the curves or trajectories that describe the evolutionary change of group interactions. Change that is random would have produced data points that equally fill all sectors of the state space, and trajectories that evolve randomly in the state space, indicating that there is no order. A "chaotic" ordered system of changing interactions would have a concentration of data points around focal regions and an orderly but complex evolution of trajectories within those regions (chaotic attractors) related to the dynamical properties of the therapeutic process.

One measure of the complexity of a chaotic attractor is the fractal dimension. This fractal dimension is defined by many algorithms. Three of the most popular, for example, are the correlation dimension, the information dimension, and the capacity or Hausdorf dimension. The focus of this illustration of therapeutic interaction will be on the correlation dimension, an estimate of fractal complexity of how points in state space cluster.

The computation of correlation dimension [d] depends on the correlation integral [Cr(I)], which in turn depends upon the number of areas, spheres, or hyperspheres required to cover the points within the state space as the radius of the spheres [I] is systematically varied. The d is the slope or ratio of log[Cr(I)] to log[I]. For a single variate state space such as we have here (HIM), a lagging technique is used to create increasing dimensionality (embedding dimension) of the state space for "attractor reconstruction." The correlation integral is recomputed for each increase in dimensionality (producing the family of curves as seen in Fig. 6.2) until d (the slope of those curves) becomes asymptotic ("saturates," which it will fail to do for truly random points). To help understand this procedure, picture a single data point in

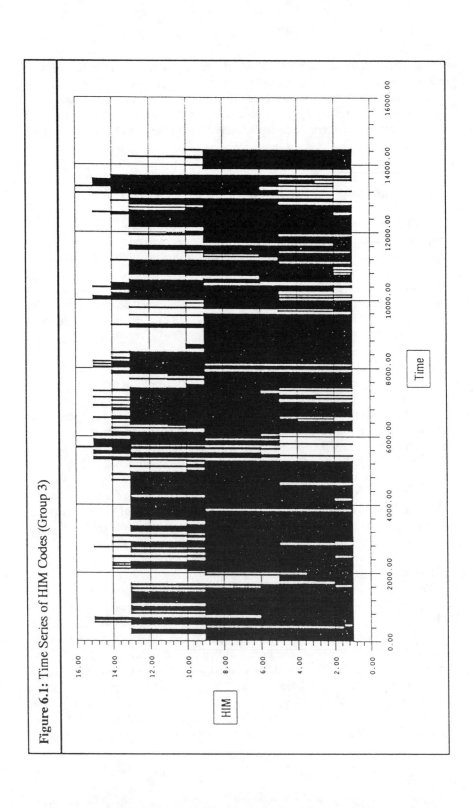

Figure 6.1: Time Series of HIM Codes (Group 3)

state space. Consider a radius as a radar beacon that emanates from this point and sweeps through the multidimensional state space creating a hypersphere. By varying the length of the radius, more or less points are captured within this hypersphere. By counting the number of points associated with different radii (or embedding dimensions), and by consecutively moving the radii to every data point in state space, one eventually ascertains the topographical density of data points in state space. Given that each data point in this illustration represents a unique group participant statement, and that its numeric value represents information regarding the therapeutic quality of utterance, then the relevance of examining the aforementioned time series for evidence of chaos is essentially an attempt to understand the density or clustering of similar statements among the group participants.

Figure 6.2a shows the correlation analysis from the group therapy time series using ten different embedding dimensions. Figure 6.2b reflects a comparable and arbitrary (from a Monte Carlo scrambling) time series that illustrates random change. The saturation evident in the lines associated with embedding dimensions 4-10 in Figure 6.2a, exhibits a form that is a cardinal characteristic of a chaotic system. In contrast, lines in Figure 6.2b, though not appearing truly random, show a much higher dimensionality. The average slope of the lines in Figure 6.2a indicates a fractal dimension of 2.12, which was cross-validated by analyzing the same time series with a similar algorithm from Sprott and Rowlands' (1992) chaos analyzer software. In short, the convergence of the two methods of analysis suggests a complex, nonlinear pattern of change inherent in the time series describing the group participant interactions in the short-term therapy group (Figure 6.1).

Exploration of the Fractal Dimension

The fractal dimension discovered by the aforementioned methods reveals two general and important findings. First, the changing pattern of participant interactions over the life of the thirty-hour time-limited therapy group does appear to have a complex, nonlinear order. This order signifies that some sectors of state space are more active, or are more dense with data points, thus suggesting the presence of a chaotic attractor. Second, the relative size of the fractal, estimated from the correlation integral, denotes the topographical density of data points, or the nonlinear, complex order of interaction. Additional findings that are directly related to the correlation integral cast light on the significance of these two overall observations.

A comparison of individual session fractal estimates with the total fractal dimension calculated for all fifteen sessions reveals several intriguing findings (Table 6.1). Initially, the intent was to ascertain if a single session could be used to estimate the fractal dimension of an entire group and, if so, what would be the best sessions to estimate the total fractal dimension.

Figure 6.2A: Correlation Integral (Group 3) Same data as in Figure 6.1.

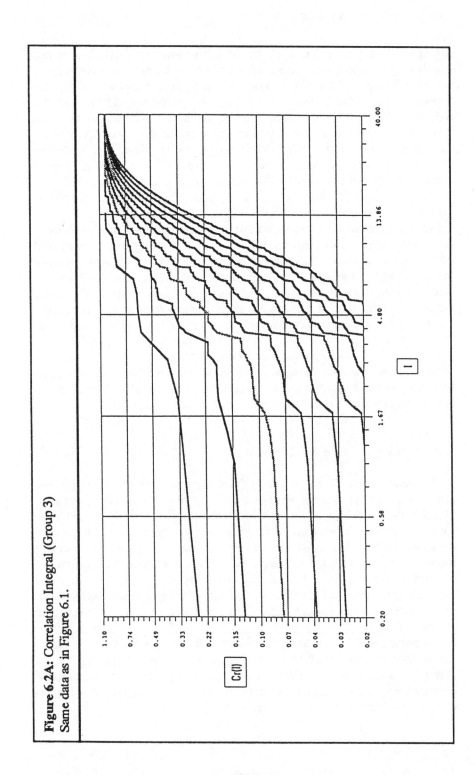

Figure 6.2B: Correlation Integral (Group 3)
Monte Carlo (Same data as in Figure 6.1, but order randomized).

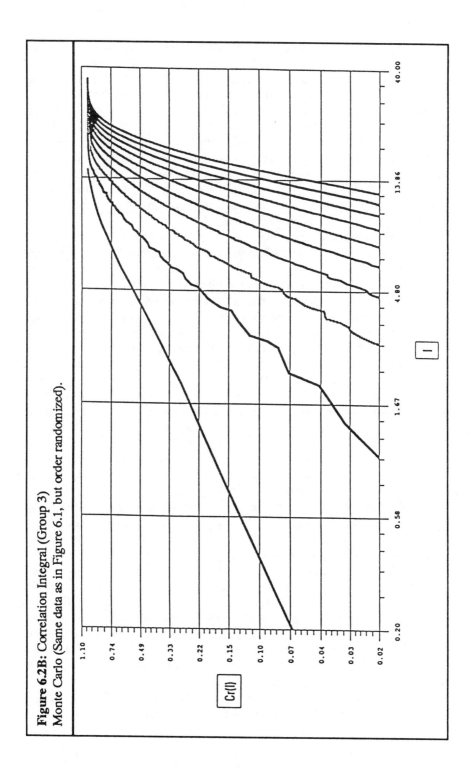

The values plotted in series 1 (Figure 6.3a) are the individual session fractal estimates for each session, excluding one statistically significant outlier that fell outside a 99 percent confidence interval (session 15, cf. Table 6.1). It is of note that the average deviation of session fractal estimates in the first half (sessions 1-7) of the group (.94) is approximately 168 percent of that of the average deviation in the second half (.56). In short, nearly two-thirds as much variability exists in the underlying order of interactions during the early life of the group than in the latter. Group maturation (what clinicians often describe as the internal rhythm of a group) is reflected in a more stable session by session fractal estimate during the latter half of the group. If such findings are replicated in other groups, it becomes clear that selecting later sessions for fractal estimates will result in better overall estimates of group development and change over time.

The second series in Figure 6.3a displays a complementary developmental trend for the HIM session averages. Although there is some variability, a significant linear trend exists ($r\{14\}=.36$), indicating an overall increase in therapeutic quality of group participants' interactions over the life of the group. This finding, although unrelated to chaos theory, is encouraging for a number of reasons: It corresponds to group development theory and what is hoped for in effective group process; it is grounded on moment-to-moment process measurement; and it gives greater assurance regarding the integrity of the data set being analyzed.

The final analyses focus on the relationship between fractal estimates and the HIM values (Figs. 6.3b & 6.4). These graphs display the relationship between fractal estimates and average HIM ratings for individual sessions. The first (Fig. 6.3b) shows a trajectory idealized through the points of the scatterplot in the two-dimensional state space. It is to be admitted that this is an unusual state space, since one of the two interactive variables is itself already a measure of the interactive therapeutic process; that is, the two measures are not independent by definition. Nonetheless, it is exciting to see a pattern emerging that, although necessarily present in the time series (Fig. 6.3a), is more evident in the trajectory (Fig. 6.3b). More specifically, there seems to be some oscillation between higher and lower regions of the state space. This suggests that the group is seeking several successive modes of interaction, exploring one and achieving some success, and then abandoning it to try a new mode. Finally, there is a decline in d and HIM, then a rise in HIM with first an increase in d and then a decline. Then, despite its success, there is a decline in both as if a better process were being sought by the group; but after that failure, comes a return to the previous process, with a high HIM and low fractal character, as the group seeks a final integration toward the end of therapy. It is possible to conceive of the therapeutic process as a Lorenzian-like dynamical system, or as a dynamical scheme undergoing bifurcations, as new strategies are being sought, with members' experience or therapists' manipulations as control parameters. The latter seems to be a more promising explanation.

The more traditional linear analysis of the same scatterplot (Fig. 6.4) yields a strong positive relationship ($r\{14\}=.46$) between fractal estimates and average

Table 6.1: Analysis of Group 3 Sessions sorted by z-score from the total fractal dimension.						
Session Number	Number of Interactions	Fractal Dimension	z-score Deviation from Total Fractal Dimension	R2 of the Fractal Estimate	Average Hill Codes	Standard Deviation of Hill Codes
12	1033	2.160	.07	0.988	6.27	4.12
5	808	2.168	.08	0.995	6.90	5.01
11	584	2.368	.42	0.984	9.63	4.16
9	1263	2.378	.43	0.991	7.21	4.97
1	717	2.394	.46	0.993	6.25	4/61
13	1052	2.435	.53	0.989	7.16	4.87
2	968	1754	−.61	0.989	5.84	5.02
10	1306	1.645	−.80	0.992	4.25	4.10
14	1020	1.642	−.80	0.998	10.38	3.88
8	1199	2.638	.87	0.994	9.11	4.39
6	894	2.654	.89	0.986	7.32	4.89
3	826	1.245	−1.46	0.991	4.19	4.11
4	904	3.011	1.49	0.982	6.54	4.26
7	1119	1.178	−1.57	0.994	9.50	4.58
15	760	0.905	−2.03	0.979	2.75	3.10

Total Fractal Dimension: 2.119
Standard Deviation: 0.598

Average Fractal Dimension z-score Deviation
First half: .94
Second half: .56

Figure 6.3A: Development of Patterns of Fractal Values and HIM Averages Time series of each variable.

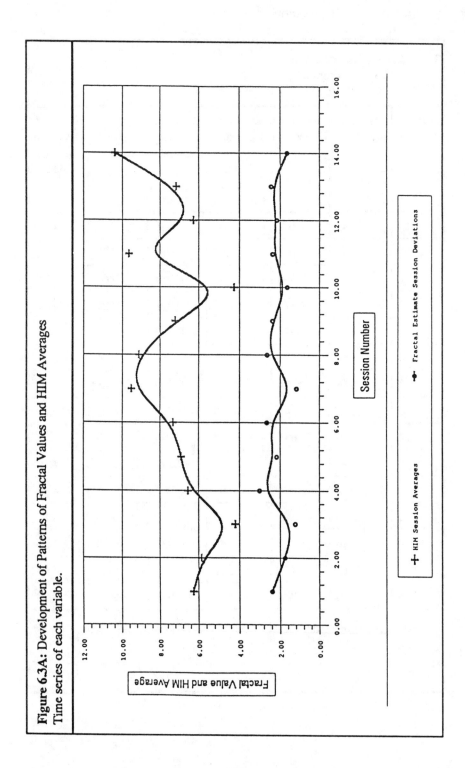

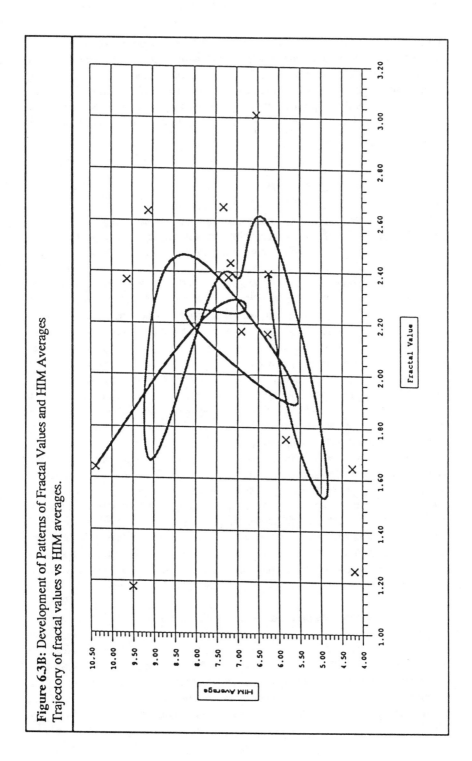

Figure 6.3B: Development of Patterns of Fractal Values and HIM Averages
Trajectory of fractal values vs HIM averages.

HIM values. As therapeutic quality increases in a session, so does the fractal estimate. A much higher relationship ($r\{11\}=.80$) is uncovered when the two outlying sessions are removed from the analysis. Thus, the increase in complexity parallels in a significant fashion the pattern of therapeutic interaction. This linear analysis supports the nonlinear one (Fig. 6.4 vs. Fig. 6.3b), but its inadequacy, especially in discarding the richness of the time-dependent components of information in the data, is very apparent.

SUMMARY AND DISCUSSION

Overall, the preceding findings are encouraging, particularly as they relate to both the applicability of chaos methodology to research on the therapeutic process and the observance of the evolutionary change of the group as a whole. Analysis of the time series from both single sessions as well as the entire interactional history of the therapy group suggests that the group gradually developed a stable, yet complex, nonlinear pattern of interaction that was related not only to time in group but also to the therapeutic quality of participant interactions. These findings correspond with clinical understanding in that one expects group therapy participants, especially the client members, to exhibit behavior that is low risk (lower average HIM scores), yet volatile (higher variability of fractal estimates) in the beginning phase of a time-limited group. Moreover, one expects later sessions to exhibit higher therapeutic quality and complexity of interaction that, in this instance, is demonstrated by the findings. The application of chaos theory and methodology in this case illustration provides preliminary support for their utility in research on the psychotherapeutic process.

At the same time a host of limitations must be kept in mind in applying this type of research methodology to psychotherapeutic research. To begin with, no precedent exists in the psychotherapeutic process literature and little that can be directly drawn from other disciplines to assist in deriving straightforward, intelligible implications. Given the lack of precedent, attempts were explored to triangulate different analyses and methods in order to arrive at a convergence of findings. An additional method is to compare the results from this study with dynamical systems that have known properties (e.g., random vs. chaotic systems) to develop a baseline for interpretation. Indeed, the embryonic nature of the field makes circumspection the order of the day.

Although there is good precedent and empirical support for the HIM, caution is suggested when directly interpreting the absolute value of the HIM ratings. Cell values are not entirely orthogonal from one another and hence must be viewed as gross indicators of interactional quality of group participants. We are currently exploring alternative measures as well as psychometric transformations of the existing HIM data. Interactional process research is a tedious, expensive, and time consuming endeavor that does not readily lead to immediate products. Additionally,

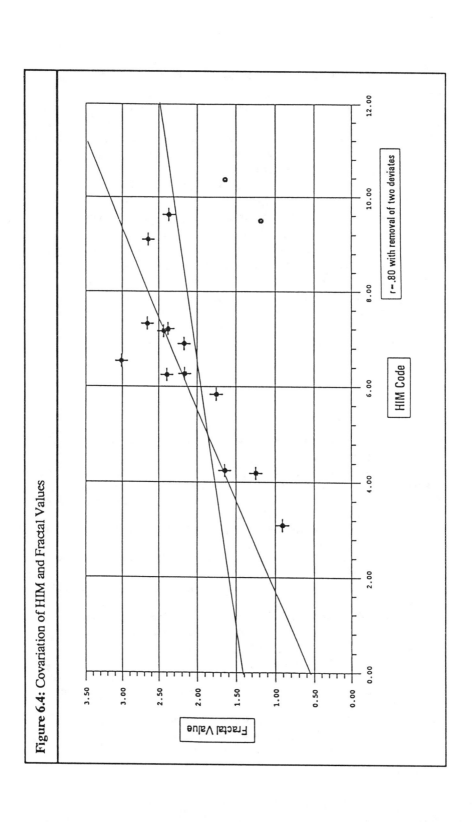

Figure 6.4: Covariation of HIM and Fractal Values

the paucity of measurement tools grounded in sound psychometric properties further exacerbates an already vexatious situation.

The current stage of this research involves fitting a mathematical model to the time series in order to capture the changing properties of group interaction. Assuming that we are able to derive a model that mirrors interactional change in psychotherapeutic groups, a fair question is: Are there any practical applications to the practice of mental health? We think so. A great deal of training in other disciplines revolves around the importance of pattern recognition in deciphering complex behavior and systems. Capturing and modeling complex patterns that are associated with both good and poor outcomes in group therapy could prove to be an invaluable aid in recognizing and changing deleterious patterns *during the course* of therapy. A clinician's ability to do so could result in a calibrating effect that could yield better overall outcome for treatment. In other words, it could improve the self-organizational feature of the process.

The application of chaos methods to research on the psychotherapeutic process is new, intriguing, and—very messy! Nevertheless, this preliminary experience suggests it to be a promising venture. Further investigations and replications should provide the requisite data to arrive at a firmer conclusion regarding its long-term relevance and heuristic value.

REFERENCES

Bakeman, R., & Gottman, J. M. (1989). *Observing interaction: An introduction to sequential analysis*. Cambridge: Cambridge University Press.

Berthelsen, C., Glazier, J., & Skolnick, M. (1992). Global fractal dimension of human DNA sequences treated as pseudorandom walks. *Physical Review A, 45*, 8902–8913.

Briggs, J., & Peat, F. D. (1989). *Turbulent mirror: An illustrated guide to chaos theory and the science of wholeness*. New York: Harper & Row.

Burlingame, G. M., & Fuhriman, A. (1990). Time-limited group therapy. *Counseling Psychologist, 18*, 93–118.

Crutchfield, J. P., Farmer, J. D., Packard, N. H., & Shaw, R. S. (1986). Chaos. *Scientific American, 255*, 46–57.

Fuhriman, A., & Burlingame, G. M. (1994). Hill Interaction Matrix: Therapy through dialogue. Unpublished manuscript, Brigham Young University.

Fuhriman, A., & Burlingame, G. M. (1990). Consistency of matter: A comparative analysis of individual and group process variables. *Counseling Psychologist, 18*, 6–63.

Fuhriman, A., Drescher, S., & Burlingame, G. (1984). Conceptualizing small group process. *Small Group Behavior, 15*, 427–440.

Garfield, S. L., & Bergin, A. E. (1986). Introduction and historical overview. In S. L. Garfield & A. E. Bergin (Eds.), *Handbook of psychotherapy and behavior change* (3rd ed., pp. 3–22). New York: Wiley.

Gottman, J. M., & Roy, A. K. (1990). *Sequential analysis: A guide for behavioral researchers*. Cambridge: Cambridge University Press.

Greenberg, L. S., & Pinsof, W. M. (1986). Process research: Current trends and future perspectives. In L. S. Greenberg & W. M. Pinsof (Eds.), *The psychotherapeutic process: A research handbook.* New York: Guilford Press.

Hill, W. F. (1965). *Hill Interaction Matrix.* Los Angeles: University of California Youth Study Center.

Prigogine, I., & Stengers, I. (1984). *Order out of chaos: Man's new dialogue with nature.* New York: Bantam Books.

Rice, L. N., & Greenberg, L. S. (1984). *Patterns of change: Intensive analysis of psychotherapy process.* New York: The Guilford Press.

Richards, D. (1990). Is strategic decision making chaotic? *Behavioral Science, 35,* 219–232.

Sprott, J., & Rowlands, G. (1992). *Chaos Data Analyzer.* New York: American Physics Society.

Weick, K. (1982). Affirmation as inquiry. *Small Group Behavior, 13,* 441–450.

7

Psychocardiological Portraits: A Clinical Application of Process Theory

Hector C. Sabelli, Linnea Carlson-Sabelli, Minu K. Patel, Joseph P. Zbilut, Joseph V. Messer, and Karen Walthall

Complex and beautiful patterns of cardiac rhythmicity are associated with psychobiological processes. Empirical correlations with emotions and behavior (Figs. 7.3, 7.4, 7.6) as well as apparent differences between psychotic and nonpsychotic patients (Table 7.1) suggest that such portraits may potentially have clinical value. This technique, which we call *electropsychocardiography* (Carlson-Sabelli, Sabelli, Patel, Messer, Zbilut, and Walthall, in press), illustrates the process method, a two-pronged approach that gives priority to the biological and supremacy to the psychological, in diagnosis and treatment as well as in research (Sabelli & Carlson-Sabelli, 1989, 1991). More generally, *process theory* postulates the priority of the simple (energy-rich) and the supremacy of the complex (information-rich) (Sabelli, 1989). Accordingly, the function of the cardiac energy-delivering system should reflect the supremacy of neurophysiological processes in organizing the behavior of the organism as an integrated whole. Some relations between cardiac timing and the content of their speech during psychotherapeutic sessions have already been observed in two patients (Reidbord & Redington, 1992). Cardiac timing is easy to measure in freely behaving subjects and provides a digital ruler to quantify how behavior consumes energy. The increasing availability of computers renders this type of methodology applicable to clinical research and practice.

PROCESS SCIENCE: THEORY AND METHOD

Process theory attempts to integrate mathematical, biological, and psychological dynamics through process philosophy (Heraclitus, Empedocles, Hegel, Engels, Teilhard de Chardin, Whitehead). A conservative bias led classical science to focus on static structures, isolated systems, reversible mechanical processes, and decay toward equilibrium, rest, disorder, and entropy, when in fact progressive and creative evolution is evident in nature as well as in history. The newly evolving science of complex dynamical systems (chaos and catastrophe theories, far-from-equilibrium thermodynamics, fractal geometry) provides powerful methods to study processes without the methodological limitations imposed by the static views of mechanics (classic, statistical, relativistic, quantic) and of logic (traditional and mathematical), and it has thus advanced from consideration of isolated systems and events to open and integrated processes. Yet a focus on stationary processes, stable attractors, and deterministic causation may bias the interpretation of dynamic systems toward a conservative philosophy. Process theory focuses on uninterrupted and creative processes that rise and fall, rather than on stable attractors, because both the clinical and the social contexts lead us to consider change as more fundamental than stability, and interactions more productive than self-organization.

Universal Laws

Our methodology is based on process theory (Carlson-Sabelli et al., in press; Sabelli, 1989; Sabelli & Carlson-Sabelli, 1989; Sabelli, Carlson-Sabelli, & Messer, 1994). In brief, process theory postulates a set of universal laws that apply to all processes, and to all levels of organization within a process, which so acquire a self-similar fractal geometry. All processes and structures have the following simple components or form:

0. *Randomness*, such as quantum flux, chance, luck.
1. *Asymmetry*, such as the temporal flow of energy (action=energy x time), the universal asymmetry of structures (Pasteur's cosmic asymmetry), and the expansion of the universe from a hypothetical point repellor (Big Bang). In contrast, mechanics portrays time as reversible.
2. *Union of opposites*, the necessary coexistence of opposites such as rise and fall, positive and negative, woman and man, right and left, sympathetic and parasympathetic, synergy and struggle, union and separation, similarity and difference, symmetry and asymmetry. Opposites cannot be accommodated in mutually exclusive categories (as in logic) or as poles in a linear continuum, but each must be represented as an independent dimension; the sum of opposites is the energy of change, and their difference provides information as to the direction of change.
3. *Trifurcations*, such as tridimensional matter. The existence of these simple and universal cosmic forms (asymmetry or lattice order, opposition or group inverse, hierarchy of topologically embedded forms) is given credence by their fundamental role in mathematics (Bourbaki) and by their empirical demonstration in thinking (Piaget) and in natural, social, and psychological processes (Sabelli, 1989).

Process theory postulates that all these simple forms coexist, and interact to create higher dimensional processes; left to themselves, processes increase in diversity and complexity. Hence natural processes have multidimensional components created by the interaction of the simpler ones, such as the widespread spiral organization of the Fibonacci series (0,1,1,2,3,5,13, ...), galaxies, and positive feedback processes, and more complex and varied novel forms, which are unique in all individual entities, from snowflakes to humans. Process theory thus builds upon and expands deterministic models according to which processes flow toward thermodynamic equlibrium or to other low-dimensional, stable, and mutually exclusive attractors. According to process theory, simple processes are universal in time and space (priority of the simple), whereas complex processes predominate in the short-lived and localized systems in which they exist (supremacy of the complex); this is in contrast to both materialism and idealism, which give primacy to one or the other pole of the hierarchy.

Methodological Implications

These theoretical developments have methodological implications. Process theory studies processes from the double perspective of the simple and the complex, as illustrated here by the study of cardiac physiology from the views of both mathematical form and psychological concomitants, and elsewhere by the biosociopsychological clinical approach (Sabelli & Carlson-Sabelli, 1991). Viewing processes as open and interacting, process theory studies systems and organisms in their natural interactions, considering their experimental isolation as a distortion that invalidates the data. Process theory interprets two-dimensional plots of lagged-time series (such as heartbeat interval) as portraying the interaction between partially synergic and partially antagonistic opposites (sympathetic acceleration and parasympathetic deceleration). Postulating that everything is a process, process theory studies time series as more natural, rather than comparing snapshots of time limited samples. Stable attractors and bifurcations between them describe relatively simple nonlinear processes; more complex natural processes require the identification of evolving complexes (organized transients), the characterization of their time course (beginning, rise, fall, and ending), and the description of the dimensional distribution of their components. We thus expanded the recurrence method (originally used to plot portraits of stationary attractors) to construct the time graph of recurrences. Instead of attempting to measure the single dimension of a hypothetical low-dimensional attractor, process theory investigates the contribution of the simple and the complex components of a process in a wide range of dimensional frameworks (1 to 500 here).

Hence, to identify patterned processes and to reconstruct their components from a time series (dimensional reconstruction), process theory uses embeddings of sequential lags in an increasing numerical order 1,2,3, . . . N of embedding dimensions. We begin with the search of low-dimensional components because every process and every level of organization in each process has the one dimension of time, the two dimensions of information, and the three dimensions of physical space. But we also study higher dimensions of organization, attempting to investigate the process of co-creation of complexity. In this chapter we explore the possibility that the notions of priority and supremacy may be rendered operational by examining complex processes using frameworks with a wide range of dimensions: The simpler components may be revealed by mathematical portraits in few dimensions, and the more complex ones by portraits of higher dimensions. Psychobiological processes may be expected to be high-dimensional, complex, and creative—that is to say, organized but not "deterministic" (in the strict meaning of the term), lying between and including the processes produced by a low-dimensional deterministic source and the components of infinite-dimensional stochastic origin. Given such a large number of dimensions, it is impossible to measure all the relevant variables, but high-dimensional plots can be obtained by examining changes in one variable at various lags and embeddings, to infer the complexities introduced by the interaction of the many variables that affect the process. Each variable necessarily reflects to some extent the influence of all others; conversely each variable influences many others. One is many and many is one, said Heraclitus. The embedding theorem shows that a vector of time-delayed copies of the observable will generate a trajectory in the dimensional space so created that it is similar to the original (Packard, Crutchfield, Farmer, & Shaw, 1980), and the Whitney embedding theorem indicates that it is possible to make quantitatively meaningful inferences about the dynamical structure of a complex, multidimensional dynamical system by measuring one variable for a sufficiently long period of time (Gershenfeld, 1992; Guillemin & Pollack, 1974).

Modules

At every level of organization, processes are made of units of finite duration or *modules*, such as atoms, action potentials, organisms, and words. As the processes of co-creation are generic (Thomson's principle of mass production), there are a limited number of classes at each level of organization (Mill's principle of the uniform structure of nature). The members of each class are exchangeable regarding many forms of interaction (hence the term *module*), even if unique in their specific characteristics; even snowflakes are unique in form, and even human beings may replace one another regarding social roles. Modules belong permanently to their class and transiently to a system (Sabelli, 1989).

Semantic Hypothesis

Within the context of a living organism, probably also in the physical world, modules can also be symbols. The classes of modules can thus represent an alphabet, which spells out messages meaningful at a higher level of organization. For instance, neuronal action potentials codify feelings and ideas. At the simplest level, the cardiac action potential is a module with a distinct message—contraction—

with the interbeat interval the most basic punctuation; at a more complex level, cardiac action potentials are grouped into sequences with similar beat intervals, as required by the ongoing behavior.

Modular and Semantic Analysis

Process theory thus compares levels of organization, attempting to decode the meaning of modules as letters of an alphabet in which complex messages are written. The behavior of the organism consists of well-organized, patterned processes, such as sleep and wakefulness cycles, feeding, sexual behavior, and emotional behaviors such as fear, anger, submission, and dominance; these are *action patterns*. Each of these genetically inherited behaviors, embodied in brain structure and available for activation by the release of synaptic transmitters and modulators, includes a subjective state, an outward behavior, and physiological changes. Since by necessity cardiac activity is part of each of these integrative patterns of behavior, we have explored methods to reveal the behavioral alphabet of the heart. Our objective is to provide a physiological method to study emotions in clinical practice. To this effect, we explored several methods of interpreting the pattern of R-R intervals (the timing of heart action potentials) in day-long dynamic recordings of the electrocardiogram.

ELECTROPSYCHOCARDIOGRAPHY: METHOD

Electrocardiographic recordings (twenty-four to forty-eight hours) were obtained during the course of daily activities from normal volunteers and psychiatric patients with anxiety, depressive and psychotic disorders diagnosed according to DSM-III R. Data were sampled at the rate of 128 Hz to determine the interbeat (R-R) intervals. While wearing the Holter monitor, subjects recorded in a diary their activities (working, driving, eating, sex, sleep) and emotions (glad, sad, angry, fearful, each zero to five), physical and psychological symptoms, and medications. Data were studied by means of time graphs of R-R intervals; two-dimensional phase plane portraits (RRI_i versus RRI_{i+1}); factor processing (factor analysis of a time series using the time delay method, see later); and recurrence plots (Eckmann, Kamphorst, & Ruelle, 1987), which construct N dimensional vectors from one variable using the delay method. Using a program developed by Zbilut and Webber (1992), a recurrence plot was generated from the time series by constructing a square matrix in which the R-R intervals were plotted along the horizontal and the vertical axes. For each beat, we constructed a vector that included the R-R interval itself and each of the following intervals up to a number N, the number of embeddings. When two vectors were equal (within 10 percent), a dot was plotted in the graph; a diagonal line was thereby formed because the vector corresponding

Figure 7.1: Twenty-four-hour Time Graphs of Heart Rate
A. Normal thirty-six-year-old woman; B. Anxious thirty-two-year-old woman; C. Depressed thirty-three-year-old woman; D. Psychotic fifty-six year-old manic man.

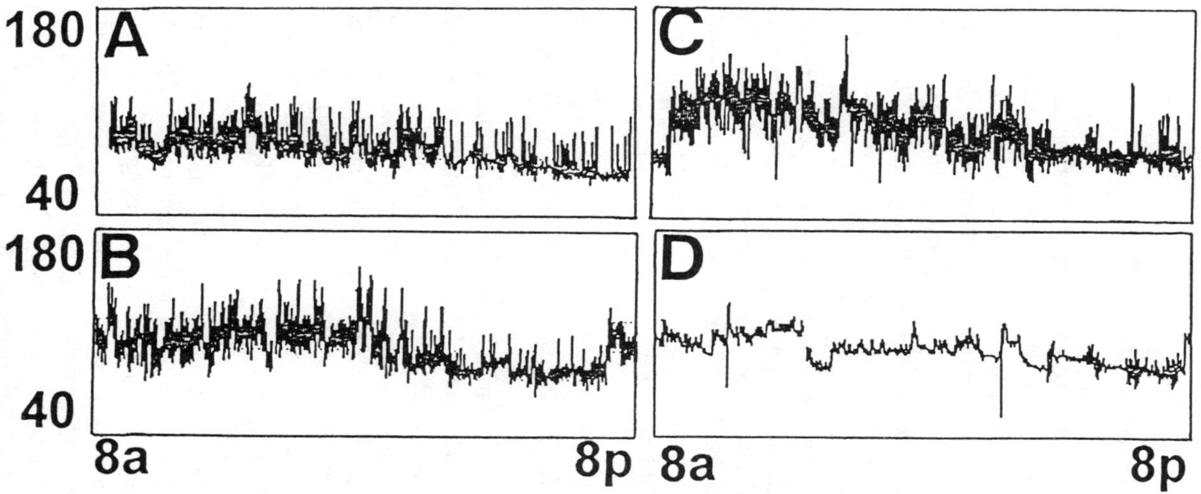

to each R-R is identical to itself. Guided by process theory, here we extend the use of recurrence plots in two directions: We studied twenty-four hour recordings rather than short, relatively stationary samples, constructing time graphs of recurrences, and we analyzed them with a wide range of embeddings (from 1 to 500 embeddings), a technique that provides graphic and distinct portraits of long and complex processes.

RESULTS

Time Graphs of Heart Rate

Psychotic subjects had faster heart rate and lower variability, changes that appear to be relevant regarding cardiac function and that are only in part secondary to anticholinergic drug effects. Heart rate variability was increased in comparison to normals in some depressed subjects also treated with anticholinergic agents (Fig. 7.1). Further, psychotic subjects also showed qualitative changes, including a paradoxical increase in cardiac variability during sleep, major shifts in rate during the day, and the occurrence of oscillatory patterns of R-R variation in some subjects.

State Space

Trajectories of instantaneous heart rate (RRI_i) versus (RRI_{i+1}) form irregular shapes (Fig. 7.2). Additional analyses of the difference between successive beats determined by the opposing processes of adrenergic acceleration and cholinergic deceleration (difference of opposites), versus the joint variation of successive beats as parts of a pattern that determines the major axis (union of opposites), provide more interesting results. There were significant reductions in the range of patterned variations in the depressed and the anxious patients, and even more in manics, without change in the beat-to-beat variations. Such trajectories do not reveal specific differences, which are apparent in recurrence plots.

Recurrence Plots of R-R Intervals

In contrast to the uniform plots of computer-generated pseudo-random numbers, recurrence plots of cardiac data were highly organized into heterogenous configurations of recurrences, that differ in various types of patients (Fig. 7.3). To investigate the possible clinical significance of these patterns, we compared recordings obtained from six schizophrenic and schizoaffective subjects and from six depressed and anxious subjects by measuring: the number of recurrences; the

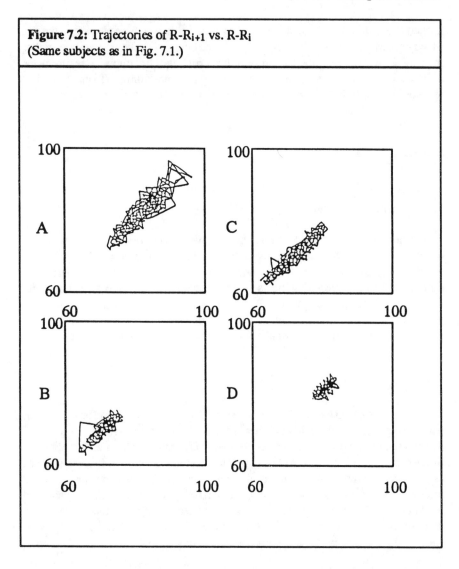

Figure 7.2: Trajectories of R-R$_{i+1}$ vs. R-R$_i$
(Same subjects as in Fig. 7.1.)

number of *patterned recurrences* contained in lines (Zbilut's determinism); Shannon's entropy; and arrangement ratio, that is, the ratio between percentages of patterned and total recurrences. Psychotics had a significantly greater number of patterned recurrences, a higher entropy, and a lower arrangement than nonpsychotics. In both groups the proportion of patterned recurrences was lower during sleep; the difference between sleep and wakefulness was statistically significant in the larger samples (Table 7.1).

Figure 7.3: Recurrence Plots
(7000 windows, 480 embeddings, cut-off 1) during day (left) and night (right).
(Same subjects as in Figs. 7.1 & 7.2.)

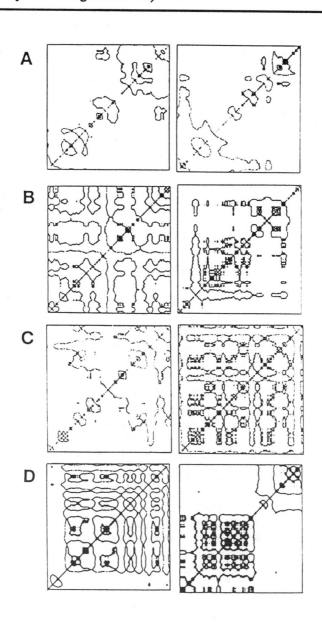

Table 7.1: Comparison Between Psychotic and Nonpsychotic Patients
(Six patients in each group. 1000 beats, lag 1, 50 embeddings.)
mean ± S.E.M., 3 p.m. above, 3 a.m. below.
* p < .02 psychotic vs nonpsychotic; ** p < .02 asleep vs awake.

Measurements	Psychotic	Nonpsychotic
Percentage of Recurrences	3.9 ± 1.2 12.5 ± 7.2	2.4 ± 0.9 3.2 ± 0.9
Percentage of Patterned recurrences	83.0 ± 5.0 86.0 ± 6.0	70.0 ± 9.0 61.0 ± 8.0*
Entropy	2.97 ± 0.27 3.14 ± 0.38	2.69 ± 0.31 2.00 ± 0.37*
Arrangement Ratio	34.9 ± 10.0 12.6 ± 2.9**	42.5 ± 11.7 23.6 ± 5.0**

Time Graph of Recurrences: Complexes and Bifurcations

The distribution of recurrences in plots changed at different times (Figure 7.4). Assuming that patterns of change carry significant information led us from "snapshots" of "stationary processes" to the time graph of recurrences of dynamic electrocardiograms. We thus constructed twenty-four-hour sequences of recurrence plots, taking advantage of the fact that the diagonal of each matrix (from first to last beat in the "window") represents time. The time graph of recurrences was clearly different during sleep (Fig. 7.4, M to N) and wakefulness. These visual differences were confirmed statistically: During sleep there is an increase in the number of recurrences and a decrease in the proportion of patterned recurrences, without significant changes in entropy, indicating a decrease in variability and in patterning. Over and above these overall changes between the opposite phases of adrenergic and cholinergic predominance, the recurrence graphs are naturally divided into shorter phases or *complexes*, different in form and in the number of patterned recurrences, variable in duration, and separated from each other by short or long interruptions of recurrences that represent bifurcations. Complexes have characteristic forms, which repeat from individual to individual. Using windows of different size, it was observed that the same forms repeated with various magnitudes, indicating a self-similarity characteristic of fractals.

Figure 7.4: Twenty-four-hour Time Graph of Recurrences
From an electrocardiographic recording of a female inpatient with generalized anxiety disorder (B of Figures 7.1-7.3). Lag 1; 480 embeddings; 7000 points; 1 cutoff. A: Start recording at 4:00 P.M.; B: Group therapy. C-D: Man in her room makes her anxious. E-F: Dinner. G-H: Reading, phoning. I: Scared by another patient. J: Mood transition, from anxious to relaxed; note the symmetric circle of recurrences indicating change in polarity of complexes. K: Going to bed. L: Difficulty falling asleep. M: Falling asleep. M-N: asleep. N: Waking up from frightening dream. N to end: Jittery, crying intermittently, anxious; note the anxiety lattice (expanded in Fig. 7.6) and the sadness square. Between O and P: During art therapy; there is a pattern also observed in other subjects during play.

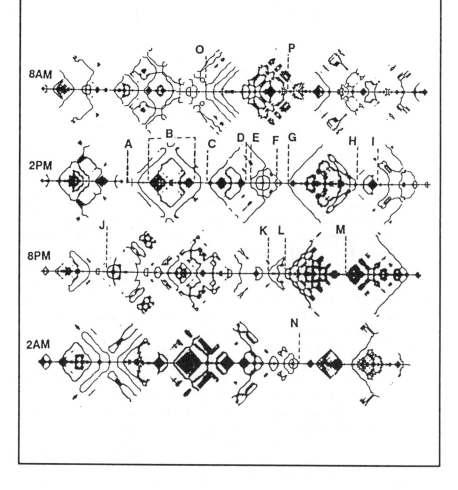

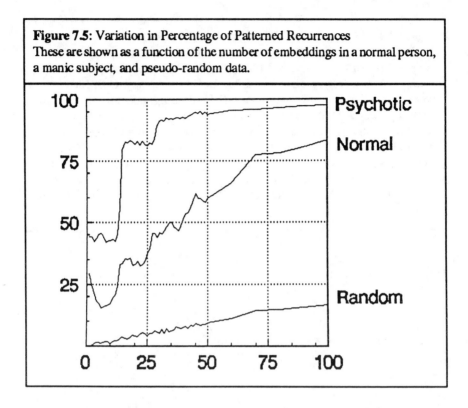

Figure 7.5: Variation in Percentage of Patterned Recurrences
These are shown as a function of the number of embeddings in a normal person,
a manic subject, and pseudo-random data.

Embedding Dimensions

The number of patterned recurrences increases in a complex manner with the
number of embeddings, up to almost 100 percent at 100 embeddings (Fig.7.5). The
median embedding dimension (Embedding 50, E_{50}) is calculated as an estimate of
the complexity of the processes under study. We observed that schizophrenic,
schizoaffective, and manic subjects treated with antipsychotics had low E_{50} (15 to
25) whereas normal, depressed, or anxious subjects had much higher values (30 to
100). Graphs obtained at high embeddings (100-500) portray the configuration of
complexes more sharply: Each complex has a fluid topology, that is, changes within
continuity, and the interruptions of recurrences that we interpret as bifurcations
between complexes are longer and clearer. Within a complex one can see modules
that combine to form complexes. Each complex has an initial and a last element, a
beat, and the pattern between them consist in a series of forkings of lines of
recurrences from the diagonal of identity and their subsequent reunion; in this
manner, the overall shape of any complex resembles a lattice. In high-embedding
graphs we have identified a number of modules and complexes that recur in many
individuals.

Cardiac Language: Alphabet and Punctuation

The identification of a relatively small number of distinct modules and complexes suggests the idea of an alphabet in which messages can be written; bifurcations between complexes would represent punctuation. In fact, complexes appear to have meaning. First, there is a correlation between the form of the complex and the activity of the individual as reported in the diary. The initiation, development, and ending of group therapy coincided with a distinct complex (Fig. 7.4). Likewise, art therapy was represented by a complex pattern that was surprisingly similar to that observed during play in other adults and children. There were also distinct patterns without a concomitant report of an event or symptom; for instance a symmetric, circular pattern (Fig. 7.4, E to F), marking a change in the apparent "polarity" between the patterns that preceded and followed it, occurred between an earlier period in which the subject was anxious (Fig. 7.4, C to D) and a later period of mood relaxation (Fig. 7.4, G to H); the same pattern was also noted later (J), and in other patients, concomitantly with shifts in mood.

Cardiac Meanings: The Lattice of Anxiety

A lattice pattern of recurrences was observed in this and a number of other patients who concomitantly reported brief feelings of fear or anxiety. Note the striking similarities in form and duration in two cases (Fig. 7.6). We have also noticed distinct changes that may be associated with sadness and anger, as well as with changes in activity (working versus playing). Also note the great differences in the patterns associated with sadness and play (Figure 7.4, N). Opposite emotional patterns appear to correspond to opposite polarities in the cardiac complexes. There is an opposite polarity of the pattern observed when the patient found it difficult to fall asleep because of anxiety (Fig. 7.4, L), similar to the complex accompanying anxiety in other patients (Fig. 7.6), and the pattern observed during art therapy. A number of other patterns recur in many subjects, but we have been unable to correlate them with behavior.

Factor Processing: Extending the Phase Plane of Opposites to Time Series

What creates internal changes in a complex, and what determines a bifurcation separating two complexes? Assuming that the evolution of a process is a function of nonlinear interactions between opposing factors, we introduced factor processing as a method to identify them from the data contained in a time series. To this effect we studied the correlation of the original time series with time-delayed replicas from one to thirty *lags* or variables, for samples of 1,000 consecutive beats. We identified the statistically significant factors that describe these thirty variables, and

Figure 7.6: Anxiety

Cardiac complexes associated with reports of transient feelings of fear or anxiety in a cardiac patient (left) and an anxious patient (right). Focusing on the feeling portrait with smaller window sizes (top to bottom); 480 embeddings, at 7,000 (A&D), 2,000 (B&E), and 126 (C&F) beat windows. I indicates an interruption, presumably a bifurcation; LC indicates a complex.

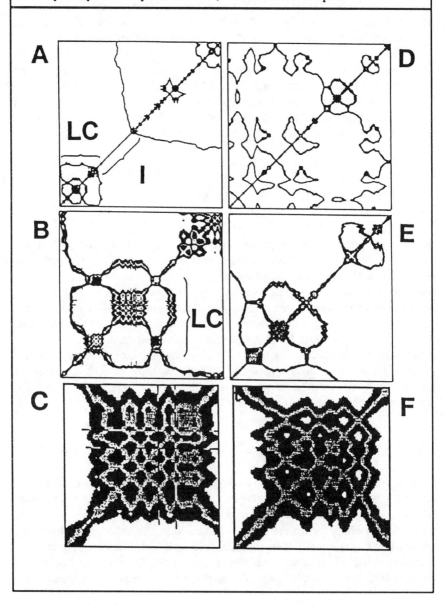

Figure 7.7: Factor Processing
The three statistically most significant factors from factor analysis of lagged time series at 3:00 p.m. (left) and 3:00 a.m. (right). A: Normal (2 factors); B: Anxious (7 factors at 3:00 P.M., and six at 3:00 A.M.); C: Depressed (3 factors at 3:00 P.M., and 6 at 3:00 A.M.); D: Manic (3 factors at 3:00 P.M., and 6 factors at 3:00 A.M.).

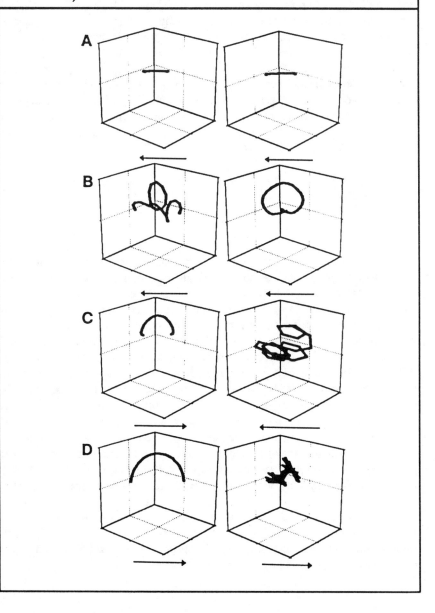

rotated them to separate orthogonal opposites. Using a symbol to indicate the order in which each variable (lag) appeared in each factor, we plotted the factor loadings for each factor against the factor loadings of the other. Plotting the trajectory determined by the three most significant factors in a three-dimensional space produced a disorganized cluster of points for pseudo-random data (corresponding to thirteen factors) and a unidirectional trajectory for patterns (cardiac or computer generated), with a lesser number of factors. The shape of the trajectory changes in time, indicating the presence of gradual and sudden bifurcations. The trajectories themselves represented change, such as from the predominance of factor 1 to that of its opposite factor 2 (Fig. 7.7, A & B), or vice versa (Fig. 7.7, C & D); often the trajectories folded partially (Fig. 7.7, A) or markedly (Fig. 7.7, B), even cycling between the opposites. Often the flow from factor 1 to its opposite, factor 2, was mediated by nonlinear changes in factor 3 (the ∩ of Fig. 7, C & D, awake). In manic, anxious and depressed individuals, daytime records were often simpler (two to three factors), and similar to those observed in many normal persons, whereas nighttime recordings were more disorganized (Fig. 7.7, B-D).

DISCUSSION

Clinical

The differences between various physiological states, the changes that accompanied emotions, and the statistically significant differences between psychotic and nonpsychotic subjects indicate that the cardiac patterns detected in recurrence plots have biological significance. Hence, these methods of interpreting dynamic electrocardiograms may assist cardiologists to study the influence of emotions on cardiovascular illness, and mental health professionals to devise a system of physiological, rather than phenomenological, diagnosis. However, the differences reported here are also influenced by treatment with psychotropic agents that may be expected to affect cardiac complexes associated with neuropsychological patterns (in contrast to peripherally acting autonomic drugs that would affect only cardiac rate or variability). Cardiac complexes that reflect both illness and drug action might serve for rational selection of drug treatment. If the various patterns of emotional behavior may be recognized through monitoring of their peripheral physiological components, cardiac activity probably is one of the best indicators because of the simplicity with which recordings can be obtained, its medical relevance, its clear connection with emotions, its fundamental role in providing energy for the performance of behavior by the entire organism, and finally because of its discrete timing, which provides a natural clock and a digital coding for the information. The identification of a specific pattern associated with anxiety opens an avenue to study objectively anxiety states.

Physiological

The sequence of patterned complexes indicates that cardiac behavior is governed by the sequence of integrated patterns of behavior of the organism, each with a distinct beginning and end, rather than being organized into a single attractor, whether homeostatic, periodic or chaotic, or simply being regulated on a beat-to-beat basis by a number of independent factors (respiration, blood pressure, endocrine, etc.). Hence, one needs to study the influence of emotions to understand the dynamics of the heart. In our view, cardiac complexes represent transient attractors, which include three internal stages: rise, stationary (*attractor*), and fall. This is in contrast to a structural model of deterministic dynamics that assumes that processes tend to stable patterns (attractors) maintained in the absence of transients created by external interactions.

Theoretical

These studies support and refine the ongoing attempt to reformulate the tenets of process philosophy as scientific hypotheses, tenets mathematically formulated and empirically testable (Sabelli, 1984, 1989). Regarding the *unity of action*, the results illustrate that cardiac behavior is made of integrated moments (such as cardiac modules and complexes), as Hegel portrayed dialectic processes, not by a series of independent and instantaneous events (beat-to-beat regulation). Recurrence plots detect an overall lattice form, which we see in a condensed form during periods of fear. Frankly speaking, we were moved by seeing in these graphs the mental images that had inspired us to postulate, based on Pasteur's cosmic asymmetry, that processes are lattices. We speculate that this lattice organization represents the bifurcation of one process into many, and the subsequent reunion of many processes into one. Mathematical logic has a lattice structure: Processes are lattices because they are logical. Regarding the *union of opposites*, we found that complexes associated with opposite emotions or activities (e.g., falling asleep and waking up) have opposite polarities. The various classes of complexes might form a group in which every pattern has one polar opposite, because every process necessarily has a rise and a fall. Regarding the *creation of higher dimensional structures*, the fractal appearance of recurrence time graphs supports Mandelbrodt's view that nature has a fractal geometry, implying the isomorphism of lower and higher levels of organization in the organism. Chaotic attractors are fractal, but obviously more complex processes can also be fractal. That fifteen to sixty embeddings are required for 50 percent of recurrences to be patterned and that the form of cardiac complexes sharpens with the increasing number of embeddings suggest to us that we are dealing with processes of high dimensionality. The complexity of physiological and psychological processes probably cannot be reduced to low-dimensional chaotic attractors, much less explained by a unidimensional tendency to equilibrium, entropy, and disorder, or toward homeostasis and health. Process theory postulates that the interaction of processes creates complexity, moving them from the low-dimensional attractors to the higher dimensions of biological matter; to the "hearty" dimensions, if the pun be forgiven, of an organ that gives the energy supply to the brainy body of a person; and to the infinite dimensions of the cosmic attractor of the universe (Sabelli, 1989). The elusive concepts of quality and complexity may be conceived as dimensions, and fitted within the context of a numerical order of nature. Physical dimensions are universal, but dimensions can multiply locally. Biological, social, and psychological dimensions are as real as physical dimensions. We cannot as yet identify these complex dimensions in the way in which we can recognize the physical dimensions of time and space, but by comparing recurrence plots obtained at a wide range of number of embeddings, we can estimate the dimensions of the process under study. Evolution is a process of dimensionogenesis: Catastrophes and other bifurcations generate dimensions, not just new forms. Reformulating the second law of thermodynamics, processes move toward symmetry and complexity, not only toward disorder (Sabelli, 1989).

A theory is not tested at the single point of experimentation. Experiments test complex sets of hypotheses, any one of them can be changed, saving the others from refutation (Quine, 1969). A theory is tested by practice, that is, by the ability of the theory to generate methods and inventions. Electrocardiography is hence also a test for process theory. Electrocardiography serves also as a model to develop the theory itself, as the practical study of cardiac complexes has clarified for us our conceptions of natural processes in general. Turning around conventional wisdom and traditional practice, we can illuminate the simpler processes by studying their complex manifestations.

ACKNOWLEDGMENTS

The authors gratefully thank Ms. María McCormick of the Society for the Advancement of Clinical Philosophy for her indispensable support, to Olga Zdanovics, Cynthia Tom, and Renée Luecht for their invaluable collaboration in this project, to Peter Fink and Arthur Sugerman for helpful discussion of the data, and to the Scientific Computer Workstation and the Biostatistics Facility of the Research Resources Center, University of Illinois at Chicago, which provided the equipment and assistance necessary to conduct some of our computations.

REFERENCES

Carlson-Sabelli, L., & Sabelli, H. C. (1984). Reality, perception and the role reversal. *Journal of Group Psychotherapy Psychodrama and Sociometry, 36*, 162–174.

Carlson-Sabelli, L., Sabelli, H. C., Patel, M., Messer, J., Zbilut, J., & Walthall, K. (in press). Electropsychocardiography. Illustrating the application of process methods to comprehensive patient evaluation. *Theoretic and Applied Chaos in Nursing, 1.*

Eckmann, J. P., Kamphorst, S. O., & Ruelle, D. (1987). Recurrence plots of dynamical systems. *Neurophysics Letters, 4*, 973–977.

Gershenfeld, N. A. (1992). Dimension measurement on high-dimensional systems. *Physica D, 55*, 135–154.

Guillemin, V., & Pollack, A. (1974). *Differential topology.* Englewood Cliffs: Prentice-Hall.

Packard, N. H., Crutchfield, J. P., Farmer, J. D., & Shaw, R. S. (1980). Geometry from a time series. *Physical Review Letters, 45*, 712–716.

Quine, W. V. O. (1969). Natural kinds. In *Ontological relativity and other essays* (pp. 114–138). New York: Columbia University Press.

Reidbord, S. P., & Redington, D. J. (1992). Psychophysiological processes during insight-oriented therapy: Further investigations into nonlinear psychodynamics. *Journal of Nervous and Mental Diseases, 180*(10), 649–657.

Sabelli, H. C. (1984). Mathematical dialectics, scientific logic and the psychoanalysis of thinking. In R. S. Cohen & M. W. Wartofsky (Eds.), *Hegel and the sciences* (pp. 349–359). New York: Reidel.

Sabelli, H. C. (1989). *Union of opposites. A comprehensive theory of natural and human processes.* Lawrenceville: Brunswick.

Sabelli, H. C. (1992). *From process theory to electropsychocardiography.* Plenary lecture, *American Society of Hispanic Psychiatry,* Chicago.

Sabelli, H. C. & Carlson-Sabelli, L. (1989). Biological priority and psychological supremacy, a new integrative paradigm derived from process theory. *American Journal of Psychiatry, 146*, 1541–1551.

Sabelli H. C., & Carlson-Sabelli, L. (1991). Process theory as a framework for comprehensive psychodynamic formulation. *Genetic, Social, and General Psychology Monographs, 117*, 5–27.

Sabelli, H. C., Carlson-Sabelli, L., & Messer, J. (1994). The process method of comprehensive patient evaluation. *Theoretic and Applied Chaos Theory in Nursing, 1*, 33–41.

Zbilut, J. P., & Webber, Jr., C. L. (1992). Embeddings and delays as derived from quantification of recurrence plots. *Physics Letters A, 171*, 199–203.

Part III
DYNAMICAL ANALYSIS OF COGNITION

8

Psychology, Chaos, and the Process Nature of Consciousness

Allan Combs

The foolish reject what they see, not what they think;
the wise reject what they think, not what they see.

Huang Po

CHAOS THEORY, PROCESS THINKING, AND PSYCHOLOGY

Chaos theory is not simply a set of novel procedures that can be imported into the existing establishment of scientific psychology; it in fact represents a fundamental revolution in viewpoint. One of the most important features of this revolution is a shift away from the current emphasis on group data with its stress on the analysis of error variance toward an examination of sequences of observations made on single individuals, a shift from a nomothetic to an idiographic orientation.

Another shift is away from theoretically plain models in which hypothetical functions are represented as straight lines or curves centered in clouds of real data points, each representing an inextricable mix of treatment effect and error. Chaos theory tries to recover much information from what has traditionally been considered as "error," the cumulative influence of unknown variables, by viewing evident irregularities as complex chaotic processes. Many such processes, despite their intricacy, have been shown to be potentially comprised of surprisingly few actual variables interacting in nonlinear ways (e.g., Crutchfield, Doyne, Packard, & Shaw, 1986).

Most important to the present discussion, chaos theory carries implicitly a shift from a structuralist perspective of psychological phenomena to a process view. The main purpose of this chapter is to show that chaos theory and its foundational antecedent, dynamical systems theory, yield a process view of psychological events, and particularly of consciousness, and that such a view is revolutionary in perspective and rich in possibilities. Process thinking has existed since at least the time of Heraclitus in the West and Lao Tzu in the East. It sees reality as flux, a flow of events in which stationary patterns arise as secondary phenomena. Such a view would seem especially appropriate for psychology, a discipline that embraces such fluid phenomena as thought, emotion, memory, and perception. A hundred years ago William James (1890/1981), for example, observed that one vital aspect of the life of the mind is its tendency to manifest as a stream of thought: "Consciousness, then, does not appear to itself chopped up in bits. . . . It is nothing jointed; it flows. A 'river' or a 'stream' are the metaphors by which it is most naturally described. *In talking of it hereafter, let us call it the stream of thought, or consciousness, or of subjective life*" (p. 233; italics are from the original text).

Philosophers, too, during and since James's time have observed that human subjective life unfolds as a continuous event (e.g., Bergson, 1907/1983; Guenther, 1989; Heidegger, 1962). I would also note that the behaviorist's interest is likewise a concern with process, as behavior is not an object to be scrutinized but an event to be noted. Unlike physics, which in some instances seems to study stationary items, psychology is virtually always concerned with the unfolding of events.

Only recently has it become possible to create a thoroughgoing process perspective in psychology. This is to a large extent because of the nature of psychology's history. Almost since its inception, certainly since the advent of behaviorism, psychology has been a philosophical and methodological tag-along to physics, the "queen of sciences." It has worked diligently to emulate the theoretical purity, mathematical consistency, and most of all the empirical objectivity of physics. As is so often the case, however, when one discipline tries to emulate another, the latter is eventually found to have its own problems. This is precisely the case with physics, whose very foundations have been profoundly unsettled since the advent of quantum theory in the early decades of this century. Ironically, however, psychology seems to have modeled itself after the previous "classical" physics.

A central feature of classical physics was its grounding in an ontology that placed numerical quantities and their seemingly eternal regularities above the day-to-day flow of sensory experience. This ontology dates all the way back to the inception of scientific laws in the minds of the architects of the Age of Enlightenment, particularly René Descartes and Isaac Newton. The central idea was that natural law is eternal and logically consistent because it derives from the mind of God, himself a mathematician and incapable of contradictory thought. The notion that God is a mathematician is as old as Plato and perhaps even Pythagoras.

The absolute authority of God's laws could not be seriously questioned after a millennium of domination by the Church. Thus natural law was seen to be the higher ontological truth—these were the laws of motion and of celestial mechanics—standing above the ever-changing phenomenal world of experience. By the beginning of the nineteenth century mathematicians such as Laplace were ready to omit God from their agendas, arguing that mathematics and the science of mechanics was all that was needed for a "complete" view of nature. This doctrine, which became know as positivism, empowered the work of figures as diverse as Mach,

Poincaré, and Einstein, to pursue a "science of nature" rather than the older seventeenth-century "natural philosophy" of Descartes and Newton (Leclerc, 1988).

It is well to keep in mind that the material side of the cosmos created by cartesian dualism was comprised of discrete objects shoved about by inanimate forces acting with machinelike regularity. In such a universe, imaged in the likeness of a clock, structure is basic in the ontological order of things and process is secondary, much like the cogs and wheels of a clock are what the clock is really made of, and the motion ensues from their arrangement. This way of thinking of the world, in which objects have the upper station and process is derivative, might be called the logic of stones. On the other hand, it is perhaps not surprising that process thinkers since Heraclitus and Lao Tzu have built their metaphors from images of water in what might be called the logic of water.

With the development of quantum theory the positivist program began to unravel in a serious way, but psychology did not relax its grip on the old concepts until well past the midpoint of the twentieth century. Even today it proceeds as if in a universe of separate pieces in which "objective" observation is the *sine qua non* of science. Just as important, it continues to search for qualitative relationships between variables that are either essentially static by nature or uncomfortably driven by the evolution of some independent control variable such as numbers of learning trials, hours of food deprivation, or accumulated experience in psychotherapy.

Today the time is ripe for a revisioning of psychology's fundamental perspective, not in the direction that physics or some other discipline might lead, but in a direction that does honor to psychology's own processual content.

SYSTEMS THEORY

Process thinking was evident in the work of John Dewey (1896) and Henri Bergson (1907/1983), though it was most systematically developed in the philosophical writings of Alfred North Whitehead (1929/1978). The latter drew heavily on ideas from the modern physics of his day but had little direct influence on psychology because his work was metaphysical. Over the past few decades, however, a more pragmatic set of concepts for understanding the world in process terms emerged almost unnoticed in the development of systems theory. Early cybernetic concepts such as self-correction through feedback, and progress through feed-forward, combined with an increasingly sophisticated understanding of complex systems to yield concepts of multifaceted systems in control of their own destinies.

An especially important advance in the understanding of complex systems was the idea of *autopoiesis*. In 1974 Humberto Maturana and Francisco Varela noted that certain systems, particularly living cells, are continuously involved in the business of creating themselves. The net product of the varied metabolic processes of a cell, for example, is that very cell. Actual molecular material changes over time, but the pattern of processes that constitutes the cell's identity continues throughout its life. It is this constellation of identity-creating processes and not the cell's material structure that defines it. The human being can likewise be regarded as an autopoietic system, ceaselessly transcending its momentary material structure in a continuing event of self-creation. Thus we come to see the human, like other organic entities and even like entire ecological systems up to the global Gaia system itself (Lovelock, 1988; Lovelock & Margulis, 1974), as a process rather than an object.

Such self-organizing systems maintain themselves and even evolve toward greater complexity by utilizing ordered energy from their environments—food and sunlight for biological organisms, sunlight and occasionally geothermal energy for ecosystems—before releasing it again in less ordered forms (Jantsch, 1980; Kampis, 1991; Laszlo, 1987; Prigogine & Stengers, 1984). This amounts to the dissipation of ordered energy as less ordered waste (fecal matter from animals, heat radiation from the Earth), yielding a net increase of information within the system in the form of complexity.

The study of autopoietic systems reveals numerous nonlinear processes. Many of these appear to be chaotic in the sense that they are complex beyond linear description, seem to be nonrepititious, and are unpredictable in detail though constrained within knowable boundaries. Such processes can often be modeled surprisingly well qualitatively using the new mathematics of chaos (e.g., Abraham, Abraham, & Shaw, 1990; Abraham & Shaw, 1982; Casti, 1992). The latter has exhibited a meteoric assent in recent years. It includes Edward Lorenz's discovery of the first chaotic ("strange") attractor in the 1960s and the subsequent mapping of several others. It includes René Thom's catastrophe theory, which continues to evolve as an important aspect of the understanding of many nonlinear processes. And it also includes Benoit Mandelbrot's discovery and the subsequent mapping of the exquisitely complex fractal geometry.

CONSCIOUSNESS AND AUTOPOIESIS

It is my belief that numerous facets of consciousness are likewise nonlinear and, though we as yet do not understand their energetics, in many instances autopoietic. For instance, certain mental processes seem not only to be self-sustaining but self-creating.

Consider Piaget's stages of mental development, each of which is constructed of a matrix of schemata functioning in coordination, and which in turn are actually cognitive *operations* or processes (Piaget, 1977; Flavell, 1963). In a particular stage, each schema tends to support other schemata in boot-strap fashion. For instance the schema or concept of *conservation*, which proclaims that matter does not appear or disappear out of nowhere, is supported by the schema of *reversibility*, the ability to run mental operations in reverse. For example, if a child is confronted with the puzzling observation that a thin glass of water poured into a wide glass does not fill it to the level of the original, he or she can imagine the water poured back again into the tall glass and note that its level is at the original height. The point here is that such schemata form processual autopoietic networks that conspire to mutually support and create each other and thus the network itself. This notion can be expanded further to state that the schemata of a given developmental stage form the fabric that in turn supports each individual schema. This is equivalent to saying that a living cell is the milieu that supports the various metabolic and other processes of which, taken as a whole, it is constituted.

States of mind such as moods seem as well to exhibit clear autopoietic features. For instance, when feeling sad or melancholy one tends to reminisce over sad or melancholy events, sustaining and deepening the mood. One entertains melancholy thoughts and even engages in outward activities all but designed to continue to make one melancholy. The same can be said of joyful moods. Indeed, there is evidence that particular emotional states are associated with memories formed in those states (Bower, 1981; Eich, 1980). For instance, when angry, one remembers personal affronts and offenses, whereas when happy one tends to recall pleasant events.

STATES OF CONSCIOUSNESS AND CHAOTIC ATTRACTORS

If moods are nonlinear autopoietic processes, then it may not be surprising that they seem to fluctuate in time in a manner that appears to be truly chaotic (Combs, Winkler, & Daley, 1994; Hannah, 1991; Hannah, cited in Casti, 1992; Sabelli & Carlson-Sabelli, 1992; Winkler, Combs, Dezern, Alstott, Burnham, Rand, & Walker, 1991). This means, for example, that they follow an irregular but roughly cyclic rhythm that plots out very much like a chaotic attractor (see Fig. 8.1). Moreover, calculations of their fractal dimension point to a level of roughness or irregularity characteristic of true chaos. Such observations support the idea that states of mind such as moods are features of nonlinear mental or neurological systems.

One type of system to which moods seem to belong is the inclusive processes commonly called a state of consciousness. Perhaps the most systematic examination of states of consciousness was undertaken some years ago by Charles Tart (1975). He considered each to be an entire system composed of subsystems such as emotion, but also including memory, cognition, perception, a sense of self, and so on. In any particular state of consciousness, such as ordinary wakefulness, these form a mutually compatible whole. Other examples include dream and nondream sleep, drug-induced states, advanced states of meditation, and shamanic trances. Tart noted that certain activities tend to reinforce a particular state of consciousness whereas others tend to disrupt it. For instance, goal-oriented work bolsters ordinary

Figure 8.1: Attractor Reconstructions

These represent the continuous mood fluctuations of a single observer during a three week period. The left trajectory traces fluctuations in the pleasant versus unpleasant dimension of mood, and the right trajectory traces fluctuations in the excitement versus relaxation dimension. They are indicative of a low-dimensional chaotic attractor. The sampling interval, τ, is one hour. The fractal (information) measures for them are 1.59 and 1.60 respectively, also suggestive of a chaotic process (© Combs).

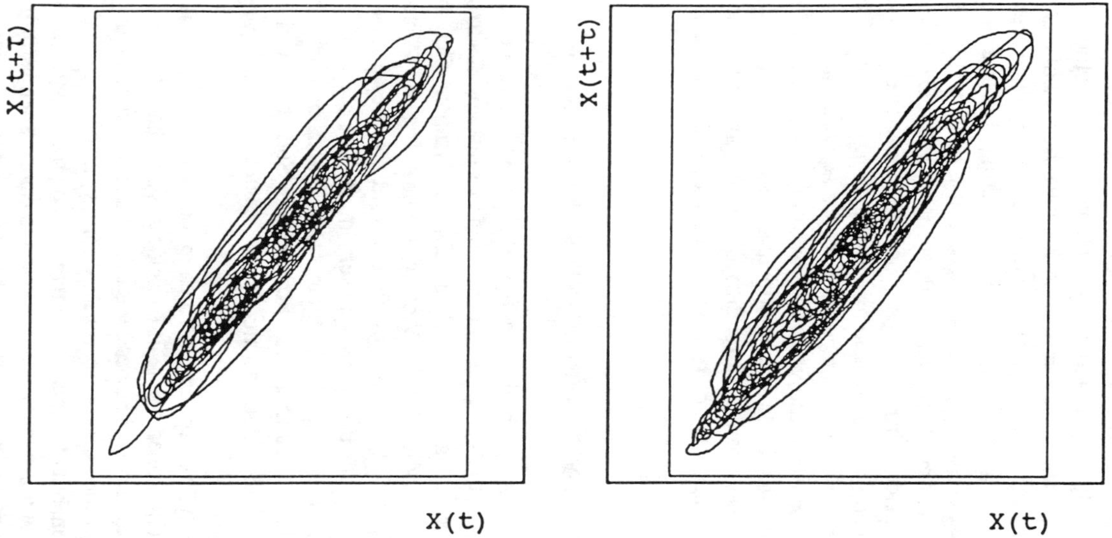

waking consciousness, and chanting augments certain ecstatic religious states. On the other hand, lying down and closing one's eyes disrupts ordinary wakefulness and moves consciousness toward sleep. Dull pragmatic tasks such as paying monthly bills are likely to disrupt ecstatic states.

On close inspection states of consciousness appear to exhibit the same quality of autopoiesis seen above in Piagetian stages. The entire matrix of subsystems that form a particular state—emotion, memory, cognition, and so on—combine in Möbius strip fashion to weave the very fabric that supports them. The moods, thoughts, and perceptions of each state are unique and conspire in the formation of this fabric. Outward activities likewise contribute to and strengthen the states of consciousness that evoke them. Ordinary waking reality, for instance, is inducive of the energetic activity that in turn sharpens the thoughts, perceptions, and the sense of a productive self of which the state is comprised. Ecstatic religious states, on the other hand, are inducive of a worshipful disposition, prayer or meditation, silent contemplation, and so on, all of which tend to reinforce those states. All these activities, needless to say, are processes, whether they be of thought, reminiscence, perception, the play of emotions, or external behavior, and they weave together forming process fabrics rather than inert structures.

The fact that states of consciousness can be understood as complex coherent processes suggests the usefulness of conceptualizing them as attractors (Combs, 1995). Like mathematical attractors, they unfold from moment to moment within certain broad boundaries, but never in a straightforward linear fashion and never returning to exactly the same location twice. Attractors representing various processes of consciousness may bifurcate under the influence of a variety of control parameters. Such is the case of a tired person who closes his eyes and suddenly falls away from waking consciousness toward sleep.

Pulling together these thoughts yields a powerful metaphor of states of consciousness as chaotic attractors in higher-dimensional state space. Indeed, it is more than a metaphor, it is a valid conceptualization of the events of consciousness itself. Each state of consciousness is an autopoietic process woven from lower-order processes such as emotion, memory, and cognition. These have their own system properties and, as noted above, in some instances, at least, are also autopoietic. The picture that emerges from all this is that of consciousness as a hierarchical processual structure, self-creating as it unfolds in time, but in each state constrained to definite and knowable boundaries.

REFERENCES

Abraham, F. D., Abraham, R. H., & Shaw, C. D. (1990). *A visual introduction to dynamical systems theory for psychology*. Santa Cruz: Aerial Press.

Abraham, R. H., & Shaw, C.D. (1982). *Dynamics—The geometry of behavior; Part I: Periodic behavior*. Santa Cruz: Aerial Press.

Bergson, H. (1907/1983). *Creative evolution.* (A. Mitchell, Trans.). Lanham: University Press of America.

Bower, G. H. (1981). Mood and memory. *American Psychologist, 36,* 129–148.

Casti, J. L. (1992). *Reality rules I: Picturing the world in mathematics—the fundamentals.* New York: Wiley.

Combs, A. (1990, February). *Concepts of consciousness: A historical survey.* Paper presented at the First International Conference on the Study of Consciousness in Science, San Francisco.

Combs, A. (1995). *The radiance of being: Complexity, chaos, and the evolution of consciousness.* Edinburgh: Floris Books.

Combs, A. L., Winkler, M., & Daley, C. (1994). A chaos systems analysis of thythms in feeling states. *Psychological Record, 44,* 359–368.

Crutchfield, J., Doyne, F., Packard, N., & Shaw, R. (1986). Chaos. *Scientific American, 225,* 46–57.

Dewey, J. (1896). The reflex arc concept in psychology. *Psychological Review, 2,* 13–32.

Eich, J. E. (1980). The cue-dependent nature of state-dependent retention. *Memory and Cognition, 8,* 157–173.

Flavell, J. H. (1963). *The developmental psychology of Jean Piaget.* New York: Van Nostrand.

Guenther, V.H. (1989). *From reductionism to creativity: rDzogs-chen and the new sciences of mind.* Boston: Shambhala.

Hannah, T. (1991, August). *Mood fluctuations and daily stress: The contribution of a dynamical systems approach.* Paper presented at the Inaugural meeting of The Society for Chaos Theory in Psychology, San Francisco, CA.

Heidegger, M. (1962). *Being and time.* (J. Macquarrie & E. Robinson, Trans.). New York: Harper & Row.

James, W. (1890/1981). *The principles of psychology.* New York: Holt/Cambridge: Harvard University Press.

Jantsch, E. (1980). *The self-organizing universe.* New York: Pergamon.

Kampis, G. (1991). *Self modifying systems: A new framework for dynamics, information and complexity.* New York: Pergamon.

Laszlo, E. (1987). *Evolution: The grand synthesis.* Boston: Shambhala.

Leclerc, I. (1988). The relation between science and metaphysics. In R.E. Kitchener (Ed.), *The world view of contemporary physics.* Albany: S. U. N. Y. Press.

Lovelock, J. E. (1988). *Ages of Gaia.* New York: W.W. Norton.

Lovelock, J. E., & Margulis, L. (1974). Biological modulation of the Earth's atmosphere. *Icarus, 21.*

Maturana, H. R., Varela, F. J., & Uribe, R. (1974). Autopoiesis: The organization of living systems, its characterization and model. *Biosystems, 5,* 187–196.

Piaget, J. (1977). *The essential Piaget.* (Gruber & Voneche, Eds.). New York: Basic Books.

Prigogine, I., & Stengers, I. (1984). *Order out of chaos: Man's new dialogue with nature.* New York: Bantam Books.

Sabelli, H. C., & Carlson-Sabelli, L. (1992, August). *Co-creative trifurcations and chromodynamics of emotions.* Paper presented at the meeting of the Society for Chaos Theory in Psychology, Washington, DC.

Tart, C. T. (1975). *States of consciousness.* New York: E. P. Dutton.

Whitehead, A. N. (1929/1978). *Process and reality.* (D.R. Griffin & D.W. Sherburne, Eds.). New York: Free Press.

Winkler, M., Combs, A., Dezern, D., Alstott, T., Burnham, J., Rand, B., & Walker, S. (1991, August). *Cyclicity in moods: A dynamical systems analysis.* Paper presented at the Inaugural meeting of the Society for Chaos Theory in Psychology, San Francisco.

9

A Search for Bifurcations in the Psychological Domain

Albert R. Gilgen

The analytical power of contemporary nonlinear metamodeling techniques suggests that as psychologists we should be especially interested in psychological bifurcations, that is, in rapid transformations of sensory, perceptual, cognitive, and affective experiences that may radically alter our lifestyles. As the following preliminary list illustrates, there are many experiences that may serve this function.

1. Routine changes in mindset or intention.
2. "Ah ha" or insight experiences when rapid perceptual or cognitive restructuring takes place in the context of working on a difficult problem (emphasized by Gestalt theorists).
3. Times when there is a serious mismatch between the cognitive state of expectancy and subsequent dynamics of the psychological domain (an anticipated promotion does not materialize).
4. Situations when we are forced to make decisions too quickly.
5. Times when we make decisions but overlook something apparently trivial that turns out to be very significant.
6. Instances when we experience overwhelming emotional transformations (we fall in love; we suddenly realize that we hate someone close to us).
7. Instances when a specific sensory experience resurrects a segment of the past (a whiff of a particular perfume or aftershave vividly brings back an event that happened many years ago); usually referred to as redintegrations.
8. Situations wherein a specific complex psychological experience restructures the entire psychological domain (we attend a Beethoven concert that reminds us of a person important to us in the past).
9. Instances when a small sensory change elicits powerful negative affects (trivial environmental disturbances such as the sound of a person chewing while we are trying to read in an otherwise quiet atmosphere capture attention and make it impossible to think; annoyances).
10. Times when we experience sensory overload (a bright light blots out everything else; a car stereo is so loud that it overwhelms our conscious state).

11. Times when "of the body" information rises to attention (we have a back ache, we feel hungry, we are thirsty, we experience genital pleasure).
12. Times when we experience significant general changes of outlook that are a function of psychological, environmental, or physiological changes (we have a psychotic break; we develop a phobia, compulsion, or hysterical symptom, all of which narrow the focus of attention; or we are affected by changes in hormonal chemistry or ingested substances).
13. Times when we totally or partially lose a particular category of psychological information (we go blind; we develop amnesia; we suffer from aphasia).

It is important to remember that the types of changes inventoried are bifurcations only if they result in significantly restructuring the pattern of our lives and are due to changing values of control parameters in our psychological space rather than to some chance external event.

With such a list in hand, where do we go from here? What do we have to do in order to engage in the type of metamodeling made possible by chaos theory? First, we should review some of the basic terms involved, and then we have to identify the system we want to model.

SOME DEFINITIONS REVIEWED

A *system* is a set of related or interacting variables that change over time. Some variables are observable, but others may be hypothetical. A *bifurcation* occurs when a phase portrait changes dramatically, qualitatively, into some topologically nonequivalent form, as a control parameter moves through a bifurcation point. A *phase portrait* is the state space, filled with trajectories (only a few representative ones are usually shown), with a *state space* being a geometric model of all the possible states of a system. Finally, a *control parameter* is a parameter of a dynamical system that may be varied, changing the dynamical system. Its change past a critical value, the bifurcation point, is responsible for a bifurcation (reviewed from Abraham, this volume, Introduction to Dynamics).

These definitions remind us that if we want to take advantage of nonlinear metamodeling, there are some formal requirements.

THE SYSTEM TO BE MODELED

As I have already indicated, I want to devise a strategy for investigating relatively discrete psychological changes that lead to significant lifestyle reorganizations. In that sense the system I am interested in representing is what I refer to as the "psychological domain."

This domain, as I have previously argued, can be viewed as the total-person-relevant information each of us has available that makes it possible to move with direction and control (Gilgen, 1987). This realm (for adults) has a dynamic structure consisting of such features as focus-background, complex change, discriminable subdomains with specific functions, redundancy of information, the availability of markers (i.e., signs and symbols), and a self-world distinction. A generally accepted taxonomy of informational subcategories consists of: the sensory-perceptual, cognitive, and affective. The sensory-perceptual is "of the immediate surround and present state of the body"; the cognitive is a highly structured domain distinguishable from the sensory-perceptual that brings with it a sense of past and future and limitless informational contexts. The affective is made up of diffuse information that biases behavioral probabilities and gives the dimension of intensity to our actions, thoughts, and perspectives.

Although the cognitive state can be subdivided into such categories as images, thoughts, intentions, and ideas, we shall for our purposes consider this aspect of psychological functioning as essentially undifferentiated. With regard to the sensory-perceptual, however, it is useful to consider separately the functions of visual, tactile-haptic, auditory, olfactory, gustatory, and somatic (of the body) information and to partition the affective realm into positive and negative "components."

At any particular time some of the information is highlighted (that comprising the attentional focus) while the rest consists of complex and interrelated, sensory-perceptual, cognitive, and affective backgrounds. Some of the background information represents an aspect of consciousness but much of it is at the ready below the level of awareness. The background information that is part of the conscious state can be subdivided into primary and secondary categories, with the former being more closely associated with the attentional focus than the latter.

Underlying physiological mechanisms, involving feedback, feedforward, and other operations, are apparently "programmed" to quickly determine the relative importance of the various psychological modalities for a particular situation and reset priorities as needed. There appear to be separate, but interconnected, "relevance" or "importance" controls for the cognitive, sensory-perceptual, and affective aspects of the informational "display" that are adjusted when circumstances change. No homunculus residing in the skull is in charge here; this control function operates by responding to the patterns of activity taking place in the central nervous system that reflect bodily and environmental changes.

For example, when there is light and precise actions are called for, the interplay of visual and tactile-haptic information may be highlighted. On the other hand, when information is received that one should "be on the look out," all information about events at a distance, that is, visual, auditory, and olfactory, is brought to the fore. Or when certain intimate personal interactions (i.e., those sexual in nature) become central, tactile, and perhaps olfactory information rises to prominence within consciousness. Since the information in focus changes relatively quickly and backgrounds regularly reconstruct, it is very difficult to predict the course of informational flow when all modalities are in play. There is, in other words, a high degree of complexity to the psychological domain and its individual subdomains over time. Many factors (control parameters) are associated with the system.

DEPICTING THE SYSTEM AND
IDENTIFYING PSYCHOLOGICAL BIFURCATIONS

To begin with we need to find a way of representing the structure of the psychological domain that is sensitive enough to be useful yet that does not bog us down in complexity. One such approach is to determine the relative importance of cognitive, visual, tactile, haptic, auditory, olfactory, and affective (positive and negative) information in the context of specific situations. In general, we can consider the information that predominates in the attentional focus and primary background as most important, with the rest constituting an essential but less important framework. Sometimes it is possible to subdivide the contextual information into additional categories. For example, we have to be able to see where we are going when we run through a complex environment at noon. Therefore, the information foremost in our attention and primary background is visual, with perhaps, tactile next in importance and the rest constituting a more general background. An actual profile (scale) might look something like this (R = Relative Importance of Information; v = visual, t = tactile, o = other sensory-perceptual, c = cognitive, a+ = positive affect, and a– = negative affect):

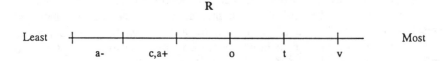

In dynamical modeling, we would view these categories as control parameters, each with its own scale. Each profile generated, therefore, becomes a point in a multidimensional control space, and the response diagram would include a phase portrait for each point in that control space.

One can with little effort construct profiles for situations involving every conceivable type of informational combination, each one thus with its own unique dynamical properties obeying the same set of equations, but with unique values for the control parameters. It is especially easy to depict instances when a particular complex of information clearly predominates in the attentional focus and in the primary background. For example, cognition predominates when we sit and think.

Auditory-affective information is primary when we quietly listen to music that we like on the radio. Gustatory-olfactory-tactile-affective information captures attention as we eat a good meal. Negative affect monopolizes consciousness when we are overcome with anxiety. Each of these situations represents a change in values of the control parameters.

Because familiarity with tasks and situations changes what we attend to and what constitutes background information, our profiles will have to differentiate between information directly associated with the task or situation and that not directly associated. This complicates our task but does not derail our strategy. We just have to recognize that familiarity also represents a major psychological control parameter and account for it.

If we develop a reasonable technique for profiling psychological information, we shall, of course, be able to represent the informational transformations characterizing each of the thirteen types of experience, which may significantly change our lives, listed earlier. For example, we can, in turn, profile going blind, becoming overwhelmed with emotion, suffering sensory overload, experiencing a redintegration, temporarily losing our capacity to think when we are annoyed by a sound, and so forth. Times when cognitive restructuring takes place would require that our informational profiles indicate not only the relative importance of the various types of information (e.g., cognitive or affective), but that the actual structure of the cognitive component had changed significantly. Notice that with such very complex multidimensional psychological systems and their multidimensional control spaces as well as their multivariate state spaces, there are hypersurfaces in the control space, comprised of bifurcation points, so that there is a family of similar bifurcations that may occur crossing anywhere on that surface. Thus there are many ways that "becoming overwhelmed with emotion" may occur.

One of the main problems we face is trying to define and model lifestyles in terms of complex psychological changes. Yet we need to do this in order to generate relevant phase portraits and response diagrams and reveal the geometry of the system. One approach would be to identify the sequence of meaningful segments comprising a person's routine before and after hypothesized bifurcations and then determine informational profiles. (A meaningful segment could be considered any portion of the day governed by a major plan or intention; determining informational profiles means estimating parameters to establish the nature of the control space.) Comparing the topology of an ongoing lifestyle profile with that following a dramatic change in the psychological domain would allow us to determine whether or not significant psychological restructuring (a bifurcation) has taken place.

Identifying "meaningful segments" of a person's routine can be facilitated by developing a taxonomy of prototypical situations, that is, basic activities we perform with some regularity in order to survive. Such a taxonomy might be based on the following very general categories: moving from place to place; manipulating aspects of the environment; processing information without engaging in much physical activity; sleeping. To make useful distinctions among the psychological information categories associated with the specific activities people engage in, however, the taxonomy would have to be expanded to include subcategories reflecting the various aspects of the environment (social and physical) with which manipulations and interactions occur, and the major environmental and bodily states under which these actions are performed.

In summary, in order to recognize psychological bifurcations we need to identify relatively short-term transformations of the psychological domain that lead to significant long-range restructurings of that domain. This entails understanding what is required to depict complex systems, having a working model of the psychological domain, and devising ways to profile defining aspects of that domain. This is a challenging but fascinating undertaking and one that may fail; however, the effort itself should provide useful insights. Certainly, more sophisticated strategies for depicting the dynamics of the psychological domain will be forthcoming.

PSYCHOLOGICAL VS BEHAVIORAL SPACE, A FINAL NOTE

We may now have the analytical tools to investigate the flow of information that makes it possible for each of us to act with direction and control. I am sure that Gottfried Leibniz, Johann Herbart, William James, Kurt Lewin, and perhaps even Sigmund Freud, would encourage us to use the full potential of those tools to investigate the ebb and flow and turbulences of consciousness that have to a large extent evaded depiction.

Psychologists uncomfortable with attempts to create profiles of private experience, can probably devise research strategies to investigate the complexities of lifestyles based entirely on comparing patterns of behavior. The problem with such an approach, however, is that the bifurcational dynamics of interest are psychological in nature. The course of human actions is a function of what people sense, perceive, think, and feel. Understanding changes in psychological terms is not only important in and of itself, but is required to link the dynamics characterizing total-person actions with those taking place in the nervous system. I agree with those who maintain that progress in the neurosciences depends more on identifying dynamics at the psychological level of analysis than vice versa.

REFERENCE

Gilgen, A. R. (1987). The psychological level of organization in nature and interdependencies among major psychological concepts. In A. W. Staats & L. P. Mos (Eds.), *Annals of theoretical psychology* (Vol. 5, pp. 179-209). New York: Plenum Press.

10

Fractal Geometry and Human Understanding

Thomas A. Gentry

This is a survey of the still short history of fractals and fractal dimensions, especially how these concepts are changing our understanding of human cognition. Thinking in terms of fractal dimensions represents a change in our concept of space and spatial thinking and is a central feature in the emerging study of deterministic chaos. Algorithms are available for computing a growing variety of fractal dimension types providing new quantitative methods for describing the complex features of the natural world. A review of the literature suggests that psychology has not kept pace with these developments, but an alternative interpretation indicates that psychologists have been computing fractal dimensions for many decades before the term *fractal* was invented. It is proposed that one consequence of fractal geometry is the resolution of a long-running debate over the proper mathematics for data from the psychophysical research that originated with the birth of modern experimental psychology. In this view, the exponents in power functions can be considered as dynamic measures for the complexity of individual experiences rather than constants in the quest for psychological laws. Fractal geometry provides both an improved quantification of nature and enhances our insights on how thoughts about the world are created. Examples from the available literature are used to outline how fractal measurements can advance psychological research applications.

Imagine that the year is 1543 and you have just completed reading the newly published *De Revolutionibus Orbium Coelestium (On the Revolution of the Heavenly Spheres)*, which has attempted to convince you that the daily experience of a stationary earth being illuminated periodically by the moving sun is an illusion. What do you think the chances are that you would have accepted the Copernican argument that violates your direct perceptions?

Now look up at a corner of a room where two walls and the ceiling meet and think about your beliefs concerning the three dimensional nature of space. If you are fortunate enough to be reading this chapter in an environment other than a box shaped room substitute this book by closing the covers and reflecting on its three dimensional construction. Does the idea that three-dimensional space is an illusion violate your direct perception?

The point here is to suggest that we are currently faced with cognitive challenges concerning the notions of space and dimension on a par with the mental effort needed to accept the idea that it is the earth turning on its axis as it orbits the sun that yields the days and seasons of our lives. The concepts of fractal and fractal dimension will be presented as being central to the themes in this book and as going beyond being new mathematical methods in their fundamental implications for human understanding.

GEOMETRY AS A WAY OF THINKING

As with the heliocentric theory of the solar system the individual credited with the discovery of our illusions about dimensionality is actually continuing a line of thinking that began in antiquity. Important new insights often take hundreds or even thousands of years before they become accepted by enough people to be considered true. The idea that life on earth has a long evolutionary history with inorganic origins is another example. Copernicus had many like minded predecessors going back as far as Aristarchus in the third century B.C., but it has become convenient to speak of the Copernican revolution. Similarly, the contemporary mathematician Benoit Mandelbrot may become identified as the discoverer of the fractal nature of nature, which seems fair given that he coined the term. However, unlike Copernicus who had the good fortune to die in the same year his controversial work was published, Mandelbrot has had to endure considerable criticism, but he has demonstrated a vigorous style in defending his views (Mandelbrot, 1992).

Geometry is as much a way of thinking as it is a branch of mathematics. Tiles (1987) has summarized this dual nature in her definition of geometry:

> Even the earliest history of geometry as a theoretical study of spatial relationships and spatial structures reveals that it had, in addition, a powerful symbolic role in both imaginative and theoretically speculative thought. Thus, although the history of geometry can be told in purely mathematical terms, it is also, from another point of view, a history of forms of representation, of ways of thinking about the world and of views on the nature of thought itself.

As with any cognitive characteristic there are also individual differences, and some have suggested that with respect to geometry this variation can be profound. Price (1975) has suggested that these differences played an important role in the development of Western science and that in "psychological terms, we may have here a problem in which we should do well to distinguish between the visualists and the verbal thinkers" (p. 21).

West (1991, 1992a, 1992b) makes a parallel argument that the emergence of computer graphics favors visual thinkers to the extent that some who have previously been labeled dyslexic are demonstrating cognitive advantages in these new visual environments. Poincaré (1905/1958) can be cited not only for his contributions to nonlinear dynamics but also as among the observers of human nature who have commented on these two types of mathematical thinking, what he called the analytical and geometrical minds, which he regarded as distinctly different. Price's (1975) thesis is that it is the collaboration between these two types of mathematical styles that provides an essential ingredient for science. The expanding utilization of nonlinear dynamics with its powerful combination of analytical and geometrical methods appears to support the Price hypothesis. The availability of desktop computing and graphics can be considered prosthetic aids for both of Poincaré's types of mathematical minds. The rendering of strange attractors on monitors enables visualization of patterns in seemingly chaotic numerical data, and the computation of fractal dimensions provides analytical assistance in quantifying complex patterns. Consequently, the emergence of fractal geometry can be viewed as much more than techniques to create (or compress) exotic patterns and naturalistic images; it represents a new way to think about everything, including "thinking" itself.

THE POST-EUCLIDIAN MIND

The meaning of *space* can be fairly placed among the group of terms, such as *time* and *energy*, which constitute the tough nuts to be cracked in any theory of knowledge. If our notions of space should be the most basic element in conscious thought, as suggested by Mach (1886) and more recently by Jaynes (1976), then any change in our spatial concepts could alter all of the intellectual superstructure that rests on this bedrock of cognition. Such is the proposition defended herein. For it will be argued that the concepts of fractal and fractal dimensions will significantly change a way of thinking that has dominated most human thought for over two millennium.

The invention of non-Euclidian geometries is impossible to date precisely due to the many contributions and meanings of *non-Euclidean* (Kline, 1972). With some exceptions, psychology has been indifferent to the cognitive implications of the early non-Euclidean works by Gauss (1777–1855), Lobatchevsky (1793–1856) and Bolyai (1802–1860) which established by the middle of the last century that "Euclidean geometry is not necessarily the geometry of physical space, that is, is not necessarily true" (Kline, 1972).

Some exceptions have been in developing models for psychometric spaces to describe human judgments (Torgerson, 1958) and the proposal by Luneberg (1947) that human binocular vision would necessarily result in non-Euclidean perception. Support for the non-Euclidean approaches to perception have been reviewed by

Blank (1959), Dodwell (1982), and Gentry and Wakefield (1991). But it is the work of Mandelbrot that has provided compelling demonstrations that geometry was using a confounded concept when invoking the unitary idea of a dimension.

Mandelbrot coined the word *fractal* in 1975, but his *Fractals: Form, Chance, and Dimension* (1975/1977) and *Fractal Geometry of Nature* (1982) provide the clearly stated challenge to our conventional notions about the meaning of dimension. Quoting him (1982) will provide the basis for what follows:

> Anyone who writes a mathematical book on *the* theory of dimension implies that this theory is unique. But to my mind the main fact is that the loose notion of dimension turns out to have many mathematical facets that not only are conceptually distinct but may lead to different numerical values. Just as William of Occam says of entities, dimensions must not be multiplied beyond necessity, but a multiplicity of dimensions is absolutely unavoidable. Euclid is limited to sets for which all the useful dimensions coincide, so that one may call them *dimensionally concordant* sets. On the other hand, the different dimensions of the sets to which the bulk of the Essay is devoted *fail* to coincide, these sets are *dimensionally discordant*.
>
> Moving on from the dimensions of mathematical sets to the 'effective' dimensions of the physical objects modeled by these sets, we encounter a different sort of inevitable and concretely essential ambiguity. (Mandelbrot, 1982, p. 14)

Mandelbrot also makes an unambiguous claim for the importance of the fractal dimension (D) concept and his role in its development: "I was the first to use D successfully in the description of Nature. And one of the central goals of this work is to establish D in a central position in empirical science, thereby showing it to be of far broader import than anyone imagined" (Mandelbrot, 1982, p. 16).

It is clear from the general scientific literature that Mandelbrot's ambitions for D are being realized at an impressive rate. Based on standard library reference sources, the estimated number of articles with the keyword *fractal(s)* has grown from an average rate of about one article per day in the mid-1980s to a publication rate that is now in the vicinity of three new reports daily. Table 10.1 provides a sample of two reference databases covering the period since *fractal* was invented.

An examination of Table 10.1 suggests that psychology is severely lagging behind the trend in the hard sciences to adopt fractal thinking. It will be suggested in a following section on psychological laws that this fractal gap is not as extreme as it seems if we are willing to reconsider a very large body of existing data from another point of view. Also, there has been a good deal of conference-based activity not reflected in the PsychINFO database that has included fractal thinking and the first book for psychologists on dynamical systems theory included the concept of fractals (Abraham, Abraham, & Shaw, 1990). In addition, the early general popularized accounts of dynamics (Briggs & Peat, 1989; Gleick, 1987) included the implications of fractal concepts for the study of behavior.

Table 10.1: Publication Frequencies for Articles with *Fractal(s)* as a Keyword In two databases: INSPEC, which reviews over 4,000 journals and other publications in physics, electronics, and computing, and PsychINFO indexed by the American Psychological Association from 1,300 journals and other publications in psychology and related social sciences.

Year	INSPEC	PsychINFO
1993	*512	*4
1992	991	10
1991	886	6
1990	853	8
1989	846	[1]3
1988	668	[2]2
1987	642	[3]1
1986	490	0
1985	281	0
1984	273	0
1983	18	0
1982	38	0
1981	22	0
1980	9	0
1979	7	0
1978	5	0
1977	2	0
1976	0	0
1975	[4]2	0
TOTAL	4098	35

*	Incomplete
[1]	Craven & Watt / Skinner / Michaels
[2]	Miyashita / Marchais
[3]	Cutting & Garvin
[4]	Mandelbrot

Before proceeding, an understanding of fractals and fractal dimensions will be needed. Fortunately, there are several good sources for learning about fractal geometry, including computer programs and textbooks spanning the difficulty range from high school to graduate school. The two-volume series *Fractals for the Classroom* and associated workbooks by Peitgen, Jurgens, and Saupe (1992) provides an extensive introduction, and each chapter includes programs in BASIC that demonstrate the principles being explained. For the visual thinkers—those who do not want to enter code into a computer—there are several software packages with helpful documentation (Barnsley, 1992; Oliver, 1992; Sprott & Rowlands, 1992; Wegner & Peterson, 1991).

A quick and inexpensive way to get an intuitive grasp for fractals and the concept of fractal dimension can be achieved with a piece of paper and pen or pencil. Regress to your childhood and begin scribbling on the paper by drawing a continuous line in a wildly random fashion so that as the line continues to grow in length it begins to fill in most of the space. As your random walk line progresses, the traditional mathematical (or topological) dimension remains one, but the fractal dimension is increasing in size from one toward the two dimensional value of the plane of the paper. It is now possible to compute the fractal dimension of your scribble, which will be some value between one and two dimensions.

Next, take the piece of paper and wad it up into a tight paper ball. Place the ball on something (this is best done outside) and walk away from the paper wad until it is no longer visible. At that distance the ball has zero dimension, but as you begin to walk back toward it the dimensionality will go from zero to three. It is this second demonstration that shows the importance of the observer to the thing observed in determining the effective dimension of anything. It is this "subjective" feature of fractal geometry that Mandelbrot emphasized.

The growing interest in fractals has numerous origins, but one commonality that makes this literature understandable is the advantage D has in describing the complexity of sensory experiences. In psychological terms, D provides an improved match between our perceptions and the numerical systems we use to describe perceptions of natural forms. Three characteristics of improved measurement methods are (1) sensitivity to changes in the things measured, (2) reliability with repeated measures, and (3) robustness or scaleability of the general method. Using measures of fractal dimensions of irregular visual patterns and just noticeable differences (JNDs) of threshold responses, Westheimer (1991) found that his observers could detect a 0.0085 shift in the fractal dimension of borders that began with D = 1.15. The JND increased to 0.015 with standard stimuli of D = 1.25. This sensitivity in measurement in the 1/100 to 1/1000 range is uncommonly good for psychological research. Similar sensitivity when using D as a dependent variable is suggested in our work on imagination (Gentry & Wakefield, 1991; Kern, 1991).

Barnsley (1988) states that the "fractal dimension of a set is a number which tells how densely the set occupies the metric space in which it lies. It is invariant under various stretchings and squeezings of the underlying space. This makes the fractal dimension meaningful as an experimental observable; it possesses a certain robustness, and is independent of the measurement units" (p. 3).

In psychological terms these qualities are akin to the perceptual constancies, and it is suggested that this is a homology reflecting the fractal properties of brain function at all levels of observation.

On reflection, D is very familiar as it reflects the questions that gave rise to experimental psychology beginning with the work of Fechner (1860/1966). The questions concern the best ways to compute numerical values for our subjective experiences. Since the work of S. S. Stevens it has been possible to consider Fechner's solution to have been only half right in the sense that power functions often provide more satisfactory fits to the data than the semi-logarithmic functions used by Fechner. However, the traditional psychophysics literature remains largely focused on the "best" function for a "psychophysical law" (e.g., Krueger, 1989).

PSYCHOLOGICAL "LAWS"

When Stevens (1961) simultaneously honored and repealed Fechner's law, he accelerated an already acrimonious literature on quests for the proper mathematics to characterize relationships between the physical and the psychological. In more than one way Stevens improved on Fechner's (1860/1966) semilogarithmic plot to make curved functions linear. Uttal (1973) reviews this literature to the year of Stevens's death, but the debates to that point were lacking the key insight needed to understand that these psychophysical experiments were exhibiting the signature of deterministic chaos.

Stevens's law can be restated as the discovery that power laws provide a means to estimate the fractal dimensions of our cognitive experiences. Debates about the stability of Stevens's Law over wide ranges of stimuli or between observers become moot when fractal thinking is adopted. It is now possible to reexamine the psychological literature where the local slopes of power functions reflect the fluctuating dimensionality of how organisms experience their world.

Until the advent of thinking about fractal dimension, the discussions focused on the validity of power functions for describing experimental results. A textbook example of this is exemplified by the following selection from Uttal (1973):

> Stevens' notions have been extremely influential in stimulating research in the last few years, to say the least. In fact, as Zinnes (1969) puts it, "the number of papers purporting to show that the correct psychophysical law is a power law or a logarithmic law is probably increasing exponentially."
>
> In spite of this enormous amount of activity, it cannot be said that there has been general agreement forthcoming about the validity of the power law, and Stevens' formulation has been challenged on many grounds. Even though his theory is a descriptive one and is not based on any specific mathematical assumptions comparable

Table 10.2: Psychophysical Magnitude of Exponents of Power Functions
These are indicative of the psychophysical dynamics of the various senses.
(From Uttal, 1973.)

Paradigm	Exponent
Brightness of 5 degree target (in continuous darkness)	0.33
Brightness of brief flash	0.5
Smell of heptane	0.6
Vibration of 250 Hz on finger	0.6
Loudness of 3000 Hz tone	0.67
Visual area	0.7
Tactal hardness	0.8
Vibrations of 60 Hz on finger	0.95
Temperature	1.0
Visual length	1.0
Duration of white noise	1.1
Pressure on palm	1.1
Vocal sound pressure	1.1
Thickness of blocks	1.3
Taste of sucrose	1.3
Taste of salt	1.4
Temperature (warmth on arm)	1.5
Tactual roughness	1.5
Handgrip	1.7
Electric stimulus in hearing	2.0
Electric stimulus to skin	3.5
Electric stimulus to teeth	7.0

to those of the Fechner formulation, power function fits often seem to be dependent upon a rather specific experimental procedure. (p. 266)

Although replicating these results may indeed be "dependent upon a rather specific experimental procedure" the data can now be viewed in a new way. These exponents are estimated from the slopes of linear functions derived from the logarithms of reports on subjective magnitude as a function of the logarithmic intensity of the physical stimulus. From the advantage of our time we can reconsider Table 10.2 as a sample of the dimensionality for perceptions during different types of laboratory experiences. It says that the cognitive dimensionality of having an electrical stimulus applied to one's teeth is likely to be more complex than reporting on the brightness of a homogeneous five-degree visual target under dark adaption conditions.

Complex systems can be quantified by the dimensionality of the space needed to describe their behavior. If fractional dimensions are employed, new and more subtle descriptions can be derived. Also, the fractal geometry measures of nature have the additional consequence of bringing the role of the observer into mathematics, completing the relativistic revolution of twentieth century science.

Mandelbrot (1982) states that "effective dimension inevitably has a subjective basis. It is a matter of approximation and therefore of degree of resolution" (p. 17).

The emerging use of dynamics and fractals in science is providing a cognitive resolution between the Aristotelian and Platonic, the bottom-up and top-down debates (e.g., Lewin, 1992). On a logarithmic paradigm shift scale, where 10.0 equals a once-in-a-thousand-years event, a 10.2 magnitude change of thinking is in progress. The severity of this alteration in the intellectual landscape is due to alterations in the concept of dimension and consequently such things as space and time. This shift in the bedrock of our conceptions of nature provides a unique opportunity for psychologists as observer-participants in a rare cognitive transformation.

REFERENCES

Abraham, F. D., Abraham, R. H., & Shaw, C. D. (1990). *A visual introduction to dynamical systems theory for psychology.* Santa Cruz: Aerial Press.

Barnsley, M. F. (1988). *Fractals everywhere.* New York: Academic Press.

Barnsley, M. F. (1992). *The desktop fractal design system.* IBM version 2.0 & Macintosh version 2.0. San Diego: Academic Press.

Blank, A. A. (1959). The Luneberg theory of binocular space perception. In S. Koch (Ed.), *Psychology: A study of a science (Vol. 1), Sensory, perceptual and physiological formulations.* New York: MacGraw-Hill.

Briggs, J. & Peat, F. D. (1989). *Turbulent mirror: An illustrated guide to chaos theory and the science of wholeness.* New York: Harper & Row.

Dodwell, P. C. (1982). Geometrical approaches to visual processing. In D. J. Ingle, M. A. Goodale, & R. J. W. Mansfield (Eds.), *Analysis of visual behavior*. Cambridge: MIT Press.

Fechner, G. T. (1860/1966). *Elemente der Psyhophysik (Vols. 1 & 2)*. Leipzig: Breitkopf U Härtel. *Elements of Psychophysics (Vol. 1)*. (H. E. Adler, Trans.). New York: Holt, Rhinehart & Winston.

Gentry, T., & Wakefield, J. (1991). Methods for measuring spatial cognition. In D. M. Mark & A. U. Frank (Eds.), *Proceedings: NATO Advanced Study Institute on the cognitive and linguistic aspects of geographic space* (pp. 185–217). Dordrecht: Kluwer Academic.

Gleick, J. (1987). *Chaos: Making a new science*. New York: Viking.

Jaynes, J. (1976). *The origin of consciousness in the breakdown of the bicameral mind*. Boston: Houghton Mifflin.

Kern, K. (1991). *The geometry of imagination: Using the fractal dimension to search for relationships between a new measure of spatial cognition and individual differences in personality and intelligence*. Unpublished master's thesis, California State University, Stanislaus.

Kline, M. (1972). *Mathematical thought from ancient to modern times*. Oxford: Oxford University Press.

Krueger, L. E. (1989). Reconciling Fechner and Stevens: Toward a unified psychophysical law. (Thirty-one peer commentaries follow.) *Behavioral & Brain Sciences, 12*, 251–320.

Lewin, R. (1992). *Complexity: Life at the edge of chaos*. New York: Macmillan.

Luneberg, G. (1947). *Mathematical analysis of binocular vision*. Princeton: Princeton University Press.

Mach, E. (1886/1959). *Die Analyse der Empfindungen und das Verhaltnis des Psychischen zun Physischen (The analysis of sensations and the relation of the physical to the psychical)*, (5th ed.). New York: Dover.

Mandelbrot, B. B. (1975/1977). *Les objets fractals: Forme, hasard et dimension*. Paris: Flammarion. *Fractals: Form, chance, and dimension*. San Francisco: W. H. Freeman.

Mandelbrot, B. B. (1982). *The fractal geometry of nature*. New York: W. H. Freeman.

Mandelbrot, B. B. (1992). Forward: Fractals and the rebirth of experimental mathematics. In H. O. Peitgen, H. Jurgens, & D. Saupe (Eds.), *Fractals for the classroom, Part One: Introduction to fractals and chaos* (pp. 1–16). New York: Springer-Verlag.

Oliver, D. (1992). *Fractal vision: Put fractals to work for you* (includes *FractalVision* software). Carmel: Sams.

Peitgen, H. O., Jurgens, H., & Saupe, D. (Eds.) (1992). *Fractals for the classroom, Part One: Introduction to fractals and chaos. Part Two: Complex systems and Mandelbrot Set. Strategic Activities (Vols. 1 & 2)*. New York: Springer-Verlag.

Poincaré, H. (1905/1913/1958). *La valeur de la science*. Paris: Flammarion. *The value of science*. (G. B. Halsted, Trans.). New York: Dover, 1958.

Price, D. de S. (1975) *Science since Babylon* (enlarged ed.). New Haven: Yale University Press.

Sprott, J. C., & Rowlands, G. (1992). *Chaos data analyzer*, IBM version 1.0. Raleigh: Academic Software Library and American Institute of Physics.

Stevens, S. S. (1961). To honor Fechner and repeal his law. *Science, 133*, 80–86.

Tiles, M. E. (1987). Geometry. In R. L. Gregory (Ed.), *The Oxford companion to the mind*. Oxford: Oxford University Press.

Torgerson, W. S. (1958). *Theory and methods of scaling*. New York: Wiley.

Uttal, W. R. (1973). *The psychobiology of sensory coding*. New York: Harper & Row.

Wegner, T., & Peterson, M. (1991). *Fractal creations*. Mill Valley CA USA: Waite.

West, T. G. (1991). *In the mind's eye: Visual thinkers, gifted people with learning difficulties, computer images, and the ironies of creativity*. Buffalo: Prometheus.

West, T. G. (1992a). A return to visual thinking: In education and in the workplace, we'll see a higher regard for visualization skills and talents. *Computer Graphics World, 15*, 115–116.

West, T. G. (1992b). A future of reversals: Dyslexic talents in a world of computer visualization. *Annals of Dyslexia, 42*, 124–139.

Westheimer, G. (1991). Visual discrimination of fractal borders. *Proceedings of the Royal Society, London Series B, 243*, 215–219.

Zinnes, J. L. (1969). Scaling. *Annual Review of Psychology, 20*, 447–478.

11

Erodynamics and the Dischaotic Personality

Ralph H. Abraham

Dedicated to Kurt Lewin (1890-1947)
and
Gregory Bateson (1904-1980)

The binary dichotomy of chaos/dischaos is used in place of that of disorder/order in modeling the psyche in the style of Kurt Lewin. Application is made to several ideas of Gregory Bateson.

HISTORICAL INTRODUCTION

The new field of erodynamics consists of applications of the mathematical theories of dynamics, chaos, and bifurcations to models in the social sciences, including economics. Here we give a capsule history of the field. Complex dynamical systems theory provides a new modeling strategy for social systems, which are usually too complex to model without a theory that allows chaos and bifurcation. These new models contribute to the hermeneutical circle for evolving social structures, in which mathematical help in understanding may be very welcome. Even the simplest social systems, such as two persons or two nations, tax our intuitive cognitive strategies. Dynamical models may be used as navigational aids for cooperation or conflict resolution in many situations in which good will prevails, yet does not suffice.

An early dynamical model for social systems, the first we know of, is the (1837) Verhulst model for population growth. Later, in the context of the Great War, came Lanchester's (1914) model for war, and Richardson's (1919) model for the arms race. Next came dynamical models for economic systems, with Keynes, Schumpeter, and von Neumann in the 1930s. Rashevsky, the founder of mathematical biology and editor of Richardson's papers, invented mathematical sociology during World War II. This sequence accelerated after World War II with the syntheses of general systems theory and cybernetics. In the mathematical branch of these movements, systems dynamics, we have the extensive development of models for factories, cities, nations, the world monetary system, and many other complex systems. The work of Jay Forrester was central to this growth. The independent development of dynamical systems theory after Poincaré remained aloof from social applications until recently, and now a reunion of these two branches of mathematics is underway. In the Poincaré lineage came the development of applied singularity theory by René Thom, its extensive application to social systems (as catastrophe theory) by Christopher Zeeman, and new dynamical models for economic systems by Radnor, Smale, and Chichilnisky in the 1970s. Since then, chaos theory has discovered systems with complex structure, and systems dynamics has discovered chaos.

THE PIONEERS

Here are some milestones in the evolution of erodynamics.

Lanchester, 1914

Frederick William Lanchester (1868-1946) was an English engineer. A creative genius interested in economics, physics, military strategy, automobiles, and airplanes, he was of one of the first to grasp the military advantage of aircraft. In this context, he conceived a dynamical model for armed conflict, in which numerical strength, firepower, strategy, and attitude were counted (Lanchester, 1914).

Richardson, 1919

Lewis Frye Richardson (1881-1953) was an English physicist, meteorologist, and Quaker. A conscientious objector in the World War I, he served as an ambulance driver on the frontlines in France, and saw a great deal of death and suffering. He decided to devote his life to the elimination of war. He developed a linear model for the arms race between two nations, in which a spiral of increasing armaments in each nation resulted from mathematical laws. He felt that the individual nations caught in this kind of dynamic were innocent victims of an out-of-control global system. He submitted a paper on this model to a journal, fully confident that another war could be averted. However, the paper was rejected, and the second World War began. After this rejection Richardson continued his work, trying to justify the model on the basis of actual armament statistics. In these efforts, he founded the field of politicometrics. Richardson's life work was published posthumously in 1960.

Von Neumann, 1932

The word *economics* is derived from the Greek *oikos nomos*, meaning the management of a household. This is also the source of oikonomia, the Christian doctrine of the economy of salvation. In the last century, economics became an important social science. Because economics is naturally equipped with numerical data, it was one of the first of the social sciences to receive a mathematical treatment. In 1932 John von Neumann (1903-1957) created one of the first dynamical models for an economic system, giving rise to a whole industry of mathematical analyses, computer simulations, and data collection (econometrics) (see Goodwin, 1991, Chap. 3).

Bateson, 1935

Gregory Bateson (1904-1980) adapted the Richardson arms race model to the process of the division of a culture into subcultures, analogous to differentiation in biological systems. He called this universal dynamical process for the development of a schism a Richardsonian process of schismogenesis (Bateson, 1972, p. 68). In fact, schismogenesis, a social form of bifurcation, was one of Bateson's main themes (Bateson, 1972, pp. 61, 107). Later he would apply it to schizophrenia (see "The Double Bind" below).

Lewin, 1936

Kurt Lewin (1890-1947) was influenced by the hermeneutics of Dilthey, with whom he had contact in Berlin, and Wertheimer, who had developed a *field* concept in Gestalt psychology as early as 1923. This was extensively developed by Lewin. His *life space* is a sort of psychological field, extending over a group of animals (Lewin, 1951/1975). He modeled social psychological objects by shapes within the life space, or field. He also introduced concepts of dynamics and bifurcations in these shapes, under the name *topological psychology* (Lewin, 1936). The rigorous development of Lewin's ideas had to await complex dynamical systems theory, or chaos theory, in the 1960s and 1970s.

Rashevsky, 1939

Nicholas Rashevsky (1895-1964) escaped from the Russian revolution to become the indefatigable pioneer of mathematical biology at the University of Chicago (Karreman, 1990) . He published an early erodynamics paper (1939) and a book (1947) applying the methods of mathematical biology to sociology. He edited the writings of Lewis Frye Richardson, the founder of erodynamics, for posthumous publication in 1960. In *Looking at History through Mathematics* (Rashevsky, 1968), he offers steps toward a mathematical model for Arnold Toynbee's theory of history. A tentative prevision of catastrophe theory is included to explain revolutions:

> Whenever we have threshold phenomena, whether in physical, biological, or social systems, the configuration of the system at the moment when the threshold is reached becomes unstable and the slightest, even infinitesimal, displacement of the configuration in a proper direction leads eventually to a finite change in the configuration of the system. Therefore, a change in the behavior of a single individual, no matter how small, may precipitate in an unstable social configuration, a process that leads to a finite, sometimes radical, change. (Rashevsky, 1968, p. 119)

An explicit recognition of the hermeneutic circle is presented in the Preface of this book, as part of an extensive defense of mathematical modeling.

Jung, 1952

Carl G. Jung (1875-1961) came late in his life to some fractal awakening, expressed in his book *Answer to Job* (1952). This presents an astonishingly bold psychoanalysis of the god Yahweh, in which good and evil are combined in a fractal binary. Further, his concept of *enantiodromia* (oscillation) admits a Lewinian model (Abraham, Abraham, & Shaw, 1990, pp. III-11 ff.).

Thom, 1972

In the 1960s René Thom developed catastrophe theory; he published the theory in 1972, along with a number of ideas for its application in the sciences, linguistics, philosophy, and so on. The final chapter of his work sets out the modern formulation of erodynamics in the context of proposed applications to sociology and psychology.

Zeeman, 1976

In the 1970s Carlos Isnard and Christopher Zeeman replaced the linear model of Lewis Richardson and Gregory Bateson with a nonlinear model, the cusp catastrophe of Thom's theory. They applied their model to the original arms race context of Richardson's work, showing how the model fit a situation of schismogenesis, in which the voting population of a democratic nation split into hawks and doves. Zeeman also adapted the cusp to model anorexia nervosa, an emotional disease in which phases of gluttony and fasting alternate (Postle, 1980; Zeeman, 1977).

Kushelman-Kadyrov, 1985

Mark Kushelman (under the pseudonym Kadyrov), a mathematician and systems' scientist then in Moscow, put together two of these cusp models into a double-cusp model for two nations engaged in an arms race, completing the nonlinear version of Richardson's original model. It provides a map, in the two-dimensional space of sensitivities of each nation to armaments of the other, showing regions of different behaviors, such as hawks and hawks, hawks and doves, doves and hawks, and doves and doves. Surprisingly, in the north-west and south-east sectors of this map, Kushelman found oscillating behavior. This might be significant in situations of codependence or addictive behavior (Abraham, Mayer-Kress, Keith, & Koebbe, 1991). A slightly different double cusp map was used by Callahan and Sashin (1987) in the treatment of anorexia nervosa and affect-response. Some other nonlinear adaptations of Richardson's model for the arms race have been studied by Saperstein and Mayer-Kress (1988), who found chaotic behavior in their model.

Haraway, 1985

In *Manifesto for Cyborgs*, Donna Haraway (1985) analyzes the cyborg, an integral being who is part human, part machine. Without explicit reference to fractal geometry, Haraway's vision is essentially fractal. She describes three critical cases of the fractal deconstruction of a binary: human/animal, animal-human/machine, and physical/nonphysical. She extends these examples to a long list of fractured identities: self/other, mind/body, culture/nature, male/female, and so on, of political significance. This pathfinding analysis leads the way to a fractal method for the deconstruction of all binaries as well as to the reconstruction of self-images (and scientific categories) as fractal identities. Thus, she introduced fractal geometry into anthropology, beginning a transformation ongoing today. Since 1985, there has been an erodynamic explosion. (See also Eglash, 1992.)

Figure 11.1: Fractal Separatrix
Formed by coupled oscillators, and seen in Poincaré section.
(Grebogi, Ott, Varosi, & Yorke, "Fractal Basin Boundary 2," displayed at an
exhibit at the Fine Arts Museum of Long Island, April 1-June 24, 1990.)

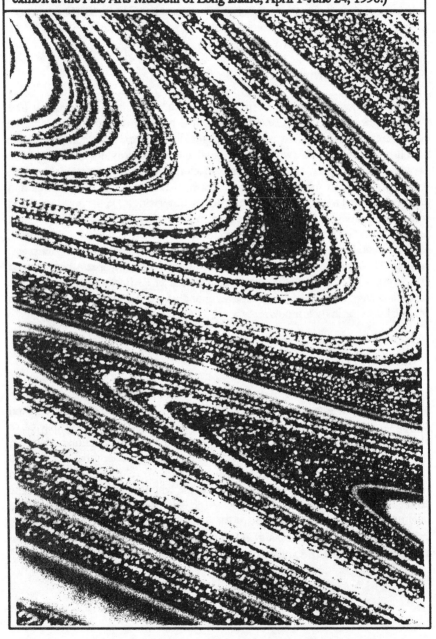

DISCHAOS: DYNAMICAL MODELS

The fractal concept introduced into anthropology by Haraway and subsequent works by Wagner, McWhinney, and Strathern are epitomized by the idea of the sandy beach. We begin the description of our model by recalling this static concept, then extending it to the dynamical model of Lewin, Thom, and Zeeman as the fractal separatrix or basin boundary (Fig. 11.1). Finally we will use the model to introduce the concept of the dischaotic personality.

The Sandy Beach

In Benoit Mandelbrot's classic text, the second chapter is titled, "How long is the coast of Britain?" We will describe the sandy beach in the two-dimensional context of a map. Thus, the ocean and the land are mostly two-dimensional. Before fractal geometry, the map showed the boundary between the ocean and the land as a smooth curve, a one-dimensional coast. But now, thanks to Mandelbrot (he gives credit to Richardson), we may zoom in on the coast and see that it has very small islands, even pebbles, in a densely packed structure. Zooming in again, we see grains of sand on the beach, and in the ocean close to the beach. All this is the coast: It has a fractal dimension. Land penetrates into the ocean in a frothy structure of sand; ocean penetrates into the land in a frothy structure of water in the wet sand. Not only is the coast a fractal, with a dimension more than one but less than two, but it is a fractal region: the coastal zone. The ocean and land are not divided by the coast in a binary fashion; they interpenetrate in a fractal geometry. The fractals of chaos theory—attractors, separatrices, and bifurcations—are all of the sandy beach variety.

Fractal Separatrices

We now make a jump to the dynamical model of Lewin (1936), who imagined the life space or psychological field of a person as the state space of a (continuous) dynamical system. The observable behaviors in this model are the attractors, and the significant regions of life space, then, are the basins of attraction of these attractors. Further, the separatrices (the boundaries of these basins) are crucial to the Lewinian view of psychology (Abraham, Abraham, & Shaw, 1990). In many important examples, these separatrices are fractal (Kennedy & Yorke, 1991; Ueda, 1992). This means that the sandy beach concept applies to the boundary between two different behavioral regions. This will be our basic model in this chapter. We should point out, however, that the improvement of the Lewinian model due to Thom and Zeeman is more complex: the attractor-basin portrait in the state space (life space of Lewin) is replaced by the response diagram, in the product of the state space and the control space of a dynamical scheme (morphogenetic field of Thom).

The Dischaotic Personality

We now assume a Lewinian dynamical model for the self or life space of an individual. Different aspects of the personality, depending critically on the individual, are represented in this model by groups of basins of attraction. These may be slowly changing in time under the effects of learning, adaptation, stimuli, and so on. Now that chaos theory and fractal geometry have emerged, we expect that fractal boundaries of these psychological regions are the rule, rather than the exception. Following the lead of chaos theoretic models in medical physiology, we may expect that chaotic attractors and fractal separatrices are important for health. Specifically, we may suggest that thick fractal separatrices in the psyche have an integrating effect. For under the effect of random or chaotic stimuli, the trajectory of the Lewinian model jumps about in small discontinuities, landing in different basins because of the fractal boundaries. This has the effect of integrating the different behaviors of the different attractors into a strongly associated or mixed personality. On the other hand, when the boundaries have become (perhaps in a pathological situation) too ordered, or *dischaotic*, or if the fractal dimension is too small, there would be a tendency to manifest one attractor for some time, until an exceptional stimulus pushes the trajectory over the edge into the basin of another aspect of the self and there is a dramatic change in behavior. Posing *dischaos/chaos* as a binary dichotomy instead of *order/disorder*, we may call this situation *personality dischaos*, rather than the more patriarchal *personality disorder*.

BATESONIAN APPLICATION

In a number of papers, Bateson anticipated the fractal and chaotic models of the psyche. Here, we consider three examples.

Logical Types

First, consider Bateson's work on logical types and communication theory (Bateson, 1972, p. 177). Each type may be viewed, in the Lewinian model, as a region of life space, a union of basins of several attractors, which enjoys some isolation from other similar regions. A message is interpreted by each category, unless it contains an identifier, or address, specifying one category as its intended destination.

Paradoxes

Next, consider Bateson's analysis of paradox, in which the meaning of a message in one category denies its meaning in another category, and vice versa. He likened this situation to a door buzzer, one of the first models of a negative feedback oscillator (Bateson, 1979, p. 65). The exemplary paradox (which is closely related to the double bind, see below) is the liars paradox ("this sentence is false"), which has recently been shown to generate a chaotic attractor in truth space (Mar & Grim, 1991). We may regard paradox as a fundamentally chaotic process.

The Double Bind

In 1952, with coworker Jay Haley at Stanford University, Bateson developed the double-bind theory of schizophrenia based on his theory of logical types, multiple levels of learning, paradoxes, and communications theory (Bateson, 1972, p. 201). The basic idea of this theory is a cycle involving two people, the dominator and the victim, in which a signal from the dominator is interpreted by the victim on two levels, and each interpretation contradicts the other. See Eglash (1992, chap. 4) for a relevant characterization of mental states in terms of fractal dimension.

In all these examples, an aspect of the individual psyche is divided into multiple levels, a normal structure. But in the pathological situation, a dynamical communication loop is set up between them, like a door buzzer: a disabling oscillation (or chaotic attractor). In our model of the normal psyche based on a dynamical system with fractally intertwined basins (the levels), a small amount of communications noise would be sufficient to stabilize the oscillation. But in a dischaotic psyche, however, the basins are separated by a clean boundary, rather than a sandy beach. Thus, in this model, dischaos is a precondition for schismogenesis, and thus, unwanted oscillations. In this picture a useful property of the psyche might be the *Wada property*: Each point on the boundary of one basin is on the boundary of all (Kennedy & Yorke, 1991). This is known to occur in the dynamical system for the forced damped pendulum. If a psyche has the Wada property, then environmental noise can effect a synthesis of all the levels into a unique self. Alternatively, periodic forcing (turning the pages of a book, for example) may suffice to restore chaos.

CONCLUSION

These examples should suffice to give an idea what chaos theory can do for the evolution of Lewinian and Batesonian models for the individual or the group psyche. This is as far as a mathematician can go; the next steps are up to the psychologists. By learning a modicum of the mathematical theory of chaotic dynamical systems and their bifurcations, one can develop new theories of dischaotic personality, and therapies too, that can spontaneously pop up. It may be, for example, that electric shocks might be replaced by computer-generated foot massage as a treatment for depression.

In future work we may use the fractal boundary model to suggest some therapies for multiple personality dischaos (MPD), bipolar personality dischaos (BPD), and other dischaos phenomena. These would utilize *forces of chaos*, such as chaotic music or exposure to nature, perhaps in a workshop setting. Further, we might try to identify some of the *forces of order*, cultural causes, or concomitants of dischaotic personality such as: urbanization, organized religion, patriarchy, monotheism, the Bible, monogamy, marriage, nuclear families, and childrearing practices.

ACKNOWLEDGMENTS

It is a pleasure to acknowledge critical discussions with Deena Metzger, Jerry Rasch, and Ray Gwyn Smith and the generosity of Fred Abraham, John Allen, Matt Clinton, Jonathan Cohen, Catherine Heatley, Robert Langs, and Marsha King in sharing their ideas and resources.

REFERENCES

Abraham, F. D., Abraham, R. H., & Shaw, C.D. (1990). *A visual introduction to dynamical systems theory for psychology.* Santa Cruz: Aerial Press.

Abraham, R. H., Mayer-Kress, G., Keith, A., & Koebbe, M. (1991). Double cusp models, public opinion, and international security. *International Journal of Bifurcations and Chaos, 1*, 417–430.

Bateson, G. H. (1972). *Steps to an ecology of mind.* New York: Ballantine.

Bateson, G. H. (1979). *Mind and nature: A necessary unity.* New York: Bantam Books.

Callahan, J., & Sashin, J. I. (1987). Models of affect-response and anorexia nervosa. In S. H. Koslow, A. J. Mandell, & M. F. Shlesinger (Eds.), *Perspectives in biological dynamics and theoretical medicine, Annals of the New York Academy of Sciences* (Vol. 504, pp. 241–259). New York: New York Academy of Sciences.

Eglash, R. B. (1992). *A cybernetics of chaos.* Ph.D. thesis, University of California, Santa Cruz.

Goodwin, R. (1991). *Chaotic economic dynamics.* Cambridge: Cambridge University Press.

Haraway, D. (1985). Manifesto for cyborgs: Science, technology, and socialist feminism in the 1980s. *Socialist Review, 80*, 65–108.

Jung, C. G. (1952/1954/1969). *Antwort auf Hiob/Answer to Job.* English translation by R. F. C. Hull in *Psychology and religion: West and East, Vol. 11. The collected works of C. G. Jung* (2nd ed.). Zurich: Rascher. London: Routledge & Kegan Paul. Princeton: Princeton University Press, Bollingen Series XX.

Karreman, G. (1990). Memories of Rashevsky. *Dynamics Newsletter, 4*, (1), 3–4, (2) 3–4, (3) 3–5.

Kennedy, J., & Yorke, J. A. (1991). Basins of Wada. *Physica D, 51*, 213–225.

Lanchester, F. W. (1914/1956). Mathematics in warfare. Reprinted in J. R. Newman, *The world of mathematics* (pp. 2138–2157). New York: Simon & Schuster.

Lewin, K. (1936). *Principles of topological psychology*. New York: McGraw-Hill.

Lewin, K. (1951/1975). *Field theory in social science: Selected theoretical papers*. Westport: Greenwood Press.

Mar, G., & Grim, P. (1991). Pattern and chaos: New images in the semantics of paradox. *Nous, 25*, 659–693.

Postle, D. (1980). *Catastrophe theory*. London: Fontana.

Rashevsky, N. (1968). *Looking at history through mathematics*. Cambridge: MIT Press.

Saperstein, A. M., & Mayer-Kress, G. (1988). A nonlinear dynamical model of the impact of SDI on the arms race. *Journal of Conflict Resolution, 32*, 636–670.

Thom, R. (1972/1975). *Stabilité structurelle et morphogenèse (Structural Stability and morphogenesis)*. (H. Fowler, Trans.). Reading: Benjamin.

Ueda, Y. (1992). *The road to chaos*. Santa Cruz: Aerial Press.

Zeeman, E. C. (1977). *Catastrophe theory and its applications*. Reading: Addison-Wesley.

12

Evolutionary Dynamics in Minds and Immune Systems

Ben Goertzel

What do attention disorders have to do with immunological chaos? What does an infant's learning to walk have in common with an antibody class learning to recognize an antigen? From the the point of view of conventional psychology, there is no reason to consider these questions worth asking. But if, on the other hand, one adopts the perspective of the newly emerging discipline of complex systems science, then one obtains quite a different attitude. Both the mind/brain and the immune system are complex, evolving, self-organizing systems. Therefore, according to complex systems science, one should expect there to be significant points of commonality between mental function and immune function. From this point of view our two questions are good ones, well worth exploring.

More specifically, the theory of self-organizing optimization implies that there are three main processes common to all complex systems: multilevel control, form creation by "crossover," and differential reproduction based on "structural fitness" (Goertzel, 1993a, 1993b, 1993c). This chapter uses this perspective to explore two issues: The role of neural chaos and the optimization processes underlying motor control. First, we look at the relationship between chaos in immune systems and chaos in the mind/brain. It is concluded that psychological chaos may have something to do with various attention disorders. A similar conclusion was reached by Marks (1992) on the basis of totally different considerations. Then we explore the connection between learning in the immune system and learning in the mind/brain. In particular, it is proposed that the process of learning to walk is mathematically and conceptually similar to the process by which the immune system learns to recognize an antigen. Both learning processes involve a simple "evolutionary mutation" algorithm. This idea is shown to explain the qualitative character of recent data regarding treadmill stepping (Thelen & Ulrich, 1991).

PATTERN, COMPLEXITY, AND COMPUTATION

My main interest here is in concrete, empirical questions, but my path toward these questions begins on the level of abstract philosophy. In the introduction to *Mind and Nature* (1979), Gregory Bateson enounces a basic epistemological/ ontological axiom, which he calls "the Metapattern." This axiom, central to the philosophy of Charles S. Peirce and the anthropological linguistics of Benjamin Whorf, states very simply that the living world is made of pattern. In Goertzel (1993b) this idea is taken literally and placed on a rigorous mathematical footing. A *pattern* is defined as a representation that that is something simpler. More explicitly: a process w is a *pattern* in an entity x if

the result of w is a good approximation of x, and
w is simpler than x

The *degree* to which w is a pattern in x may be defined as the product AB, where A is the ratio of the simplicity of w to the simplicity of x, and B is 1 plus the error of the approximation of x by w. The easiest way of specifying these concepts is to take a computational point of view. For example, if an entity is a binary sequence, and a process is a computer program, then their *simplicity* may be defined as their length. This definition ties in nicely with Chaitin's (1987) algorithmic information theory: The algorithmic information $I(x)$ is the simplicity of the simplest pattern in x. A simple example is the binary sequence x=1000100010001000100010001000 1000100010001000100010001000100010001000100010001000100010001000. The program w = "Repeat '1000' 21 times" is a pattern in x because it results in x and is shorter.

One good way to think about the concept of pattern is to look at two-dimensional images rather than binary sequences. Suppose one has a picture on the computer screen. If the screen is 400 by 600 pixels, then to store this picture in a bit-by-bit way requires at least 240,000 bits. But using fractal image generation techniques, one may generate many very complex pictures from very short programs. In this case the program is a pattern in the picture; it is a process that results in the output of the picture, and it is simpler than the picture, where simplicity is measured in terms of storage requirements. The concept of pattern is not limited to the formalism of computational complexity; it may be generalized to quantum computers (Deutsch, 1985), hypersets (Goertzel, 1993b), and so on. Algorithmic information theory is merely the simplest approach.

One may define the *structure* of an entity as the set of all patterns in that entity. This is a fuzzy set, since different patterns provide different degrees of simplification. Formally, I denote the structure of x as $St(x)$. One may then define the *structural complexity* of an entity x as the size of the fuzzy set $St(x)$. This is a measure of the total amount of pattern in x: It captures formally the sense in which a person is more complex than a flower, which is more complex than a virus. The definition of size here is a little bit subtle as one has to subtract out for overlapping patterns.

Next, consider the operation of emergence relating patterns with fuzzy sets of patterns. Most simply, a process is *emergent* between x and y if it is a pattern in the union of x and y but not in either x or y individually. More generally, a process is emergent between x and y if the degree to which it is a pattern in the union of x and y exceeds the sum of the degree to which it is a pattern in x and the degree to which it is a pattern in y. The set of all patterns emergent between x and y is denoted Em(x,y), and it is defined by the equation Em(x,y) = St(x∪y)–St(x)–St(y). Mathematically astute readers will notice a coding routine being smuggled in here: Somehow the joint entity x∪y must be mapped into a single binary sequence. But this presents no major problems.

THE STRUCTURE AND DYNAMICS OF INTELLIGENCE

Intelligence can be defined as able pattern formation and recognition. More explicitly, an entity is intelligent if it is capable of achieving complex goals in an environment that is, though unpredictable in its microscopic details, roughly predictable on the level of macroscopic structure.

Mind can be defined as the structure of an intelligent system. It follows that a mind is a mathematical form, a certain fuzzy set of processes that are patterns in a certain entity. This definition of mind does not resolve age-old puzzles of the philosophy of mind, but it does give us something to work with. At the very least it gives one license to use the word mind without being ashamed.

It follows from these definitions of intelligence and the mind that prediction and pattern recognition are necessarily based on *analogical reasoning*, that is, on reasoning of the form: If the same pattern occurs in two situations, then related patterns may also occur in both situations. This requirement leads to a crucial observation. If a long-term memory is to be useful for analogical reasoning, it must have the property such that once one has accessed a certain pattern, it is generally easy to access other patterns related to that pattern. If analogy had to use a memory without this property, it would be uselessly slow. Analogy requires continual search for related patterns.

These considerations yield the idea of a *structurally associative memory* in which some entities are stored near to entities related to them by common patterns. In particular, if w is a pattern emergent between x and y, then a structurally associative memory should usually store w, x, and y near one another. This is a very natural idea. It is just the old idea of associative memory, with association defined in terms of pattern. The pattern-theoretic approach resolves a weak point in the associationist theory of memory, because the structurally associative memory is emphatically made of dynamical processes, not static images or tokens.

It has been convincingly demonstrated by Rosenfeld (1988) that we remember something by applying a complex array of interacting processes, rather than by accessing a record stored as in a file cabinet or a library. Historically, most associationist theories have assumed an imagist view of memory. But the definition of pattern provides a natural, general way to talk about association of processes. It is important to note that nearby is defined in terms of memory access, not physical memory structure. If w is near x in the structurally associative memory, this means that accessing w primes the memory for access of x.

Finally, it must not be forgotten that every mind is continually recognizing new patterns, both in external data and among the patterns in its own memory. Furthermore, every real associative memory is only approximate. There are always errors; a new pattern may not immediately be placed in the proper location. It follows that the memory network is always shifting itself around, experimenting with new locations not only for particular patterns but perhaps for whole clusters of related patterns. Goertzel (1993a) shows that this process of relocation may be interpreted, in true Darwinian style, as a process of fitness maximization. Memory may be understood to operate by natural selection.

IMMUNODYNAMICS

The immune system recognizes bacteria, viruses, and other foreign antigens by a lock-and-key mechanism. An antibody class Ab recognizes an antigen Ab if the shape of the surface of Ag is complementary to the shape of the variable region of the surface of Ab. One main use of the immune system is for killing antigens. But killing is always preceded by recognition.

The actual definition of complementary is complicated, as one must compute a bunch of free energies. Alternatively, there is a simple way of visualizing the process (e.g., de Boer, 1992; de Boer & Perelson, 1991), modeling antigens and antibodies as one-dimensional finite sequences of bumps and indentations, which can also be represented by numbers such as 1,4,–5,6,–7. Positive numbers correspond to bumps, negative numbers correspond to indentations, and the magnitude of the number indicates the height of the bump or the depth of the indentation. For an antibody class to be complementary to an antigen, it must have bumps when the antigen has indentations, and vice versa. So the ideal complement to the antigen given above would be –1,–4,5,–6,7; these two fit together just like a lock and a key. But approximate matching is all right too. The antibody class corresponding to –4,0,4,–5,5 might well be able to grab on to the antigen corresponding to 1,4,–5,6,–7. This "shape space" idea highlights what is for me the most interesting aspect of immune behavior: *If Ab recognizes Ag, then Em(Ab,Ag) is significant.* If two sequences are (approximately) complementary, then one can (approximately) compute either one from the other.

Burnet's theory of clonal selection, the foundation of modern immunology, states that immune systems evolve by natural selection, where "fitness" is defined as "amount of emergent pattern generated in conjunction with the environment." New antibody classes are created by the bone marrow; and antibody classes that are successful in "grabbing onto" something that has an appropriate concentration in the bloodstream are not only systematically reproduced but also mutated (e.g., in the germinal center of the spleen). For instance, given a large concentration of $Ag = 5,0,0,0,5$, then, all else being equal, $Ab_1 = -5,0,0,0,-5$ will reproduce much more than $Ab_2 = 1,2,3,4,5$. And mutants similar to Ab_1 will be much more common than mutants similar to Ab_2.

Two antibody classes can recognize each other. This can result in complex behavior. For example, each one attacks the other, thus depleting the other but also stimulating the other to reproduce, mutate, and attack. This self-reactivity of the immune system leads immediately to the concept of the immune network: the idea, first presented by Niels Jerne, that the immune system is continually acting on itself, even in the absence of external stimulation. This is a controversial idea within theoretical immunology, but it has received a great deal of support from computer simulations (de Boer & Perelson, 1991). Dynamical models inevitably lead to rich patterns of fluctuations (phase portraits) among the variables of the immune network.

Taking this line of thought one step further, de Boer and Perelson (1991) have mathematically demonstrated that even in an immune system consisting of but two antibody types, chaos is possible. Also, experiments indicate the presence of chaotic fluctuations in the levels of certain antibody types in mice (Stewart, 1992). These chaotic fluctuations are proof of an active immune network, proof that the theoretical possibility of an interconnected immune system is probable in real living systems. Stewart and Varela (Stewart, 1992; Stewart & Varela, 1991) have conjectured that this network may provide communication links between other systems, such as that which connects a neurotransmitter to a hormone.

Suppose that some fixed fraction of antibody types participates in the richly interconnected network. Then these chaotic fluctuations ensure that at any given time a pseudo-random sample, a Poincaré section, of this fraction of antibody types is active. If the conjecture of Stewart and Varela (1991) is correct, then this is a very valuable thing for it provides raw material for the formation of new chains. Chaotic dynamics accentuates the Darwinian process of mutation, reproduction, and selection in the sense that it causes certain antibody types to pseudo-randomly reproduce far more than would be necessary to deal with external antigenic stimulation. Then these excessively proliferating antibody types may mutate and possibly connect with other antibody types, forming new chains.

Of course, chaos in the narrow mathematical sense is not necessary for producing pseudo-random fluctuations. Complex periodic behavior or aperiodic behavior that depends polynomially but not exponentially on initial conditions would do as well. But since we know mathematically that immunological chaos is possible, and we have observed experimentally what looks like chaos, calling these fluctuations chaos is not exactly a leap of faith.

CHAOS AND ATTENTION

Admittedly, the role of chaos in immune systems is somewhat speculative. But the very possibility of a role for immunological chaos is pregnant with psychological suggestions. What about chaos in the human memory network? Chaos in the immune network may, for example, be caused by two antibody types that partially match each other. The two continually battle it out, neither one truly prevailing, the concentration of each one rising and falling in an apparently random way. Does this process not occur in the psyche as well? Competing ideas, struggling against each other, neither one ever gaining ascendancy?

To make the most of this concept requires the idea of multilevel control. Careful analysis of pattern recognition dynamics leads to the idea of a perceptual hierarchy of recognitive processes, a sort of pyramidal architecture consisting of a level 1 containing processes that recognize patterns in sense data, a level 2 containing processes that recognize patterns emerging from the patterns recognized by level 1 processes, a level 3 containing processes that recognize patterns emerging from the patterns recognized in level 2 processes, and so on (Goertzel, 1993c). Of course, this structure need not be strict and orderly. Some processes may recognize patterns emerging between patterns on different levels.

Inversely, close study of pattern-creation dynamics gives rise to the concept of a motor control hierarchy. Suppose the mind wants to carry out a complex plan of action. It needs to somehow build this complex action out of tiny, simple actions, out of elementary muscle movements and the like. This is a very difficult problem, and I propose that the only generally workable way to solve it is hierarchically. The complex action must be decomposed into a collection of simpler actions, which in turn must be decomposed into a collection of simpler actions, and so on down until a sufficiently elementary level is reached. An act like throwing a football or massaging a shoulder is then a pattern emergent among patterns emergent among ... patterns emergent among muscle movements.

Of course, these two networks need not be distinct; quite the opposite, they must be intricately interconnected. Furthermore, they must be deeply interconnected with the structurally associative memory. This interconnection leads to the idea of the mind as a *dual network*, a network of processes interconnected simultaneously according to a perceptual-motor hierarchy and according to a structurally associative memory.

Now consider the interactions between a set, say, a pair, of processes that reside on one of the lower levels of the perceptual-motor hierarchy. These processes themselves will not generally receive much attention from processes on higher levels. A process will be considered important only if it is useful for dealing with something that is considered important, that is, if it matches something important. This is implicit in the logic of multilevel control. However, chaotic dynamics is a tool by which two cooperatively matching processes could simultaneously increase one another's importance, just as two matching antibody classes can cause each other to proliferate. Thus we have a mechanism by which pseudo-random samples of lower-level processes may put themselves forth for the attention of higher-level processes. And this mechanism is enforced, not by some overarching global program, but by natural self-organizing dynamics.

This idea obviously needs to be refined (Goertzel, 1993b). Even in this rough form, though, it has important implications for the psychology of attention. If one views consciousness as a process residing on the intermediate levels of the perceptual-motor hierarchy, then in chaos we have a potential mechanism for pseudo-random changes in the focus of attention. This ties in closely with the speculation of Terry Marks (1992) that psychological chaos is the root of much impulsive behavior.

HOW DO INFANTS LEARN TO WALK?

Chaotic attention is an enchanting but rather speculative idea. Let us now turn to a more concrete question, closer to the level of empirical data. How is the ability of independent upright locomotion acquired? How do infants learn to walk? The immunological analogy suggests a specific neurological hypothesis: Infants learn to walk by a simple mutation/selection process. If this hypothesis is correct, it will be a strong point in favor of the analogy between mind/brains and immune systems. Furthermore, the hypothesis provides an excellent illustration of the difference between conventional psychology and psychology inspired by complex systems and science. Over the last half century there has been considerable research on the acquisition of independent upright locomotion. However, much less effort has been devoted to the question of the neural and psychological dynamics underlying this acquisition process. In the words of Thelen and Ulrich (1991), "The great bulk of Western developmental science has proceeded to make significant empirical gains documenting new behavioral forms and their precursors, successors and variants while remaining less concerned, and for the most part atheoretical, about issues of fundamental processes of change."

This aversion to speculation about dynamical processes has encouraged theories that explain development without invoking active learning. For example, the maturationist approach to the development of independent upright locomotion, pioneered by McGraw (1945), views learning to walk as a microgenetic process: As a new portion of the brain matures, a new component of walking skill is acquired. This approach is far from obsolete (e.g., Forssberg, 1985). The most important exception to this antidynamics trend has been the work of Jean Piaget (1970). Piaget's constructivist point of view places a great deal of emphasis on underlying dynamical processes. Piaget's concept of equilibriation, although somewhat vaguely defined, is an extremely important one, for it connects developmental psychology with the study of mathematical, physical, and chemical dynamical systems (Prigogine & Stengers, 1984; Devaney, 1988). Schwalbe's (1991) four-stage dynamical theory of development is more explicitly dynamical, but it has not been developed thoroughly as yet, and it has not been applied specifically to walking behavior.

The Piagetan perspective leaves the connection between developmental psychology and dynamical systems theory on a purely intuitive level; Schwalbe's, while metaphorical, on a more explicitly dynamical level. Others have also striven to remedy this deficiency. For example, Bruncks (personal communication, 1992) has proposed to use nonlinear dynamics to explain the convergence of disparate early walking styles to a more standard, "mature" walking style. And Thelen and Ulrich (1991) have provided a dynamical-systems-theoretic analysis of the development of treadmill stepping during the first year. Their work must be classified as an unqualified success. Based on a study of nine infants, they were able to determine a specific control parameter (leg strength) of the dynamics underlying the process of learning to walk on a moving treadmill and were able to portray the dynamical interaction of exploration and various component perceptual-action processes. In contrast to the Piagetan mentalism, their approach was strictly behavioral.

Thelen and Ulrich are certainly correct in studying developmental processes using the tools of dynamical systems theory. However, I suspect that their attitude toward structural explanations may be undesirably severe. The Piagetan concept of developmental scheme is a valuable one, and it does not contradict the presence of active learning and complex mathematical dynamics. In order to really understand the dynamics underlying motor development, I suggest, the viewpoint of dynamical systems theory must be integrated with the framework of developmental schemes. If we are to comprehend the hidden neuropsychological strategies underlying motor learning, we must use every tool we can get our hands on. Schwalbe represents the amalgamation of both approaches.

The gap between dynamical systems theory and Piagetan psychology might appear to be a huge one. On the one side, there are vaguely defined psychological structures such as schemes and representations. On the other side, there are differentiable functions of real variables, obeying specific differential or difference equations. But, in fact, recent developments suggest that this gap is not so large at all. More and more cognitive scientists have begun thinking about the computational representation of psychological schemes. More and more researchers concerned with complex systems have come to realize that the fundamental concepts of dynamical systems theory may be studied in a purely discrete, computational setting. The theory of computation has brought structure-oriented thinking and dynamics-oriented thinking much closer together. Evolutionary theory (Goertzel, 1993a) completes this unification process; it gives an abstract model of mental process according to which representational schemes and self-organizing dynamics can coexist and interact.

So let us return to the issue at hand: Learning to walk. According to Bruncks's (personal communication, 1992) study, beginning walkers use a wide variety of styles. Then little by little, as they become more adept, their walking styles converge to a relatively standard, "mature" walking style. The dynamical pattern Thelen and Ulrich (1991) observed in the context of treadmill stepping is essentially quite similar:

> Our observations showed that, with age, infants stepped more on the treadmill, their repertoire became increasingly dominated by alternating steps, their steps were more sensitive to the belt speed, and the coordination between the two legs became more symmetrical. In short, the infants increasingly "settled in" to a preferred motor regime while on the treadmill; alternating stepping is a behavioral attractor state for infants when placed on a treadmill.

Tracking step-cycle duration and relative phase lag between the legs, Thelen and Ulrich observed treadmill walkers proceeding through an initial period of high variability, followed by a period of low variability as they settled into the attractor regime.

One might explain these empirical observations by modeling the task of learning to walk as a discrete optimization problem. In this perspective, any possible strategy for learning to walk may be represented as a discrete optimization technique. Conversely, every discrete optimization technique may be considered as a potential strategy for learning to walk. The problem is then determining which discrete optimization algorithm is actually implemented in the brain. For the class of all discrete optimization techniques is a very large one. Of course, not every optimization technique is a viable candidate. One requires, at the very least, an algorithm that satisfies two criteria: Effectiveness at solving the particular optimization problem of learning to walk and simplicity of neural representation. If a certain technique is very effective but has no convenient neural representation, then it is a poor candidate. On the other hand, if a certain technique has a simple neural representation but does not work very well, it is also a poor candidate. The technique used by the brain must satisfy both criteria to a reasonable extent.

In particular, I suggest that at least one of the following three optimization strategies is probably at work here: *evolutionary mutation, simulated annealing,* or *genetic optimization.* This point of view poses three main questions.

1. Which of these three algorithms is most relevant?
2. How much parallelism is involved in the implementation of these algorithms?
3. What degree of multilevelization is involved in the implementation of these algorithms?

Evolutionary mutation, as briefly discussed above, is the optimization routine implemented by the immune system. Simulated annealing is a simple variant of this routine; it is evolutionary mutation with a random element, which sometimes causes the less fit of two competing entities to survive. The trick is that the degree of random error decreases as time goes by. Thus, in the early stages of optimization, fitness determines survival only weakly; but in the later stages fitness determines survival very strongly. It is possible (Goertzel & Ananda, in press; Hagen, Macken,

& Perelson, 1991) that immune systems make use of a simple version of simulated annealing; this speculation remains unproven.

It is certainly not inconceivable that genetic optimization plays a role in the selection of walking styles. However, as a working hypothesis, learning to walk may be understood as a process of evolutionary mutation, or perhaps as a process of simulated annealing with a moderately small initial random element. In a nutshell, what this means is as follows. Given a small set of psychological schemes representing initial walk styles, the infant mutates these walk styles to obtain a larger pool of styles. Those styles that work best, that give the fastest, most reliable locomotion, are retained; the others are eliminated. Eventually this process results in the evolution of an approximately optimal walk style, a "mature" style that permits quick, stable locomotion. This "mature" style is the scheme for walking that will be retained into adulthood.

This point of view synthesizes scheme-oriented thinking with dynamics-oriented thinking. It also gives rise to two neurological questions: What sort of brain structures represent walk styles? And are these structures amenable to optimization by evolutionary mutation? If the answer to the latter question is yes, then we have demonstrated that the immunological analogy is a good one.

CONCLUSION

We began with abstract mathematical philosophy, but we ended up with hypotheses regarding some very concrete scientific issues. What causes attention disorders? How is independent upright locomotion acquired? These questions allow us to put complex systems science to the test. If the hypotheses proposed here turn out to be empirically correct, then we will have a strong argument in favor of complex systems science, which draws our attention to potential powerful parallels between different self-organizing systems. On the other hand, if some of these hypotheses turn out to be wrong, we will have evidence in favor of serious limitations on the parallels between various self-organizing systems.

Complex systems science may be out of its infancy, but it is still in its childhood. The hallmark of an adult science is the application of general principles to yield testable hypotheses about specific real-world phenomena. For those of us who wish to aid in the continued maturation of complex systems science, the task at hand is clear.

REFERENCES

Bateson, G. H. (1979). *Mind and nature: A necessary unity*. New York: Dutton.
Bruncks. (1992). Personal communication.
Chaitin, G. (1987). *Algorithmic information theory*. New York: Cambridge University Press.

de Boer, R. (1992, August). Lecture at workshop on mathematical immunology, MSRI, Berkeley, CA.

de Boer, R., & Perelson, A. (1991). Size and connectivity as emergent properties of a developing network. *Journal of Theoretical Biology, 149*, 334–365.

Deutsch, D. (1985). Quantum theory, the Church-Turing principle and the universal quantum computer. *Proceedings of the Royal Society, London Series A , 400*, 97–117.

Devaney, R. (1988). *Chaotic dynamical systems.* New York: Addison-Wesley.

Forssberg, H. (1985). Ontogeny of human locomotor control. *Experimental Brain Research, 57*, 480–493.

Goertzel, B. (1993a). *The evolving mind.* New York: Gordon & Breach.

Goertzel, B. (1993b). *Chaotic logic: Language, thought and reality from the point of view of complex systems science.* Unpublished manuscript.

Goertzel, B. (1993c). *The structure of intelligence.* New York: Springer-Verlag.

Goertzel, B., & Ananda, M. (in press). Simulated annealing on uncorrelated energy landscapes. *Journal of Mathematics and Mathematical Sciences.*

Hagen, M., Macken, C., & Perelson, A. (1991). *Evolutionary walks on rugged landscapes.* Unpublished manuscript.

Marks, T. (1992, August). *Chaos and impulsivity.* Paper presented at the Second Annual Conference of the Society for Chaos Theory in Psychology, Washington, DC.

McGraw, M. B. (1945). *The neuromuscular maturation of the human infant.* New York: Columbia University Press.

Piaget, J. (1970). *The child's conception of movement and speed.* London: Routledge & Keegan Paul.

Prigogine, I., & Stengers, I. (1984). *Order out of chaos.* New York: Bantam Books.

Rosenfeld, I. (1988). *The invention of memory.* New York: Basic Books.

Schwalbe, M. L. (1991). The autogenesis of the self. *Journal for the Theory of Social Behavior, 21*, 269–295.

Stewart, J. (1992, August). Lecture presented at the Workshop on Mathematical Immunology, MSRI, Berkeley, CA, August 1992.

Stewart, J., & Varela, F. (1991). Morphogenetics in shape space. *Journal of Theoretical Biology, 153*, 78–86.

Thelen, E., & Ulrich, B. D. (1991). Hidden skills: A dynamic systems analysis of treadmill stepping during the first year. *Monographs of the Society for Research in Child Development, 56* (1, Serial No. 223).

13

Freedom in Chaos Theory: A Case for Choice in a Universe without a Bottom Line

Frank Mosca

This discussion will focus on the age-old question of human freedom and whether that question has, from the perspective of chaos theory, become clarified in the direction of the affirmation of the reality of choice or whether while speaking the language of indeterminacy, uncertainty, and spontaneity some are using their high tech, mathematically driven models to capture and reduce these newly discovered exotic cosmic and microcosmic rhythms and resonances and place them in a variety of deterministic cages, all to be sure, for the betterment of humankind.

My view of the universe is that it is entropic, in the sense of dissipation, diffusion, and all the whirling processes that create the divide of irreversibility; but at the same time it is informationally negentropic, that is, that all around—us and principally, as a microcosm of all, in ourselves—is unfolding in ever-burgeoning orders of greater complexity a process that is made optimal in us through the exercise of freedom. We as tiny self-reflective mirrors of that universal permanent turbulence are the very essence of uncertainty itself. Therein do I align myself with those like Fyodor Dostoevsky and with the wonderful tightrope walk that is life, with all its manifold variations that can never, like the universe itself, be encaged in mathematical formulae or therapeutic techniques; that nature is an asymptotic reality, the ultimate variable that will remain variable no matter what.

My own background combines years of work as a professor in philosophy, Russian literature, and linguistics with decades as a therapist. For me therapy is an art in the sense that Martin Buber (1970) describes art as a meeting, a fortuitous, unpredictable, sometimes ineffable resonance between two entities capable of such an encounter. Indeed, it is the philosophy of "in-betweenness" that I have, I think, been the first to coin to describe how creative life issues forth from the cracks and crevices, the fractional margins as it were, of our linear, explicate order to invite us to venture to far-from-equilibrium states with ourselves, with others. To the degree that we nonjudgmentally choose truth and happiness, to that degree do we acquire the maximum amount of openness to the chaotic matrix that echoes in the poetic cry of another adept of chaos, Friedrich Nietzsche: "Yea verily, I say unto you: A man must have chaos yet within him to birth a dancing star."

What I propose to present is a therapeutic model of chaos, or the near to chaos condition known as complexity, as the omnipresent zone of potential transition and transformation that invites people to embrace indeterminacy as the paradoxical means of achieving the greatest possible certainty and clarity of mind. I will be identifying the process in myth, literature, language, and clinical vignettes. First I look at freedom as the ground of being; then at certainty and uncertainty; next at dialogue, play, language, and memory, and finally the relevance to helping others through chaos, under the headings of information, in-betweenness.

FREEDOM AS THE GROUND OF BEING

I begin with a quote from a little-known Russian philosopher and connoisseur of creative chaos, Nicholas Berdyaev, as he reviews the impact of the thought and work of Dostoevsky:

> Man came forth out of freedom and issues into freedom. Freedom is a primordial source and condition of existence, and characteristically, I have put Freedom, rather than Being at the basis of my philosophy. . . . The mystery of the world abides in freedom. . . . Freedom is at the beginning and at the end. . . . Men, as Dostoevsky has shown with such amazing power often renounce freedom to ease their lot. (Berdyaev, 1951, pp. 46, 47, 24).

I assert that choice, will, truth, and happiness are coextensive when they are phase locked, that is when they are superposed in the service of implicate order creativity. It is my thesis that this occurs in the commonplace motion of everyday life when we choose to be happy, that is, to be consonant with the basic chirality or spin of the universe that I posit as the "will to happiness," which is the ultimate strange attractor in human experience. This derives from the primal in-betweenness of reality that implies asymmetries, discontinuances, and therefore, strangely, hope. Hope is the understanding that since flux underlies all that is, nothing is unchangeable or fixed. The universe in its unfolding will never stop at any one informational level. Complexity is the product of the creative accumulation and structuring of information. It warrants that this moment's vision never has to be an icon, around which a stagnant pool of linear invariance is formed. Happiness is the potential to be totally consonant with what is as it unfolds. It implies the nonjudgmental transcendence of the linear blandishments of point, limit cycle, or carefully tesselated tori attractors. It is allowing oneself to choose to go with the ontogenetic or intuitive drift of the aforementioned "vacuum" of the missing information described in Gödel's incompleteness theorem.

That missing information in the unpredictable interstices of any apparently stable, logical system draws us, to the degree we allow it, to fill in the blanks of the universe as it unfolds with us and through us. Each one of us creates the universe in a real sense, since no other knows reality in precisely the way that we do; thus our creative weaving of ourselves and all the projects of self out of our loving, family, art, and work are woven into the larger fabric—even design, if understood as an unfolding without limits or prediction—of the universe. Living and choosing is an aesthetic process; so a beautiful life is a truthful life lived out of one's happiness, one's open-ended consonance with the implicate order's subtle promptings, as we come to know it. Thus, as I have said, we graph our existence from point to point in our own strange attractor sequence, randomly, unpredictably, but always uniquely and unmistakeably us.

CERTAINTY AND UNCERTAINTY: STABILITY AND CHANGE

If, as I have posited, freedom, choice, and happiness are the strange attractors I have described, then what about the counter arguments against freedom. Freedom has been seen through the ages as the enemy of human security, as the random variable that spoils all the hopes and schemes of those who would want utopian invariance, many times in order to stem what is perceived as the inevitable destructiveness of choice.

What has defined tragedy is precisely the conflict between the demands of a culture-bound explicate order with its security operations creating myths to bind and limit, through the entropic internal programming of the cultural logic envelope, and the Promethean assertions of freely choosing entities who either transcend the entropy of culture, or become a minion of its apriorisms. In his endless perspicacity Shakespeare puts forth these words through one of his characters: That one should look not to the stars for causes of our unfolding, but to ourselves. Even more telling is the response of Hamlet, coming from his own affirmation of limitation and unhappiness to be sure: "For there is nothing either good or bad, but thinking makes it so" (1936, p. 1162). The line of demarcation between the old order of culture-bound security and the new order of open ended self-determining, self-organizing autonomy marks an end to the mythologies that subordinate the individual to the community as Joseph Campbell notes: "People have begun to take the existence of their supporting social orders for granted, and instead of aiming to defend and maintain the integrity of the community have begun to place at the center of concern the development and protection of the individual—the individual, moreover not as an organ of the state, but as an end and entity in himself" (1972, p. 22).

Freedom was tolerated with a knowing smile as at best a localized illusion that evaporated in the ineluctable glare of the perfect symmetries of the trajectories wrought by gravity. It is to literature, then, that we must look for the preservation of the intuitions of nonlinearity, in an historical context. Shakespeare might seem an unlikely point of departure simply because we know how his age required, like that of Sophocles, obeisance to the primacy of hierarchy and static order. Yet is it not true that Shakespeare's worst villains, though dutifully coming to their doom as prescribed by the rules of hierarchy and precedent, were covert strange attractors in that their greatest appeal was in their use of chaos, however unsuccessful that might have turned out to be. And is not the arch anarchist Jack Cade of Henry VI, that representative of all that hierarchy fears the most, the bearer of perhaps the most telling statement when he responds to his aide's observation about the king's forces advancing on them:

DICK: They are all in order and march toward us.
CADE: But then are we in order when we are most out of order.
                              (Shakespeare, Henry VI, Part 2, Act IV, Scene 2)

Dostoevsky (1962), possessed of a keen interest in science, particularly psychology, probed the issues from the sidelines, as it were, even as disturbing anomalies were building in the nineteenth-century nonlinear discoveries in thermodynamics and the contrasting view of light as a wave or a particle. What he saw were two equally limiting visions of reality burgeoning into the state space of the twilight of the old order of religion, hierarchy, and monarchy. They were twin attractors, sometimes fixed point, sometimes cyclic, but always predictable. The one was the rise of the bourgeoisie, the middle class, a wave of cultural instantiation that desired the certainty of nonreflectivity about the meaning of life. Life was to have no sharp edges, no awe, no real subtlety, no essential creativity. All of that was inimical to the heavily enmeshed, superficially concerned attitudinal set that was involved only in narcissistic pursuits following the attractors of money, success (not too much of that), and ego massaging. The Russian word *meschanstvo* or *poshlost*, describes this phenomenon of linear aimlessness without depth or intensity. This in turn spawned the notion of the superfluous person, or *lishny chelovek*, a person addicted to the meretricious flow of the explicate order, willingly allowing himself or herself to be orchestrated by the pseudo-serious, pseudo-playful kitsch of fashions and *mitwelt* pressures.

Equally illusory in Dostoevsky's view was the rising tide of radical revolutionaries, who were quite certain about everything and fueled their certainties with hatreds, class jealousies, and ultimately violence. This Scylla and Charybdis of mediocrity created a phase portrait, a "material frame" to use Bohm's (1982) term, that was information poor and was designed culturally to maintain that informational impoverishment as the linchpin of the structure's stability. These were intransitive systems, nongenerative, precisely because of their rootedness in mythologies of certainty, whether it be the shallow optimism of the middle class or the furious syllogisms of the revolutionaries.

To counter this he created in his novels, phase portraits of characters with the growing dimensions of strange attractors, that is, they may ultimately be on a trajectory that would live out the predictability of other attractors, but at some point they come into an awareness, often of symmetry-breaking proportions, about life in freedom, allowing the development of their own unique information-rich determinist-but-probabilistic strange attractor to unfold. In the swirling grid of the artistic state space one finds the archetypical Underground Man, so called to bring to mind an insect-like existence of blind determinate quality. This basic character, in his (mainly male) guises traverses the grid with a combination of the assumptions mentioned above, but with an additional destabilizing "butterfly effect" awareness of his own superfluousness in living life out this way. The character in *Notes from Underground* manages to be a strange attractor enough to raise the consciousness of a young prostitute into self-compassion, while he himself remains in endless cyclical oscillation between accepting or rejecting her, or anyone's, love. In the end he proclaims the truth about the fear and stasis that bind the classical world: "Come, try, give any one of us, for instance, a little more independence, untie our hands, widen the spheres of our activity, relax the control and we. . . . Yes, I assure you, . . . we should be begging to be under control again at once" (Dostoevsky, 1960, p. 140).

DIALOGUE, PLAY, LANGUAGE, AND MEMORY

The question arises of how to maintain equanimity in an open-ended state of an increasingly high order of complexity, improbability, and uncertainty. One important component of the answer lies in *play* and *dialogue*. We all recognize the importance of what we call play among children, that is, their ability to utilize their environment with utter delight and infinite plasticity. There is an ongoing "willing suspension of disbelief" that lends itself to creative fantasy with self, as in "imaginary friends" and with others as in games, sports, and so on. Following Jerome Bruner's (1986) views, children can be seen to live in the "narrative mode," an order of experience marked by strange attractor states of fancy, whimsy, and silliness that are then made more intransitive by bifurcation into the "paradigmatic mode" of what we call maturity, so called because of its greater dependence on linear modes of self-referencing. There are reasons given by cultures for this transition, and yet the strange attractor call to become as little children hangs in the air with interrogative resonance.

Hence play and dialogue, where dialogue is understood in its root meaning of *dia*, through, *logos*, the word; so we end up with a process of playing through words, with "logos," of course, being a concept that we know paradoxically goes far beyond words. This is thwarted by cultures that subordinate creative play to external goals. In educative processes, particularly, and almost anything in a given culture can serve that purpose directly or indirectly, setting up unchallengeable authority leads to a fundamental loss of self-confidence, the blockage of free movement which in itself can lead to a subsequent fear of free inquiry, a chronic looking to experts, gurus, and "geniuses" to solve problems whenever a difficulty is encountered. Difficulties are seen as a threat to linear stability, not as a potential for embracing the unknown. According to Bohm and Peat: "Specifically, rigidity in the generative order, to which control through rewards and punishments makes a major contribution, prevents the free play of thought and the free movement of awareness and attention. This leads to false play which ultimately brings about a pervasive destructiveness while at the same time blocking natural creativity of human beings" (1987, p. 234).

Logos, meaning language, is a crucial component in both linear and nonlinear self-systems. We know that limiting information in the service of certainty is to create misinformation. Often this linear mode is seen in advertising or propaganda of many types. The uses of the technological proliferation of information has been employed ideologically to limit information, as Bohm and Peat point out: "Words expressing totality, such as all, always, forever, never and only are the key ingredients of many popular songs, which weave their words together in a context whose meaning is aimed at stirring up all sorts of strong feelings" (1987, p. 218).

The entrainment of logos in the service of linear thinking has been used by charismatic speakers for their own personal ends. One has only to recall Benito Mussolini or Adolph Hitler, their apodictic manner, their absolute certainty. Throughout history the maximalistic cry *"Aut Ceasar, aut nihil"* has fueled the linear drive to power and formed the fabric of linear moral imperatives. Eschatology, that theological science that preceded scientific learning but which combined the elements of the classic frame and of genuine chaos can offer us some insights here, both with respect to language and with respect to the issues of certainty and uncertainty.

Will people change when they learn that their passive yearnings for solutions are but another illusion or false play? In the history of eschatology, this disconfirmation phenomenon is a potential bifurcation point, though many will seek another linear charismatic process, or "cultural logic envelope," as I like to call it, as they live out their lives as passive vessels waiting to be magically filled up with salvation of one kind or another.

We who are clinicians know the effect of the unyielding, inflexible, intransitive form of speech and dialogue that flows from the unhappy people who seek us out for relief. They accuse themselves and others in conditioned, accusatory, imperatives, with pseudo causal attributions to explain their existential plight. It is interesting in examining the syntax of such unhappy talk that inevitably it shifts from the personal, active voice, transitive verb status to either the impersonal construction or to some form of passive voice modality. Here, the joke of the comedian Flip Wilson, "The devil made me do it!" is relevant. It never failed to draw a laugh precisely because it touched a deep intuitive "bone" of understanding about how we create ourselves. The pain or anxiety is an "out there" reality; the depression is a reified entity. One speaks of one's unhappiness much like one talks of being infected by a virus: It just happens to us. That is what we believe, or are beloved of, in Bohm's understanding. And our beliefs are the actual feelings and sentiments we express. There is no artificial separation into cognitive process that then spawns belief; rather, the belief is the wholeness of the thought-feeling complex itself. This periodic attractor of entrapment through speech is illustrated in a clinical vignette in which a family presented itself, in one dimension at least, much like characters in a Chekhov play. Each one was the cause of the other's unhappiness and each believed he or she could not be happy until the other decided to be happy. To encapture the pseudo causal pattern in a kinetic phase portrait, I had them line up in a circle, with each one facing the back of the other person. Then in a continuing round of repetition I had each repeat in sequence, "I cannot be happy until you are happy because you're being unhappy is the cause of my unhappiness." This went on for about five minutes, until one of the sons paused, stepped out of the circle, and said in a smiling but knowing way, "You know, I don't really believe that." The breaking of the symmetry of that pseudo-causal circuit, that periodic attractor in endless repetition, helped the others to begin to move toward that realization as well.

In such speech, then, there is little art because there is a lack of nonlinear flexibility, of play, of subjunctivity that renders life into art and art into life. Such language, interestingly enough, can be part of art when it is organically part of a work of dramatic dialogue, such as a play by Chekhov; but there language, however linear in a character's mouth, serves the nonlinear end of at least a potential, bifurcating catharsis.

Play, in short, brings us to an awareness of life as an aesthetic process, an ongoing praxis of self-creation and ever changing fictional states, a process that proceeds not *krono*tically, but *kairo*tically, with major far-from-equilibrium leaps into ever-burgeoning states of new potentials. *Kairos* is another word in Greek for time, the time of awe-filled in-betweenness and epiphanies of self unfolding. Information leavens this process, and truth is the ultimate quality of information that brings the consonance of the beautiful, of love, into each moment. Bohm and Peat describe dialogue as the "immune system of society" and as a process in which "people . . . face their disagreements without confrontation and be willing to explore points of view to which they do not personally subscribe . . . without evasion or anger" (1987, p. 242).

Futher, beliefs understood in their Old English origins as that which is beloved can stand in the way and so, "the danger in belief should therefore be clear, for when the 'love' for a set of assumptions and their implications is strong, it may lead to playing false in order to defend them" (Bohm & Peat, 1987, p. 264).

So the first order of business, again, is the willing suspension of disbelief in the ability to suspend or change one's beliefs. The reenchantment of nature can only be wrought through free play, to use Prigogine & Stengers's phrase (1984). His emphasis on the "entropy barrier" as the key to the introduction of "irreversibility" and hence the possibility of history is a major concept in chaos theory. Derivative from that, memory holds a special place precisely because time irreversibility gives a meaning to the process of life that it otherwise would not have in the light of the classical dispensation of certainty. What possible difference would one moment have from the next? The determinative quality of each instant would rob history of meaning in the same way that the worker on an assembly line loses awareness of any individual car that comes by. Language assumes a special place as well, as noted in the process of dialogue or playing with words. In a determined order, one word would weigh as well as another, since basically there would be nothing new to say! The order would have said it, all and our voices would be at best mere footnotes to the obvious and the inevitable.

Exactly! But what we have seen is that the child still possesses to a large and still unspoiled degree the flavor of the implicate order with its corresponding greater tolerance of randomness, silliness, free play, and joy. Additionally, just as we create art, so art creates us in a mutual feedback of loving interactivity. Bruner underlines this inimitable value of art as life.

> I have tried to make the case that the function of literature as art is to open us to dilemmas, to the hypothetical, to the range of possible worlds that a text can refer to. I have used the term "to subjunctivize," to render the world less fixed, less banal, more susceptible to recreation. Literature subjunctivizes, makes strange, renders the obvious less so, the unknowable less so as well, matters of value more open to reason and intuition. Literature in this spirit, is an instrument of freedom. (Bruner, 1986)

TIME AND MEMORY

Having said that, let us turn our attention to the issue of the role of memory and time within the purview of our discussion of freedom and consciousness. Again, I refer to literature to illustrate the difference between linear and nonlinear understandings of these themes.

Time in its "kronotic" variant can present a difficulty because the essence of freedom is in discernment, because through discernment comes the knowing that allows the creative intelligence the ability to see the radical "in-betweenness" of things, to unfold the gyres and gimbals of the implicate order. Here is only the unchanging, uniform (even if in a multiform way) silence of Newtonian space, where time has no meaning because whatever evolves is squeezed into insignificance by the determinate weight of certainty. This is truly *krono*tic time in the sense of the total lack of any amplitude in the numbered progression of seconds, minutes, hours, eons; they are all exchangeable, one for the other; no ripples arise on the infinite horizon of the time space continuum because no matter how many details there are in this phase portrait, without the potential for symmetry-breaking innovation, which requires chaos and uncertainty, the picture remains an icon, reflected in the description of a metaphorical library, in a story of Jorge Luis Borges, derivative of the theorems of classical physics: "illuminated, solitary, infinite, perfectly motionless, equipped with precious volumes, useless, incorruptible, secret" (1962, p. 58).

In yet another work by a South American writer, the Peruvian Mario Vargas Llosa, *The Storyteller*, time and memory exhibit a mixture of linear and nonlinear perspectives. The narrator tells a tale of an alienated soul, part native Indian, part

Jewish, born with a prominent blotchy birthmark that distorts his face, making him an anomaly among anomalies. His study of native Amazonian tribes eventually leads to his abandoning his own "tribe" of David and to his acquiring a central role for a still hidden Amazonian tribe, living in the flow of their ancient mythologies about life, the role of the *hablador* or storyteller.

In the tribe's mythology each person is responsible for the maintenance of reality on a cosmic level. Their answer to the orginal chaos that entered when their version of Eden dissolved and death entered the world was as follows: "Start walking. . . . Walk, keep walking. And remember this: The day you stop walking, you will disappear completely. Dragging the sun down with you" (Llosa, 1989, p. 39).

What a fascinating mixture of certainty and uncertainty is therein contained; what an amazing solution to grasp at the kinetic, dynamic, motion of reality and harness it to their sense of choice, of freedom to be able to have an impact, nay, to hold the cosmos in balance by the movement of their bodies. The storyteller's role is to be the memory of the tribe; to communicate in an ongoing way these primal truths about contingency and uncertainty, so that they will indeed remain in motion because stasis is death. Here memory and time are united in a kairotic, not a kronotic, manner. The amplitudes of their collective memory are selective mythological peaks that prophetically outline the potential pitfalls of equilibrium. And though their lives as, in Campbell's (1972) words, "a mythologically instructed people" are limited by the inevitable linearity of any a priori construction of reality, still their inventiveness at connecting their dissipative processes with their own individual and tribal activity far exceeds the passivity and helplessness of much more contemporary myths presently widely in currency.

INFORMATION, IN-BETWEENNESS

There is folk saying that a person with two watches will never know the right time. Perhaps the dividing line between the linear response and the nonlinear response to this folksy dilemma can be described in informational terms. The saying implies that one has too much information; hence the linear thinker would say, Take away one of the watches and the time one has will be the only time there is. A decrease in information is the solution. The chaoticist would say, Give one a truckload of watches and let's see what happens. Perhaps the search for the right time will become so destabilized by one's examination of all the watches that one will attain the far-from-equilibrium conditions necessary to put us in contact with our own strange attractor; thereby one may begin a journey into one's own state space that will graph a design of such unpredictable and endless beauty that one's earlier concerns about approximating the right time will pale into insignificance. In other words, we would continue to enrich, not deplete the informational field.

In therapy, it seems to me, this is of paramount importance. Where is the play in all the dour patterns of pathology? An example comes to mind of my work with a man who was paranoid because of his use of a substance employed to treat the symptoms of Parkinson's disease. This was a brilliant, eccentric scholar who would come in to share the "horrors" of what the voices had told him to do that day. At times they told him to kill everyone in the department or to destroy New York. Often, as you might imagine, he was quite distraught. Part of our interactions revolved around jokes; when the voices permitted, he was an excellent raconteur with a large repertoire of truly funny stories. Now these voices represented a kind of internal committee of grim individuals given to bloody and mirthless imperatives. On one occasion I said to him, "Look, why don't you tell them some jokes?" He first looked at me rather aghast, underlining how irreverent that might be taken to be, much like getting silly in church during a sermon about hellfire and damnation. But with encouragement he undertook to do what I suggested. At first as he would "go inside" in a typical paranoid movement of head and eyes, and returning to say that nothing had changed. I urged him to keep at it. He did. Finally, many minutes later he returned to his "normal" facial set and broke out into a broad puckish grin "You know the one on the very end, well, he just cracked a smile." We collapsed into peals of laughter, and he then understood that there was an in-betweenness even in his psychotic inscape; and so, he became a standup comic for his internal paranoid self, with, I might add, ever-increasing success.

For me, then, the key question in therapy is this: Is the therapy we practice nonlinear in the sense of enriching the information flow, of encouraging the free choice of happiness? More accurately, does it encourage a choice simply to be (since in my view being and happiness, properly understood, are coextensive), thereby, spurring the optimal use of creative intelligence? Or is therapy in the service of some ideological conception, which may have a lot of information but paradoxically be impoverished because that information represents distillates from the explicate order of apriorisms that are a procrustean bed of assumptions, a closed logic envelope subject to the law of the equifinality of systems, not a gridwork of open-ended inquiry about human state space?

Why would one want to encapture human behavior in a net of definitive observations anyway? When I see chaos theory being used to "figure people out" or to discover certain patterns of "pathology," I wonder if in fact a covert attempt is going on to put Humpty Dumpty back together again. Is not pathology, if it has any real meaning at all, the denial of freedom, the personal mythology of unhappiness through self-limitation? When therapists or clinicians of whatever ideological stamp cast out their nets, their gridwork of apriorisms, into the infinite informational ocean, they will indeed "catch" those of us who through our painful assumptions about self and the world are truly suffering, but more importantly those of us who have created a material frame, a form that will lend itself to the characterological features that make up a particular therapist's version of what a fish should look like.

And so we are hauled into the boat and lie breathing heavily on the deck, awaiting the analytic dissections that will perhaps, at least temporarily, assuage our miseries; or as often happens, we will be tossed back into the sea with the admonition that we are living out only the ineluctable misfortunes of causality—genetic, familial, interpersonal, political, environmental and so on, and so on—and in that gridlock of causality we are dependent on something else for our well-being. This may be accompanied by the intake of substances that by their manipulation of our brain chemistry, reinforce that understanding of ourselves as passive structures awaiting the New Jerusalem of technololgical salvation. But, the fisherperson knows the size of the fish he or she wishes to catch and weaves a net to fit that dimension. We can be a fish formed to the size of the net, or we can be like the water that eludes any net's encapturement because we are so information rich that our subtlety drips maddenly through the empty nets, creating confusion and panic in those who have made assumptions about the existence of fish in the first place.

The first loving imperative is to create thyself in freedom, truth, and happiness, and thereby to lend a resonant support to the creation of another through truth in information-rich languaging and mutually enriching superposition or mapping to create a subjunctive context for the implicate order to unfold within us and within those we attempt to help. Finally, then, to take the most ancient symbol of unpredictability, fire, and speak in chorus with the sages of old: truly *ignis mutat res*, fire changes things. We are the fire, the flame that consumes to create and to perpetuate what we create and to know that what we create and cocreate with all others remains with us for all time.

REFERENCES

Berdyaev, N. (1951). *Dream and reality.* (K. Lampert, Trans.). New York: Macmillan.

Bohm, D. (1982). *Wholeness and the implicate order.* New York: Simon & Schuster.

Bohm, D. & Peat, D. (1987). *Science, order and creativity.* New York: Bantam Books.

Borges, J. L. (1962). *Labyrinths.* New York: New Directions.

Bruner, J. (1986). *Actual minds, possible worlds.* New York: Harvard University Press.

Buber, M. (1970). *I and Thou.* New York: Scribner's.

Campbell, J. (1972). *Myths to live by.* New York: Bantam Books.

Dostoevsky, F. (1960). *Notes from underground.* (C. Garnett, Trans.). New York: Dell.

Dostoevsky, F. (1962). *The idiot.* (C. Garnett, Trans.). New York: Dell.

Llosa, M. V. (1989). *The storyteller.* New York: Farrar Straus Giroux.

Prigogine, I., & Stengers, I. (1984). *Order out of chaos.* New York: Bantam Books.

Shakespeare,W. (1936). *The complete works of Shakespeare.* (G. Kittredge, Ed.). New York: Ginn & Co.

Part IV
NEURAL NETS

14

Introduction to Artificial Neural Networks

Paul S. Prueitt, Daniel S. Levine, Samuel J. Leven, Warren W. Tryon, and Frederick David Abraham

Artificial neural networks (ANNs) could be considered a category of dynamics, albeit one of the most well developed mathematically, especially with respect to its relevance for psychology. Part IV of this book presents the nature of the use of ANNs in psychology and explores the closeness of the relationship between dynamics and ANNs, including the use of the dynamical principles of bifurcation, chaos, and self-organization in neural networks and the use of networking within complex dynamical systems. As such, this section attempts to display the maturing state of dynamical neural networking as a modeling strategy for psychology. This chapter reviews some of the basic principles of ANNs assumed in this section.

It is important to take a broad view and to place ANNs within some kind of historical perspective (Levine, 1991). Over the period of five or six decades a few well-defined ANN principles have emerged: (1) associative learning, to enable strengthening or weakening of connections between events; (2) lateral inhibition, to enable selection between competing percepts, drives, categorizations, plans, or behaviors; (3) opponent processing, to enable selective enhancement of events that change over time; (4) interlevel resonant feedback, to enable reality testing of tentative classifications; and (5) neuromodulation, to enable contextual refinement of attention (Levine, Parks, & Prueitt, 1993).

ASSOCIATIVE LEARNING

Associative learning strengthens or weakens the connections between representational events. As a dynamic principle, associative learning has a rich heritage. Neurobiological or neurochemical research has suggested improvements to the initial formulation of associative learning. Synaptic plasticity was proposed by Hebb (1949) to explain Pavlovian conditioning data and had even been hinted at much earlier by Freud (1895/1966). Experimental demonstration of synaptic plasticity in a biological nervous system was first provided by Kandel and Tauc (1965), working in the sea slug, Aplysia. The first widely accepted demonstration of plasticity in mammalian synapses was by Bliss and Lomo (1973) in the rabbit hippocampus. More recently, indirect cause has been indicated in the associative mechanisms that enable synaptic plasticity. One such manifestation of indirect cause is seen in allosteric protein dynamics and the role that allosteric protein plays in mediating long term modifications of synaptic connection (Changeux & Dehaene, 1989).

Synaptic plasticity is a neural basis for the psychological idea of associative learning (Aristotle; Estes, 1950; Guthrie, 1935; Hull, 1943; Voeks, 1950). Variations of associative learning with models of neural networks (Levine, 1991, Chaps. 3 & 5) are represented here (Fig. 14.1) by one such model, the outstar (Grossberg, 1968). In the outstar, one node x_i projects to the other nodes $x_2, x_3, \ldots,$ x_n called sinks. There is an input I_1 to x_1 and a pattern (vector) of inputs $I_2, \ldots, I_n$ to the sink nodes. Grossberg's differential equations include connection weights w_{1i} that increase with paired activities of x_1 and x_i. He showed that if the sink inputs are presented often enough and remain in the same proportion, the vector $w_{12}, \ldots, w_{1n}$ of weights converges to the values proportional to the sink inputs, the activities x_i represent short-term memory, whereas the weights w_{1i} represent long-term memory.

LATERAL INHIBITION

Lateral inhibition is in some ways complementary to association and, like it, has been recognized since the last century (Hartline & Ratliff, 1957; von Békésy, 1967). The closeness of its role in models of neural network to physiological evidence has matured considerably (Levine & Leven, 1991). One role is to stabilize network activity. Another is to enable making choices (not always all or none). These choices might, for example, be between input patterns for short-term storage, between categories for classifying an input, or between drives. Hence this principle is also called competition. There are various kinds of competitive networks— recurrent (feedback) versus nonrecurrent (feedforward) and shunting (multiplicative) versus subtractive (Levine, 1991). An example of a shunting recurrent network, typical of many current theories of cortical short-term processing, is shown in Figure 14.2. These systems converge to limits (Cohen & Grossberg, 1983), with the limits interpreted as a transformed and stored pattern.

The expression of lateral inhibition produced by local control centers will pull apart those global-system components that are least strongly connected. If these local units have a self-reinforcement mechanism, and most living systems do, the result is contrast enhancement. A class of models of this type of dynamics are the on-center, off-surround network architectures of the visual system (Hartline & Ratliff, 1957; Grossberg, 1972a, 1972b).

Figure 14.1: Outstar Architecture
(Reprinted and modified by permission of the publisher from Neural population modeling and psychology: A review, by D. S. Levine, *Mathematical Biosciences, 66,* 1–86. © 1983 by Elsevier Science, Inc.)

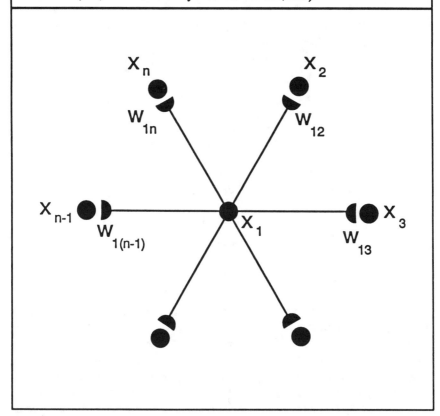

OPPONENT PROCESSING

Grossberg (1972a, 1972b) defined a very important dynamical relationship, the *gated dipole,* that embodies a principle of opponent processing, already a common idea in psychology. Processes defined by this relationship have the property that attention to or involvement in an activity will enhance activity of the opposite nature following the activity. For example, a warm stimulus may yield a brief sensation of cold (paradoxical cold). One perception of a biological basis for opponent processing involves a transmitter depletion at synapses (Levine & Prueitt, 1989). Opponent processing is also seen in the actions of allosteric receptors found at postsynaptic membranes (Changeux, 1981) and is the basis of what Dehaene and Changeux (1989) have called "episodic memory."

Figure 14.2: Example of a Recurrent Lateral Inhibitory Network
+ = excitation; – = inhibition.
(From Levine, 1991; courtesy Erlbaum.)

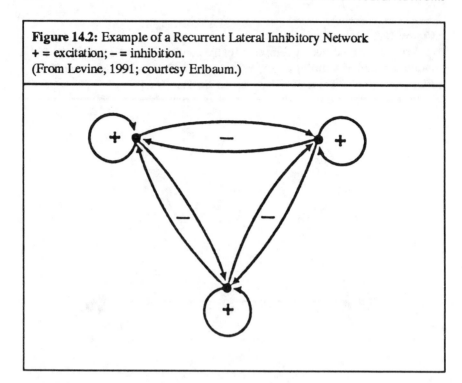

This principle is more controversial than is associative learning or competition, but it is just as important to our models. Hence we describe its instantiation as the gated dipole, introduced by Grossberg (1972a, 1972b). Escape learning can be modeled by such a neural network (Fig. 14.3). Synapses marked by squares may undergo transmitter depletion or attenuation of receptor activity (by downregulation or overcongregation), which may be counteracted by transmitter synthesis or receptor recovery. The input J represents aversive stimulation, for example. I is a nonspecific arousal to both channels, $y_1-x_1-x_3$ and $y_2-x_2-x_4$. While the aversive stimulation is occurring, the left channel receives more input than the right, hence w_1 is more inactivated than w_2. The greater input overcomes the more depleted transmitter, so the left channel activity x_1 exceeds the right channel activity x_2. By competition this leads to activity of the left channel output node x_3. However, just after shock ends, both sides receive equal inputs but the right channel is less inactivated. Hence x_2 now exceeds x_1, leading to activity of the right channel output node x_4. The active output node excites or inhibits x_5, thus enhancing or suppressing some motor or cognitive response.

Figure 14.3: Schematic of Gated Dipole Network
The signs of the outputs from x3 and x4 indicate that the input J is a negative
reinforcer; the signs are reversed if instead J is a positive reinforcer.
(From Levine, 1991; courtesy Erlbaum.)

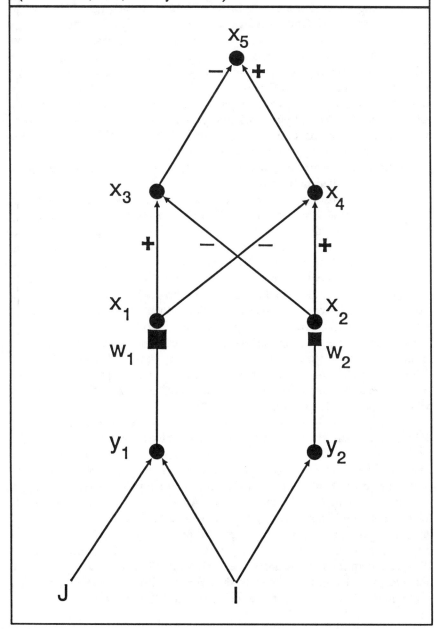

INTERLEVEL RESONANT FEEDBACK

The principle of interlevel resonant feedback has not yet been fully exploited within the artificial intelligence literature. It was developed as part of a larger theory of embedding fields (Carpenter & Grossberg, 1987; Grossberg, 1972a, 1972b, 1976). Many networks for classifying patterns are two-layer and feedforward with feature and category representation layers. This combines associative learning and competition: When an input vector reaches the feature layer, each category node receives a weighted bottom-up signal, and the node receiving the largest signal determines the input's classification. Grossberg (1976) showed that in such a network, a long input sequence might not reach a steady categorization. He achieved stability by adding feedback from the category down to the feature layer, as in the adaptive resonance theory (ART) network (Fig. 14.4). The node for each category stores a prototype pattern that can change with learning. If the node for the winning category perceives the input as different enough from its prototype, a top-down mismatch signal occurs that suppresses bottom-up signals.

Within the neuroscience tradition feedforward processing involves a reentrant loop before a signal is propagated to a new area, as opposed to a simple reflex arc in which nothing is added to be fed forward. This reentrant loop is a mechanism that adjusts local system observables to influences of global observables, and is thereby a feedback mechanism. The notion of reentrant feedforward is quite different from the feedforward network architecture of the early ANNs (Pitts & McCulloch, 1947). In the simplest case, the feedforward networks only distribute information. Reinforcement can be added to this distribution process, but that is an associative learning paradigm, not part of the network feedforward dynamic. Feedforward paradigms have been used in numerous models, perhaps the first being the model of feature detection in the visual cortex by von der Malsburg (1973) and Grossberg (1976). The notion of reentry in Edelman's (1987) work on neuronal group selection brings the network notion of feedback in line with the neuro-psychological literature.

Some of the underlying issues relating the notion of reentrant feedforward and the principle of interlevel resonant feedback are (1) the nature of feedback, (2) the modulation of local dynamics by reentrant loops, (3) multilevel processing within layers partitioned by time scale, and (4) the nature of a level. Each of these issues is strongly nonstationary at transition times and strongly stationary during a processing episode (Prueitt, this volume). Another characteristic of the feed-forward network is that a purely feedforward network is likely to be unstable (Carpenter & Grossberg, 1987). Principles of control theory have lead to advanced theories of mismatch-detecting mechanisms serving as adaptive critics (Werbos, 1974) or pattern classifiers (Carpenter & Grossberg, 1987). It should be clear in the presentation above that the theory of deterministic chaos is the central pivot on which much of the future theoretical development in this area will turn.

Figure 14.4: An Adaptive Resonance Theory (ART) Network
(See Chapter 15, this volume, for an interpretation in the context of learned helplessness.)
(From Carpenter & Grossberg, 1987; courtesy Academic Press.)

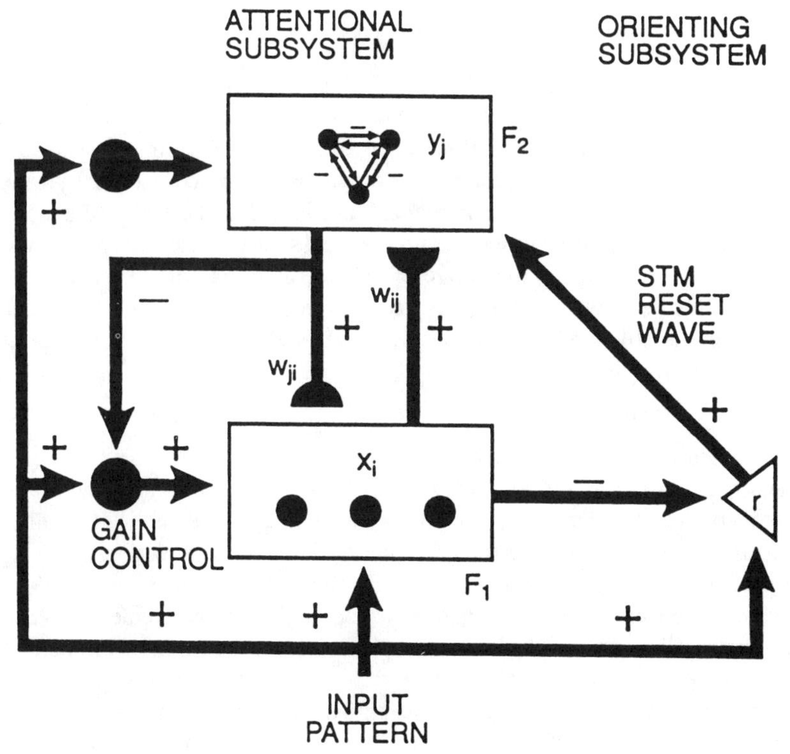

NEUROMODULATION

Neuromodulation of local processing units adds a cognitive dimension. Contextual shifts influence what sensory features or stimuli are attended to by the organism (Rashevsky, 1960; Grossberg 1972a, 1972b). These shifts are probably due to intersystem modulation. Modulation can arise either externally, for example, from changes in reinforcement (field) contingencies, or internally, from changes in drive levels. Both modulation and feedback in complexes of locally defined dynamical systems can lead to deterministic chaos and suggest the natural role that sensitivity to initial condition must play in brain function, including language processing. The term *neuromodulation* derives from "the ability of neurons to alter their electrical properties in response to intracellular biochemical changes resulting from synaptic or hormonal stimulation" (Kaczmarek & Levitan, 1987, p. 3), and from the ability of neural circuits to change their behavior and architecture due to circulating biochemical environmental conditions (Harris-Warrick, Marder, Selverston, & Moulins, 1992).

DYNAMICS AND NEURAL NETS

For both dynamics and neural nets, sets of differential equations represent the basic variables and their interaction over time. The difference historically has been one not of substance but of emphasis and terminology. The nodes of neural nets are the variables of the state space for dynamical systems, and each node and each variable has its tendency to change over time, as represented by a differential equation; the equations are played by vector calculus. The differential equation for any given variable may be a function of itself and/or any other variables in the system/network. Such as

$dx/dt = f(x_1) + f(x_2,x_3...)$

In dynamics those terms of the differential equations that makes the equation a function of other variables, that is, $f(x_2,x_3...)$, are *coupling* terms, and any parameters associated with them are *coupling parameters* which represent the strength of the couplings. In neural networks these features are known as connections and weights, respectively. Complex dynamical systems also use network representations. In dynamics, feedback (self-organization) usually refers to involvement of a *control parameter*. Feedback is when a control parameter is a function of the state of the system or of a component subsystem. Feedback for neural networks, and for general systems theory, may simply refer to the mutual coupling of nodes, which is simply the normal interaction of variables in the dynamical systems approach.

When some of the differential equations are nonlinear, bifurcations and chaos are enabled. This is normal for most systems of any degree of complexity (higher-dimensionality) for a large share of the parameter space. Dynamics has emphasized the graphics of the phase portrait and the response diagram to represent patterns of the behavior of the interacting variables over time, as well as the importance of bifurcations and the parsimony involved in using a single model to explain very different patterns of results. It emphasizes the saltatory, punctuated nature of evolution and development, and it emphasizes the ubiquity of chaos. Neural nets have stressed the nature of very clear models of complex neural, biological, psychological, and social processes, capturing more and more of their real complexity. Their graphic emphasis has been on the network pictures of the basic nature of the model, with numerical computation providing verification of the model without emphasizing the temporal patterns in the data. With dynamics having helped make modeling of neural nets more aware of the power of their models by possessing bifurcational and chaotic properties, the cross-fertilization and convergent evolution of these two approaches will accelerate. The combination of the visualization of both the model and the temporal patterns of data they produce should provide a powerful and unifying language and metamodeling strategy for psychology and, indeed, all sciences of complexity.

REFERENCES

Békésy, G. von. (1967). *Sensory inhibition*. Princeton: Princeton University Press.

Bliss, T. V. P., & Lomo, T. (1973). Long-lasting potentiation of synaptic transmission in the dentate area of the anaesthetized rabbit following stimulation of the perforant path. *Journal of Physiology* (London), *232*, 331–356.

Carpenter, G. A., & Grossberg, S. (1987). A massively parallel architecture for a self-organizing neural pattern recognition machine. *Computer Vision, Graphics, and Image Processing, 37*, 54–115.

Changeux, J.-P. (1981). The acetylcholine receptor: An "allosteric" membrane protein. *Harvey Lectures, 75*, 85–254.

Changeux, J.-P., & Dehaene, S. (1989). Neuronal models of cognitive functions. *Cognition, 3*, 63–109.

Cohen, M. A., & Grossberg, S. (1983). Absolute stability of global pattern formation and parallel memory storage by competitive neural networks. *IEEE Transactions on Systems, Man, and Cybernetics, SMC-13*, 815–826.

Dehaene, S., & Changeux, J.-P. (1989). A simple model of prefrontal cortex function in delayed-response tasks. *Journal of Cognitive Neuroscience, 1*, 244–261.

Edelman, G. M. (1987). *Neural Darwinism*. New York: Basic Books.

Estes, W. K. (1950). Toward a statistical theory of learning. *Psychological Review, 57*, 94–107.

Freud, S. (1895/1966). *Project for a scientific psychology*. London: Hogarth.

Grossberg, S. (1968). A prediction theory for some non-linear functional-differential equations. II. Learning of patterns. *Journal of Mathematical Analysis and Applications, 20*, 490–522.

Grossberg, S. (1972a). A neural theory of punishment and avoidance. I. Qualitative theory. *Mathematical Biosciences, 15*, 39–67.

Grossberg, S. (1972b). A neural theory of punishment and avoidance. II. Quantitative theory. *Mathematical Biosciences, 15*, 253–285.

Grossberg, S. (1976). Adaptive pattern classification and universal recoding, II. Feedback, expectation, olfaction, and illusions. *Biological Cybernetics, 23*, 187–202.

Guthrie, E. R. (1935). *The psychology of learning*. New York: Harper & Row.

Harris-Warrick, R. M., Marder, E., Selverston, A. I., & Moulins, M. (Eds.). (1992). *Dynamic biological networks*. Cambridge: MIT Press.

Hartline, H. K., & Ratliff, F. (1957). Inhibitory interactions of receptor units in the eye of Limulus. *Journal of General Physiology, 40*, 351–376.

Hebb, D. O. (1949). *The organization of behavior*. New York: Wiley.

Hull, C. L. (1943). *Principles of behavior*. Englewood Cliffs: Prentice-Hall.

Kandel, E. R., & Tauc, L. (1965). Heterosynaptic facilitation in neurones of the abdominal ganglion of Aplysia depilans. *Journal of Physiology* (London), *181*, 1–27.

Kaczmarek, L. K., & Levitan, I. B. (1987). *Neuromodulation: The biochemical control of neuronal excitability*. New York: Oxford University Press.

Levine, D. (1989, December). The third wave in neural networks. *AI Expert*, 26–33.

Levine, D. (1991). *Introduction to neural and cognitive modeling*. Hillsdale: Lawrence Erlbaum.

Levine, D., & Leven, S. J. (1991). Inhibition in the nervous system: Models of its roles in choice and context determination. *Neurochemical Research, 16*, 381–395.

Levine, D., Leven, S. J., & Prueitt, P. S. (1992). Integration, disintegration, and the frontal lobes. In D. S. Levine & S. J. Leven (Eds.), *Motivation, emotion, and goal direction in neural networks* (pp. 301–335). Hillsdale: Erlbaum.

Levine, D. S., Parks, R.W., & Prueitt, P.S. (1993). Methodological and theoretical issues in neural network models of frontal cognitive functions. *International Review of Neuroscience, 72*, 209–233.

Levine, D. S., & Prueitt, P. S. (1989). Modeling some effects of frontal lobe damage: novelty and perseveration. *Neural Network, 2*, 103–116.

Pitts, W., & McCulloch, W. S. (1947). How we know universals: the perception of auditory and visual forms. *Bulletin of Mathematical Biophysics, 9*, 127–147.

Rashevsky, N. (1960). *Mathematical biophysics* (Vols. 1 & 2). New York: Dover.

Voeks, V. W. (1950). Formalization and clarification of a theory of learning. *Journal of Psychology, 30*, 341–363.

von der Malsburg, C. (1973). Self-organization of orientation sensitive cells in the striate cortex. *Kybernetik, 14*, 85–100.

Werbos, P. (1974). *Beyond regression: New tools for prediction and analysis in the behavioral sciences*. Unpublished doctoral dissertation, Harvard University.

15

Of Mice and Networks: Connectionist Dynamics of Intention Versus Action

Daniel S. Levine and Samuel J. Leven

The good that I would I do not; but the evil that I would not, that I do.

St. Paul (Romans 7:19)

The best laid schemes of Mice and Men gang aft agley.

Robert Burns, "To a Mouse"

THE ENIGMA OF OPTIMALITY

Poets, clerics, and scientists have often lamented that human will is not synonymous with human action ("The road to Hell is paved with good intentions"). Yet belief in ultimate control of our own destiny ("Where there is a will there is a way") continues to have wide appeal. We take a position that in the short run looks pessimistic. We believe that in every endeavor wrong decisions are often made when right decisions are available. Yet if these patterns are analyzed, normative proposals emerge about how to structure interactions to make constructive decisions more likely. Our quotation from Paul can be paraphrased "If I am now doing evil, I can do good," or "what you get is more than what you see." Hence our conclusions will lead not to despair, but to deeper optimism about human potential. Our optimism is buoyed by advances in two fields, neuroscience and dynamical systems theory, and the interface between them, neural network (connectionist) modeling. These advances enable partial scientific answers to the will and action questions for the first time in recorded human history.

The relationship of neuroscience and neural networks to "will versus action" is the main topic of a book in progress (Levine, 1995). In the space available, we can outline just our neural network methodology and its application to two model systems. The data these systems model are perseverative errors in card sorting and self-reinforcing learned helplessness. Both are examples of dissonance between actual and "optimal" behavior. To understand this dissonance, we must challenge notions of optimality that pervade many disciplines and even popular culture.

Optimality ideas have been central to disciplines ranging from physics to economics (Schoemaker, 1991). Neural network modelers (Klopf, 1972; Werbos, 1974, 1993) have sought to explain behavior broadly as maximizing reward and/or minimizing punishment. These scholars were inspired by the analogy with maximizing revenue and/or minimizing cost in economics; in fact, Rosenstein (1972) treated net biological reinforcement as "net income." They were also inspired by evolutionary theory (cf. Sober, 1988); biologists since Darwin have tended to see prevailing behavior as serving some evolutionary purpose. Yet there is a competing tendency to see rationality as flawed, to see Edgar Allan Poe's imp of the perverse in some of our actions (Stedman & Woodberry, 1894). Using optimality alone, how can we explain addictive gambling, neurotic self-punishment, sexual attraction to criminals, or election of dishonest politicians? Evolution need not imply "progress"; Gould (1980) said that "organisms are integrated systems and adaptive change in one part can lead to nonadaptive modifications of other features" (p. 50).

Schoemaker (1991) asked whether optimality is "(1) an organizing principle of nature, (2) a set of relatively unconnected techniques of science, (3) a normative principle for rational choice and social organization, (4) a metaphysical way of looking at the world, or (5) something else still" (p. 205). Our view is a hybrid of (1) and (3) of Schoemaker's choices (cf. Levine & Elsberry, 1995). Optimality is *an* organizing principle of nature but not *the* organizing principle. A neural system may be optimal in overall organization but suboptimal in parts, or vice versa. The idea that all behavior is in some way optimal (maximizes a "utility function") is now out of fashion in academic psychology. Optimality theory is still the norm in academic economics, however (see Leven & Levine, Chapter 16, this volume), and continues to guide much psychotherapy. For example, therapists often describe inability to discard a destructive or stagnating behavioral pattern as *wanting* to maintain that pattern. We believe this interpretation is both incorrect and insulting (see *Psychotherapy* section below).

Dynamical system thinking leads away from strict optimality theory. If one's thoughts, feelings, beliefs, concepts, memories, decisions, and so on, are viewed as a dynamical system, no two subsystems, even if strongly connected, are likely to have identical states at all times. Hence, the subsystem that intends or wills strongly influences the subsystem that acts, but it may compete with other influences. This is why will is not synonymous with action. To flesh out these system ideas, we now introduce elaborations of the introductory principles of neural networks (Chap. 14, this volume) that seem to underlie both rational and irrational behavior. These are applied to specific model systems, one involving perseveration on a cognitive task and the other involving learned helplessness.

MODEL SYSTEMS

Concept Learning and Perseveration

Wisconsin Card Sorting Task

A common neuropsychological test is the Wisconsin Card Sorting Test (WCST) (Milner, 1964). A sequence of cards is given, each displaying a number, color, and shape (Figure 15.1). The subject must match the card shown to one of four template cards and is told whether the match is right or wrong, no reason given. After ten correct matches in a row based on color, without warning the criterion is switched to shape. Then if ten correct matches are made to shape, the criterion shifts to number, then back to color, and so on. Patients with damage to the dorsolateral frontal cortex can learn the color criterion as fast as normals but tend to perseverate in color choices even after the criterion is changed. By contrast, normals tend to change criteria three or four times over 128 trials.

These results were simulated (Leven & Levine, 1987) using the network of Figure 15.2, which combines the feature and category layers of ART (Carpenter & Grossberg, 1987) with modulation of feature-to-category signals. In our network, nodes in F_1 code features (four numbers, four colors, four shapes). Nodes in F_2

Figure 15.1: Cards Used in the Wisconsin Card Sorting Test
(Reprinted from *Neural Networks*, 2, Levine & Prueitt, Modeling some effects of frontal lobe damage: Novelty and perseveration, 103-116, © 1989, with kind permission from Elsevier Science Ltd, The Boulevard, Langford Lane, Kidlington 0X5 1GB, UK.)

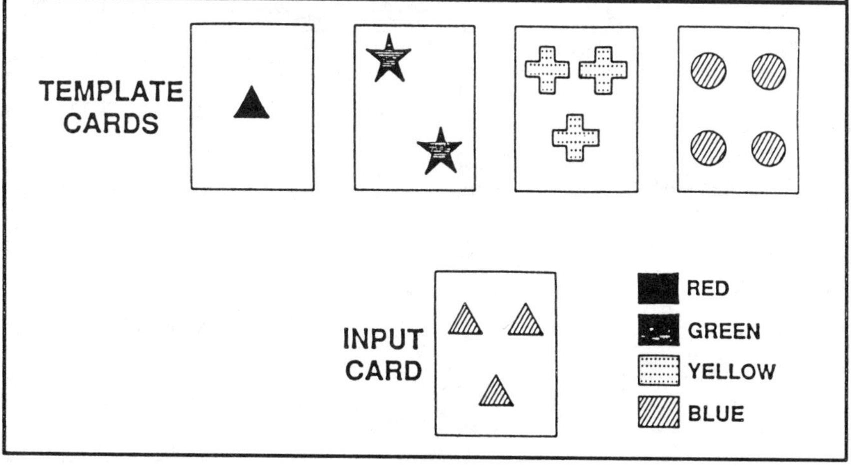

code template cards, each defining a category of cards "similar" to it. For each criterion there is a "habit node" and a "bias node." Habit nodes detect previous choices based on the given criterion. The weights w_{ij} and w_{ji} between F_1 and F_2 are large when node x_i represents a feature present in card j. When a card is input, the match is made to the template card whose activity y_j is largest. If input and template cards share a feature, a match signal is sent to the bias node for that feature; this signal is excitatory or inhibitory depending on the sign of reinforcement. Frontal damage is emulated by reduced reinforcement signals to bias nodes (cf. Fuster, 1989). Bias nodes in turn selectively enhance F_1-to-F_2 signals.

Perseveration is an example of suboptimal behavior. Of course, lesioned people are not likely to act optimally, but we believe that frontally damaged behavior is one end of a behavioral continuum (Figure 15.3). In our model frontal damage is

Figure 15.2: Network Used To Simulate Card Sorting Data
Frontal damage is modeled by reduced gain from the reinforcement node to bias nodes i (i=1 for number, 2 for color, 3 for shape).
(Adapted from Leven & Levine, 1987; © 1987 IEEE.)

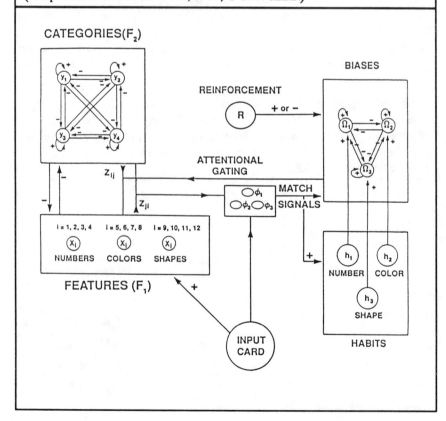

treated as weakening of a connection, not breakage. Hence, optimal cognitive function depends on a certain balance of activities and connection weights in many brain areas. This balance, we believe, is disrupted not only by focal brain damage but by many other effects, such as bad education or entrenched maladaptive social customs.

At the other end of the continuum from frontal damage is *self-actualization* (Maslow, 1968), or functioning at the highest level of conceptual and behavioral synthesis; a tentative theory of frontal lobe involvement in self-actualization appears in Levine, Leven, and Prueitt (1992). In the middle are various forms of stereotyped behavior, or behavior that has become a habit after it ceases to be adaptive, due to positive feedback such as in the network of Figure 15.2. Clearly, perseverative behavior or perseverative ideation constantly occurs in people, and analogs occur in institutions and societies. For example, Harris (1977) discussed societies, such as late pharaonic Egypt, that stagnated in rigid hierarchies because institutions were reinforced by popular beliefs. Ghemawat (1991) discussed corporations, such as International Business Machines (IBM), that failed when they maintained entrenched patterns despite evidence in favor of strategic change. We shall now see that maladaptive habits can sometimes be reinforced even by adaptive behaviors!

Adventitious Reinforcement of "Bad" Habits

We noticed an effect in our simulations of the WCST. The template cards are: one red triangle, two green stars, three yellow crosses, four blue circles. Suppose the test is at a stage when the criterion has just been switched from color to shape, but the subject has not yet learned the shape criterion. During this stage, if a card is shown that matches a template on *both* color and shape—say, four red triangles—and the subject correctly matches the input card to the one-red-triangle template card, both the color and shape habit node activities increase. Hence, color habit unlearning is retarded. This does not appear to be an artifact of our network; clinicians giving the WCST find cards that match on two criteria to make the test harder.

Other analogs of this phenomenon lead to normative clues, for example, in psychotherapy and in public policy. In psychotherapy, most neurotic patterns are perseverated from an earlier time, such as childhood. Yet the pattern usually involves a tendency that covers a wide range of situations; hence, perfectly healthy behavior may happen to fit into that general pattern. For example, suppose one became, as a single person, overly cautious in entering sexual relationships, which led to blocks against creativity in other areas of life. Then suppose one gets into a good marriage, and AIDS is epidemic. Caution in sex outside of marriage is now appropriate for marital stability and the health of the two partners. But on some brain level, the current appropriate behavior reinforces the earlier timidity that suppressed creativity.

Figure 15.3: Continuum of Behavioral Patterns from Frontally Damaged to Self-actualized, with Stereotyped or Entrenched Behavior in Between

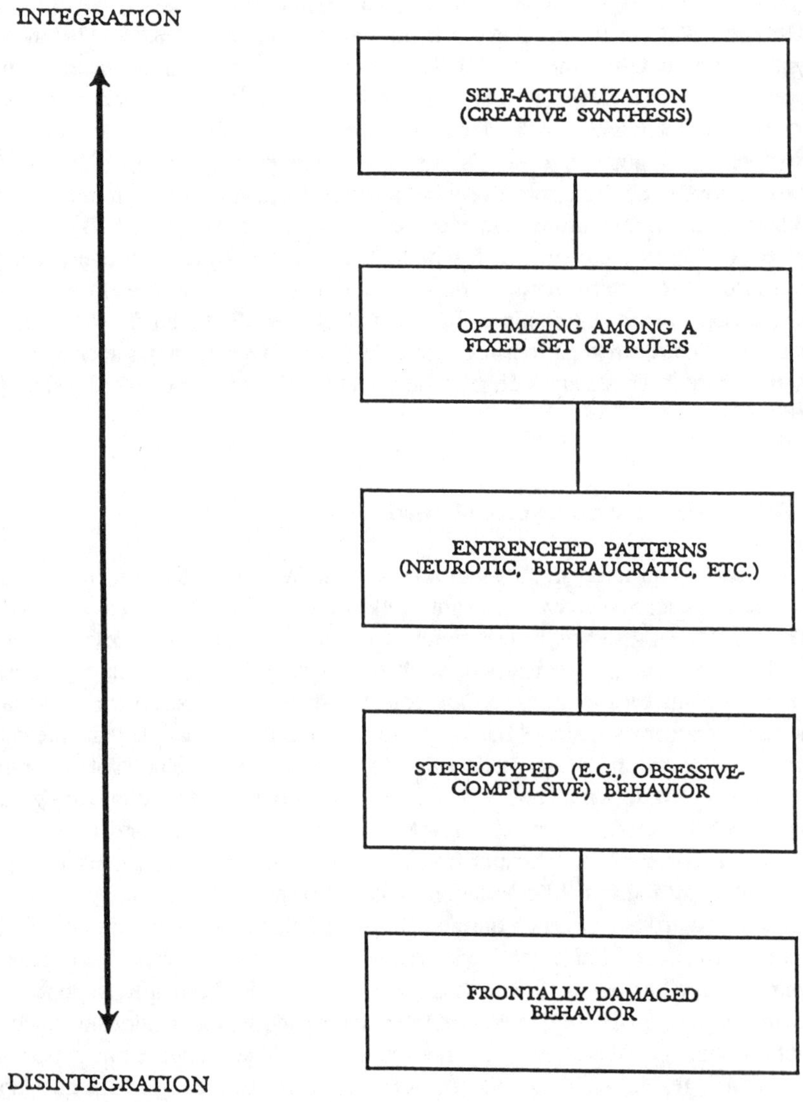

INTEGRATION

SELF-ACTUALIZATION
(CREATIVE SYNTHESIS)

OPTIMIZING AMONG A
FIXED SET OF RULES

ENTRENCHED PATTERNS
(NEUROTIC, BUREAUCRATIC, ETC.)

STEREOTYPED (E.G., OBSESSIVE-
COMPULSIVE) BEHAVIOR

FRONTALLY DAMAGED
BEHAVIOR

DISINTEGRATION

We spoke earlier about the tendency of some therapists to say that the client "wants" to stay neurotic. In our sexual caution example, such a statement is inappropriate because the client's behavior is justified by non-neurotic personal goals. The normative lesson is that there is a world of difference between wanting to do X and wanting to do Y which has consequence X (even if the wanter *knows* it has consequence X), and that one should honor this difference to enhance the client's self-respect.

An example from public policy concerns the Boston school busing crisis of the mid-1970s. The city was segregated by race and ethnicity. Hence, Boston Irish-Americans, like most white Americans, had some degree of racism. Then a judge imposed a busing plan requiring white children from many ethnic enclaves to travel to currently segregated schools in black neighborhoods. Most Boston Irish objected to busing for appropriate reasons: they did not want their children to travel far from home, nor to attend schools in unsafe areas. When the media and academicians accused them of racism, the Irish denied any anti-black sentiment. As accusations persisted, however, they became publicly hostile to blacks.

The stands taken by the Boston Irish, some of them as poor as the blacks, led many liberals to write off an entire group of people as racist. Here, as elsewhere in the country, these liberals lost many potential allies, which was one of the main causes of the Democratic Party's decline in the 1980s (cf. Dionne, 1991). The normative lesson is that it would have been wiser to empathize with the motivations of the Irish that were based on community and family pride.

Learned Helplessness

The Basic Nature of Learned Helplessness

Learned helplessness occurs in humans and animals; in the latter, it is the most widely accepted animal analog of depression. Seligman (1975), for example, noted that rats who had no control over shock they received showed characteristic autonomic responses, such as freezing. On later trials when the rats did have control, they were less able than normal rats to make successful escape responses. These same rats had, at times, other pathologies: depressed ability to learn unrelated tasks; indifference to novelty; low arousability; low sociability; and reduced motivation to solve problems.

There are at least three separate qualitative theories of learned helplessness. We shall outline these three theories, which stress emotional, cognitive, and automatic aspects respectively. Then we shall show that a neural network theory introduced in Leven (1992) might bridge these three accounts.

Seligman (1975) said: "When organisms experience events . . . in which the probability of the outcome is the same whether or not the response of interest occurs, learning takes place. Behaviorally, this will tend to diminish [efforts] to control the outcome; cognitively, it will produce a belief in the inefficiency of responding . . . ; and emotionally, when the outcome is traumatic, it will produce . . . depression" (pp. 46-47). We call this theory *Seligman One*, since Seligman later changed his emphasis to a different theory that we call *Seligman Two* (Miller & Seligman, 1982): "People who attribute the causes of their helplessness to *stable* factors expect to be helpless whenever the original situation recurs. . . . People who attribute the causes of their helplessness to *global* factors expect to be helpless even when the situation changes. . . . People who make *internal* attributions . . . exhibit low self-esteem" (p. 152). Depression involves making internal, stable, global attributions for failure, and external, unstable, specific attributions for success. A third view of helplessness is that of Weiss, who maintains that *anxiety* and *stress* in helpless situations induce depression. In this model (Glazer & Weiss, 1976), a struggle occurs between motivation to escape and frustration from seeking to master the unsolvable. The result is stress, thence deficits in motor activity, appetitive behavior, grooming, and sleep.

Seligman One is affective, Seligman Two cognitive, and Weiss visceral (autonomic). These three models lead to different physiological emphases. However, some agreements among the models are clear. All three acknowledge the role of stress, require helplessness to be perceived and frustration suffered, and accept the result to be depressed affect. These agreements suggest a unitary condition but with different aspects more prominent at different times. The three aspects of helplessness reflect the three parts of the familiar *triune brain* (MacLean, 1980). Triunity informs our network effects, as as we saw earlier with the WCST. The frontal lobes mediate between emotional, cognitive, and visceral subsystems, and in the decision network of Leven and Levine (Chapter 16, this volume), changing emotional and visceral variables alters cognitive categorizations. Let us first pave the way by discussing some of the biochemistry of helplessness.

Henn (1987) found a biochemical basis for Seligman One in mediation of helplessness by a specific anatomical pathway. The locus ceruleus (LC) sends norepinephrine (NE) signals to the hippocampus, which largely through serotonin synapses influences the hypothalamus, septum, and frontal cortex. Henn found that under stress, abnormal NE signals lead to distorted levels of receptors for that transmitter, which in turn produces depression via the endocrine system. Petty (1986) found a basis for Seligman Two in that one antidepressant (desipramine) applied intracranially reversed helplessness only when injected into frontal cortex. It works along the pathway from frontal cortex to hippocampus to septum (the last two areas of the limbic system); the transmitters are serotonin in the cortex, GABA in the hippocampus, and again serotonin in the septum. Finally, a basis for the Weiss theory is the successful treatment of Weiss-helpless rats by dexamethasone suppression. As reviewed by Willner (1985), dexamethasone is an inhibitor of serotonin. This confirms that some forms of depression come from a deficit in that transmitter, for which Hestenes (1992) posited the role of testing tentative classifications.

All these results point to unity of the three types. We now discuss Leven's (1992) "triune" neural network approach to modeling depression. As Leven's network gets elaborated into computer simulations, it will include network roles suggested by Hestenes (1992) for the three monoamine transmitters: for norepinephrine, selective enhancement of novel or significant inputs; for serotonin (5-HT), matching between two patterns; for dopamine, potentiation of reward signals.

A Network Theory of Helplessness

MacLean (1980) said: "There exists . . . a hierarchy of three-brains-in-one, or what I call . . . a triune brain. . . . Each cerebrotype has its own special kind of intelligence, its own special memory, its own sense of time and space" (p. 14). He treated brain evolution as involving an ancient "reptilian" center for instinctive, primary motor, and basic sensory functions; a later "paleomammalian" or "limbic" center for emotion and orientation; and a late "neomammalian" center for planning and memory coordination.

How can we include all this in a network theory? Figure 15.4 shows a possible network basis for the *Weiss* helplessness theory. Reward is mediated by LC's NE and punishment by limbic 5-HT pathways. The network looks like a gated dipole, in which one channel "beats" the other, but now both channels are equally active, leading to "freezing." The choice between J_1 (NE, fight) and J_2 (5-HT, flight) is made at x_5. As NE depletion tends to be faster than that of 5-HT, J_2 should win. This assumption is based on the evolutionary notion that fleeing is usually preferred to fighting. The reuptake rate of NE is lower than that of 5-HT, perhaps for other evolutionary reasons (readiness to fight). However, the J_2 signal is strong enough that despite NE activity and the input J_1, no fight takes place—and no flight either. After a time, NE production at x_2 sinks so low that x_2 can no longer fire. That is the *depressive* outcome of helplessness. This failure leads to reduced choosing of alternatives and worse accuracy of choices.

The results of Petty (1986) suggest adding a "frontal" filtering layer. We introduce a parameter to represent attentional demands, which increase when the environment is more important or stressful; call this parameter *arousal*, A. Another parameter emulates filtering of irrelevant inputs; call it *gain control*, G. The resulting model is much like the ART network of Figure 14.4 in Chapter 14. The input I is perceived at layer F_1. At cortical F_2, an existing category for I is recognized (generating appropriate behavior) or a new category emerges (generating new plans). Mismatch between F_1 and F_2 generates a signal that suppresses the failed match possibility. When G is too low, however, old mismatches continue and correct categorizations fail to emerge. Either problem can stem from inability to maintain stable NE levels under stress.

Figure 15.4: Gated Dipole Model of Helpless "Freezing"
J_1 and J_2 are inputs to opponent channels representing flight and fight respectively. Left channel uses serotonin (5-HT) as a depletable transmitter; right channel, norepinephrine (NE). The greater signal at J_1 than at J_2 balances greater depletion of NE than of 5-HT, causing "deadlock" at x_5 in which neither channel wins.
(Adapted from Grossberg, 1980; © 1980 by the American Psychological Association. Adapted by permission.)

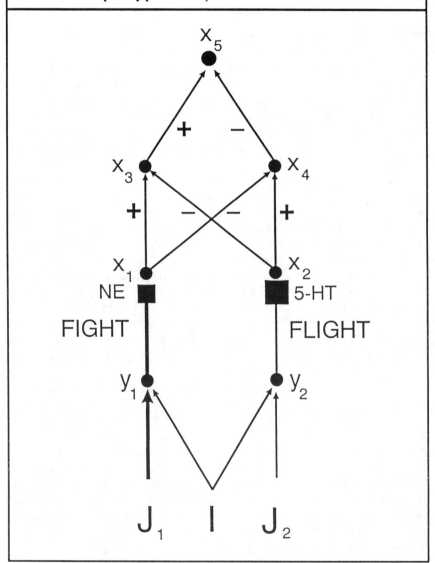

One can combine the models of Figure 15.4 here and Figure 14.4 of Chapter 14 by treating the input stimulus I as part of a system: LC levels may affect hippocampal or forebrain areas. Combining these two networks follows Carpenter and Grossberg's (1987) idea that ART may output to a field of dipoles.

Our network analysis is supported by data from Minor, Dess, and Overmier (1991). In rigorous 3 x 3 tests Minor et al. showed three flavors of helplessness: "This organization suggests a matrix of distress indexes, with cognitive, vegetative, and motor categories crossed with observations from molecular to molar.... Three major systems were distinguished" (p. 127). They also tested 5-HT levels of patients diagnosed as depressed. Patients fell into two groups, one suffering extreme external locus of control, the other feeling sad. The sad-feelers had extreme 5-HT deficiency, whereas the others had none. Both these types of helplessness, and our third, are discussed more fully in Leven (in preparation).

POTENTIAL APPLICATIONS

We have shown examples of irrational behavior and the framework in which they are modeled, a dynamical framework with implications in every discipline. We now discuss two examples in the behavioral sciences. Examples in economic behavior, such as the choice of Old Coke or New Coke, appear in Leven and Levine (Chapter 16, this volume).

Psychotherapy

The suggestions from the section on the *Adventitious Reinforcement of "Bad" Habits* that people don't always do what they "want" to do, and that what you get is more than what you see have implications for how to treat human emotional problems. Broadly, these notions point to the importance of giving clients credit for previous growth, even if that growth is not reflected in current outward behavior. A dynamical systems approach brings within reach a psychotherapy that takes a positive view of people's deep yearnings and treats the "whole person" rather than reacting to current imbalance, the goal set forth by Maslow (1968) but rarely achieved in practice.

Like many economists (see Leven & Levine, Chapter 16, this volume) and academic psychologists, late twentieth-century American therapists often ignore context. They reflect the individualist bias that people *have traits*, that so-and-so tends to be aggressive, courageous, selfish, or overgenerous. By contrast, the discussion earlier (on *Learned Helplessness*) hinted that the brain can simultaneously hold patterns for two or more incompatible traits. These patterns may have been learned at different times and under different conditions, and they may concern unlike matters: The Marine shell-shocked into helplessness in Vietnam may seem normal except when loud noises remind him of his earlier fear. He may suddenly become depressed at Yankee Stadium and not know why. All too often, his therapist does not know why either.

Competing behavioral patterns can both be hard-wired from birth. One theme of Levine (1995) is that every person, starting from childhood, can act in either a cooperative manner or a selfishly destructive manner. Although both patterns are innate, environmental conditions such as family structure, economic status, or job situation, can selectively enhance one or the other pattern. Our multiattribute decision model (Leven & Levine, Chapter 16, this volume) suggests how context can alter which pattern is expressed—whether the patterns are innate, learned, or some of both. One can be drug-free in the country and an addict in the ghetto, or confident while dancing and panicky while doing mathematics (or the reverse). To understand and treat such a system, one must give a person credit for contexts in which he or she is most effective, even if those contexts are currently absent. At stages where self-esteem is low, a client can benefit from accessing a remembered emotional state from a more favorable context. At stages where self-esteem is high but conflicting values are activated by different contexts, the client can benefit from synthesizing emotional states that are already accessible.

The dynamical system nature of the human mind means that there are generic classes of emotional and behavioral problems but no single treatment for all of them. Therapists who hold to one preferred treatment for everyone (cognitive, Freudian, Gestalt, etc.) are analogous to car mechanics who always look for battery trouble. These issues will be discussed more fully in Levine (1995), but we hope we have at least outlined some questions to ask in pursuing a more systematic approach to psychotherapy.

Social Psychology

If dynamical system analysis leads away from thinking that people simply have traits, it should do the same for groups or societies. Hence, the approach that we take can help in combating harmful stereotypes. Contrary to the view that mathematics leads to dehumanization, the mathematics of neural networks can thus be a deeply humanizing and liberating force.

How do incorrect stereotypes arise? Snyder (1983) found that subjects cued to believe that a person is an extrovert asked that person questions phrased to encourage him or her to respond as an extrovert. He concluded that people build hypotheses about others, then engage in "preferential soliciting of behavioral evidence whose presence would tend to confirm" their theories (p. 281).

The behavior of Snyder's subjects is reminiscent of the "frontally damaged" version of the card-sorting network of Figure 15.2. They develop positive feedback between categorizations and perceptions, similar to the feedback between categories and habits on the card-sorting test. Combatting stereotypes depends on study of social dynamical systems, which are in many ways like the neural dynamical systems of individuals. Leven and Elsberry (1990) discuss a network model of American-Arab oil trade; their model includes formation, development, and crumbling of one group's stereotype about the other. Perseverative feedback loops can be broken when a change in need changes the context (see the model of buying Coke in Leven & Levine, Chapter 16, this volume). When white racists and blacks must fight on the same side together in war, the racism diminishes. When male sexists encounter a woman performing a needed job well, the sexism diminishes.

GENERAL CONCLUSIONS

Frontal lobe patients sorting cards, consumers sampling soft drinks, and rats freezing due to inescapable shock may not appear to have much in common. All provide examples, however, of similar interplay between habit, affect, and novelty in nonrational decision making.

Although the examples herein are of suboptimal decisions, some decisions *should* not be made rationally. Often, spontaneous periods and impulsive activities lead to creative ideas that elude more directed search. The alternative to domination by reason need not be "naked ape" enslavement to instincts. Rather, liberation from the confines of strict rationality can free the mind to use a combination of intuition and reason to solve problems in subtle and innovative ways. We share the view of Maslow (1968) that the deepest human desires are for stimulating experiences and cooperation.

Under the laments of Robert Burns and Edgar Allan Poe, and the neural dynamics that explain them, is a message of hope. Modern science can be used to expand human potential and alleviate the part of human suffering caused by faulty decisions (cf. Tuchman, 1984). Progress in neural networks (Levine, 1991) and in other technical areas like PET scanning, multiple electrode recording, EEG analysis, and high-speed computing, tells us these problems are difficult but solvable. Let us strive to be as wise and subtle as nature is.

REFERENCES

Carpenter, G. A., & Grossberg, S. (1987). A massively parallel architecture for a self-organizing neural pattern recognition machine. *Computer Vision, Graphics, and Image Processing, 37,* 54–115.

Dionne, E. J. (1991). *Why Americans hate politics.* New York: Simon & Schuster.

Fuster, J. M. (1989). *The prefrontal cortex.* New York: Raven.

Ghemawat, P. (1991). *Commitment.* New York: Free Press.

Glazer, H. I., & Weiss, J. M. (1976). Long-term and transitory interference effect: An alternative to learned helplessness. *Journal of Experimental Psychology: Animal Behavior Processes, 2,* 191–201.

Gould, S. J. (1980). *The panda's thumb*. New York: W. W. Norton.

Grossberg, S. (1980). How does a brain build a cognitive code? *Psychological Review, 87*, 1–51.

Harris, M. (1977). *Cannibals and kings*. New York: Random House.

Henn, F. (1987). Models of self-helplessness and melancholia in animals. In U. Halbreich (Ed.), *Hormones and depression* (pp. 255–262). New York: Raven.

Hestenes, D. (1992). A neural network theory of manic-depressive illness. In D. S. Levine & S. J. Leven (Eds.), *Motivation, emotion, and goal direction in neural networks* (pp. 209–257). Hillsdale: Erlbaum.

Klopf, A. H. (1972). Brain function and adaptive systems: A heterostatic theory. *Air Force Cambridge Research Laboratories Research Report AFCRL-72-0164*, Bedford, MA.

Leven, S. J. (In preparation). *The neural networks of helplessness: A systems approach.*

Leven, S. J. (1992). Learned helplessness, memory, and the dynamics of hope. In D. S. Levine & S. J. Leven (Eds.), *Motivation, emotion, and goal direction in neural networks* (pp. 259–299). Hillsdale: Erlbaum.

Leven, S. J., & Elsberry, W. R. (1990). Interactions among embedded networks under uncertainty. *IJCNN International Joint Conference on Neural Networks* (Vol. 3, pp. 739–742). San Diego, CA: IEEE.

Leven, S. J., & Levine, D. S. (1987). Effects of reinforcement on knowledge retrieval and evaluation. In M. Caudill & C. Butler (Eds.), *Proceedings of the First International Conference on Neural Networks* (Vol. 2, pp. 269–279). San Diego, CA: IEEE/ICNN.

Levine, D. S. (1991). *Introduction to neural and cognitive modeling*. Hillsdale: Erlbaum.

Levine, D. S. (1995). *Common sense and common nonsense*. New York: Oxford University Press.

Levine, D. S., & Elsberry, W. R. (Eds.). (1995). *Optimality in biological and artificial networks?* Hillsdale: Erlbaum.

Levine, D. S., Leven, S. J., & Prueitt, P. S. (1992). Integration, disintegration, and the frontal lobes. In D. S. Levine & S. J. Leven (Eds.), *Motivation, emotion, and goal direction in neural networks* (pp. 301–335). Hillsdale: Erlbaum.

MacLean, P. D. (1980). Sensory and perceptive functions in emotional functions of the triune brain. In A. Rorty (Ed.), *Explaining emotions* (pp. 9–36). Berkeley: University of California Press.

Maslow, A. H. (1968). *Toward a psychology of being*. New York: Van Nostrand.

Miller, S., & Seligman, M. E. P. (1982). The reformulated model of helplessness and depression: Evidence and theory. In R. Neufeld (Ed.), *Psychological stress and psychopathology* (pp. 149–178). New York: McGraw-Hill.

Milner, B. (1964). Some effects of frontal lobectomy in man. In J. M. Warren & K. Akert (Eds.), *The frontal granular cortex and behavior* (pp. 313–334). New York: McGraw-Hill.

Minor, T. R., Dess, N. K., & Overmier, J. B. (1991). Inverting the traditional view of "learned helplessness." In M. R. Denny (Ed.), *Fear, avoidance, and phobias* (pp. 87–133). Hillsdale: Erlbaum.

Petty, F. (1986). GABA mechanisms in learned helplessness. In G. Bartholini, K. Lloyd, & P. Morselli (Eds.), *GABA and mood disorders* (pp. 61–66). New York: Raven.

Rosenstein, G.-Z. (1972). Doctoral dissertation, Moscow State University. Edited and reprinted in 1991 as a book, *Income and choice in biological systems*. Hillsdale: Erlbaum.

Schoemaker, P. J. H. (1991). The quest for optimality: A positive heuristic of science? *Behavioral and Brain Sciences, 14*, 205–245.

Seligman, M. E. P. (1975). *Helplessness*. New York: W. H. Freeman.

Snyder, M. (1983). Seek and ye shall find: Testing hypotheses about other people. In E. Higgins, C. Herman, & M. Hanna (Eds.), *Social cognition*. Hillsdale: Erlbaum.

Sober, E. (1988). *Reconstructing the past: Parsimony, evolution, and inference*. Cambridge: MIT Press.

Stedman, E. C., & Woodberry, G. E. (Eds.). (1894). *Works of Edgar Allan Poe* (Vol. 2, pp. 37–47). Freeport: Books for Libraries Press.

Tuchman, B. (1984). *The march of folly*. New York: Knopf.

Werbos, P. J. (1974). *Beyond regression: New tools for prediction and analysis in the behavioral sciences*. Unpublished doctoral dissertation, Harvard University.

Werbos, P. J. (1993). The roots of backpropagation: From ordered derivatives to political forecasting. New York: Wiley.

Willner, P. (1985). *Depression: A psychobiological synthesis*. New York: Wiley Interscience.

16

Parts and Wholes: Connectionist Dynamics of Economic Behavior in Context

Samuel J. Leven and Daniel S. Levine

How do you eat an elephant? One bite at a time.

Beverly Johnson, after climbing the rock
face of El Capitan, Yosemite National Park

THE CRISIS IN ECONOMIC THEORY:
PSYCHOLOGISTS TO THE RESCUE?

The notion that human behavior is in some sense optimal, or maximizes a utility function, has gone somewhat out of fashion in academic psychology, as discussed in Chapter 15 of this volume. Yet this notion continues to dominate economic decision theory in the form of what is broadly called subjective expected utility (SEU) theory. Its roots lie in the fact that economists have shared with some psychologists an "imperial" view of mind. This is a view grounded in the following assumptions (Weintraub, 1979):

1. There exist economic agents.
2. Agents have well-defined, preexistent preferences among available current and future outcomes.
3. Agents independently optimize subject to constraints.
4. Choices are made in interrelated markets.
5. Agents have full relevant knowledge.
6. Observable economic outcomes are coordinated, producing equilibrium conditions (fixed-point attractors).

Why these assumptions should have been more tenacious in economics than in other social sciences is clear. Economics is, after all, the science of "dollars and cents," of "hard practicality." But this outlook has been increasingly challenged in recent years from both within and without the field. Arrow (1990), Heiner (1983),

Leven (1987), and others have argued that economic decisions, being a subset of human behavior, are subject to as many nonrational influences as any other kind of behavior. R. Heiner (personal communication) said that although economists are cognizant of emotional attachments, panics, habits, attraction to novelty, and so on, many still believe that one can construct predictive economic models that ignore all those factors. We disagree; continued errors in traditional economic forecasting argue that nonrational "psychological" factors cannot be ignored, indeed should be included at the very foundation of theory in economics as well as in all other social sciences. It was to move toward that goal that Samuel J. Leven founded the *Foundation For a New Social Science* in 1988. We return to this point later when we discuss an example from microeconomics (consumer preferences for soft drinks) and one from macroeconomics (trade relations between the United States and the Organization of Petroleum Exporting Countries (OPEC) in the oil industry).

Profit maximization and cost minimization have a strong influence on economic decisions but cannot fully explain all decisions that are finally made. This is analogous to the general thesis of Levine and Leven (Chapter 15, this volume) that intention has a strong influence on action, but not an all-powerful influence. Of course, intention is a more complex phenomenon than utility maximization and is not solely rational. Nevertheless, the economic example is an object lesson for avoidance of simplistic theories that explain all behavior by a single overarching principle rather than a set of interrelated principles. Regularity and order do not entail exact, minute predictability.

The theory of decision making is now in the midst of a paradigmatic crisis created by its reliance on SEU theory (Edwards, 1992). In this chapter we argue that neural network theory as the quantitative basis for understanding cognitive function in general provides a partial way out of this crisis. We give a detailed neural network model of one instance of consumer decision making (soft drink preferences) and sketch a model of one instance of producer decision making (American-Arab oil trade). The resulting models will turn out to have implications beyond economics itself, in social psychology and psychotherapy, for example. These models assume a familiarity with the general principles of neural nets (Chapter 14, this volume).

OLD AND NEW COKE

When the Coca-Cola Company introduced New Coke, the new flavor had decisively outscored all its competition in blind taste tests. Its popularity seemed to be based on the fact that it was sweeter than Old Coke, as Old Coke had been losing ground among younger buyers because Pepsi was sweeter. Further tests suggested that fewer than 10 percent of the Old Coke-drinking public would object to the new flavor combined with the old name. As most Americans know, the actual market had vastly different results. New Coke was so unpopular that after its introduction, the company had to bring back Old Coke (see Oliver, 1986, for the history).

Coca-Cola had asked people to imagine future states of mind. But the influence of emotional states, which depend heavily on context, means that mental projections of the future may be inaccurate (Holbrook, Moore, Dodgen, & Havlena, 1985). Specifically, in the test situation people based preferences mostly on the direct appeal of taste. In the actual market indirect emotional factors, such as memories associated with the expected taste and its familiarity, became more important than taste itself.

Moreover, the market was different from tests in that *the alternative, of Old Coke, was unavailable.* The public's reaction against buying New Coke can be seen in psychological terms as a *frustrative rebound.* The Coke label created an expectation of a particular taste, and the secure feeling it evoked, which led to cognitive mismatch when the expected security did not occur. This theory is supported by data from Pierce (1987). Pierce studied responses to advertisements of both old and new versions of the drink by people who had been habitual Coke drinkers and by people who had been habitual drinkers of other drinks, such as Pepsi. He found that by a small but statistically significant margin, habitual Coke drinkers were more hostile to products they perceived as New Coke than were non-Coke drinkers.

Frustrative rebound is an example of comparing current with expected or ongoing reinforcement. Just as cessation of a negative reinforcer is positively reinforcing (provides relief), cessation of a positive reinforcer, or its absence when expected, is negatively reinforcing (provides frustration). Both can be modeled using opponent processing in a gated dipole neural network (see chapter 14, this volume). Our network for modeling the Coke data includes many submodules of dipoles denoting sensory features, categories, and drives. Grossberg (1980) extended the dipole idea from the reinforcement domain to the sensory domain, with on and off channels coding presence or absence of specific sensory stimuli; a *dipole field* is a collection of on and off channels for different stimuli. Levine and Prueitt (1989) used a dipole field (Figure 16.1) to simulate hyperattraction to novel objects by monkeys with frontal lobe lesions. In Figure 16.1, two dipole channel pairs are shown, one corresponding to a previously rewarded cue and one to a novel cue. The nodes $x_{1,5}$ and $x_{2,5}$ of the dipoles (and $x_{3,5}$ for a third dipole, not shown) represent competing tendencies to approach the given cues. The cue with the largest $x_{1,5}$ at a given time is approached.

In the network of Figure 16.1, the "on" channel for the novel cue is less depleted of transmitter than the "on" channel for the old cue because the one for the novel cue has not been active as long. Hence, competition among $x_{i,5}$ nodes favors novel cues, all else equal. On the other hand, each $x_{i,5}$ connects with the reward node via synapses that learn which cues have been rewarded. Hence, competition also favors previously rewarded cues, all else being equal. As in our card-sorting model, the winner depends on the gain of signals from the reward locus to sensory loci. If this gain is high, as in a normal monkey, the rewarded cue is favored. If gain is low, as in a frontally damaged monkey, the novel cue is favored.

Figure 16.1: Dipole Field Used To Simulate Novelty Data
Semicircles denote modifiable weights.
(Adapted from *Neural Networks*, 2, Levine & Prueitt, Modeling some effects
of frontal lobe damage: Novelty and perseveration, 103-116, © 1989; with kind
permission from Elsevier Science Ltd, The Boulevard, Langford Lane,
Kidlington OX5 1GB, UK.)

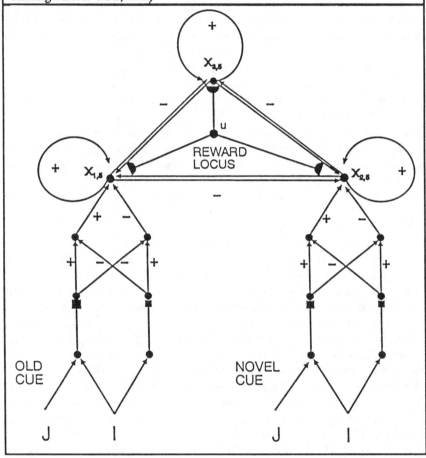

Leven and Levine (1987) noted that the Coke data can be approximated by the
network of Figure 16.1, with New Coke analogized to "novel cue," Old Coke to
"old cue"; testing to "frontally damaged," and market to "normal." Of course, most
people taking the taste test are not frontally damaged. The analogy is plausible,
though, because frontally damaged people tend to be less goal-directed than
normals (Fuster, 1989); hence their day-to-day life is closer to a play than a serious
situation. Karl Pribram (personal communication) notes that nondirected play in

frontally damaged subjects constitutes aimless wandering, whereas in normals it may lead to insight, because normals engage in play partly to break or reformulate existing rules and patterns.

Yet the network of Figure 16.1 is inadequate to model the Coke data for two reasons. First, the market did not pose a choice between New Coke and Old Coke as did tests. Hence, relative affective values attached by buyers to the two drinks must be inferred indirectly from their relative preference for New Coke and for non-Coke drinks. Second, the reaction of consumers to the change in Coke showed they were not making buying decisions on taste alone. Hence, a realistic model of the Coke data requires loci for two competing drives: one for taste, the other for a broad range of feelings that we call security.

Our network replaces the single reward node of Levine and Prueitt (1989) by two entire gated subnetworks of dipoles representing the two drives. We make another change to model the public's reaction, not to a new taste alone, but to a new taste *combined with an old label*. As Pierce (1987) showed, the reaction was stronger in people who attached greater positive affect to the old label. Hence we treat both Old Coke and New Coke not as atomic stimuli but as vectors of attributes, each attribute represented by its own gated dipole (Figure 16.2). The minimal set of attributes needed are Coke label, familiarity, taste, and Pepsi label. The latter is introduced to model the switch in preference from New Coke to non-Coke drinks (lumped together as Pepsi for simplicity) or to no soft drinks when Old Coke was unavailable.

How does this explain Pierce's data? For a network to represent principles of human cognitive functioning, it should also account for individual differences. In the network of Figure 16.2, connection weights between attributional dipoles and motivational dipoles can vary. Suppose the (bidirectional) connection weights between the on side of the Coke label dipole (sensory attributes) and the positive side of the security dipole (motivational loci) are higher in copy 1 of the network than in copy 2, and the corresponding weights to and from the Pepsi label dipole (sensory attributes) are higher in copy 2. Copy 1 can be taken to model the group of habitual Coke drinkers, whereas copy 2 models habitual Pepsi drinkers. (We assume all weights are now fixed but have been learned in the past by an associative learning law.) Because of differences in motivational-to-sensory weights in the two network copies, the expectation of positive affect from seeing the Coke label is greater in the habitual Coke-drinking group. Hence, frustrative rebound upon mismatch with that expectation is also greater among habitual Coke drinkers.

The network of Figure 16.2 also contains two competing motivational dipoles. In Figure 16.1, we treated testing as a low motivation context that disinhibited attraction to novelty. But what really seems to differ between the two contexts is not the *amount* of motivation but, rather, the *focus* of motivation. The Taste attribute plays a larger role in categorizations and decisions during the tests than does the Familiarity attribute, and these roles are reversed during the market.

Figure 16.2: Network Used To Simulate Coke Data
A total of eight gated dipoles are included: four for the attributes of taste, familiarity, Coke label, and Pepsi label; two for the Coke and Pepsi categories; two for the excitement and security drives. Darker lines denote connections with higher weights.

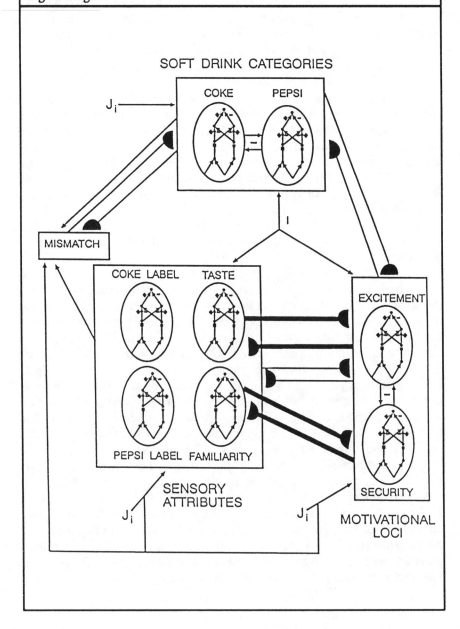

The motivational dipoles in our network are labeled "excitement" and "security." "Excitement" is a shorthand for the desire for experiences that please the traditional five senses; "security," for the desire for experiences that promote a sense of affiliation or rootedness in society or relationships (McClelland, 1961). We assume that drive loci, like the positive sides of the taste and security dipoles in Figure 16.2, compete, the winner changing with context. If connections between the Excitement dipole (motivational locus) and the taste dipole (sensory attribute), and between the security dipole (motivational locus) and the familiarity dipole (sensory attribute), are much stronger than the cross-connections, the current winner of the drive competition determines which sensory attributes receive the network's attention.

Finally, the network includes dipoles representing the Coke and Pepsi *categories*, which are connected to attribute nodes via resonant feedback as in ART (Carpenter & Grossberg, 1987). The habitual Coke drinker's positive affect toward the Coke category as well as toward the attribute of the Coke label enhances the expected positive affect from drinking Coke products and the frustrative rebound that occurs when New Coke mismatches that expectation.

In ART, a sensory attribute vector is compared with stored prototypes for the categories and placed in the same category as a prototype that it matches to within some prescribed amount, called *vigilance*. We suggest that the brain's motivational system uses a dynamically feature-selective vigilance criterion, perhaps involving the amygdala of the limbic system (Pribram, 1991, Chap. 8). This could be done by means of *bias nodes* (Levine & Leven, Chap. 15, this volume). The network of Figure 16.2 does not include bias nodes but simulates their effect as follows. The stored prototype for the Coke category is the sensory attribute vector corresponding to Old Coke. The network multiplies both input and prototype vectors, componentwise, by an attribute weight vector before comparing them. During tests, the familiarity attribute on which these two vectors mismatch has low weight; hence New Coke passes the match test. In the market, familiarity has high weight, so

Table 16.1: Simulation Results from the Network of Figure 16.2
Numbers are obtained from applying the given inputs for a fixed time interval and then adding the outputs x_5 of the positive sides of the motivational excitement and security dipoles.

Input	Old Coke	New Coke	Pepsi
Testing (Cokephile)	4.6601	5.0019	——
Buying (Cokephile)	——	4.6119	6.3006
Buying (Pepsiphile)	——	4.8055	6.3555

mismatch is perceived. The mismatch-orienting signal inhibits activity on the positive side of the category, Coke dipole. This in turn inhibits activity on the positive side of the Security drive dipole, leading to frustrative rebound on the negative side of the security dipole. The results of the simulation using the network model for Coke, shown in Table 16.1 indicate how different the preferences for the New Coke can be depending on the context.

DISCUSSION

This model for preference for Coke, new and old, shows that our approach to cognition and behavior, grounded in neural networks and dynamical systems, is applicable to decision making in an economic context. This is likely to provide some fundamentally new answers in economic decision theory (Edwards, 1992).

The assumption of full knowledge and rationality for economic decision makers, the basis for SEU theory, has been challenged by much recent psychological and economic data. Tversky and Kahneman (e.g., 1974, 1992) have especially been notable in showing that preferences are not linearly related to the expected value, in the mathematical sense, of a measurable monetary gain or loss. Such preferences are particularly sensitive to comparison between expected and actual outcomes. This has been modeled by Tversky and Kahneman (1992) themselves using a nonlinear construct known as prospect theory. However, prospect theory does not seem to us to capture many of the contextual and dynamic influences fundamental to the phenomena being studied. Grossberg and Gutowski (1987) capture much more of these dynamic influences using a variant of the gated dipole neural network discussed in these chapters. Our Coke model is in the spirit of Grossberg and Gutowski's, with the addition of modeling effects of multiple attributes and multiple motivational sources.

The notion of the gated dipole as a method of comparing ongoing with expected outcomes can potentially underlie models of macroeconomic phenomena as well. Blackwood, Elsberry, and Leven (1988) and Leven and Elsberry (1990) constructed an extensive network model that simulates bargaining between two "agents." Each agent's decision making is composed of and affected by affective, automatic/instinctive, and semantic/cognitive components in a manner reminiscent of the triune brain of MacLean (1990). Context sensitivity and affective response in this network are modeled by a variant of adaptive resonance theory. During the negotiation process in this network each agent sets up expectations, based on its own past experience, of the other agent's likely response to its actions; then the other agent's actual responses occur and are compared with expectations via a dipolelike mechanism.

Leven and Elsberry (1990) suggested that their multiagent, multimodule expectation-comparison mechanism could mimic interactions between principals in international trade. The composition of each agent in their network, consisting of three modules with separate functions, emulates some of the processes that affect bargaining responses such as acculturation/socialization, accommodation to environment, and belief engendered by education. An example is the interactions between the United States and Third World oil-producing countries (OPEC). Growing U.S. control of the oil market from the 1920s to 1973 engendered U.S. expectations that Arabs and other OPEC members were less competent and sophisticated than Americans. In 1973 the Arabs reduced the amount of oil available on the world market, inducing panic in the "sophisticated," "competent" nations. The element of surprise in the Arabs' newly asserted control led to a gated dipole effect, amplifying the perceived power of the Arabs and thereby diminishing that of the Americans. In a manner reminiscent of the spreading incompetence in the learned helplessness paradigm (Leven, 1992; Levine & Leven, Chapter 15, this volume), this diminution of U.S. economic power spread from the oil industry to other industries (cf. Carter, 1977).

Now let us return to the version of SEU described by Weintraub (1979), whose assumptions were listed earlier. The Coke model was successful precisely because it violated Weintraub's assumption (2), that agents have preexisting and invariant preferences. Likewise, the OPEC-related model of Leven and Elsberry (1990) was successful because it violated Weintraub's assumptions (3) and (5). Assumption (3), that agents independently optimize subject to objective and easily observable constraints, breaks down because differences in cultural experience and education cause Americans and Arabs, for example, to perceive constraints differently. Assumption (5), that agents always possess full relevant knowledge, breaks down because the negotiation dynamics themselves can increase the knowledge (accurate or false) that each agent has of the other and challenge beliefs previously held by each agent about the other.

Neural network studies such as our Coke and OPEC models point to potential ways out of some paradigmatic crises in economics. Rosenberg (1992) criticized what he called rational choice theory as follows: "The explanatory variables of economic theory ... are not linked to physical mechanisms in a way that will enable us to discover where and how they go wrong. The relationship between beliefs, desires, and behavior just does not permit us to isolate one of these variables from the others" (p. 239). The complex interplay of values, affect, beliefs, and so on, in our models begins to address Rosenberg's criticisms (see also Leven, 1987). Although we have not yet identified measurable physical variables relevant to actual economic behavior, further network studies, informed by psychological and neurobiological data, should facilitate finding these variables in the relatively near future.

Edwards (1992) described a recent academic conference on decision theory and the attitudes of its participants toward SEU theory: "I ... asked for a show of hands on the following question: Do you consider SEU maximization to be the appropriate normative rule for decision making under uncertainty? Every hand went up.... Do you feel that the ... evidence has established ... the assertion that people do not maximize SEU, that is, that SEU maximization is not defensible as a descriptive model of the behavior of unaided decision makers? Again, every hand went up, including my own" (pp. 254–255). Clearly, decision theorists, who come from a mixture of disciplines including economics, business, management theory, and psychology, are hungering for better descriptive theories to supplant SEU (alias rational choice theory or economic man [*sic*] theory). The work discussed herein suggests that neural networks, far from being mere computational devices, can provide the basis for such an improved decision theory.

The work herein, particularly the Coke model, has implications in other fields as well. The ability to map radical differences in preference based on different motivational contexts has implications for psychotherapy and social psychology, which were discussed more fully in the preceding chapter. In fact, as stated there, this approach argues for a more favorable view of human needs and desires along the lines of Maslow (1968). If context can selectively enhance one or another attribute of our behavior, then "what you get is more than what you see": People tend to be far richer and greater in potential than the ways they are acting at any moment. The economic man in which some thinkers take refuge is actually a rather impoverished version of the human spirit, one without frontal lobe function, for example (see Levine, Leven, & Prueitt, 1992, n. 1). Under our apparent perversity is a much more creative and innovative organism. Our goal is to make all the social sciences reflect our real power.

REFERENCES

Arrow, K. J. (1990). Economic theory and the hypothesis of rationality. In J. Atwell, M. Milgate, & P. Newman (Eds.), *The new Palgrave: Utility and probability* (pp. 25–37). New York: W. W. Norton.

Blackwood, D. J., Elsberry, W. R., & Leven, S. J. (1988). Competing neural network models and problem solving. *Neural Networks, 1,* Supplement 1, 10.

Carpenter, G. A., & Grossberg, S. (1987). A massively parallel architecture for a self-organizing neural pattern recognition machine. *Computer Vision, Graphics, and Image Processing, 37,* 54–115.

Carter, J. E. (1977, April 18). Presidential address to the nation on the energy problem.

Edwards, W. (Ed.). (1992). *Utility theories: Measurements and applications.* Dordrecht, Netherlands: Kluwer.

Fuster, J. M. (1989). *The prefrontal cortex.* New York: Raven.

Grossberg, S. (1980). How does a brain build a cognitive code? *Psychological Review, 87,* 1–51.

Grossberg, S., & Gutowski, W. (1987). Neural dynamics of decision making under risk: Affective balance and cognitive-emotional interactions. *Psychological Review, 94,* 300–318.

Heiner, R. (1983). The origin of predictable behavior. *American Economic Review, 73,* 560–585.

Holbrook, M. B., Moore, W. L., Dodgen, G. N., & Havlena, W. J. (1985). Nonisomorphism, shadow features, and imputed preferences. *Marketing Science, 4*, 215–233.

Leven, S. J. (1987). *Choice and neural process*. Unpublished doctoral dissertation, University of Texas at Arlington.

Leven, S. J. (1992). Learned helplessness, memory, and the dynamics of hope. In D. S. Levine & S. J. Leven (Eds.), *Motivation, emotion, and goal direction in neural networks* (pp. 259–299). Hillsdale: Erlbaum.

Leven, S. J., & Elsberry, W. R. (1990). Interactions among embedded networks under uncertainty. *IJCNN International Joint Conference on Neural Networks* (Vol. 3, pp. 739–742). San Diego, CA: IEEE.

Leven, S. J., & Levine, D. S. (1987). Effects of reinforcement on knowledge retrieval and evaluation. In M. Caudill & C. Butler (Eds), *Proceedings of the First International Conference on Neural Networks* (Vol. 2, pp. 269–279). San Diego, CA: IEEE/ICNN.

Levine, D. S., Leven, S. J., & Prueitt, P. S. (1992). Integration, disintegration, and the frontal lobes. In D. S. Levine & S. J. Leven (Eds.), *Motivation, emotion, and goal direction in neural networks* (pp. 301–335). Hillsdale: Erlbaum.

Levine, D. S., & Prueitt, P. S. (1989). Modeling some effects of frontal lobe damage: Novelty and perseveration. *Neural Networks, 2*, 103–116.

MacLean, P. D. (1990). *The triune brain in evolution*. New York: Plenum Press.

Maslow, A. H. (1968). *Toward a psychology of being*. New York: Van Nostrand.

McClelland, D. (1961). *The achieving society*. Princeton: Van Nostrand.

Oliver, T. (1986). *The real Coke, the real story*. New York: Random House.

Pierce, W. D. (1987). Whose Coke is it? Social influence in the marketplace. *Psychological Reports, 60*, 279–286.

Pribram, K. H. (1991). *Brain and perception*. Hillsdale: Erlbaum.

Rosenberg, A. (1992). *Economics—Mathematical politics or science of diminishing returns?* Chicago: University of Chicago Press.

Tversky, A., & Kahneman, D. (1974). Judgment under uncertainty: Heuristics and biases. *Science, 185*, 1124–1131.

Tversky, A., & Kahneman, D. (1992). Advances in prospect theory: Cumulative representation of uncertainty. *Journal of Risk and Uncertainty, 5*, 297–323.

Weintraub, E. (1979). *Microfoundations*. New York: Cambridge University Press.

17

System Need, Chaos, and Choice in Machine Intelligence

Paul S. Prueitt

Chaos theory itself tells us very little about the world we live in unless we understand the nature of transient structures that make a living between chaotic transitions. What appears to be a periodic and radical restructuring of the architecture of biological processors can be understood in the context of multiple and dynamic circuits embedded in a temporally stratified hierarchy, as suggested is a wonderfully perceptive paper by Pattee (1972). In fact, emergent structure at several levels of organization may be used to support cognition.

The notion that cognition requires several levels of process support is advocated by several leading scholars (Pribram, 1991; Hameroff, 1987; Hameroff, Dayhoff, Lahoz-Beltra, Rasmussen, Insinna, & Koruga, 1993). Pribram has hypothesized that the neuron is not the primary computational element of cognitive processing and has advanced the alternative hypothesis that the computational element of human cognition is an emergent field coherence that is physically established in dendrodendritic field interactions. Hameroff's work on intracellular microtubulin dynamics suggest that the dynamics of protein metastable states form the basement level to a computational hierarchy. Structural stability at the level of anatomical features has been conjectured to be the basis for the episodic and prospective features of human cognition (Pennington 1992; Prueitt, 1993).

Emergent structures arising in the region of the prefrontal cortex are conjectured to provide a perceptual organization to internal and external "information" within the context of a present moment. Such structures could well be composed of associations between a small number of dendrodendritic coherent fields as hypothesized by Pribram (e.g., Schempp, 1993). Binding messages from the posterior association cortex and the limbic structures could help shape a dynamic relationship that correlates with cognitively attended perception of the world. The messages themselves could very well take several forms, chemical or electromagnetic, and propagate in several media.

Clearly, maintaining an exact cognitive correspondence to a nonstationary world has some energy cost associated with it, resulting in real-time approximation when forming the perception and in reliance on past perceptions. This chapter addresses how human intelligence might manage this cost and suggest a computational architecture for machine intelligence based on the model of biological intelligence. The most important characteristic of this architecture is its ability to form and dissolve a fixed set of formal invariances by the creation of transient phenomena. During the period of existence, the transient phenomena correlates with episodic phenomena.

A complete description of biologically encoded information will have syntactic, semantic, and pragmatic dimensions. The maintenance of each of these informational dimensions is important when forming a perception of the external world. Syntax will relate primary to the "sign localization" as expressed in an invariant form. Semantics and pragmatics are a little more difficult to understand. A prospective feature, from the interpretation of temporally existing structures, provides for expectation and error correction based on acute measurement and feedback. Thus it is possible that semantics and pragmatics are carried in a distributed fashion.

The prospective feature of cognition and the need to form, and collapse, structural invariances within a stable window suggest that a dynamical continuum is involved. A computational model using a dissipative system is suggested herein. It is reasonable to expect that processing by the emergent invariances of a dissipative system will be sensitive to environmental variables present at the beginning of the window, will be closed to environmental influences during the episode, and will depend indirectly on other processes for the energy that sustains them. Energy flows from other parts of the temporal hierarchy could establish a complex interface with internal emergent structures. Subsystem processes could then create and control within-episode phenomena to reflect a fusion of environmental variables and internal information.

NEXT GENERATION MACHINE INTELLIGENCE

The theory of deterministic chaos is relevant to many areas of research: economics, collaborative-cooperative theory, linguistics, and machine intelligence. The related theory of emergent phenomena has been studied in physics for three decades (Haken, 1977; Nicolis & Prigogine, 1977). These two research areas have produced a basic capability to unwrap the mechanics of complex phenomena, at least approximately, and with this capability comes new technology. One of the critical emerging technologies is human-mediated machine translation (MT) of natural language.

A broad-scope taxonomy summarizing functional capabilities that might be incorporated into MT design is given in Table 17.1. First-generation systems perform well only if addressing a limited set of sentences, having known one-to-one

Table 17.1: Functional Taxonomy of Machine Translation Systems	
Generation	**Functions**
First	sign substitution with dependency on well-formed formulas and linguistic structuralism, mainframe/batch-processing based, limited application to special domains.
Second	script-based reasoning and connectionism, minimal interlingua and knowledge representation, primitive episodic reasoning, workstation and microcomputer based, primitive interfaces, text only.
Third	episodic reasoning, expectation and automated error correction, machine-based representation of structural ambiguity, intercomponent interfaces with response degeneracy, user profiles, hybrid digital/analog computational elements, handheld computational system, speech and text.
Fourth	full conversational capability, biological processing elements, existence of a pragmatic link to the present moment.

correspondences between well-formed morphology, and lexical and grammatical structure in the source language (SL) and the target language (TL). This invariance is expressed in case grammars, syntactically oriented trees, concordant lexical statistical information, and some primitive notions of scripts and frames.

Second-generation machine translation systems can be defined by the MT history. Beginning in the mid-1980s, renewed interest developed in machine-mediated language processing. Much of this interest was embodied in Japan's MT projects. Although far from accomplishing the stated goal of universal translation, these projects opened up new possibilities for building large-scale practical MT projects. Some theoretical work stimulated by this effort links the methods of deterministic chaos, distributed reasoning, and language processing (Tani, 1992).

Episodic reasoning is useful in delineating differences between first- and second-generation MT systems. Event-based reasoning is involved in some of the early systems, but the scope of a representative event was local in nature, was implemented in conditional logic, and employed only a knowledge of language-specific morphology, syntax, and grammar. Semantics is only partially captured through a class of transformational grammars that are said to transfer meaning from SL to TL. Scripts, frames, and explanatory patterns extend this scope but has restricted and often nongeneralizable domain application (Rich & Knight, 1991; Schank, 1986). More general approaches to knowledge-based machine translation (KBMT) is being developed (Nirenburg, Carbonell, Tomita, & Goodman, 1992). Second-generation MT systems are envisioned that will adaptively select domain-specific dictionaries and knowledge-domain models.

It has been conjectured that compositional structure present in human language can be identified by distributed processing (Pollack, 1990; Smolensky, 1990; Chrisman, 1991; Nigrin, 1993; Prueitt, 1993). These structures may be either purely semantic (language independent) or language dependent and may correlate with the deep structures associated with human cognition. Using distributed computation to identify a class of dynamic structures that correlate well with linguistically deep structure will extend the scope of primitive machine-based episodic reasoning as well as provide the computational architecture for adaptive-domain specificity.

Experimental evidence suggests that the prefrontal cortex is functionally involved in a pragmatic selection of cognitive resources (Pennington, 1992; Levine, Parks, & Prueitt, 1993). It should be noted that "system needs, chaos, and choice" are not critical descriptors in defining second-generation MT systems. They are, however, of central importance in describing the episodic reasoning, structural ambiguity, and response degeneracy characteristics of third-generation systems. The Levine-Prueitt model of prefrontal involvement in selective attention begins to develop computational constructs that address system choice issues and, to a lesser extent, system needs. The next step for us is the embedding of this model in a dissipative system that admits to deterministic chaos and thus sets up the systemic requirements for the expression of choice.

LIMITED CAPACITY PROCESSING

A limited capacity processing (LCP) paradigm accounts for behavioral data from the study of frontal lobe mediation of limbic and posteriori association cortex (Levine & Prueitt, 1989; Pennington, 1992; Levine, Parks, & Prueitt, 1993). LCP provides a computational rationale for episodic reasoning because the quantity of information considered relevant at any one moment is greatly reduced. It is likely that subsymbolic selection occurs offline and is then integrated together in the formation of within-episode behavioral rules. Furthermore, the spectrum of substrate events in the human brain indicates that the inherent stratification of support processes is important to overall brain functionality. It is thus conjectured that distributed structures are mediated by centers of control at multiple levels within a temporal hierarchy. This mediation is the basis for distributed episodic reasoning whose potential scope is global and unrestricted by knowledge domain or natural language but produces a sharply focused computational basis for language generation within a specific pragmatic context.

The LCP paradigm addresses a general pragmatic deficit that exists in the approach to second-generation system design seen in Nirenburg et al. (1992). In this design, semantics is carried from an SL text to a TL text in three ways: (1) A transfer of linguistic structure is employed. The specifics of this transfer have been defined by computational linguistics to identify well-formed expressions (wfe) in the TL that serve semantically similar purposes to wfes in the SL. (2) Lexical semantics is used to provide semantic links between SL and TL lexicons. These links can be established based on ad hoc, statistical or distributed judgments. (3) An artificial unambiguous knowledge representation language (interlingua) is used to mediate semantic transfer. In Nirenburg's design, meaning in the SL text is represented unambiguously in interlingua and then meaning is expressed using the lexical units and syntactic constructs of the TL.

The preselection of computational resources is of great importance in keeping the system tuned to the task at hand. This selection must depend on information provided in or with the text to be translated as well as on "learned" machine-based representations of prototypes from past experiences. This implies that interlingua must be a set of constructs and that each of these constructs must be underconstrained. These conditions must allow environmental and auxiliary information to influence linguistic disambiguation during the TL text generation.

Human intervention is anticipated by Nirenburg et al. during disambiguation, and this will require computer interfaces whose actions correlate well with subsymbolic choices that occur in the minds of human translators. Automated choices between lexical units cannot be expected to address inadequacies in deep-structure analysis. In fact, the acceptance of MT by human translators depends on the degree to which MT systems reflect the actual mental processes involved in human translation. For example, disambiguation is in most cases a many-to-one transformation. Thus there is the logical requirement for a one-to-many ambiguation process (this would relate to exploratory behavior in humans). Translation involving deep structure should therefore be seen as the repeated composition of one-to-many-to-one processes, or something slightly more complex. MT with both SL-TL and TL-SL should also have conditional fixed-point computation where translated text can be retranslated to the original language to the same lexical units in the same grammar. The study of iterated translation and fixed points has not been reported in the literature but should give a measure of the completeness of a KBMT system.

Levine and Prueitt (1989) provide a top-down sketch of the relation between frontal and limbic axonal connections and influence. The local nodes, and associations between them, are subject to encoded categorization based on experience and to present-moment environmental variables. Conditioned on architectural, associational, and real-time constraints, the dynamics of emergent dissipative structures in the prefrontal cortex gives rise to temporary memory elements. The Levine-Prueitt network model begins to reflect some qualitative characteristics of emergent behavior, but it has not yet been expressed as a dissipative system.

When the Levine-Prueitt model is unified with the work of Pennington (1992), the result is an LCP model with some degree of biological feasibility. The resulting model implies that dissipative structures far from equilibrium support a multiplexing of information, derived from more posterior associational cortex and limbic regions, within a prefrontally maintained working memory. This multiplexing occurs after a selection of a few (from potential many) processes. The outputs of these selected processes are then fused together into a single limited-capacity processor. Relevance to the real world, in a present moment, is kept tuned through episodic formation and collapse.

The LCP model relies on the selection of substructure computational elements in the formation of an "analog information manifold" stable only within an episode. These informational manifolds support perception and reaction. Perception and action have been expressed in terms of a cooperative ensemble that jointly maintains the dissipative structures through nonconservative induced gradients (Kugler & Turvey, 1987). This ensemble provides a joint representation of the conditions supporting behavioral capacity and the conditions that define an intentional objective. The temporal span of the ensemble is measured by the one dimensional continuum of time, $t \varepsilon [t_0, t_f]$. This representation is degenerate, that is, one to many, inside the cell, $t \varepsilon (t_0, t_f)$, with singularities at each end. The LCP model predicts that the ensembles themselves correspond to basins of attraction that form in the prefrontal cortex due to the action of second-messenger-correlated intersystem binding activity in the limbic system. Similar structures in the limbic system could give rise to cognitive coherence, judgment, and motivation (see Pribram, 1971, 1991).

Neurocircuits composed of neurons and connections between neurons is a simplification of the complete organization of the brain, an organization stratified in spatial and temporal dimensions. This oversimplification, called the *neuronal model*, is criticized by Pribram. In fact, specific synaptic connectivity may change as a function of electrical and/or chemical stimulation, substrate processes, and field dynamics. Substrate processes are, in this case, those processes supporting synaptic connectivity expressing characteristic shifts in stability. Central to the LCP model is the conjecture that the functional stability of cognitive support processes is maintained within a certain stratification level by exploiting the relative stability of slower processes (providing semantics) and the emergent properties of faster processes (providing syntax). The argument for this is still highly conjectural, in light of as-yet-incomplete work on emergent processes going back to the earlier work of Prigogine and Haken. Moreover, the issue of the origin of control has not been settled.

The network principles of competitive selection, cooperative reinforcement, feedback, intrasystem modulation, and opponent processing (per Chap. 14, this volume) are operational in a specific form as long as the functional stability of a level is maintained, that is, as long as symmetry between complementary forces continues to support an episodic structure. Certain cross-scale interaction also conforms to these five principles and thus leads to indirect cause. Mechanisms of indirect cause establish the conditions necessary for the creation and drive of reflex arcs or other output processes of neuronal systems and lead to a holographic view of sensory processing. Indirect causes also lead to a theory of cognitive depth supported by a hierarchy of processes whose "basement" is microtubulin-related processes and/or protein conformation (Hydén, 1970; Hameroff, 1987; Hameroff et al., 1993). In the hierarchical model, an ecological approach is suggested by the creation and maintenance of affordance (Gibson, 1979) during the span of perception/ action cycles (Kugler & Turvey, 1987). Recently Freeman (1990, 1993) has been able to show that sensory input representation does not produce the invariance that has been predicted by classical object-recognition theorists (Marr, 1982). Richmond (1993) has shown the other side of this coin by pointing out that the interpretation of sensory input deeper in the brain also does not produce invariance (Pribram, 1993). These findings are directly related to the discussion above on the absence of structural ambiguity in KBMT architectures suggested by Nirenburg et al. (1992).

The question of representational invariance between perception and stimulus-response still lacks sufficient experimental demonstration (Freeman, personal communication), but support for an ecological approach to theories of computational vision or behavioral theory is strongly suggested. It seems clear from the research data that behavioral consistency observed in stimulus-response studies consist of at least two parts, neither of which has any obvious invariant measurement taken by itself. The analogue to holographic processing is further complicated by the underlying complexity of the biological medium. However, the requirements of a "reference" beam and a structural substrate is unmistakable even if optical holography is not endowed with the nonstationary dynamics required of autonomous models (Beek, Turvey, & Schmidt, 1992).

DISSIPATIVE SYSTEMS AND STRATIFIED PROCESSES

Table 17.1 presented a taxonomy for machine intelligence. The upper tier of that taxonomy relies on a distinction between what can be instantiated in the present moment and what can reasonably be part of the past or the future. The existence of a pragmatic link to the present moment is a property shared with human consciousness. A moment's reflection informs us that the notion of consciousness, at least for mortals, is vacuous except in a present moment. However, the taxonomy suggests not that machines will become conscious but that fourth-generation machine intelligence will share a distinguishing feature with human consciousness.

The present moment has interesting instantiation properties in quantum mechanics (Bohm, 1980). In the many-worlds hypothesis of some quantum mechanical paradigms, the present moment is produced from a set of potential choices in a many-to-one fashion. If an action is initiated at a macrolevel, for example, as a response action to visual stimulus in the receptive cellular layer of the retina, then substrate systems require sufficient time to sort out reactions to the perturbations that have been imposed. It is reasonable that these reactions occur in a substrate where "layered" activity rates are separated by several time scales. In each layer there are emergent phenomena and between layers there are dissipation and escapement flows of energy and information. This implies that some "player" is involved on coordinating the many-to-one collapse of higher-order potentials in present moments. Again, the theory of deterministic chaos provides a framework for the description of this collapse within a global, but temporally stratified, dynamic.

A theoretical framework can be established having a formal link between (1) perception in a nonstationary environment having objects with nonlocalizable semantic entailment and (2) natural systems having multiple levels of organization and a range of genetic information available to its mechanisms of system control. Having nonlocalizable semantic entailment means that context becomes critically important to the choices the systems will make at bifurcation points. In terms generally used in artificial intelligence, the logic of the system is being determined by nonsyntactic constraints. In text retrieval, machine translation, and natural language processing, the context of a symbol can be partially described through the distributed encoding of experience, as in machine learning or memory-based reasoning (Waltz, 1988). Of course, this distributed encoding is necessary but not sufficient to describe natural intelligence.

The prefrontal cortex supports the formation of a working memory that has a future-oriented semantic dimension (Goldman-Rakic & Friedman, 1991; Pennington, 1992) and thus provides essential cues as to how biological systems place experiential stimulus in context to global needs and projects these cues into the future. In machine intelligence the relevant analog is a mission-oriented system that is sensitive to environmental input, including input passing through a human/computer interface and information derived from learning. The filtering of data by current-generation automatic target-recognition systems is not optimal, since the emergent organization of dynamic interactions between environmental variables and internal "genetic" information is lost in precisely those cases where real time stimulus is most interesting.

The nano level (Hameroff, 1987; Hameroff et al., 1993), the neurosystem level (Pribram, 1991; Levine & Prueitt, 1989), and the ecosystem level (Gibson, 1979; Kugler & Turvey, 1987) are places where the linkage between natural systems and machine intelligence can be made. Information is distinguished from data by measuring retrospective and prospective semantic and pragmatic properties. Selective filtering and organization of data into information involves some type of semantic encapsulation, either through generic constraints or through a nonlocal prospective expectation.

To place a little more structure on this speculative discussion, it is useful to give a general mathematical model that will support stratified nonstationary processes. Let H be an operator whose domain set is the formal cross-product of the replacement set for the variables $x = (x_1, x_2, \ldots, x_n[t])$ with the replacement set for the rates of change, dx/dt. $n(t)$ is an integer depending on a specific episode. H will be used to represent a parameter, such as total energy, that is useful in measuring the state of a physical system.

For the simple harmonic oscillator, H is a Hamiltonian and may be written:

$$H(x,dx/dt) = 1/2\, m\, [dx/dt]^2 + 1/2\, k\, x^2. \tag{1}$$

In our model, H is generalized to

$$H(x,dx/dt) = 1/2\, m\, [dx/dt]^2 + V(x), \tag{2}$$

and then to

$$H(x,dx/dt) = 1/2\, m\, [dx/dt]^2 + V(x) + D(dx/dt) + E(x) + I(x) + O(x,dx/dt), \tag{3}$$

where $D(dx/dt)$ is dissipative term under the influence of a slower time scale and $E(x)$ is an escapement term under the influence of a faster time scale. $I(x)$ is environmental input to the observables represented by x. $O(x,dx/dt)$ is a higher-order cross-scale term that exists only during transitions. D and E are regarded as positive and negative energy flows on the manifold

$$H(x,dx/dt) = 1/2\, m\, [dx/dt]^2 + V(x), \tag{4}$$

with $V(x)$ representing the informational manifold produced by learning that partitions the domain set into attractor domains, that is, in a classical connectionist fashion. It is important to restate the assumption that within episodes $V(x)$ is autonomous, whereas at the transitions points, $V(x)$ becomes highly nonautonomous and subject the a renomination of observables. This will generally change the dimension of the measurement vector.

H is a scalar-valued operator whose domain set is the formal cross-product of the replacement set for the variables $x = (x_1, x_2, \ldots, x_n)$ with the replacement set for the variable rates of change dx/dt. The variables are formal constructs that take on the scalar values from naturally arising observables and their rates of motion, which in turn reflect the degrees of freedom of the thermodynamics as represented in Equation 4. The Schrödinger equation also represents such a solution set, which when given an initial condition produces a system trajectory. An analysis of the system's trajectory provides a new observable, the probability that a particle will be at a particular place and time, and thus provides a mathematical theory of expectation that links the mathematics of dissipative systems to quantum mechanics (Yasue, Jibu, & Pribram, 1991; Dawes, 1993).

The formation of episodic boundaries, and even decisive events within these episodic windows, is sensitive to the state of symmetry-forming mechanisms. Sir John Eccles (1993) has pointed out that the geometrical arrangement of synaptic boutons supports a femto-second process controlling the release of the transmitter vesicle mediated by Ca+ influxes. The control is provided by a process evolved to conserve the neurotransmitter but having the effect of creating a homogenous probability distribution measuring the likelihood that any one of six boutons will carry a gradient field interchange between the pre- and postsynaptic process. Eccles sees this mechanism as the interface in which the mind couples to the brain by changing the probability and timing of synaptic events. These events are then seen to play a role in the formation of network connections at a high level of organization. Hameroff (1987; Hameroff et al., 1993) has identified similar symmetry-generating mechanisms in the geometric structures of the microtubulin assembly as well as in the temporal dynamics of microtubulin formation. Microtubulin play important roles in cell mitosis and have the potential to direct the connectivity of neuronal ensembles through the fine alteration of dendritic connections. They also influence second-messenger cascades guiding long-term potentiation.

Underconstrained systems provide the degeneracy needed for an interactive specification of the proper observables that arise as measurements are made by the system (Rosen, 1985). The resulting inferential actions produced by the episodic constraints has a direct analogue to the motion of a trajectory constrained to exist in a "solution set" as defined by a energy manifold and is thus not symbolic in the sense of Fodor and Pylyshyn (1988). However the inferential entailment is quantial in the sense that entropy has been denied locally. From the work of Walter Freeman on olfactory perception and cognition, it may be possible to generalize and conjecture that newly emergent observables alter the topology of a low-dimensional solution set or change the dimension of the state space itself.

SUMMARY

In contradistinction to mechanics, experimental evidence from biology and medicine does not yet support mathematical formalism. This deficit is particularly evident when inquiring about the goal orientation and cognitive mechanisms of the brain or immune systems. The deficit also exists in computational linguistics, particularly when context-free grammars are used without coming to grips with real-time pragmatics. The deterministic models of information processing may unpredictably fail to approximate human cognition.

Language processing by living systems involves a decentralization of the control of a complex system at one time scale and a more localized control originating from transient emergent structures at a slower time scale. Subsystem indeterminism and intersystem modulation provide a basis of behavioral bifurcations in the substrate organization during cognitive activity. Episodic bifurcations are thus implicated in human cognition activity. The forces driving evolution include the struggle of individual life forms to fulfill a spectrum of needs and to more fully exercise choice. As a consequence, mechanisms sensitive to external modulation and to internal, self-organizational modulation of episodic-based structures have developed.

REFERENCES

Beek, P. J., Turvey, M. T., & Schmidt, R. C. (1992). Autonomous and nonautonomous dynamics of coordinated rhythmic movements. *Ecological Psychology, 4*, 65–95.

Bohm, D. (1980). *Wholeness and the implicate order*. London: Routledge & Kegan Paul.

Chrisman, L. (1991). Learning recursive distributed representations for holistic computation. *Connection Science, 3*, 345–366.

Dawes, R. (1993). Advances in the theory of quantum neurodynamics. In K. H. Pribram (Ed.), *Rethinking neural networks: Quantum fields and biological data* (pp. 131–142). Hillsdale: Erlbaum.

Eccles, J. (1993). Keynote address. In K. H. Pribram (Ed.), *Rethinking neural networks: Quantum fields and biological data* (pp. 1–18). Hillsdale: Erlbaum.

Fodor, J. A., & Pylyshyn, Z. W. (1988). Connectionism and cognitive architecture: a critical analysis. In S. Pinker & J. Mehler (Eds.), *Connections and symbols* (pp. 3–71). Cambridge: MIT Press.

Freeman, W. (1990). On the problem of anomalous dispersion in chaoto-chaotic phase transitions of neural masses, and its significance for the management of perceptual information in brains. *Synergetics of cognition*. New York: Springer-Verlag.

Freeman, W. (1993). The emergence of chaotic dynamics as a basis for comprehending intentionality and experimental subjects. In K. H. Pribram (Ed.), *Rethinking neural networks: Quantum fields and biological data* (pp. 467–474). Hillsdale: Erlbaum.

Gibson, J. J. (1979). *The ecological approach to visual perception*. Boston: Houghton Mifflin.

Goldman-Rakic, P. S., & Friedman, H. R. (1991). The circuitry of working memory revealed by anatomy and metabolic imaging. In H. S. Levin, H. M. Eisenberg, & A. L. Benton (Eds.), *Frontal lobe function and dysfunction* (pp. 72–91). New York: Oxford University Press.

Haken, H. (1977). *Synergetics: An introduction*. Heidelberg: Springer-Verlag.

Hameroff, S. R. (1987). *Ultimate computing: Biomolecular consciousness and nanotechnology*. Amsterdam: Elsevier–North Holland.

Hameroff, S. R., Dayhoff, J. E., Lahoz-Beltra, R., Rasmussen, S., Insinna, E. M., & Koruga, D. (1993). Nanoneurology and the cytoskeleton: Quantum signaling and protein conformational dynamics as cognitive substrates. In K. H. Pribram (Ed.), *Rethinking neural networks: Quantum fields and biological data* (pp. 297–360). Hillsdale: Erlbaum.

Hydén, H. (1970). The question of a molecular basis for the memory trace. In K. H. Pribram & D. E. Broadbent (Eds.), *Biology of memory* (pp. 101–119). New York: Academic Press.

Kugler, P. N., & Turvey, M. T. (1987). *Information, natural law and the self-assembly of rhythmic movements*. Hillsdale: Erlbaum.

Levine D. S., Parks, R. W., & Prueitt, P. S. (1993). Methodological and theoretical issues in neural network models of frontal cognitive functions. *International Journal of Neuroscience, 72*, 209–233.

Levine, D. S., & Prueitt, P. S. (1989). Modeling some effects of frontal lobe damage: Novelty and perseveration. *Neural Network, 2*, 103–116.

Marr, D. (1982). *Vision: A computational investigation into the human representation and processing of visual information*. San Francisco: W. H. Freeman.

Nicolis, G., & Prigogine, I. (1977). *Self-organization in nonequilibrium systems*. New York: Wiley.

Nigrin, A. (1993). *Self-organizing neural networks for pattern recognition clustering, segmentation and synonyms*. Cambridge: MIT Press.

Nirenburg, S., Carbonell, J., Tomita, M., & Goodman K. (1992). *Machine translation: A knowledge-based approach*. San Mateo: Kaufmann.

Pattee, H. (1972). The nature of hierarchical controls in living matter. In R. Rosen (Ed.), *Foundations of mathematical biology, Vol.1. Subcellular Systems* (pp. 1–22). New York: Academic Press.

Pennington, B. F. (1992). The working memory function of the prefrontal cortices: Implications for developmental and individual differences in cognition. In M. Haith et al. (Eds.), *Future oriented processes in development*. Chicago: University of Chicago Press.

Pollack, J. B. (1990). Recursive distributed representations. *Artificial Intelligence, 46*, 77–105.

Pribram, K. H. (1971). *Languages of the brain*. Englewood Cliffs: Prentice Hall.

Pribram, K. H. (1991). *Brain and perception: Holonomy and structure in figural processing*. Hillsdale: Erlbaum.

Pribram, K. H. (Ed.). (1993). *Rethinking neural networks: Quantum fields and biological data*. Hillsdale NJ USA: Erlbaum.

Prueitt, P. S. (1993). Network models in behavioral and computational neuroscience. In *Non-animal models in biomedical & psychological research, testing, and education*. New Gloucester: PsyETA.

Rich, E., & Knight, K. (1991). *Artificial intelligence* (2nd ed.). New York: McGraw-Hill.

Richmond, B. (1993). Neuronal encoding of information related to visual perception, memory, and motivation. In K. H. Pribram (Ed.), *Rethinking neural networks: Quantum fields and biological data* (pp. 437–448). Hillsdale: Erlbaum.

Rosen, R. (1985). *Anticipatory systems, philosophical, mathematical and methodological foundations*. New York: Pergamon Press.

Schank, R. C. (1986). *Explanation patterns, understanding mechanically and creatively*. Hillsdale: Erlbaum.

Schempp, W. (1993). Analog VLSI network model: Cortical linking neural net models and quantum holographic neural technology. In K. H. Pribram (Ed.), *Rethinking neural networks: Quantum fields and biological data* (pp. 213–278). Hillsdale: Erlbaum.

Smolensky, P. (1990). Tensor product variable binding and the representation of symbolic structures in connectionist systems. *Artificial Intelligence, 46*, 159–216.

Tani, J. (1992). The role of chaos in processing language. In *International Joint Conference on Neural Networks, 1992* (pp. 444–448). Salem: IEEE.

Waltz, D. (1988). The prospects for building truly intelligent machines. In S. R. Graubard (Ed.), *The artificial intelligence debate*. Cambridge: MIT Press.

Yasue, K., Jibu, M., & Pribram, K. H. (1991). Appendices: A theory of nonlocal cortical processing in the brain. In K. H. Pribram (Ed.), *Brain and perception: Holonomy and structure in figural processing*. Hillsdale: Erlbaum.

18

Synthesizing Psychological Schisms through Connectionism

Warren W. Tryon

Psychology has been divided since its inception by a series of theoretical schisms described by Staats (1983). The purpose of this chapter is to describe how neural networks and the underlying connectionism of parallel distributed processing provide a perspective from which ten important psychological schisms disappear as nonissues. The resulting unification is the consequence of true dialectic synthesis where seemingly contradictory positions are shown to be consistent aspects of a more general perspective.

Evidence of disunity within psychology abounds everywhere (Altman, 1987; Churchland, 1986; Rychlak, 1981; Skinner, 1987; Spence, 1987; Staats, 1983, 1987, 1991; Tulving, 1983). Although the case has been made for the corrosive effects of disunity within psychology (Staats, 1983, 1987, 1991), diversity has some advantages (cf. Altman, 1987). Variation (diversity) and selection ensure that most, if not all, possibilities are explored and compete against one another for publication space and consequently the attention of present and future scientists. Kuhn (1970) correctly observed that theoretical change comes mainly from new scientists and scholars rather than from converts of established investigators.

Preparadigmatic disciplines, as described by Kuhn (1970), are extremely diverse because they agree on practically nothing. They make different assumptions about what questions are important, about what methods to employ, and about what results are persuasive. The opposing positions have so little in common that they do not take their divergent colleagues seriously. When they address their "misguided" peers, it is to criticize the questions they ask, and the methods they use; thus they trivialize their results as either methodologically flawed or conceptually flawed. As much time is spent debating the merits of each other's approach as is devoted to discovering and systematizing new knowledge. In short, too much diversity, like any good thing, has undesirable consequences.

Diversity becomes corrosive when it serves to define schools and paradigms that cannot work constructively together. If two groups disagree on the primary content to be studied, on what constitutes proper modes of inquiry, on what type of evidence is persuasive, then they do not have a basis for mutual discussion. Their differences set the occasion for making pejorative remarks about the content, methods, and findings of each other's discipline. Without critical common elements no constructive collaboration is possible. The resulting competition is corrosive to what might otherwise be positive productive science.

Diversity will remain within the unified position described below but its scope will be reduced by an important common core of shared philosophy and methods to stimulate synergistic science. Investigation of the remaining alternatives will intensify, thereby setting the occasion for accelerated progress. Productive diversity will replace corrosive diversity. The resulting common context will enhance every psychologist's professional identity; whether devoted to research, clinical practice, or both. Applied and basic psychologists will have a renewed interest in each other's writings; a common intellectual nucleus will have formed around which knowledge can be systematized, applied, and refined.

Goldfried (1982), Goldfried and Padawer (1982), Beitman, Goldfried, and Norcross (1989), and Wachtel (1977) review the history of integration in psychotherapy. Although admirable, these efforts have not stemmed the proliferation of psychotherapies. The present proposal calls for fundamental changes having a much greater sphere of impact.

Connectionism describes parallel distributed processing systems of highly interconnected, biologically inspired, homogeneous computing elements. Schneider (1987) has, I believe, correctly predicted that connectionism will largely, if not completely, replace present information processing models of psychology and behavior. Donahoe and Palmer (1989), Lawson and Staver (1989), Levine (1989), McClelland (1988), and Ramsey, Stich, and Rumelhart (1991) plus Schneider (1987) discuss philosophical implications of connectionism but do not address theoretical unification through schism reduction within psychology; that is the focus of this chapter. We begin our discussion by first learning more about connectionism and the neural networks used to implement these ideas.

CONNECTIONISM AND NEURAL NETWORKS

Psychology emphasized the role of learning early on and founded the scientific study of learning on laboratory investigations of animal behavior based on behaviorist theory. Refusal to address proximal causal mechanisms led to the rise of cognitive psychology and the demise of learning as a specific area of inquiry. Information-processing theories of mediating events supported the growth of work in artificial intelligence based on rules and the digital computer with its separate memory and central processing units. Despite much progress, extremely powerful supercomputers are inferior by several orders of magnitude in their computational abilities to perceive and learn compared to a bee. Sejnowski and Churchland (1992) indicate that a honeybee's brain has only about 1 million neurons, whereas the human brain has 100 billion (100 thousand million times as many neurons), yet the bee's brain performs approximately 10,000 billion operations per second whereas the most powerful supercomputer has yet to reach 10 billion operations per second. The key to the bee's ability to perceive, learn, and respond in real time—something present supercomputers cannot come close to doing—is connectionism; that is, parallel distributed processing rather than a central processing unit.

Figure 18.1 illustrates a simple three-layer neural network. The top input layer can represent single sensory neurons or different perceptual attributes. It codes for input characteristics. The lower output layer can represent single motor neurons or response modes. The middle, sometimes called hidden, layer serves as a feature detector and is what enables the neural network to intelligently coordinate inputs (stimuli) and outputs (responses) in ways to be described shortly. The middle layer forms representations. Neural networks can learn anything that they can accurately represent (code).

Figure 18.2 represents one of the middle layers and illustrates the two fundamental properties of each computational element. These elements are

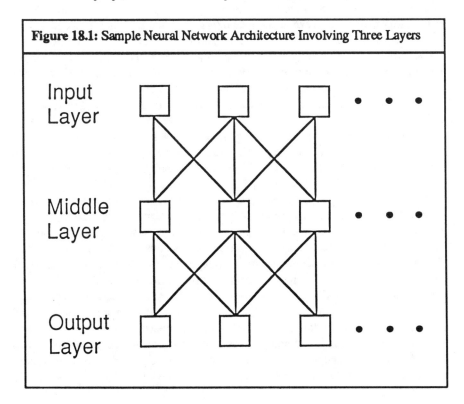

Figure 18.1: Sample Neural Network Architecture Involving Three Layers

Input Layer

Middle Layer

Output Layer

called neurons, and the resulting matrix is called a neural network because of two critical biologically inspired properties that operate similarly across the phylogenetic continuum from elementary animals through humans. The first function is summation. Real neurons have dendrites studded with ion channels. Neurotransmitters selectively open these channels, thereby letting though charged particles, and this constitutes current flow. These effects cumulate across dendrites and determine total current flow, which if large enough causes the neuron to depolarize and transmit a spike down its axon.

A "synaptic weight" is associated with each line connecting the input neurons to mediating neurons and mediating neurons to output neurons. Input summation to a mediating neuron is illustrated in Figure 18.2 and is accomplished by multiplying each incoming (upper) synaptic weight by the status of the neuron from which it came (1=on, 0=off) and summing according to an equation such as is illustrated in the top panel. The theta term added to all summations is a bias term that can be positive, negative, or zero representing the disposition of the neuron to fire (turn on).

The lower panel of Figure 18.2 determines whether the neuron fires. The 0 and 1 states can either represent off and on respectively, or they can represent probability limits governing the likelihood of the neuron firing. In both cases, the neuron will be off given small summation (Sum) values and on given large Sum values. Much of the ability of neural networks to function intelligently is due to the nonlinear nature of this threshold function. If the neuron fires, then the status of the outputs moves from 0 to 1, which means that the associated synaptic weights leading to other neurons will influence the summation processes associated with the neurons to which they are connected. If the neuron fails to fire, then the synaptic weights will be multiplied by 0, causing them to add nothing to the response neurons.

Neurobiological studies of learning indicate that synaptic weights change. Neural networks learn by changing their synaptic weights according to an equation called the learning function. One of the simplest learning functions is named after Donald O. Hebb (1949), a psychologist and pioneer in the field of learning. The Hebbian learning rule is that synaptic weights change only when neurons at both ends of a connecting line fire (are on). In that case, the new synaptic weight joining the two neurons equals the old weight plus the product of the summation calculation, excitation level, of the source neuron times the summation calculation of the destination neuron. One Hebbian variant is to replace the summation multiplications with the outputs of the two neurons. Many learning rules exist, and exploring the consequences of each one constitutes productive diversity among investigators.

Neural networks can learn through supervision or on their own. Supervised learning involves stimulating the input nodes, comparing the output with the desired or target output, and back-propagating the errors, discrepancies between output and desired output. An equation is used to change the synaptic weights connecting the middle to output layers and then to change the synaptic weights

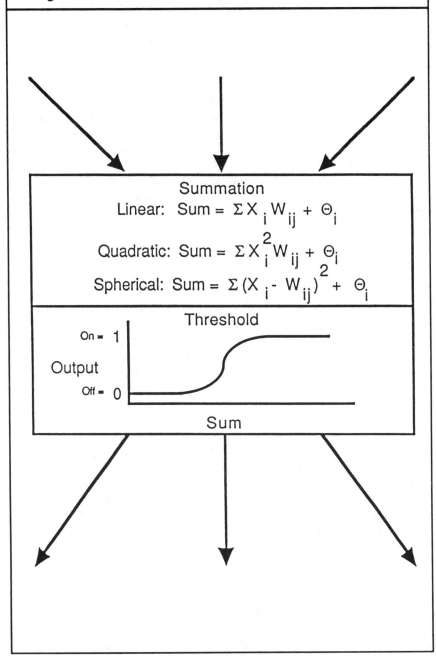

Figure 18.2: Sample Summation and Threshold Characteristics of Distributed Homogeneous Elements in a Neural Network

Summation

Linear: $\text{Sum} = \Sigma\, X_i\, W_{ij} + \Theta_i$

Quadratic: $\text{Sum} = \Sigma\, X_i^2\, W_{ij} + \Theta_i$

Spherical: $\text{Sum} = \Sigma\, (X_i - W_{ij})^2 + \Theta_i$

Threshold

On = 1

Output

Off = 0

Sum

connecting the input to middle layers. The same stimulus is again applied to the input layer and better results are obtained at the output layer if the network is capable of learning the task. The synaptic weights encode the energy state of the network. The weights change to minimize the energy state. Like water running downhill at the lowest available level, synaptic weights change according to a gradient descent algorithm, resulting in convergence on an intelligent solution. Increasingly sophisticated psychological and behavioral properties emerge from the functioning network during the developmental course of gradient descent.

Neural networks can also learn on their own. Imagine that Figure 18.1 is extended to create a cube. The middle layer now corresponds to a surface that initially is flat because all the weights from which it "hangs" from the input layers are the same length (value) and all the "poles" that extend up from the response layer are of the same length (value). Through repeated experience, the synaptic weights connecting the middle layer to both the input and output layers change in such a way that the middle layer forms a discriminant surface capable of distinguishing among the relevant dimensions of the perceptual, cognitive, or other problem to be solved. Hanson and Burr (1990) illustrate a polynomial and spherical surface capable of discriminating X's from O's.

One of the earliest applications of neural networks was as a memory formation and retrieval mechanism. Hopfield's (1982) work in this area greatly accelerated serious scientific attention to this topic. He demonstrated that a memory can be encoded by changing synaptic weights and that memories can be nondestructively encoded on top of each other up to a specified limit depending upon network size. It is remarkable that the same connection weights can be successively changed without destroying any part of any of the previously encoded memories. Moreover, presenting partial information about any one of the memories enables the correct recall of the entire memory. That memories can be nondestructively superimposed provides a mechanism for cumulative hierarchical learning as described by Gagné (1970) and Staats (1986).

Neural networks have been used to model adaptive behavior. Jones and Hoskins's (1987) "Little Red Riding Hood" simulation is a good example. Their six input ellipses represent: big ears, big eyes, big teeth, kindly, wrinkled, and handsome. Their three hidden, middle layer, ellipses represent: Wolf, Grandma, and Woodcutter. Their seven output ellipses represent: run away, scream, look for woodcutter, kiss on cheek, approach, offer food to, and flirt with. The number of hidden units must equal or exceed the number of concepts to be formed in such cases.

SYNTHETIC PROPERTIES

Before addressing the specific schisms to be synthesized, the reader requires reasons why connectionism is capable of the proposed syntheses.

Emergent Properties

Neural networks, and their underlying connectionism, would be unable to synthesize schisms if they could not instantiate a broad range of psychologically interesting emergent properties. The *Oxford English Dictionary* specifies the scientific meaning of *emergent* to be: "An effect produced by a combination of several causes, but not capable of being regarded as the sum of their individual effects" (Simpson & Weiner, 1989). Instantiate is defined as "To represent by an instance." *Webster's Ninth New Collegiate Dictionary* extends this definition as: "to represent (an abstraction) by a concrete instance" (Mish et al., 1989). For our purposes *instantiation* is the process whereby an abstract psychological state assumes physical form as a specific instance. *Emergence* refers to the fact that the specific instance arises from the interaction of neural architecture (number of elements, "neurons," and their pattern of interconnections, their synaptic weights), learning rules by which synaptic weights are modified in response to experience, and the specific sequence of training experiences.

From neural networks have emerged many psychologically interesting phenomena such as simple learning phenomena including but not limited to stimulus summation, blocking, unblocking, overshadowing, partial reinforcement effects, interstimulus interval effects, second-order conditioning, conditioned inhibition, extinction, reacquisition effects, backward conditioning, compound conditioning, discriminative stimulus effects, ∩-shaped curve in learning as a function of interstimulus interval, anticipatory conditioned responses, secondary reinforcement, attentional focusing by conditioned motivational feedback, latent inhibition, superconditioning, and learned helplessness (Gluck & Thompson, 1987; Kehoe, 1988; Sutton & Barto, 1981; Klopf, 1988; Grossberg & Levine, 1987; Grossberg & Schmajuk, 1987, 1989). Neural networks have learned to categorize patients into diagnostic groups on the basis of symptoms (Gluck & Bower, 1988a, 1988b). Interestingly, this neural network overestimated the value of a valid symptom of a rare disease in the same way that humans do.

Hopfield (1982) described a neural network capable of storing many memories and able to correctly retrieve a complete memory from just a part of it. Hopfield, Feinstein, and Palmer (1983) demonstrated that selective unlearning in Hopfield (1982) neural networks aids memory recall by reducing spurious memories. Other aspects of human memory have been effectively modeled by McClelland and Rumelhart (1985). Neural networks have shown letter perception including facilitation for letters in pronounceable pseudo-words as well as words that characterize human behavior (McClelland & Rumelhart, 1981; Rumelhart & McClelland, 1982). Neural nets are able to recognize human faces and determine if they are male or female (Sejnowski, Lawrence, & Golomb, 1991). NETalk learned on its own to correctly pronounce English words from transcriptions of a child's informal continuous speech containing 1,024 words. Playing the neural network phoneme output through DECtalk, a commercial speech synthesizer, mimicked normal human speech development. The first stage involved babbling. Then vowels were distinguished from consonants. Word boundaries were learned next, resulting in pseudo-words and then intelligible words. Errors were of the same type as made by children. Dell (1988) has shown that phonological speech error data can be simulated by neural networks. "Lesioning" normal functioning neural networks can give rise to psychopathology. Excessive pruning of a normal neural network has been shown by Hoffman and Dobscha (1989) to give rise to "loose associations." Changing a single parameter of a neural network capable of normal Wisconsin card sorting causes it to perseverate and pay excessive attention to novelty in the same way as patients with frontal lobe damage do (Levine & Prueitt, 1989).

Rule Governed but not Rule Based

Intelligent adaptive behavior appears to be rule based and the implementation of such rules seems to require the types of cognitive processes now familiar to students of information processing and artificial intelligence. Neural networks do not have a central processing unit and do not employ traditional if-then rules. Each "neuron" in the network receives input only from its neighbors; no overarching organization is imposed by an executive unit. Nevertheless, executive type functions emerge from neural networks. The ability to explain complex human behavior without regard to a central rule processing unit or self allows behaviorists to join ranks with cognitivists.

Process and Product

Behaviorism is a functional analysis in that it relates the end behavioral product to a set of environmental conditions without addressing the process enabling such changes to occur. Exploration of the biological mechanisms responsible for these changes is left to neuroscience. Cognitive psychology has largely been concerned with mediation. For example, consider adults taking the Wisconsin Card Sorting Task. Behaviorists emphasize that all subjects eventually identify the relevant dimension given consistent reinforcement for responses based on color, shape, or size. Cognitive psychologists emphasize the trial-by-trial hypothesis testing that led the subject to identify the relevant dimension.

Neural networks integrate product (functional) and process (structural) explanations. Issues concerning mechanism involve the construction of connectionist, parallel distributed processing, models to simulate psychological and/or behavioral phenomena. All mediating processes are represented by: (1) patterns of synaptic weights (the system architecture) and (2) algorithms for changing these connection weights as a result of experience. Full mechanism information is available. One vendor provides a pull-down menu to help the user identify the more important changes in a neural net associated with learning a particular task. Functional issues reflect the extent to which the system operates consistently with laboratory or clinical findings. The system must function like the research subject; human or animal.

Learning through Representation

Neural networks can learn anything they can represent through patterns of synaptic weights, weighted interconnections among computational elements. Representation is what enables learning to occur. The study of learning is coextensive with the study of representation. All representations within neural networks are embodied in the pattern of synaptic weights among the homogeneous computing elements (neurons).

Unity through Simplicity and Synthesis

Simplicity is best achieved through dialectic synthesis such that a few fundamental principles explain broadly diverse phenomena. Neural networks simulate a wide variety of animal and human behavior, including language, through variations in architecture and in how the synaptic weights are changed as a result of experience. No new fundamental principles are introduced when moving from animals to humans. Learning is taken as the central psychological process. Perception, memory, and cognition are conceptualized as specific instances of learning. Although simplifying assumptions are made in an effort to construct first approximations of biologically plausible networks, all replicated findings are deemed important. Simplicity is obtained through inclusion rather than exclusion.

UNIFYING SCHISMS

The following ten sections synthesize the eight theoretical schisms Staats (1983, p. 115) has identified as having blocked psychology from becoming a unified science plus two additional schisms. It will be shown that these schisms disappear into nonissues from the neural network perspective, thereby enabling psychology to emerge as a much more unified science.

Mind versus Body

René Descartes proposed the mind-body split because existing mechanical devices were so primitive that for intelligence and adaptive behavior to ever result from a mechanism seemed impossible. Separating mind from brain created the problem of how mind and body interacted. Answers were associated with terms such as *psychosomatic, somatopsychic, psychopharmacology,* and *psychoneuroimmunology.*

That neural networks are capable of instantiating a broad range of psychological/behavioral processes is demonstrative proof that Descartes's distinction is entirely unnecessary. Psychological states can and do emerge from functioning neural networks, making it totally unnecessary to posit separate mental functions. Avoiding the distinction between mind and brain avoids having to explain how one influences the other; the problem simply disappears. Moreover, neural network models provide psychologists with a proximal causal system for explaining how psychological states mediate behavioral events and how experience with the environment alters internal representations and subsequent behavior.

Nature versus Nurture

The biology (heredity) versus environment schism (cf. Staats, 1983, pp. 118-119) is among the most divisive in psychology. Fortunately, neural networks provide an especially elegant resolution of this issue. The architecture of a biological neural network is unquestionably constructed under genetic control. The initial synaptic weights are probably also genetically determined. Subsequent experience alters the synaptic weights and consequently changes the biological status of the neural network. The brain has been physically changed by experience (consequences).

Any degree of sophistication can be inherited depending upon the architecture and synaptic weights established during gestation. Spiders are hatched with a sophisticated neural network capable of weaving intricate webs. Humans have few skills at birth but they have an enormous capacity to change in response to their experience, that is, to learn. Neural networks illustrate how biology and experience interact to produce psychology and behavior. Just as the area of a rectangle is equally dependent upon length and width, neural networks depend equally upon their "biological" properties of architecture and learning mechanism plus environmental experience which modifies connection weights. Both factors play fundamentally important roles; neither one can be trivialized in favor of the other when discussing human behavior.

Language Learning

Language is a very important aspect of human behavior, and its development and function is of special concern to many psychologists. Skinner (1957) provided a functional analysis of language, whereas Chomsky (1975, 1980) provided an account of language acquisition based on innate grammar. The main criticism of Skinner is that language rules are not taught, per se, to the child.

The ability of neural networks to behave in accordance with rules without embodying any formal if-then structures is why they synthesize the Skinner-Chomsky schism so completely. Sejnowski and Rosenberg's (1987) NETalk learned to pronounce English words on their own after being exposed to many speech samples. The first stage involved babbling. Then vowels were distinguished from consonants. Word boundaries were learned next, resulting in pseudo-words and then intelligible words. Errors were of the same type as made by children. It is particularly important to note that the mistakes neural networks make during learning are similar to the mistakes children make thereby strengthening the neural network model of language acquisition. Dell (1988) has shown that phonological speech error data can be simulated by neural networks. In both instances, neural networks learn to speak through experience but without innate grammars of any kind or other prewired speech processing.

Subjective versus Objective

Staats (1983, pp. 114-116) describes this schism by contrasting Chomsky's (1975, 1980) emphasis on internal mental processes versus Skinner's (1957) emphasis on language as a type of behavior. Neural networks objectify subjective psychological states such as perception and cognition by creating a functional model of these states that is completely open to experimental study. Constructing a working model of a subjective process objectifies it and therefore vitiates the associated schism.

End-product behaviors and mediating processes are equally available for scientific study. For example, NETalk can be stopped at any point in its development and completely dissected to determine the properties enabling its functional abilities. Neural networks are to psychology what animal preparations are to medicine. They are a practical vehicle for representing complex systems in ways that are tractable to scientific inquiry.

Holistic versus Atomistic

Staats (1983, pp. 116-117) describes the holistic versus atomistic schism as a debate over whether it is better to study systems as a functional whole or to analyze them in terms of component parts. Neural networks synthesize this schism because they can be studied from both perspectives simultaneously due to the fact that they are implemented on a computer. The holistic functioning network can be suspended at any point in time and every constituent part examined down to the minutest detail. Because there is no need to choose one approach over the other, no schism exists.

Idiographic versus Nomothetic

Idiographic analysis examines the behavior of a single subject or few subjects over time, whereas nomothetic analysis examines two or more groups at a single point in time. The theoretical debate is whether human behavior is governed by general laws and principles or each person is truly unique (cf. Staats, 1983, pp. 117-118).

The study of neural networks is consistent with the ideographic approach because the investigator studies a single network, or a few variants of a basic network, while trying to synthesize psychological processes (perception, cognition, memory, learning, etc.) and the behaviors they mediate. Neural networks are consistent with nomothetic research because the general principles (back propagation, gradient descent, Hebbian learning rule, etc.) are general in that they can be applied to a wide variety of networks. Since neural networks are consistent with both sides of this issue, no schism exists.

Experimental versus Naturalistic

This schism is a clash between the requirements for internal and external validity (Staats, 1983, pp. 119-120). A study is internally valid when alternative interpretations of results can be excluded. This occurs when the investigator has control over all relevant experimental parameters. A study is externally valid when its results can be generalized to subjects and settings outside of the laboratory. External validity is enhanced by sampling from the population of subjects to which the results will be generalized and conducting the study under naturalistic conditions. A schism arises because increases in internal validity usually occur at the expense of external validity and vice versa.

Neural networks synthesize this schism because they simultaneously provide high levels of internal and external validity. Internal validity is high because all aspects of the network are completely controllable due to the fact that the networks are implemented using computers. External validity is high because the computer is the natural environment for the neural network. Because networks are synthesized and not taken from a larger context into the laboratory, threats to external validity never arise, thereby completely nullifying this schism.

Awareness versus Conditioning

This schism is a debate over whether the environment automatically influences behavior or whether awareness necessarily mediates all learning (Staats, 1983, pp. 120-121). Neural networks are consistent with the awareness side of the schism in that networks can learn only what they can represent. Neural networks are also consistent with the conditioning side of the schism in that experience has a highly deterministic influence on the subsequent state of all mediational processes and behaviors. Synaptic weights change with mathematical precision unless random functions are expressly created. Neural networks learn because their hidden middle layer necessarily responds to systematic features of input stimuli analogous to how statistical routines identify a discriminant surface to distinguish among two or more groups of subjects on the basis of a set of measurements. Neural networks synthesize this schism because they are compatible with cognition as well as conditioning. Both functions are embodied in every network, thereby obviating theoretical schism.

A desirable theoretical consequence of learning without awareness, and the implied rule-bound central processing unit, is that unconscious learning and dissociative processes can be explained by neural networks, thereby broadly expanding their clinical relevance and attractiveness.

Human versus Animal (Cognitive versus Associative) Learning

Human and animal learning are typically taught separately and in reference to distinctly different literature and concepts. Differences between humans and animals are often cited to explain why research on the latter is not especially relevant to the former. The debate is over phylogenetic continuity. Persons studying animal learning argue for phylogenetic continuity, whereas persons studying human behavior either dispute such continuity or argue that human higher cognitive functions dwarf whatever elements continue up the phylogenetic scale. Though Staats (1983) did not discuss this topic as a formal schism, it nevertheless clearly divides psychologists into competitive camps.

Neural networks synthesize this schism because elaborate networks capable of human categorical judgment, pronouncing English, and so on, are composed of exactly the same elements as networks capable of operant and respondent conditioning, and they work by the same principles. The differences are in architecture and complexity only. Hence, neural networks provide a unified approach to learning from the most simple through the very complex.

Learning versus Development

Developmental psychology arose at a time when learning was studied as a major discipline. Though Staats did not discuss this issue as a schism, it is clear that learning theorists are not developmentalists and vice versa, clearly demonstrating disunity on this issue. Learning and development are two sides of the same coin from the neural network perspective. Changes in synaptic weights during learning occur over time and therefore constitute development, assuming that neural architecture remains constant. The fact that memories are nondestructively superimposed upon each other over the same network elements provides an understanding of how cumulative hierarchical learning (cf. Gagné, 1970; Staats, 1986, 1991) can occur and explains the emergence of developmental stages in behavior and mediating psychological processes.

CONCLUSIONS

Repairing the above mentioned ten schisms through a synthesis that accommodates both sides of each issue demonstrates that neural networks provide a common unified perspective from which to view all psychological phenomena including perception, cognition, memory, language, representation, and learning. The resulting increase in shared orientation enables a larger proportion of research and clinical psychologists to work together more effectively. An initial contribution is to place current cognitive-behavioral approaches to psychotherapy on a firmer neuroscience footing.

Neural networks provide proximal causal models in addition to fostering theoretical synthesis. Although connectionism competes with and replaces structural psychological theories, connectionism is compatible with functional psychological theories such as psychological behaviorism (Tryon, 1990) because one cannot construct a plausible mechanism until one can specify its desired functional properties. Hence, functional psychological theory will guide neural network construction to the benefit of both. The result behaves (perceives, remembers, chooses, etc.) in accordance with available data and provides full mechanism information regarding how such feats are accomplished. Psychological science is advanced by being able to directly examine the inner action of a common class of working models rather than being restricted to drawing inferences about hypothetical structures and processes to understand and explain psychological functions and behavior.

The explosion of basic and applied empirical research generated by Wolpe's (1961) systematic desensitization model of fear reduction will be dwarfed by the availability of a common class of causal neural network mechanisms capable of complete experimental analysis of the entire psychological spectrum. The associated philosophical and methodological agreement will transform psychology into a mature science (Kuhn, 1970).

REFERENCES

Altman, I. (1987). Centripetal and centrifugal trends in psychology. *American Psychologist, 42*, 1058–1069.

Beitman, B. D., Goldfried, M. R., & Norcross, J. C. (1989). The movement toward integrating the psychotherapies: An overview. *American Journal of Psychiatry, 146*, 138–147.

Chomsky, N. (1975). *Syntactic structures*. Hague: Mouton.

Chomsky, N. (1980). *Rules and representations*. New York: Columbia University Press.

Churchland, P. S. (1986). *Neurophilosophy: Toward a unified science of the mind/brain*. Cambridge: The MIT Press.

Dell, G. S. (1988). The retrieval of phonological forms in production: Tests of predictions from a connectionist model. *Journal of Memory and Language, 27*, 124–142.

Donahoe, J. W., & Palmer, D. C. (1989). The interpretation of complex human behavior: Some reactions to parallel distributed processing, edited by J. L. McClelland, D. E. Rumelhart, and the PDP Research Group. *Journal of the Experimental Analysis of Behavior, 51*, 399–416.

Gagné, R. M., (1970). *The conditions of learning* (2nd ed.). New York: Holt, Rinehart & Winston.

Gluck, M. A., & Bower, G. H. (1988a). Evaluating an adaptive network model of human learning. *Journal of Memory and Language, 27*, 166–195.

Gluck, M. A., & Bower, G. H. (1988b). From conditioning to category learning: An adaptive network model. *Journal of Experimental Psychology: General, 117*, 227–247.

Gluck, M. A., & Thompson, R. F. (1987). Modeling the neural substrates of associative learning and memory: A computational approach. *Psychological Review, 94*, 176–191.

Goldfried, M. R. (Ed.). (1982). *Converging themes in psychotherapy: Trends in psychodynamic, humanistic, and behavioral practice*. New York: Springer.

Goldfried, M. R., & Padawer, W. (1982). Current status and future directions in psychotherapy. In M. R. Goldfried (Ed.), *Converging themes in psychotherapy: Trends in psychodymanic, humanistic, and behavioral practice* (pp. 3–49). New York: Springer.

Grossberg, S., & Levine, D. S. (1987). Neural dynamics of attentionally modulated Pavlovian conditioning: blocking, interstimulus interval, and secondary reinforcement. *Applied Optics, 26*, 5015–5030.

Grossberg, S., & Schmajuk, N. A. (1987). Neural dynamics of attentionally modulated Pavlovian conditioning: Conditioned reinforcement, inhibition, and opponent processing. *Psychobiology, 15*, 195–240.

Grossberg, S., & Schmajuk, N. A. (1989). Neural dynamics of adaptive timing and temporal discrimination during associative learning. *Neural Networks, 2*, 79–102.

Hanson, S. J., & Burr, D. J. (1990). What connectionist models learn: Learning and representation in connectionist networks. *Behavioral and Brain Sciences, 13*, 471–489, 501–503.

Hebb, D. O. (1949). *Organization of behavior: A neuropsychological theory*. New York: Wiley.

Hopfield, J. J. (1982). Neural networks and physical systems with emergent collective computational abilities. *Proceedings of the National Academy of Science, 79,* 2554–2558.

Hopfield, J. J., Feinstein, D. I., & Palmer, R. G. (1983). "Unlearning" has a stabilizing effect in collective memories. *Nature, 304,* 158–159.

Hoffman, R. E., & Dobscha, S. K. (1989). Cortical pruning and the development of schizophrenia: A computer model. *Schizophrenia Bulletin, 15,* 477–490.

Jones, W. P., & Hoskins, J. (1987). Back-propagation: A generalized delta learning rule. *Byte, 12,* 155–162.

Kehoe, E. J. (1988). A layered network model of associative learning: Learning to learn and configuration. *Psychological Review, 95,* 411–433.

Klopf, A. H. (1988). A neuronal model of classical conditioning. *Psychobiology, 16,* 85–125.

Kuhn, T. S. (1970). *The structure of scientific revolutions* (2nd ed.). Chicago: The University of Chicago Press.

Lawson, A., & Staver, J. R. (1989). Toward a solution of the learning paradox: Emergent properties and neurological principles of constructivism. *Instructional Science, 18,* 169–177.

Levine, D. S. (1989). Neural network principles for theoretical psychology. *Behavior Research Methods, Instruments, & Computers, 21,* 213–224.

Levine, D. S., & Prueitt, P. S. (1989). Modeling some effects of frontal damage: Novelty and perseveration. *Neural Network, 2,* 103–116.

McClelland, J. L. (1988). Connectionist models and psychological evidence. *Journal of Memory and Language, 27,* 107–123.

McClelland, J. L., & Rumelhart, D. E. (1981). An interactive activation model of context effects in letter perception: Part 1. An account of basic findings. *Psychological Review, 88,* 375–407.

McClelland, J. L., & Rumelhart, D. E. (1985). Distributed memory and the representation of general and specific information. *Journal of Experimental Psychology: General, 114,* 159–188.

Mish, F. C. et al. (1989). *Webster's Ninth New Collegiate Dictionary*. Springfield: Merrium-Webster.

Ramsey, W., Stich, S., & Rumelhart, D. E. (Eds.). (1991). *Philosophy and connectionist theory*. Hillsdale: Erlbaum.

Rumelhart, D. E., & McClelland, J. L. (1982). An interactive activation model of context effects in letter perception: Part 2. The contextual enhancement effect and some tests and extensions of the model. *Psychological Review, 89,* 60–94.

Rychlak, J. F. (1981). *A philosophy of science for personality theory* (2nd ed). Malabar: Krieger.

Schneider, W. (1987). Connectionism: Is it a paradigm shift for psychology? *Behavior Research Methods, Instruments, & Computers, 19,* 73–83.

Sejnowski, T. J., & Churchland, P. S. (1992). Silicon brains: Innovative computer devices are being inspired by the results of research on the brains of nature's creatures. *Byte, 17*(10), 137–146.

Sejnowski, T. J., Lawrence, D., & Golomb, B. (1991). Sexnet: A neural network identifies sex from human faces. In D. Touretzky and R. Lippman (Eds.). *Advances in neural information processing systems 3* (pp. 572–577). San Mateo: Kaufmann.

Sejnowski, T. J., & Rosenberg, C. R. (1987). Parallel networks that learn to pronounce English text. *Complex Systems, 1*, 145–168.

Simpson, J. A., & Weiner, E. S. C. (1989). *Oxford English Dictionary* (2nd ed). Oxford: Clarendon Press.

Skinner, B. F. (1957). *Verbal behavior.* New York: Appleton-Century-Crofts.

Skinner, B. F. (1987). Whatever happened to psychology as the science of behavior? *American Psychologist, 42*, 780–786.

Spence, J. T. (1987). Centripetal and centrifugal trends in psychology: Will the center hold? *American Psychologist, 42*, 1052–1054.

Staats, A. W. (1983). *Psychology's crisis of disunity: Philosophy and method for a unified science.* New York: Praeger.

Staats, A. W. (1986). Behaviorism with a personality: The paradigmatic behavioral assessment approach. In R. O. Nelson & S. C. Hayes (Eds.), *Conceptual foundations of behavioral assessment* (pp. 242–296). New York: Guilford Press.

Staats, A. W. (1987). Humanistic volition versus behavioristic determinism: Disunified psychology's schism problem and its solution. *American Psychologist, 42*, 1030–1032.

Staats, A. W. (1991). Unified positivism and unification psychology: Fad or new field? *American Psychologist, 46*, 899–912.

Sutton, R. S., & Barto, A. G. (1981). Toward a modern theory of adaptive networks: Expectation and prediction. *Psychological Review, 88*, 135–170.

Tryon, W. W. (1990). Why paradigmatic behaviorism should be retitled psychological behaviorism. *The Behavior Therapist, 13*, 127–128.

Tulving, E. (1983). *Elements of episodic memory.* London: Oxford University Press.

Wachtel, P. L. (1977). *Psychoanalysis and behavior therapy: Toward an integration.* New York: Basic Books.

Wolpe, J. (1961). The systematic desensitization treatment of neuroses. *Journal of Nervous and Mental Disease, 132*, 189–203.

Part V
APPLICATIONS TO SOCIAL PROGRESS

19

Chaos, Organizational Theory, and Organizational Development

Stephen J. Guastello, Kevin J. Dooley, and Jeffrey A. Goldstein

Chaos theory and related nonlinear systems theories are making a substantial impact on organizational science and the practice of organizational development (OD). There are three schools of thought concerning chaos in organizations (Michaels, 1991a). The linear school incorrectly uses chaos as if to characterize temporary conditions that exist between times of certainty and stability. It uses chaos nonmathematically and, at best, as a loose metaphor. The New Age school ponders the greater order of the universe on the basis of the new scientific insights, often with unrestrained conclusions that have no basis in the actual theory. The dynamical systems school, by contrast, studies real systems and the interrelationships among their parts, with the intent of applying the mathematics of chaos. We confine our remarks to applications of the third type and summarize the theoretical progress pertaining to organizational theory and OD.

In classical approaches to understanding organizational change and stability a phase of uncertainty, randomness, and innovation is sandwiched between two indefinitely long periods of stability without change in what Lewin (1947) called quasi-stationary equilibrium (Goldstein, 1991). In Lewin's formulation, the organizational change process occurs in three phases: the unfreezing, the change operation, and the refreezing. In the course of the change process the organization hypothetically finds a direction it wants to pursue, and it goes there. However, process consultation based on the Lewinian paradigm has not been successful often enough in accomplishing its missions (Hackman, 1992). Clearly a new paradigm for organizational change and stability is needed.

In the chaos paradigm of OD, times of stability are merely periods of respite within a complex dynamical process of change. The strange attractor, bifurcation, self-organizing systems, and concomitant mathematics are useful concepts for describing the nature of change processes, thereby imposing an order onto disorder, such that conditions once thought of as random processes are indeed explicable and no longer as uncertain as they once were (Michaels, 1989). Moreover, the new chaos paradigm allows for both evolutionary and revolutionary change processes. This chapter elaborates on theoretical advances in organizational processes with specific reference to self-organization, organizational learning, motivation, decision making, and implications for practice and intervention.

THEORIES OF STABILITY AND CHANGE IN ORGANIZATIONS

Beyond Lewin's Force Field

Dynamical systems theory shifts focus onto the attractors within the patterns of trajectories (phase portraits) created by vectorfields (force fields) and seeks explanations of how they change. A dynamical scheme specifies conditions controlling change in the vectorfields and phase portraits. That is, it is a dynamical system as a function of control parameters. In nonlinear dynamics, where change is inevitable, a model seeks to specify conditions that promote evolutionary versus revolutionary change (DeGreene, 1978; Goldstein, 1991). Evolutionary change is when there are only gradual changes in the vectorfield and its phase portraits as the control parameters are changed. Revolutionary change is bifurcation, whether subtle, catastrophic, or explosive. It occurs when a vectorfield and its phase portrait undergo a major change with a small critical shift in the control parameter (at a threshold known as the bifurcation point), which is usually caused when energy dispensed to the force vectors changes which changes the relative strength of their mutual interactions. Bifurcation points represent conditions of great instability; the farther from a bifurcation point, the more stable the system, which may possess stable fixed-point, periodic, and chaotic attractors, singularly or plurally, depending on the system, at any nonbifurcational point in the parameter space.

As a small amount of energy changes in the region near the bifurcation point, the control parameter may get closer to the bifurcation point, and the system begins to destabilize. As energy increases, the system experiences greater instability and propensity toward bifurcation. In the famous cusp catastrophe, a particular type of bifurcation, for a region of the two-dimensional control space (the cusp area of the two control parameters), the one-dimensional state space has two fixed point attractors rather than just one, with a repellor between them. Outside this region is but one fixed-point attractor. For one control parameter, often called the normal or asymmetrical parameter, there is a hysteresis effect when the parameter is systematically raised or lowered, so that the switch in the trajectory from one attractor to the other occurs at the second bifurcation point (at the boundaries of the cusp region). That is, the first bifurcation point is not seen because the trajectory is already to one side of the repellor and thus stays with that attractor, not being forced to the other attractor until encountering the second bifurcation, which takes the system out of the cusp region into the region where there is only one attractor (Guastello, 1992a; Thom, 1975; Zeeman, 1976).

Qualitative analysis showed that pressure for change and resistance to change themselves could be considered as two control parameters (Bigelow, 1982). They are, however, orthogonal forces, rather than opposing forces. When resistance is low, small pressures for change result in a gradual change by the organization that might even take place on a subconscious level. When resistance is high, old practices may be solidified if pressure is low. Revolutionary change is likely when both pressure and resistance are high. Furthermore, a feedback loop is thought to exist between the two control parameters such that pressure to change may result in the expulsion of resisting managers; alternatively, a compensation system that ties individual rewards to organizational success would essentially stifle resistance to change pressures.

Self-Organization

When a nonlinear system is placed in a far-from-equilibrium condition, it can undergo a process of *self-organization* or spontaneous transformation into a more complex order or pattern of functioning (Nicolis & Prigogine, 1989; Waldrop, 1992). As such, self-organization represents the system transiting into attractor regimes of increasing complexity. Such bifurcational sequences occur when the control parameters of the system (or of subsystems in a network comprising a complex system) are under the control of the system itself, which is the technical meaning of self-organization. Self-organization need not be hierarchically driven, nor does it assume that systems inherently resist change. Rather, it is self-generated and self-guiding.

This self-organization is another critical departure from the traditional Lewinian model of a shift in equilibrium levels (Goldstein, 1990, 1991, 1992, 1993). The self-organizational concept suggests that organizations do not necessarily inherently resist change, nor do they require outside pressure to force them to change. Rather, organizations or work groups become predisposed to change when they are under the appropriate far-from-equilibrium conditions. These far-from-equilibrium conditions may be those of stable conditions that are no longer satisfying because of shifts in goals, ethics, or demands of the organizational environment, or they may represent instabilities as organizational or environmental control parameters push the organization to unstable conditions that prevail at bifurcation points. The challenge facing facilitators of change, therefore, is to unleash the inherent propensity toward bifurcation by promoting the right type of far-from-equilibrium conditions. They may do this by a variety of means that get the organization to recognize a discontent, recognize relevant control parameters (profits, size of production, advertising budget, amount of internal communication), architect or imagine potential bifurcations, and get more self-organizational workforce participation in the self-transformative process. The facilitators may have to nucleate a source of energy and enthusiasm necessary to cause a bifurcation. It takes energy and courage in many instances for an organization to bifurcate creatively (Solow, 1991); failure to do so may cause disastrous, annihilative catastrophes. Catastrophic bifurcations are complex events involving the appearance and disappearance of attractors and repellors; they are usually accompanied by the creation and separation or collision and disappearance of attractors, repellors, saddles, or basins (Abraham & Shaw, 1992).

A crucial aspect of the self-organizational process is that the system amplifies, rather than dampens "organizational noise" or random (or unanticipated) departures from stability (Ciborra, Migliarese, & Romano, 1984). This happens in two ways. In one, the noise within the control parameters, as in any chaotic attractor, grows over time, spreading the trajectories out (not so relevant here, as an organization only gets one trajectory). In the other, which is more pertinent here, the noise on the control parameter pushes it over a bifurcation point, causing an organizational transformation. In classical organizational theory, managers control or limit the effect of such noise and thereby keep the organization in a stable condition. Yet for innovation to truly take place, random departures from equilibrium may become the seed of desirable transformation. Therefore, facilitators or self-organization must enable the business or institution to take advantage of, rather than, discard, some departures from stability.

In traditional OD practice, the tendency to dampen organizational noise or departures from stability shows up in the use of averaging in survey feedback, where group members' differences are hidden by using the group average. The tendency to diminish departures from stability also occurs when a group is pushed to find consensus prematurely. Therefore, Goldstein (1988) suggested the methods of "difference questioning" and "purpose contrasting," in which departures from organizational or group equilibrium are encouraged and amplified. The goal of such techniques is to identify patterns of acceptance and rejection of ideas (attractors and repellors) and to define a course of action that successfully navigates the organization's vectorfield. Further applications of the sample principle are seen in the encouragement of organizational learning.

Organizational Learning

In a neural network model of the brain, patterns constituting knowledge are embedded in a complex array of interconnected nodes and associated nodal weights. Each node acts in a nonlinear fashion, and learning occurs through self-organization (Rumelhart & McClelland, 1986). Michaels (1991b) noted that there are many similarities between neural learning and organizational learning, and uses the analogy to suggest that improvement and change efforts should focus on the interconnections within the organization. As contrasted to individual learning, "organizational learning occurs when members of the organization act as learning agents for the organization, responding to changes in the internal and external environments of the organization by detecting and correcting errors in organizational theory-in-use, and embedding results of their inquiry in private images and shared maps of the organization" (Argyris & Schön, 1978, p. 29). Dixon (1992) and Huber (1991) provided relevant reviews of research. Again, the goal of such techniques is to identify patterns (attractors and repellors) of acceptance and rejection of ideas and to define a course of action that successfully navigates the organization's vectorfield.

Some types of organizational learning are examples of self-organization (Dooley, Bush, & Johnson, 1992); these can be further understood by analogy to physical systems, where information transfer and dissipation are analogous to heat transfer and dissipation. A system of liquid, when pushed far from equilibrium by heating, will self-organize into complex patterns that dissipate heat into the environment. Similarly, as information from the "external" environment is brought into the organization, the information must be dissipated. If the information is low in "energy," the organization will process it within the context of its existing systems. As information pushes the organization further from equilibrium, existing mental models can be challenged and changed (Bush & Dooley, 1992).

An unstable system at a bifurcation point is highly sensitive to perturbation, to changes in events and the actions of individuals. These bifurcation points thus amplify small fluctuations, which leads to choice (Prigogine & Stengers, 1984). The learning organization does not despise the uncertainty of random events; rather, it attempts to learn and to create leverage from such events through the design of its information channels and systems.

Such self-organization has similarity to Argyris and Schön's (1978) concepts of single and double loop learning. When information is presented to the organization in such a manner that it conflicts with members' "picture" of the organization or team, teams can respond by either correcting for "errors" so as to maintain the features of the organization's or team's theory-in-use (single loop learning), or they can establish new norms, priorities, strategies, and assumptions (double loop learning). Their research shows that the ability to self-organize depends on an openness to reflective inquiry, among other things. The learning organization is constantly seeking reality checks to ascertain the appropriateness of its espoused theories. An organization must learn when to retreat along control parameters to previous safe forms of stability (the single loop), and when to grit its teeth, and cross the bifurcation point to a new, unexplored pattern of stability on the other side, which may help it to define new goals and to progress toward them (the double loop).

DECISION MAKING

Complex Systems Require Complex Controllers

Using systems theory and control theory, it is possible to show that the variety or complexity of a feedback control system must be at least equivalent to the complexity of the system it is trying to control. Equivalently, chaotic systems can be themselves controlled by chaos. Ashby's (1958) law of requisite variety states that when a system is subject to disturbances, the controller (regulator) must act as a communication channel so that proper corrective action can be taken. In order for the disturbance to be properly decoded and acted upon, the feedback channel must have sufficient capacity. Controller capacity can be operationalized by the ability of the controller to handle a signal's variety or entropy, that is, complexity. The practical implications are that (1) a good feedback system should be a model of the system itself and (2) strategies for control and improvement that work on simple linear systems may be grossly inadequate for more complex nonlinear systems.

Hubler (1992) showed through control theory that chaotic systems can be controlled themselves by weak chaos. He further stated that the principle of "matching" means that "interacting physical systems adjust those control parameters which are not fixed by external constraints, in such a way that their interaction is extremal" (p. 23). Thus, a control system adapts its behavior so that it interacts with its parent system in a self-organized manner; the complexities of the parent system and control system will not necessarily lead to more complexity, but can rather lead to simplicity and stability of behavior.

The key implication here for organizations is that control mechanisms (feedback systems, policies, and procedures, etc.) should have some chaotic nature to them. They should go beyond deterministic mappings of problem to solution and should contain some element of complexity and chance or experimentation. In such experimentation the organization may "entrain" to a new desired state even with small external control forces (Mayer-Kress & Hubler, 1991). Furthermore, a system can be made less controllable by added unpredictability and randomness to it; this strategy is well known in game theory (Ruelle, 1991). Thus, if the organization wants to outwit its competition, its strategy should have some element of irrationality to it, for it is unlikely that the competitor's corresponding "communication channel" has the requisite variety to handle such complexity.

Beer Distribution and Workforce Staffing

Two lines of inquiry have investigated decision making under conditions of chaotic uncertainty. Mosekilde, Larssen, and Sterman (1991) studied policy making of beer distributors in a simulation where the players had to maintain a supply and fill orders in the face of random interruptions of supply and random fluctuations in the demand for beer. The ordering policies of the gaming distributors fit a mathematical chaotic function involving embedded quasi-periodicities. There was considerable variability in the economic effectiveness of the policies generated by the players which were, as a rule, suboptimal. Only 11 percent of the players were successful at maintaining a supply that did not overflow the warehouse or run out of beer (Sterman, 1988).

A second set of experiments pertained to organizational staffing decisions where there was a shortage of qualified job applicants (Guastello, 1992b). It was shown that organizations that maintain an unchanging and linear hiring standard are destined to extinction. Rather, a successful strategy would accept a more varied workforce and prepare for substantial oscillations in the number of employees, higher termination rates, and substantial changes in the variance of work performance by individuals. A successful staffing policy would require a policy of selection and training that changes predictably approximately every four years.

Guastello (1992b) further showed that the workforce census of a small construction contractor oscillates over time in the same manner as populations of insects vary over time (May & Oster, 1976):

$$N_{t+1} = bN_t e^{-aN},$$

where N is the number of employed persons, b is a bifurcation parameter that is a function of the hiring rate, and a is a crowding parameter. The number of employed persons is the sum of new hires (X) and those who survived to a subsequent "hiring generation" (Y). Y is the result of the number of new hires from a previous generation times the survival rate. Staffing policies based on a long range view of future staffing needs (caused by chaotic dynamics) result in a more stable census than staffing policies that hired new members only as the openings occurred.

Hubler's (1992) work on chaotic controllers and Guastello's (1992b) work on population dynamics led Young and Kiel (in press) to propose that management science rethink its concepts of rationality in decision making. Under conventional rationality, causes and effects are linearly related, and future trends are anticipated through extrapolations from past events. Once established to address the expected circumstances, policies remain fixed. In a nonlinear cause-and-effect paradigm, small changes in controls can have dramatic results. Stability and predictability can often be obtained by carefully orchestrating policy changes that are responsive to dynamical and chaotic patterns of events.

MOTIVATION AND CONFLICT RESOLUTION

Successful OD strategies depend in part on working theories of motivation and conflict resolution. Abraham (1995) nonlinearized Dollard and Miller's (1950) approach-avoidance conflict work; elaborations appear elsewhere in this volume.

The approach-avoidance conflict has been considered in past applications of nonlinear dynamics to work motivation. Guastello (1981, 1987) determined that work behavior is best described as a butterfly catastrophe (five-dimensional) configuration of three stable attractor states that are separated by two repellor forces. The three attractive states on the performance variable (univariate state space) are (1) innovation, competence, and performance beyond expectations; (2) adequate performance and attendance; and (3) inadequate performance, chronic absenteeism, and imminent termination. The butterfly model has four control parameters: ability, extrinsic motivation, intrinsic motivation, and a management parameter that governs motivational conditions by controlling the other three parameters.

The management control parameter is ripe with meanings familiar to organizational theory. At one end of its continuum, management style is rigid and draconian, but it is humanistic and tolerant of individual differences at its other end. The humanistic pole allows for growth and evolution of the social system, whereas the authoritarian regime promotes stability through conformity (Guastello, 1988). As one might anticipate the management control parameter, which can also be thought of as an organizational climate or culture parameter, is largely responsible for outcomes of the dynamics of organizational change. Several theories of work motivation and much empirically derived information on performance variability in organizations can be deduced from the butterfly motivation model including equity, motivator-hygiene, opponent process, and approach-avoidance theories (Guastello, 1981, 1987).

TOTAL QUALITY MANAGEMENT

Organization-wide quality improvement known as total quality management (TQM) has become a common practice among organizations of all types. Such efforts focus on processes, variation, teamwork, and empowerment and lead to continuous improvement of the firm's products and services. Many of the technical and behavioral tools and methods used to implement quality improvement have been borne out of the paradigm of scientific management and its parent paradigm of Newtonian mechanics; while other practices appear to represent a transition to the chaos paradigm (Dooley, 1992).

Perhaps the strongest connection between the Newtonian paradigm and TQM is in its approach to problem solving. There is belief that a sequential learning model representative of the scientific method, such as Plan-Do-Study-Act, can and should be applied in all learning situations. Some companies have gone so far as to require all effort and communications concerning quality improvement to be structured in this manner. In a sense this represents classical determinism, and scientific management's belief that management can be treated as a science. In using Plan-Do-Study-Act one typically takes a very analytical view of the process and its components. The tools TQM has available for such tasks are rooted in such reductionism.

Organizational TQM practices can also be seen to be influenced by the classical paradigm. Lewin's (1947) concept of the unfreezing, learning, internalization, and refreezing sequence are very similar to current ideas in quality control (e.g., Kume, 1985), which show how process improvement must be followed by standardization and "holding the gains." These models are not counter to the classical view of equilibrium.

Equilibrium in the TQM environment is being reinforced by the development of normative practices, the most influential of these being the Malcolm Baldridge National Quality Award criteria (Dooley, Bush, Anderson, & Rungtusanatham, 1990). The criteria lay out in great detail the elements of a world-class TQM system, even to the point of allocating weights toward certain elements, such as customer satisfaction or strategic quality planning. In a similar manner, the European Economic Community is introducing the ISO 9000 quality management system criteria. The worldwide spread of these normative practices is leading to a state of maximum entropy, where there will be focus (once again) on uniformity in organizational practice, leading to probable stagnation.

Some modern practices within TQM seem to indicate that it is a stepping stone toward a new management paradigm. Organizational learning creates a focus on continuous measurement of the product, process, and customer. The capability to experiment, and thus to learn about the current reality, is becoming more valued than expertise. In TQM, great emphasis has been placed on the role of experimentation, and the continuous measurement of customer satisfaction, as means to learn and determine direction.

TQM is often implemented in a manner that contains a serious contradiction between the participative methods demanded by deeply rooted change and the nonparticipative way change is initiated by management mandate. Of course, many organizations use an "enlightened" approach in which the obvious signs of authoritarian managerial pressure have disappeared and been replaced by persuasion and participation. Nonetheless, agents of change often oversee and guide the process of change from their vantage point as planners, anticipators of resistance, "thawing" agents, and "refreezers." Even though managerial authority is moved to the background, the change agents are nevertheless indirectly representing management and hierarchically controlling the change process.

To avoid this contradiction, TQM can be installed in a way congruent with the new chaos paradigm of organizational transformation. For example, the Japanese practice of TQM espouses *hoshin kanri*, which operationally means to have a completely customer-driven organization. Thus, as customers' needs change, the organization will immediately adapt. Such changes cannot be predicted; rather, the organization must develop policies and structures to allow such adaptation. Self-organization can occur when the system opens itself to the environment. The idea of the internal customer, where people inside the organization form a chain of customers eventually reaching out to the external customer, is powerful in this regard. Customer needs are back-propagated through the system, and the organization truly becomes customer focused.

The push to the brink of unstable bifurcation conditions allowing such self-organization to take place has been accomplished primarily through the "quality crisis," or the inability for many organizations to compete with respect to quality. The influence of leadership has been essential; it is highly unlikely, however, that leadership itself without crisis could have created the organizational changes we now see taking place. It thus seems apparent that TQM may be the first indication that transformational change to a new management paradigm, a metabifurcation, so to speak, is really occurring.

SUMMARY

The new ideas emerging from chaos and nonlinear theory provide the basis for deep-rooted transformation whereby an organization can more rapidly embody new directions and strategies. A new set of assumptions guiding organizational research and practice are introduced: Organizations and work groups inherently tend toward change and development. Organizational transformation is a process much more radical than mere "unfreezing" and "refreezing." Instead of large changes requiring large efforts, small-scale efforts can facilitate large-scale changes. Instead of emphasizing planning, change is an evolving strategy utilizing change and accidental events. The study of organizational dynamics and change requires a new kind of nonlinear rationality employing the new mathematical models.

REFERENCES

Abraham, F. D. (1995). Dynamics, bifurcation, self-organization, chaos, mind, conflict, insensitivity to intitial conditions, time, unification, diversity, free-will, & social responsibility. In R. Robertson & A. Combs (Eds.), *A chaos psychology reader*. Hillsdale: Erlbaum.

Abraham, R. H., & Shaw, C. D. (1992). *Dynamics, the geometry of behavior* (2nd ed.). Reading: Addison-Wesley.

Argyris, C., & Schön, D. (1978). *Organizational learning: A theory of action perspective*. Reading MA: Addison-Wesley.

Ashby, R. (1958). Requisite variety and its implications for the control of complex systems. *Cybernetica, 1*, 1–17.

Bigelow, J. (1982). A catastrophe model of organizational change. *Behavioral Science, 27*, 26–42.

Bush, D., & Dooley, K. (1992). Team chaos. *The Chaos Network, 4*(4), 1–4. (Available from People Technologies, P.O. Box 4100, Urbana IL USA 61801)

Ciborra, C., Migliarese, P., & Romano, P. (1984). A methodological inquiry of organizational noise in sociotechnical systems. *Human Relations, 37*, 565-588.

DeGreene, K. B. (1978). Force fields and emergent phenomena in sociotechnical macrosystems: Theories and models. *Behavioral Science, 23*, 1–14.

Dollard, J., & Miller, N. E. (1950). *Personality and psychotherapy: An analysis in terms of learning, thinking, and culture.* New York: McGraw-Hill.

Dixon, N. (1992). Organizational learning: A review of the literature with implications for HRD professional. *Human Resource Development Quarterly, 3*, 29–49.

Dooley, K. (1992, June). Total quality management and chaos theory. In S. J. Guastello (chair), *Chaos theory and social-organizational dynamics.* Symposium conducted at the annual meeting of the American Psychological Society, San Diego, CA.

Dooley, K., Bush, D., Anderson, J., & Rungtusanatham, M. (1990). The U.S. Baldridge Award and Japan's Deming Prize: Two guidelines for total quality control. *Engineering Management Journal, 2*, 9–16.

Dooley, K., Bush, D., & Johnson, T. (1992, June). Quantitative models of learning: Neural, cognitive, and organizational. In M. D. Michaels (Ed.), *Proceedings of the annual Chaos Network Conference: The second iteration* (pp. 107–113). Urbana: People Technologies.

Goldstein, J. (1988). A far-from-equilibrium system approach to resistance to change. *Organizational Dynamics, 17*, 16–26.

Goldstein, J. (1990). A nonequilibrium nonlinear approach to organizational change. *Systems Dynamics '90: Proceedings of the 1990 International Systems Dynamics Conference* (Vol. 1, pp. 425–439). Cambridge: System Dynamics Society, Massachusetts Institute of Technology.

Goldstein, J. (1991). Lewin's model for organizational development. How to refashion it in light of non-linear and non-equilibrium theory. In M.D. Michaels (Ed.), *Proceedings of the First Annual Chaos Network Conference Proceedings, 1991* (pp. 43–48). Urbana: People Technologies.

Goldstein, J. (1992). Beyond planning and prediction: Bringing back action research to OD. *The Organization Development Journal, 10*(2), 1–8.

Goldstein, J. (1993). Beyond Lewin's force-field: A new model for organizational change interventions. In F. Massarik (Ed.), *Advances in Organization Development* (Vol. 2, pp. 72–78). Norwood NJ USA: Ablex Press.

Guastello, S.J. (1981). Catastrophe modeling of equity in organizations. *Behavioral Science, 26*, 63–74.

Guastello, S. J. (1987). A butterfly catastrophe model of motivation in organizations: Academic Performance [Monograph]. *Journal of Applied Psychology, 72*, 165–182.

Guastello, S. J. (1988). The organizational security subsystem: Some potentially catastrophe events. *Behavioral Science, 33*, 48–58.

Guastello, S. J. (1992a). Clash of the paradigms: A critique of an examination of the polynomial regression technique for evaluating catastrophe theory hypotheses. *Psychological Bulletin, 111*, 375–379.

Guastello, S. J. (1992b). Population dynamics and workforce productivity. In M. Michaels (Ed.), *Proceedings of the annual Chaos Network Conference: The second iteration* (pp. 120–127). Urbana: People Technologies.

Hackman, R. (1992, June). *Where the variance lives: Continuity and change in social behavior.* Paper presented to the annual meeting of the American Psychological Society, San Diego, CA.

Huber, G. P. (1991). Organizational learning: The contributing processes and the literatures. *Organizational Science, 2*, 88–115.

Hubler, A. (1992). Modeling and control of complex systems: Paradigms and applications. In L. Lam (Ed.), *Modeling complex systems*. New York: Springer.

Kume, H. (1985). *Statistical methods for quality improvement*. Tokyo: AOTS.

Lewin, K. (1947). Frontiers in group dynamics. *Human Relations, 1*, 5–41.

May, R. M., & Oster, G. F. (1976). Bifurcations and dynamic complexity in simple ecological models. *American Naturalist, 110*, 573–599.

Mayer-Kress, G., & Hubler, A. (1991). Time evolution and local complexity measures and aperiodic perturbations in nonlinear dynamical systems. In N.B. Abraham (Ed.), *Measures of complex dynamical systems* (p. 155). New York: Plenum Press.

Michaels, M. D. (1989). The chaos paradigm. *Organizational Development Journal, 7*, 31–35.

Michaels, M.D. (1991a). Three schools of chaos theory. *The Chaos Network, 3*(1), 9–10. (Available from People Technologies, Urbana, IL 61801)

Michaels, M. D. (1991b). Chaos constructions: A neuralnet model of organization. In M.D. Michaels (Ed.), *Proceedings of the First Annual Chaos Network Conference* (pp. 79–83). Urbana: People Technologies.

Mosekilde, E., Larssen, E., & Sterman, J. (1991). Coping with complexity: Chaos in human decision making behavior. In J. Casti & A. Karlqvist (Eds.), *Beyond belief: Randomness, prediction, and explanation in science* (pp. 199–299). Boca Raton: CRC.

Nicolis, G., & Prigogine, I. (1989). *Exploring complexity*. New York: W. H. Freeman.

Prigogine, I., & Stengers, I. (1984). *Order out of chaos*. New York: Bantam Books.

Ruelle, D. (1991). *Chance and chaos*. Princeton: Princeton University Press.

Rumelhart, G., & McClelland, J. (Eds.). (1986). *Parallel distributed processing*. Cambridge: MIT Press.

Solow, L. (1991). (R)evolution of employee involvement at Harley-Davidson, Inc. In M. Michaels (Ed.), *Proceedings of the First Annual Chaos Network Conference* (pp. 35–39). Urbana IL USA: People Technologies.

Sterman, J. (1988). Deterministic models of chaos in human behavior: Methodological issues and experimental results. *System Dynamics Review, 4, 148–178.*

Thom, R. (1975). *Structural stability and morphogenesis*. New York: Benjamin.

Waldrop, M. (1992). *Complexity: The emerging science at the edge of order and chaos*. New York: Simon & Schuster.

Young, T. R., & Kiel, L. D. (in press). Chaos and management science: Control, prediction and nonlinear dynamics. *Journal of Management Inquiry*.

Zeeman, E. C. (1976, April). Catastrophe theory. *Scientific American, 23*, 65–83.

20

Chaos in the Triadic Theory of Psychological Competence in the Academic Setting

Carlos Antonio Torre

THE TRIADIC THEORY

The triadic theory (Torre, 1984, 1987, 1989, 1993) proposes three domains of psychological variables that are convenient for analyzing academic competence. These domains are, roughly, intellectual, emotional, and pragmatic-contextual. It further proposes that variables within and between these domains interact as an inherently chaotic process. It stresses applications attempting bifurcations leading to improving academic success, especially for those entering higher education with inadequate pragmatic-contextual attitudes and skills. Examples of group programs at several universities are given.

Basic Psychological Processes

There is a constant and inseparable flow of interaction among the cognitive, affective/perceptive, and pragmatic mental processes. Each is associated with its own way of knowing and verifying information. Together, they interact in ways that are concerted, antagonistic, and reconciliatory and suggest a dynamical model for educational problem solving (Figs. 20.1a, 20.1b, 20.1c).

Cognitive processes are the modes of thinking associated with the scientific method and with academic knowledge and skills. Analytic, linear, and rational, they bring about knowledge by applying logic to the observed and reducing the whole to its parts. These processes are characterized by a tendency toward designing sequential step-by-step procedures toward goal attainment. Seeking to discover what the object under consideration is composed of and how its parts relate to each other may require the manipulation of the parts of the whole in order to consider them from different angles and to be able to reassemble them again before one

Figure 20.1a: Chaotic Dynamics of the Triadic Theory of Mental Functioning Cognitive, affective/perceptive, and pragmatic mental processes interact in ways that are concerted (activation), antagonistic (restraint), and reconciliatory (integration). Take formula: $z_n = z^2_{n-1} + b\bar{z}_{n-1} + c$ in which $b = 1 + .2i$ and $c > 0$ are complex parameters and z_n, z_{n-1} are complex numbers. For a complex number z_0, we have a sequence $[z_n]$, where $z_n = z^2 n-1 + b\bar{z}_{n-1} + c$. Consider those z_0 in the complex plane such that $[z_n]$ are bounded. The set of those z_0 forms a triadic figure for parameters above $c = 0$, $b = 1 + .2i$. At each node point of the figure there are three choices: one is C (Cognitive); another is AP (Affective/Perceptive); and the third is P (Pragmatic). The limit set of this triadic figure is a fractal set. This is a plot of a Jiangbar set.
(Equation and figure by Jiang Yunping, CUNY/Queens College)

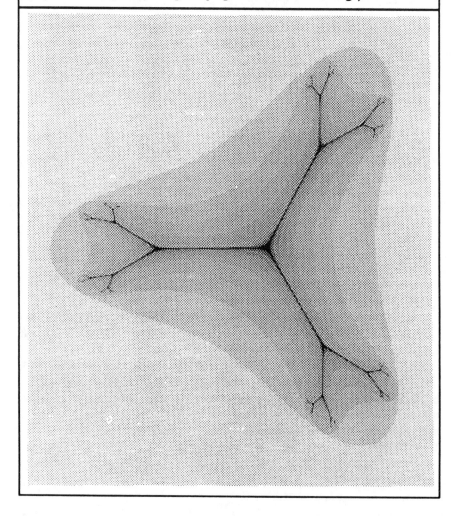

actually feels that the object is understood (Torre, 1987). For verification, the cognitive processes call for establishing formal empirical proof.

The cognitive problem-solving processes subsume three tasks: (1) *statement of the problem*, or specifying purpose, goals, and objectives in approaching the particular situation; (2) *information gathering*, or selecting sources of information, gathering, classifying, and storing of information, and assessing the quality and type of information gathered; and (3) *diagnosis*, or analyzing and synthesizing information.

Affective/perceptive processes involve creative, artistic, and emotional thinking (love, hate, fear, insecurity, doubt), as well as perceptivity (such as intuition, feelings, hunches, and keen insight). These processes enable us to discern what can be considered intangible knowledge flowing from imperceptible sources of information. Unmediated awareness of truth may also arise when we place the object of consideration in context, which in turn allows us to see the larger background of the object. To pursue this way of knowing to its logical conclusion, we progressively seek to find the context of the context (Torre, 1987). To verify, the affective/perceptive processes require probability and likelihood, that is, verisimilitude.

The main tasks of the affective/perceptive problem solving processes are (1) *prognosis*, or the forecasting of the probable future courses or trajectories of the problem; (2) *generation of solutions*, including the use of various techniques to proliferate approaches to given situations; and (3) *decision making*, or the selection of ideas that form an optimal approach to the given situation.

Pragmatic processes are experiential, observational, and tacit modes of thought. They require understanding the utilitarian nature of the object or situation under consideration and the kind of skills and knowledge acquired through implicit means or mentorship types of activities, the kind that are not taught directly, discussed explicitly, or written about. They involve the learning that takes place by being exposed to certain practices or lifestyles that implicitly and subconsciously foster particular attitudes and behaviors. To verify, pragmatic processes require concrete results and evaluation of the desirability of obtained outcomes.

Like the affective/perceptive problem-solving processes, the pragmatic problem-solving processes involve three main tasks: (1) *planning*, that is, outlining the desired outcomes, describing the process, steps, or procedures necessary for problem solution, and determining what new capabilities the problem solver needs to develop to carry out the plan successfully; (2) *implementation*, the performance of the tasks specified in the planning; and (3) *evaluation*, the pragmatic consideration of self- and other-generated feedback regarding the extent to which one's problem-solving efforts have actually produced desirable outcomes for the situation at hand.

Although in our daily experiences the cognitive, affective/perceptive, and pragmatic ways of knowing interact dynamically and consistently to form our realities, we often place more credibility on certain of these ways of knowing at the cost of others. The sciences, for example, emphasize the cognitive, logical, linear

Figure 20.1b: Magnification of the Dynamics in One of the Three Mental Processes
The triadic structure exhibits irregular self-similarity.

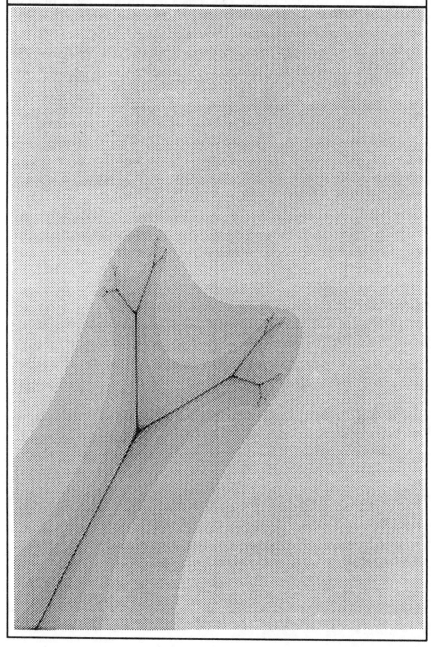

Figure 20.1c: Further Magnification
Irregular self-similar dynamics continues to be exhibited on all scales.

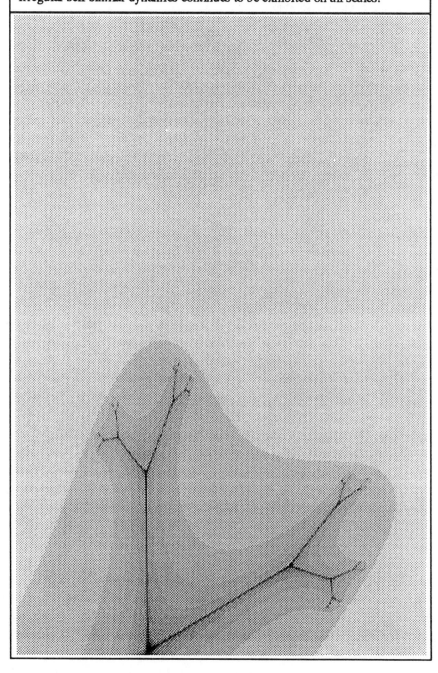

mental processes. In the arts, the affective/perceptive with its elements of inspiration and creativity, are most valued. In business the pragmatic, with its bottom-line approach, gets most credibility.

Because of these various ways of knowing, we experience the world in different ways and through different beliefs and points of view. The result is often opposition, contradiction, or other forms of conflict, which take our mental processes away from equilibrium. Thus, the energy of the interaction experienced by these mental processes increases. They begin to fluctuate between opposites until the energy is high enough to bring these opposites to polarize and bifurcate repeatedly. From further increases in energy (stress, conflict), turbulence develops; this, in turn, can seriously affect efforts at problem-solving. For this reason we need to conform these three mental processes and their interactions into our conceptions of education and educational problem solving.

Forms of Interaction among the Mental Processes

These three types of mental processes interact in several ways. One way is through *activation* and *restraint,* which can be thought of as two opposing forces that are brought together into a working relationship by *integration* (as a fulcrum creates a relationship between the two ends of a wooden plank).

More specifically, *activation* is a form of interaction among mental processes that induces movement (the motivation of thought and behavior) toward specified goals or a specific direction. It dominates, organizes, and coordinates mental functioning at any given moment.

Restraint counterbalances activation by interfering with goal attainment. Examples are the barriers that hold one back from reaching a goal or the stresses and tensions that move mental activity either toward creative bifurcations or toward incapacitating pathology. Restraint provides the necessary tension or instability that can revitalize thinking or, contrarily, throw it into higher-dimensional more disordered chaos (Torre, 1984) thus, effectively restraining greatly one's problem-solving capabilities. By forcing the individual toward bifurcation points where learning and decision making take place, restraint can initiate the creative process, the birth of new ideas, the emergence of new patterns of interaction or forms of organization, the minimizing of blind alleys, and the consideration of additional plans for optimal goal attainment. Insurmountable restraints can, however, erupt into personal disorientation, inner conflict, or stress.

Finally, *integration* is what can bind activation and restraint together into a working relationship through the reconciliation of their opposing forces. When effective, integration mediates and reconciles the opposition between activation and restraint into movement toward goal attainment or in a desired direction, in a manner similar to the interaction of a sailboat with the wind and the sea: The wind provides activation (movement in a particular direction), the boat and the sea furnish restraint (resist the wind), and the combination of rudder, movable sail, and helmsman provide integration (reconcile the opposing forces of the wind and the boat's and sea's resistance to the wind into productive movement in a desired direction or toward a desired goal). When ineffective, integration's efforts lead toward increased stress, disorientation, apathy, blunder, oversight, or wasted labor.

The interaction of cognitive, affective/perceptive, and pragmatic processes runs the gamut of behavior from static (fixed-point) to cyclical (periodic) to chaotic attractors and may involve several bifurcation sequences. Such mental activities as thinking, feeling, creativity, and action constitute this type of dynamical process. In particular, the interaction is also a dynamical process with its attendant bifurcations and waxing and waning of energy.

A DYNAMICAL MODEL OF PROBLEM SOLVING

The mental processes of the triadic theory form the specific mechanisms through which individuals make sense of their world and act intelligently within it. Moreover, each class of mental processes, and its interaction with the other two, forms a different way of knowing. In this context, any of the three can mediate between the other two. Likewise, any can be in complementary opposition to either of the others. For example, the cognitive and affective/perceptive processes may be in complementary opposition to each other, whereas the pragmatic processes may tend to mediate the consequent antagonism between them (as when we are moved emotionally to do something about what is considered an unjust civil law and the intellect and friends tell us, "You can't fight City Hall." Pragmatically, we can research the issues involved, devise a plan of action, and recruit allies for the effort).

Because each of the three mental processes involves three problem-solving subtasks, the result is a nine-task model of problem solving (Figure 20.2). As described earlier, the model encompasses (1) statement of the problem, (2) information gathering, (3) diagnosis, (4) prognosis, (5) generation of solutions, (6) decision making, (7) planning, (8) implementation, and (9) evaluation. This model facilitates understanding of the dynamical interaction among mental processes during thinking and problem-solving activity. It serves, also, as a heuristic for encouraging and nurturing creative and integrative thinking and for avoiding thinking that fosters artificial dichotomies and conflict in problem resolution.

We can think of the nine problem-solving tasks as regions in the interactive state space. Trajectories of problem solving might visit these regions in a variety of sequences, that is, not necessarily in a fixed linear order. Rather, they can be performed in any possible order that realizes the particular aim of the broader task of which they are a part. The trajectories wander, driven by their dynamics as the three basic processes wax and wane. Each of the model's tasks is recursive or iterative, in that each poses a "problem" (What type of situation am I really facing here? What kind of information do I need to get? etc.) and, therefore, may require the use of one or more of the remaining tasks. In addition, if we were to magnify any of the tasks or functions of the dynamical problem-solving model, each would contain a tiny copy of the entire model. Further magnification of any part of this copy would again result in even tinier copies of the entire model. Thus, the model is fractal typical of low-dimensional chaotic attractors when seen in Lorenz's cross-sections. More specifically, the structured irregularity of mental functions, processes, and interactions is fractal in that it continues to exhibit irregular self-similar structure on all scales.

APPLYING THE THEORY FOR BETTER EDUCATION AND SELF-IMPROVEMENT

The mind is at the core of every aspect of human endeavor. Its functioning underlies performance in any activity in which we are engaged. Improving the workings of our minds, consequently, would enable us to perform more competently in a chosen field of endeavor as well as to increase our ability to produce more meaningful results for ourselves and for others.

Nowhere are these implications more important than in the field of education. Educators need continually to address obstacles and opportunities that arise among energetic diverse students—some with difficulties in their academic skills; others who are talented and gifted, with a need to share their capabilities and experiences; still others with low self-esteem or disoriented because of fragmented academic experiences. Understanding the mental processes involved in problem-solving, teaching and learning, and self-actualization is, therefore, essential to educators and anyone interested in improving the human condition.

Toward these aims, I have tested the triadic theory in a 14-month "quality of thinking" research study at the University of Puerto Rico's Cayey University College to identify and better comprehend the elusive mental processes that tend to restrain college-level students from achieving their academic potential (see Torre, 1989, 1993); in the development and execution of activities in Yale University's Preregistration Orientation Program, the aim of which is to orient ethnic minority students to the workings of the university and to the academic skills they need to make the best use of their college experience; and in a course to help academically disoriented first-generation college students at Northeastern Illinois University overcome their fears and insecurities and improve their overall academic performance (Torre, 1984, 1987). This last example, the inaugural test of the triadic theory, serves as the basis for the following illustration of how the theory and its dynamical problem-solving model can be applied in educational settings.

Figure 20.2: The Dynamical Problem-solving Model
The iterative self-similar nature of the problem-solving process is nonlinear and can occur in any order or sequence.

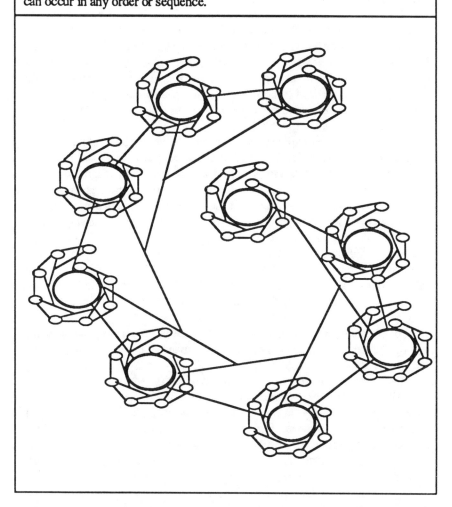

Inadequate Triadic Foundations: Disorientation, Fears, and Insecurities

Based on the triadic theory, I developed and implemented a course, entitled Problem Solving and Decision Making (PSDM), at Northeastern Illinois University between 1978 and 1985. My goal was to help students considered at risk of failing to meet the scholastic expectations of the university to improve their thinking as a way of enhancing academic performance. PSDM was eventually included in the

University's "limited list" of courses from which undergraduates were required to choose in order to graduate.

The target students, who were, for the most part, the first in their families to attend college, had weak precollegiate education. Thus, they lacked the conceptual base most of their professors presumed college students to have and were generally ineffective at applying the academic skills necessary for success in college. Because of their personal disorientation, many failed to understand the nature of a university or their own reasons for being in one. They lacked direction or goals for a postcollege career, as well as knowledge of the possibilities open to them after graduation. Of equal importance, our target students lacked role models to emulate as well as other guidance resources.

Framing the above example within the triadic theory, we see that the university placed high academic demands on the students' *cognitive* processes as a way to challenge or activate them toward scholarly achievement. The magnitude of these demands, however, was beyond the students' present capabilities to undertake them, thus revealing the inadequacy of their *pragmatic* experiences (ineffective academic skills, meager exposure to environments of higher education, lack of mentors or role models, and so on).

As the pressure and stress (*the driving energy*) exerted on them by this situation increased, their mental functioning began to bifurcate. Their observable behavior was not predictable at any given moment. At times they felt willing to try to do well in school; at other times they felt incapable of doing so and felt an urge to stop trying.

As the pressures continued, their behavior went into a period-halving (octave-jumping) bifurcation sequence. Their attention span became shorter. The range of things on which they focused narrowed considerably, and intake of environmental cues that might have helped to orient them better was reduced greatly. Repeated bifurcations caused their behavior to alternate among an increasing number of possibilities: spontaneity, improvisation, introversion, extroversion, binges of partying and/or time-consuming social activism intermixed with purges of prolonged study periods. The resultant intense level of disorientation these students experienced limited their ability to organize their time. Thus, their academic functioning became increasingly inefficient and ineffectual.

The inadequacy of the students' pragmatic experiences gave rise to fears, insecurities, and other adverse difficulties in their *affective/perceptive mental processes*. From the dynamical point of view, blame is not placed on a specific component (such as a given mental process, the individual, or the social environment) of a maladaptive system. Whatever characteristics exist or arise are characteristic of the entire system. The students' insecurities thereby affected the whole of their behavior and mental functioning. Consequently, their coursework suffered, resulting in poor grades. Progress toward a successful completion of their degree requirements was jeopardized, and their increased efforts to reconcile the situation ended in frustration. The students' poor academic performance accentuated their lack of previous experiences, skills, and capabilities, again increasing their fears and insecurities, thereby further adversely affecting academic performance.

The inability to draw on previous pragmatic experiences that could serve as a third (*mediating* or *integrating*) force resulted in a win-lose situation. Repeated interaction among the students' three mental processes (cognitive, affective/ perceptive, and pragmatic) nurtured a vicious cycle that short-circuited their learning process and brought out their potential to self-organizationally bifurcate to patterns they preferred, or at least to those with which they felt more comfortable. On the one hand, an unacceptably high-dimensional chaos ensued and their behavioral flow became turbulent; on the other hand, the degeneration of their academic functioning was also evident in simpler attractors, both periodic (binge partying with purges of prolonged studying) and fixed-point (doing no school work at all).

Too much cognitive activation, without adequate means of coping, creates enormous emotive pressures, which push individuals far away from affective/ perceptive stability. Without a mediating force to integrate the complementary opposites of activation (academic demands) and restraint (fears and emotional insecurities), the resulting discord obstructs the learning process and hinders effective cognition. Feeling out of control, individuals find that their behavior begins to bifurcate repeatedly, alternating among an increasing number of possibilities. The above description accurately portrayed our target students. For many, the prognosis was clear: dropping-out, some sort of pathology, self-destructive or self-sabotaging behavior; or the like.

Triadic Interventions and Bifurcations

Chaos theory holds that interventions or perturbations could help move people toward bifurcation points, or nudge people over them. Guess and Sailor's work (1993) indicates that such interventions are more successful when administered during transitions (bifurcations) between strong attractors because systems are less stable and thus more amenable to change during such transitionary states. Consequently, in order to deal effectively with the particular circumstances described above, at least two seemingly contradictory prerequisites had to be addressed: (1) alleviating the overwhelming affective difficulties being experienced by the students' stable but maladaptive attractors created by their fears and insecurities, and (2) finding a way to move the students' mental functioning away from those attractors and toward a less stable, and possibly even more uncomfortable, transitionary state, which is necessary for bifurcating to more adaptive educational attractors. To this extent, educational interventions imply a balancing act of inducing sufficient tension to cause a bifurcation, while making sure the instability at the bifurcation is not so great as to preclude a meaningful bifurcation to a useful attractor.

First, alleviating the students' emotional difficulties required the development of an environment conducive to a certain level of comfort and trust among its various participants. I took a number of measures in the PSDM course to develop a comfortable trusting environment and provide alternatives to more traditional, often intimidating, classroom settings. For example, the class met in an attractive ground-level room, with one entire wall of windows looking out on an aesthetically pleasing shrub and rock garden. The room's three remaining walls were covered with flip-chart paper and markers; writing tablets were readily available. A large conference table surrounded by comfortable chairs replaced traditional desks. Name tags and group-work techniques and games, encouraged dialogue and interaction among class participants.

The course called for students to apply what they learned to a situation they considered problematic, whether personal (family, financial, etc.) or academic (a term paper, selecting a major, etc.). The aim was to guide students as they worked on issues they considered crucial. Stimulating them toward self-motivated activation to acquire knowledge and upgrade academic capabilities called for more than just the passive process of providing interventions. It required helping students to develop capabilities for recognizing control parameters, for maneuvering on them, for exploring to find bifurcations, for learning and creating response diagrams, and for using self-intervention to get to bifurcations and generating the energy to pass through them into the educational world beyond.

Second, attending to some of the students' emotional difficulties produced a new set of pedagogical "initial" conditions conducive to attempts at driving the students' mental activity further toward bifurcation. We all differ widely in terms of the modalities that optimize our potential for learning. Additionally, each of us brings a variety of other variables to the learning process (culture, age, ego, previous academic experiences, physical and emotional challenges). Consequently, given that no single strategy will be effective with all students or in all situations, creating a learning environment appropriate to all class participants is essential.

To address these concerns, I pursued a multistrategy approach in the PSDM course, using feedback and feedforward for self-regulated learning, explicit group dynamics and role playing, "lecturettes," and numerous other means (for a more in-depth treatment, see Torre, 1984). In brief, feedback, feedforward, and self-regulation are concepts from cybernetics. Feedback alerts to discrepancies between intended and actual outcomes. Here, outcomes are the new attractors that emerge from problem-solving efforts, and discrepancies are the bifurcations between intended and actual outcomes. Feedforward informs future action or directions (trajectories) to be taken. Together, they comprise self-organization, the learning of generalized control parameters and dynamical schemes (that is, dynamical systems as a function of control parameters), which empowers navigation and innovation in the state space, producing an active flow of continuous feedback, feedforward, and new self-regulated learning. Feedback and feedforward produce alternating patterns of unstable tensions leading to bifurcations of problem solving and patterns of stability representing satisfactory learning processes in the educational environment.

Toward these ends, I organized the PSDM course around problem-solving or content-learning activities, placing students in cooperative learning groups of three to six. A variety of group-work techniques optimized interaction and communication among all participants. Thus, I informed students about their progress toward intended outcomes and toward their development of the capabilities required for realizing them. Their achievements became increasingly more purposeful and self-regulated rather than other-directed or left to chance.

Explicit group dynamics techniques called for sharing six basic functions of the teacher's role among class participants: (1) animator, (2) receptionist, (3) record-keeper, (4) time-keeper, (5) facilitator, and (6) provider of feedback. Along with role playing, these techniques helped the student problem solvers feel more capable of undertaking their academic work successfully. The premise was that in order to deal effectively with emotional difficulties, individuals need to develop a more capable frame of mind, building up confidence in their own talents and capabilities for approaching difficult situations and for improvising when their specific knowledge on a given issue has been exhausted. Explicit group dynamics and role playing provided opportunities to develop these kinds of dexterities through hands-on activities in a nurturing cooperative environment.

Traditionally, the lecture format has been a passive vehicle for imparting knowledge. Used creatively, however, variations of the traditional lecture can stimulate student involvement with subject matter, serve as a reflection technique, or foster healthy skepticism. In the PSDM course, "lecturettes" (five- to twenty-minute oral or audiovisual presentations) fulfilled this purpose. Content was presented in a global manner (macroanalysis), purposely leaving out many details and connections, and followed by group-work techniques designed to promote curiosity and reflections.

In the PSDM course the dynamics manifested within the cooperative learning groups, as well as in full-class discussions, appeared to mimic the above-described chaotic trajectories of the mental processes. Although the discussion seemed to have no particular sequence or order, patterns of questions, assertions, confrontations, and ideas emerged. The overall results exhibited an increase in problem-solving effectiveness beyond what these same students demonstrated at the beginning of the course or when they worked independently.

The following anecdote supports this statement and summarizes the "clinical" data: After working with the dynamical problem-solving model, I asked students to deliberate on a particular situation abstracted from an out-of-town newspaper:

> A municipality needs to provide funds for a day-care center and a fire station at the end of its fiscal year. Both agencies have requested financial support for expanding their physical plants and for the purchase of new equipment. The municipality does not have sufficient money to fund both agencies' projects, but the entire pot of available funds is in excess of what is needed to fund either project alone. The problem

is how best to meet the child-rearing and fire safety needs of the community with the available resources.

Discussions in the city council led to the expected arguments in defense of a variety of standard solutions to the predicament:

1. Allocate all funds to one project, with the expected outcome that it will be able to meet its commitments and obligations while the other is left to subside or would have to deescalate its services. As a result, either the day-care or fire-fighting needs of the municipality will not be met.
2. Divide available funds between both projects according to some formula to be negotiated. Presumably, neither project will go by the wayside but, realistically, would probably be unable to fulfill its obligations entirely.

After some deliberation, the students in the PSDM course offered a third, nonstandard approach to the above situation. They proposed that the city council:

3. Allocate all the funds to the fire station so that it could expand its physical plant beyond its needs, thereby creating sufficient room to house a soundproof (also expanded) day-care facility. The city could then sell the old day-care center's physical plant, generating the additional funds necessary for purchasing the equipment needed for both the fire station and the day-care center.

The students' proposal would solve not only the problem posed originally but also subsidiary problems not even considered in advance. It rendered the day-care center about as safe and secure as it could possibly be, for the center would now be housed in the fire station, and it provided a built-in field trip for the children in the day-care center because they could easily and frequently visit the fire station. The proposal also provided relief from the boredom the firefighters normally experienced waiting for a fire to occur, because they would now have the children around to divert them during periods of inactivity.

IMPLICATIONS AND CONCLUSIONS

Work with the triadic theory demonstrates that most college failures are held back academically not because of poor intellectual potential but because of fears and insecurities brought on by undeveloped scholastic savoir faire. Mitigating students' emotional restraints tends to perturb the stable attractors created by students' fears and insecurities, allowing for less stable transitionary states (bifurcations) that are more responsive to change as a result of intervention. It is thus an essential prerequisite for dealing with students' ineffective academic capabilities or the fragmentary ways they have attained knowledge. Additionally, using varied teaching strategies optimizes the possibilities of creating a learning environment conducive to students of widely diverse backgrounds and learning styles. A particular teaching strategy may stimulate one student while irritating another. Nonetheless, both stimulation and irritation can serve as agents for driving students' mental activities far from stable but maladaptive attractors, through unstable bifurcations, toward new stable, adaptive attractors of creative mental functioning that seeks to integrate apparent opposites. By addressing emotional restraints and developing an educational environment conducive to diversity, the necessary dynamic conditions can be generated to tap and encourage the optimal functioning and interaction of students' mental processes.

Taking the momentum of what Bohm (1980) calls the "implicate order," we can avoid getting stuck in an expediter role in which we attempt to erase the uncertainties of a given situation. This type of undertaking usually succeeds only in creating additional uncertainties, thus generating more problems than solutions. Alternatively, we can come to trust the mental and group interactive processes, understanding that (1) these processes are inherently chaotic, bringing to bear a combination of order and randomness to thinking and problem solving, and (2) the problem itself contains the solution.

Implicitly, then, the chaotic dynamics connoted in the triadic theory compel educators to leave the learning process open to the students. The atmosphere within which they are to solve problems should not be preconditioned with expectations that a right answer exists. Freeing the students to think openly about the situation and intuitively infer the solutions inherent within it can, again, tap the chaotic dynamics inherent in thinking and problem solving and encourage the optimal functioning and interaction of students' cognitive, affective/perceptive, and pragmatic mental processes.

Future investigations of mental functioning in the context of chaos theory imply a transformation in experimental designs as well as in conceptual approaches to research. Many standard multivariate techniques can continue to be useful, but we need to make greater use of such multivariate measures on individuals and to characterize the results dynamically. This might best be accomplished through a descriptive profile or portrait of the specific configurations of problem-solving strategies exhibited, along with the sequences or trajectories followed. Dynamics might thus provide a more rigorous foundation for education and problem solving. Furthermore, we need to focus on the disparity between individuals' stated problem-solving purposes and their actual practice or accomplishments. Such disparity can help us identify control parameters that influence the person's problem-solving effectiveness. In a given design the profile or portrait of a subject's mental functioning during problem solving could be considered as a dependent variable, and the control parameters as the independent variables.

Much remains to be learned about chaos theory and its applications within educational psychology. With cautioned optimism as the rule, I believe strongly that educators should be conversant with nonlinear dynamics. The examples provided in this chapter may serve to generate new understanding of mental functioning intrinsic to teaching-learning and problem-solving processes and may spawn speculations to be tested. Additionally, this growing and very promising body of literature can help educators cast new light on old issues, uncovering possibilities for approaching educational effectiveness in ways concordant with our experiences.

REFERENCES

Bohm, D. (1980). *Wholeness and the implicate order.* London: Routledge & Kegan Paul.

Guess, D., & Sailor, W. (1993). Chaos theory and the study of human behavior: Implications for special education and developmental disabilities. *Journal of Special Education, 27,* 16–34.

Torre, C. A. (1984, August). *Problem solving and decision making: An integration of cognitive, affective, and pragmatic operations.* Paper presented at the Second Biennial International Conference on Thinking, Harvard University.

Torre, C. A. (1987, January). *Thinking, culture, and education.* Paper presented at the Third Biennial International Conference on Thinking, University of Hawaii at Manoa.

Torre, C. A. (1989). *El proyecto Cayey: Una investigación sobre la calidad del pensamiento* (The Cayey project: A study on the quality of thinking). Cayey, PR: University of Puerto Rico.

Torre, C. A. (1993). *Sobre la calidad del pensamiento: El caos triádico en el proceso enseñansa-aprendisaje* (On the quality of thinking: Triadic chaos in the teaching-learning process). Manuscript submitted for publication.

21

Feminist Psychology: Prototype of the Dynamical Revolution in Psychology

Patricia L. Murphy and
Frederick David Abraham

Feminist psychology is generating a revolution in the field of psychology, not just in its demand for an egalitarian, gender-complete program for its subject matter but in the demand for an improved methodology and conceptual framework. With an emphasis on a holistic, process-oriented psychology that considers the contextual social system as well as individuals, it should find a powerful ally in the dynamical systems approach, which provides a theoretical modeling strategy and an experimental design and analysis strategy appropriate to the feminist program. In short, feminist psychology and the dynamical systems approaches share the holistic, process orientation in focusing on the patterns of change among multiple interactive variables in psychosocial systems.

FEMINIST PSYCHOLOGY

Feminist psychologists have been calling for changes within the discipline of psychology almost since its inception over 100 years ago. In the past twenty years these summonses have been documented in numerous articles criticizing the existing order for its theories (Caplan, 1984; Crawford & Marecek, 1989; Denmark, 1980; Loye & Eisler, 1987), choice of methods (Harding, 1991; Riger, 1992), and its lack of a critical history (Bohan, 1991; Shields, 1975). An examination of these reviews reveals a common grievance: the lack of a contextual approach within the science of psychology. Vicenzi (1994) notes similar needs in other health fields.

Crawford and Maracek (1989) criticize the frameworks that have guided much of the research into the psychology of gender: "The cultural emphasis on autonomy from social influences and on individual responsibility for action frequently inclines psychologists toward viewing behavior in terms of personal, internal factors rather than external social ones" (Crawford & Maracek, 1989, p. 154).

Riger's recent review of the epistemological debates concerning women in psychological science examines the many biases, one of which is "the lack of attention to social context. . . . By stripping behavior of its social context, psychologists rule out the sociocultural and historical factors, and implicitly attribute causes to factors inside the person" (Crawford & Maracek, 1989, p. 731).

Furthermore, the lack of a critical examination of psychology's history leads scientists to neglect their own social context and the effect that it has on their science. Shields's evaluation of evolutionary theory's historic effect on the psychology of women leads her to conclude, "That science played handmaiden to social values cannot be denied" (Crawford & Maracek, 1989, p. 753). Her observation that science is guided by social values, as many feminist and other psychologists would agree (Ehrlich & Abraham, 1974; Harding, 1991; Riger, 1992), makes the call to contextualize psychology all the more critical. In the context of a patriarchal system, research demonstrating gender differences possesses a distinct meaning that is unclear when the context is missing. Thus, although feminist psychologists are not a homogeneous group whose ideals are easily enumerated, one ideal appears to be to correct the gender deficiency in psychology through social contextualization of the theory, the research, and the discipline itself. In the past, psychological methods have abetted decontextualizing, partly as a result of the design and analysis methods of reductionist science, especially in the attempt to control extraneous variables. Thus dynamics suggests general benefits to psychology as well as the correction of this gender deficiency.

Objective science had lost the compassionate concern for its subject matter, namely, people, that could lead it to creatively seek new interrelationships among many social and psychological variables. Thus humanistic concerns would be included among the general benefits of the dynamical approach.

Lastly, psychologists have not, until recently (Bohan, 1991; Shields, 1975), given their history the critical examination that is imperative for understanding the sociopolitical nature of our knowledege in psychological science today. This lack of awareness as to how our theories and research are informed by our sociohistorical milieu maintains our illusion of impartiality and objectivity.

Nonfeminist psychologists are not the source of the problem, however, as these mistakes are inevitable when the dominant paradigm is a minimalist, decontextual one. In fact, feminist psychologists themselves have not been immune to this tendency to spotlight the individual (Bohan, 1991; Mednick, 1989), as many feminist theories and concepts have deemphasized the role of the environment.

In many cases, however, this aspect was not to be overlooked for long. For example, when Bem (1975) and others (Spence, Helmreich, & Stapp, 1975) first began studying androgyny theory, the focus was upon how an androgynous personality benefits the individual. Later articles demonstrate that Bem (1981, 1984) recognized that the burden of change should be not on the individual's shoulders, but on the structure of society. The androgynous personality might have an advantage given the structure of society and its propensity for valuing "maleness" and devaluing "femaleness"; however, "the feminist prescription . . . is not that the individual be androgynous, but that society be aschematic" (Bem, 1981, p. 363).

As an aside one might point out that this tendency to devalue "feminine" values, a social prejudice incorporated by the field of psychology—one of the symptoms of its lack of critical history—is even more damaging than its failure to dynamically attempt to correct social injustices. Psychology went even further, legitimizing with a scientific stamp of approval those prejudicial features of society at large (Broverman, Broverman, Clarkson, Rosenkrantz, & Vogel, 1970; Chesler, 1972; Ehrlich & Abraham, 1974).

Or one might say, "Neutrality is a myth in the sense that the pursuit and use of scientific principles are not merely contrived in a particular socio-scientific value matrix, but their very technological flavor tends to support their role in social control and conformity rather than in support of individual fulfillment" (Abraham, 1975, p. 250).

Thus until recently, with but a few notable, hardy exceptions (e.g., Lewin, 1951), the reductionist scientific paradigm dominated psychology, routinely decontextualized its subject matter, and divorced it from a concern with issues of individual, social, and cultural rights and diversity and their nurturance. Because psychology lacked the conceptual and mathematical tools for following the temporal evolution of interactive variables, it placed its focus on controlling one or a few independent variables, measuring one or a few dependent variables, eliminating the influence of other "extraneous" variables by controlling or randomization techniques, and it usually did so without daring to study temporal evolution of variables except for a few homeostatic and cyclic patterns. In other words, it was forced to limit itself and divorce itself from exactly those things of obviously the most central interest in psychology.

However, although the very nature of the scientific method, when carried to such rigorous reductionistic extremes, serves to decontextualize its subject matter, not all feminist psychologists are so reactive as to call for the demise of scientific methodology in psychology. Riger (1992) advocates using many different methods as long as the assumptions behind the different methodologies are made clear. To clarify the goals of a more feminist methodology she cites the central tenets as put forth by Mary Gergen (1988):

1. Recognizing the interdependence of experimenter and subject;
2. Avoiding the decontextualizing of the subject or experimenter from their social and historical surroundings;
3. Recognizing and revealing the nature of one's values within the research context;
4. Accepting that facts do not exist independently of their producers' linguistic codes; and
5. Demystifying the role of the scientists and establishing an egalitarian relationship between science makers and science consumers. (Riger, 1992, p. 47)

Dynamical systems viewpoints are consistent with these goals, inevitably leading to the same conclusions for some of these goals by its emphasis on how any given variable is mutually interdependent with other variables and with the ease it gives expression to this interdependence, or leads to the empowerment of the remaining goals by its emphasis on transformative and self-organizational principles.

One might be inclined to question why feminist psychologists are specifically concerned that a more contextualized approach be taken in the practice of psychology. Susan Faludi's (1991) recent analysis of the "backlash against American women" cites numerous examples of how feminist notions, which do not emphasize sociocultural features or are taken out of context, have been used to urge women's retreat to traditional roles (Murphy & Bohan, 1992). The notion that women possess a "different voice" (Gilligan, 1982), one more interpersonally oriented than that of men, suggests, without accompanying sociocultural critique, that there is a logical basis for existing sex roles. The significance of such notions is not whether or not women's voices are more or less interpersonally oriented than men's, but why they are thus. Bohan (1991) articulates the problem well with her assertion that "we need to look carefully at the consequences of cherishing qualities that derive from our oppression, lest we inadvertently conspire in its recreation."

In addition to upholding status quo beliefs concerning sex roles, the decontextualized approach to psychology can have other dire consequences when put into application. Paula Caplan's (1984) critique of the "myth of women's masochism" is just one example of how psychological theory tends to inaccurately locate the source of difficulty within the individual when it ignores the sociocultural context. In this case women's subjugation and abuse by men is attributed to the abused women's gratification in self-denial and self-destructive tendencies.

Another example is the treatment programs for individuals (usually women) suffering from anorexia and bulimia. These programs rarely examine the cultural influences underlying self-destructive behavior. Their behavior is simply explained as being deviant (Cogan, 1992). Given the emaciated look of the models presented to us as the ideal in female beauty, it seems more likely that the anorexic or bulimic individual considers her behavior as conforming rather than deviant. Women's paucity of control over their own lives (only recently undergoing change) leaves control over image as one of the most accessible and desirable avenues of social control.

Riger (1992) articulates this argument well when she explains that the prevailing ideology of decontextualization: "assume[s] that outcomes are due to choices made by free and self-determining individuals; the implication is that people get what they deserve" (p. 732; also see Kahn & Yoder, 1989).

To summarize on a positive note, feminist psychology emphasizes the following:

1. Individuals interact dynamically with their social context.
2. The study of this interaction requires a cooperative effort among individuals (including subjects and experimenters in research), psychology, and community.

3. At the heart of this cooperative effort must be a compassion for the rights and diversity of individuals, and for cultural rights and diversity.

DYNAMICAL SYSTEMS: A METAMODELING STRATEGY

It might be of value to review some of the essential features of dynamics. As with the revolution of psychology by feminist psychology,

> The past two decades have witnessed a revolution in its language, concepts, and techniques for dealing with complex cooperative systems evolving through multiple modes of dynamical equilibrium (static, oscillatory, and chaotic).... The mathematics provides models, simulation, cognitive strategies, and intuitive clear geometric representations for complex systems. It also serves as a unified philosophic view for integrative, hierarchically organized systems.... It is emerging as the metalanguage, the metaparadigm, of science. Several essential features contriubute to this developing hegemony.
>
> The *first* is that instead of looking at a static object or event as a thing to be explained, it looks to a set of complex evolving relationships as both the subject, the object, and the explanation, holistic and dynamical.
>
> A *second* ... is that [it] takes an essential set of rules defining those relationships and shows how very different types of organization in those relationships can emerge ... called bifurcations.
>
> A *third*, causality is considered multilevel and multideterminate.... Dynamical theory is very well disposed to relating several levels of observation. The language of reductionism and independent and dependent variables gives way to the language of dynamical interactive variables. Interactions include the systems concepts of feedback and control, which lead to the fourth main feature.
>
> This *fourth* feature, self-organization, derives from combining the concept of feedback and the concept of the control parameter. This occurs when the value of the control parameter depends on the state of the system, individuals and societies become aware of critical control parameters and learn to control them for self-improvement (hopefully).
>
> A *fifth* feature is that the visual geometric dynamical approach is highly communicative, ...
>
> A *sixth* ... is the importance of chaos. (Abraham, Abraham, & Shaw, 1990, Part 1, pp. 2–3)

Perhaps these features can be illustrated by an example cited above involving social context and gender identity, that of anorexia. By definition anorexia involves patterns of interaction between eating behavior, psychological variables, biological variables, and social variables with temporal parameters in ultradian, circadian, and infradian domains (first and third features mentioned above; dynamical systems). Anorexic attractors change within all these time domains as a function of social stressors and attributional theoretical aspects such as locus of control (from the second feature mentioned above, bifurcations).

Self-organizational features, from the feminist perspective, would emphasize empowerment of egalitarian opportunities and attitudes in society and changes in social attitudes toward respect for individuals based upon substantial personal values rather than upon superficial ones such as body image (from the fourth feature above, self-organization). Psychology could make a transformational contribution to society, generate needed research, and emphasize its interventive and preventive roles as among its contributions.

The dynamical scheme might emphasize the change from normal eating behavior interacting with socially imposed stress as a function of learned helplessness or social fairness as control parameters, allowing the change from a single-lobed chaotic attractor with motion within normal bounds changing to a larger, double-lobed chaotic attractor, carrying an individual into extreme eating behavior ranges of binging and starving, the fifth and sixth features (see Fig. 21.1).

THE SYNERGY SUMMARIZED

The language and conceptualization of Crawford and Maracek (1989) in feminist psychology, montaged with that of Abraham et al. (1990) illustrate their synergy. With respect to research emphasis:

> An important difference between the Psychology of Gender framework and those previously described is that the conception of gender as a process cannot be readily accommodated within conventional methods of psychological research when social organization and social relations are the subjects of inquiry; laboratory experiments are not necessarily the best means of study. (Crawford & Maracek, 1989, p. 157)

> [Dynamics] has implications for improved experimental designs emphasizing multiple measurements over time; studying changes in individual's states over time has long been considered the proper study of psychology, but previously we have been impoverished without the conceptual, empirical, and linguistic (communicative, computational, or graphic) tools with which to exploit this point of view. (Abraham et al., 1990, Part I, pp. 2–3)

Or:

> One of the major contributions of chaos theory, to focus on variance and to suggest that what is often thrown away as random or error variability (assumed by the linear analysis of variance design philosophy of much of our science), is, in fact, deterministic, with complex, intricate structure. [It should] get us to focus more on tracking changes in biosocialpsychological processes over adequate periods of time and with adequate temporal resolution in order to characterize more adequately the phase portrait which epitomizes some biosocialpsychological process. This means a revolution in our experimental designs as well as our conceptual approaches. (Abraham et al., 1990, Part 3, pp. 112–113)

Figure 21.1: Response Diagram of Attribution Model of Eating Behavior
The three-dimensional state space consists of eating (e), similar to expectancy of personal efficacy, internalization (i), and situational specificity (ss), both global and stable. The control parameter could be derived from self-confidence, learned helplessness, or social fairness.

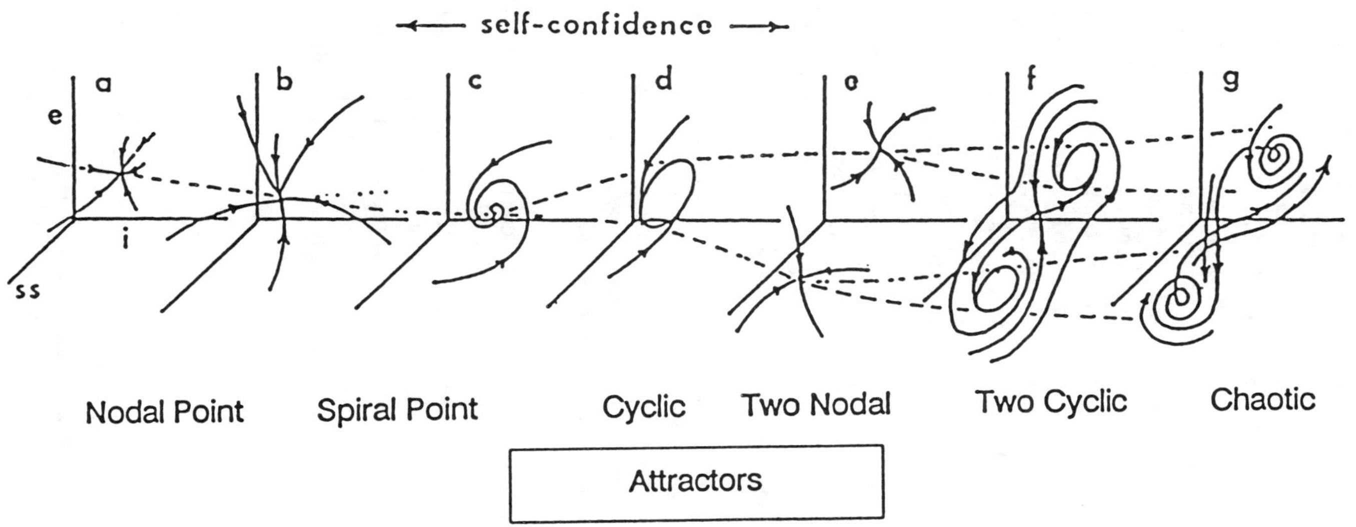

With respect to self-organizational cooperative control of critical parameters, "Feminism hold the promise of helping psychology to be more self-conscious about its values and to change them as needed in order to promote equality and social justice" (Crawford & Maracek, 1989, p. 158). Indeed, "If one holds truth to be historically and culturally situated, then methods should focus on dynamic processes and regard historical and cultural influences not as 'nuisance variance' but as legitimate objects of study (Hoffnung, 1985)" (Crawford & Maracek, 1989, p. 159). This last also relates to the comments above about error variance. Further, "revision of the research paradigm to one of mutual collaboration, in which the research participant is acknowledged as the primary interpreter of her or his experience and the research initiator is acknowledged as emotionally involved and as changed by the process of doing the research" (Crawford & Maracek, 1989, p. 159).

Note the dynamic interaction, the inseparability of points to be summarized, itself a self-reflective process whereby the self-control and bifurcational transformative aspects of psychology are tied to the changes needed in research strategy, a point also mentioned by Crawford & Maracek: "[Despite constraints of written presentation] the approaches are interactive" (1989, p. 161).

Complex dynamical networks with self-organizational capabilities can select values of control parameters that produce more desirable phase portraits. A system becomes aware of its control parameters and learns to control them to effect changes in its portraits. It learns bifurcational behavior. Packard has suggested even that a system can change the dimensions of its state space (private communication). Features of self-control provide the basis of professional, group, and personal life-style, self-help, and social consciousness-raising programs. (Abraham et al., 1990, Part 3, pp. 117–118)

As a final summary, we might note that feminist psychology has created a revolution in psychology paralleled by and synergistic with that proposed by dynamics. Contextualization is emphasized by the dynamic interrelatedness of psychosocial variables. Critical history emphasizes the need for the recognition of social values in the transformational processes in psychology and society, those viewed as self-organization, the learning of bifurcational behavior by self-reflective dynamical schemes. This is especially true for those with culturally rich diversity and a respect for individual rights.

REFERENCES

Abraham, F. D. (1975). Biobehavioral technology: Is it really neutral? *Contemporary Psychology, 20,* 250–251.

Abraham, F. D., Abraham, R. H., & Shaw, C. D. (1990). *A visual introduction to dynamical systems theory for psychology.* Santa Cruz: Aerial Press.

Bem, S. L. (1975). Sex role adaptability: One consequence of psychological androgyny. Journal of Personality and Social Psychology, 31, 634–643.

Bem, S. L. (1981). Gender schema theory: A cognitive account of sex-typing. Psychological Review, 88, 354–364.

Bem, S. L. (1984). Androgyny and gender schema theory: A conceptual and empirical integration. Nebraska Symposium on Motivation, 32, 179–226.

Bohan, J. S. (1991, November). Gilligan, Chodorow, and women's ways of knowing: Denial or diversity? Paper presented at the annual convention of the American Education Research Association, San Jose, CA.

Broverman, I. K., Broverman, D. M., Clarkson, F. E., Rosenkrantz, P. S., & Vogel, S. R. (1970). Journal of Consulting and Clinical Psychology, 34, 1–7.

Caplan, P. J. (1984). The myth of women's masochism. American Psychologist, 39, 130–139.

Chesler, P. (1972). Women & madness. New York: Avon.

Cogan, J. (1992). Fat and feminism: A dangerous liaison? Paper presented at the annual conference of the Association for Women in Psychology, Long Beach, CA, February, 1992.

Crawford, M., & Maracek, J. (1989). Psychology reconstructs the female 1968–1988. Psychology of Women Quarterly, 13, 147–165.

Denmark, F. L. (1980). From rocking the cradle to rocking the boat. American Psychologist, 35, 1057–1065.

Ehrlich, A., & Abraham, F. D. (1974, September). Caution, mental health may prove hazardous. Human Behavior, 3, 64–77.

Faludi, S. (1991). Backlash: The undeclared war against American women. New York: Crown.

Gergen, M. M. (1988). Building a feminist methodology. Contemporary Social Psychology, 13, 47–53.

Gilligan, C. (1982). In a different voice: Psychological theory and women's development. Cambridge: Harvard University Press.

Harding, S. (1991). Whose science? Whose knowledge? Ithaca: Cornell University Press.

Kahn, A. S., & Yoder, J. D. (1989). The psychology of women and conservatism: Rediscovering social change. Psychology of Women Quarterly, 13, 417–432.

Lewin, K. (1951). Field theory in social science. New York: Harper & Row.

Loye, D., & Eisler, R. (1987). Chaos and transformation: Implications of nonequilibrium theory for social science and society. Behavioral Science, 32, 53–65.

Mednick, M. T. (1989). On the politics of psychological constructs: Stop the bandwagon I want to get off. American Psychologist, 44, 1118–1123.

Murphy, P. L., & Bohan, J. S. (1992). Psychology's past as feminist prologue: Recurring women's visions. Paper presented at annual conference of the Association for Women in Psychology, Long Beach, CA, February, 1992.

Riger, S. (1992). Epistemological debates, feminist voices. American Psychologist, 47, 730–740.

Shields, S. A. (1975). Functionalism, Darwinism, and the psychology of women. American Psychologist, 30, 739–754.

Spence, J. T., Helmreich, R. L., & Stapp, J. (1975). Ratings of self and peers on sex role attributions and their relation to self-esteem and conceptions of masculinity and femininity. Journal of Personality and Social Psychology, 32, 29–39.

Vicenzi, A. E. (1994). Chaos theory and some nursing considerations. *Nursing Science Quarterly*, 7, 36–42.

Part VI
EPILOGUE

22
Commentary
Karl H. Pribram

Much of science is technologically driven. Mathematics is a technical achievement somewhat different from most in that it is essentially mental rather than material, even in its instantiations. As a form of mathematics, nonlinear dynamics and its offspring chaos theory are technical achievements and this volume examines their impact on the issues that concern psychology. The contents of the volume, however, are not just science. Rather, the volume is often metatheoretical and deals with the philosophy of applying chaos and related formulations to specific problems in psychology. My claim that this is so is based on the fact that all the contributors begin with an interest in one or another chaos-related formulations, which is then applied to their psychological concern. Except for the chapter by Gary Burlingame, Addie Fuhriman, and Karl Barnum, who compared a lag sequential analysis to one based on chaos theory, there is little testing of alternative hypotheses to detect a best fit to explain a particular finding. The assumption is that previous attempts to use linear or stochastic explanations have failed and that nonlinearity comes to the rescue.

Given this reading of the contents of this book, there are many fascinating and important contributions to be found. Sally Goerner sets the stage: There are two faces to chaos theory. One face shows that all that appears random is not stochastic and indeterminate. Deterministic chaos comes about by way of positive Liapunov exponents that reflect forces toward divergence that results in random-looking results. This face of chaos is interesting but was anticipated by information measurement theory: The greater the amount of information describing a set of entities or events, the greater the uncertainty. Also, this face, in its philosophical import, is shown when a Fourier transform is performed leading to a display in the spectral domain, as in a hologram and in the simplest of David Bohm's implicate orders. Neither information measurement theory nor the enfolding (implication) of space and time in holography demands nonlinearity to accomplish.

The second face of chaos theory is the more unique and equally far-reaching in its philosophical import. Stabilities can be achieved far from equilibrium. This insight, carefully promulgated by Ilya Prigogine, has made me wish that the formulation had been baptized turbulence theory rather than chaos theory. The formulation deals with dynamics, with the time evolution of a process. When the process becomes turbulent, nonlinearities describe it and stabilities far from equilibrium can occur.

Goerner makes an additional important point. Because history is turbulent, nonlinear dynamical descriptions are appropriate; thus hermeneutics becomes scientific. Allan Combs adds to this line of thought that chaos theory provides the tools for shifting psychology from a predominantly nomothetic science to one that allows for an idiographic orientation.

Walter Freeman's chapter is a beautifully written description of where and how nonlinear dynamics applies to the nervous system as it relates to experience. The chapter is destined to become a classic, and although here and there I have some disagreements with its author, this chapter alone makes it worth owning the book.

The promise of dynamics for the study of emotion and motivation is developed by Steve Guastello, Kevin Dooley, and Jeffrey Goldstein, who delineate the connection between current theorizing and that of Kurt Lewin (force fields are seen as attractors) and Ross Ashby's "Law of Requisite Variety."

Guastello, Dooley, and Goldstein also review the work of Hubler, which addresses one of the major concerns I have expressed with regard to the development of stabilities far from equilibrium. For almost twenty years I have argued with Prigogine regarding the brusselator and other far-from-equilibrium devices that develop stabilities. All such devices are constrained, whether by a vessel wall containing a chemical solution, a river's bank and bed, or a set of streets and buildings, as in Brussels. These constraints frame the dynamic process and are as necessary to the formation of temporary stabilities as are initial conditions (such as Liapunov functions). Fred Abraham expresses similar concerns. What Hubler has contributed is that these constraints controlling the dynamic process can also be dynamic and even weakly chaotic. When appropriately matched, the control system adapts its behavior so that it interacts with the parent system to self-organize a simplified "stable" resultant.

A related method of producing control has been developed by Min Xie at Radford University's Center for Brain Research and Informational Sciences in conjunction with Peter Kugler. Xie has shown that when a part of a large bifurcating network can come under the control of a constraining process, the entire network will stabilize. And Kugler has emphasized that such constraints are especially effective during the period of increasing fluctuation that just precedes a bifurcation.

Fred Abraham makes a valiant attempt at introducing the reader to the basic language of nonlinear dynamics. This is no easy task in a field so new that it has spawned several research groups each of which has developed its own somewhat idiosyncratic definitions of terms. On the whole, nonetheless, Abraham succeeds (although his definitions do not help much in reading his brother's chapter). Abraham takes the large view of chaos theory. He does not explicitly state this, but it is evident that he considers two forms of chaos: stochastic, or high-dimensional, and deterministic. Thus he can include stochastic resonance under the chaos rubric. (We have spent considerable effort showing that unentrained axonal spike trains in hippocampus and neocortex are stochastic and not determined.) In the same vein he uses simulated annealing as an example of a chaotic process.

In view of the use of simulated annealing by Hopfield in describing processing in his single-layered neural networks, the inclusion of several chapters on neural nets is understandable. These chapters, written mostly by Levine, Leven, and Prueitt (Part IV) use nonlinear dynamics or chaos theory in their simulations. The connection between these two technical achievements is especially well spelled out in the chapter by Guastello, Dooley, and Goldstein. These authors describe models of organizational learning by neural networks as an example of a nonlinear chaotic process leading to self-organization.

Warren Tryon, who also contributes to Part IV, makes the point in his chapter that chaos theory is a process theory and as such portrays the geometrical structure of the time evolution of the nonlinear process. This point is also made by Abraham, but Tryon apposes this structural approach to that of the behaviorists who are functionalists in their procedures. In this sense, but only in this sense, nonlinear dynamics is closer to cognitive psychology than it is to the behaviorist paradigm.

Cognitivists have been imbued with the structuralist view of linguistics since Lévi-Strauss, Saussure, and Chomsky. Miller, Galanter, and Pribram's *Plans and the Structure of Behavior* brought this view to bear on the rest of psychology. But plans were shown to emerge from images, the decision (bifurcation) nodes in treelike structures (programs). In *Languages of the Brain* I began to tackle the problem of image processing. I suggested that local field potentials in the synaptodendritic microstructure of the cerebral cortex are the responsible processes, processes that can be described mathematically as akin to Gabor's mathematical invention of holography. In *Brain and Perception* this suggestion is developed into a full-fledged data-based theory. Holography was found to be one end of a continuum, the other end being our ordinary space-time experience. In between, the best description of the process centers on Gabor's definition of a quantum of information. The holographic record is made up of coefficients representing the amplitudes of intersections among interfering and reenforcing wave forms; Gabor's quanta of information are minima of uncertainty in a Hilbert space consisting of sinusoids constrained by space-time structures. These formulations are all essentially linear and go a long way toward describing and explaining the sensory driven aspects of perception.

I have belabored this history because it bears directly on nonlinear dynamics and chaos theory. Harold Pattee has for many years emphasized a distinction between structure as it applies to linguistic processing and the dynamical formulations of physics and thermodynamics. Dynamical formulations are essentially field formulations—though this does not mean that they cannot be represented discretely, as by Fourier or Gabor coefficients. Nonlinear dynamics as practiced in chaos theory provides a new geometric representation of process that is different from that embodied in structural linguistics and symbolic programming. As in the case of Hilbert spaces and Schroedinger differential equations, these representations have not become staples in tackling problems in psychology. One of the hopes expressed repeatedly in this volume is that dynamical explanations, whether linear or nonlinear, will at least be tried in scientific psychology. But a warning needs to be heeded: Many of the early applications of chaos theory to aspects of brain function were found to be due to artifacts of the technique. Rigorous controls using split data sets and phase shifting have to be used before a process can be ascertained to be truly deterministic.

I have not covered all the proposals and applications of chaos theory put forward in these chapters. Each reader will, of course, be excited or dismayed by different chapters depending on her or his own interest and expertise. In addition, I benefited greatly not only from what I covered above, but also from Ralph Abraham's "brief history," which extends from before Kurt Lewin through Gregory Bateson to his own contributions. The reader will also see that Frederick and Ralph Abraham are by no means satisfied with the accomplishments of current chaos theory. Fred Abraham emphasizes insensitivity to initial conditions in his observations, and Ralph Abraham has embarked on a wholly new though related enterprise he calls *erodynamics*.

As a final point, however, I want to make clear one more distinction. This one regards self-organization and autopoiesis. At a dinner in my house one evening a decade ago, Ilya Prigogine and Francisco Varela were arguing vehemently about their respective views on self-organization. The argument made it clear that they were not talking about the same process. The difference was clarified for me by Heinz von Foerster, a good friend of Maturana, who was Varela's mentor. The concept of autopoiesis was generated by the observation that structural integrity, the biological form of a membrane, cell, or organism is maintained in the face of constant exchange of the components that make up that biological form. Autopoiesis deals with self-maintenance rather than with the creation of form, which is the emphasis in Prigogine's program. Chaos theory encompasses both: the creation of stabilities far from equilibrium and their maintenance by fixed-point, periodic, or fractal attractors. On the basis of this analysis Prigogine's program is at the moment incomplete. Perhaps some of the suggestions forwarded by the Abrahams will in due time formally address this important issue.

23

A Postscript on Language, Modeling, and Metaphor

Frederick David Abraham

The souls of **tohu**, *of chaos, are higher than the souls of order (they are very great). They seek much from reality, more than their vessels can endure. They seek very great illumination. Everything which is bounded, delimited, and arranged they cannot bear. . . .*
Strength appears in the form of **tohu**, *but finally it will be taken from the evil ones and given to the righteous, who with the heroism of lions, through a forceful and clear reason, with the strong feeling, in a practical clear, and ordered way, will reveal the true order of construction.*   Rav Abraham Isaac Kook

In earlier chapters we set three themes for this book. Our first theme was set in the preface on, and in large part by, Leibniz. We shared his hope for a *unified language*, in order to find a balance between unity and diversity within science and within our discipline. We have speculated before that the waxing and waning evolution of this balance itself could be viewed as a dynamical system enjoying ample amounts of chaos and bifurcation. A chaotic attractor has a multiplicity of interacting forces of convergence to the attractor and divergence away from the attractor whose resolution makes for its chaotic charm. When the forces of divergence within the discipline are great, taking the trajectory to the outer reaches of its historical attractor, the discipline appears too diversified (psychology in the 1980s), and then the forces of attraction become greater, bending the trajectory homeward again. When the forces of convergence are greater, and the attractor becomes shrunken or the trajectory is too near the center, the discipline appears too rigid and fixed, as in the days of the grand psychological theories (1940s and 1950s), and divergent forces tend to increase again (Tryon herein, and Gilgen, 1987, and Staats, 1991, for issues of unity and diversity). Our hope is that dynamics (dynamical systems theory) will provide a common language for the evolution of our discipline. It provides several major concepts packed into a few basic terms (a reasonably complete starter kit is contained in the basic concepts chapter). Even more compelling, those terms are well represented by visual-geometric forms (trajectories, phase portraits, response diagrams, bifurcation diagrams, and network diagrams) that constitute an easily communicable language, at least for those who are at home with graphic representations.

Our second theme is that dynamics provides a *metamodeling strategy* for our science. By metamodeling strategy we mean that the mathematical techniques of dynamics supply a way of developing scientific models to represent variables— observed as well as hypothetical (MacCorquodale & Meehl, 1948; Marx, 1951)— interacting over time and suggest experimental design and analysis techniques for testing those models. As the survey within this book shows, it is clear that the evolution toward a mature science is still in very preliminary stages of its development. Bringing this evolution to fruition will depend upon an appreciation of the language simplification and metamodeling generality of the dynamical approach.

Our third theme is that in addition to providing a metamodeling strategy, dynamics also provides a perspective, a *metaphorical approach*, to professional applications. That is, it forms the basis of informal models for viewing the complex nature of the universe and of various psychological phenomena, using them as a perspective for making decisions concerning therapy, social progress, and organizational development, with or without the assistance of scientific instantiation of those metaphors. The research chapters (Part II) and the neural net chapters (Part IV) and the chapter on organizations (Guastello et al., Chap. 19, this volume) depict examples where scientific support is used for such decision making, whereas the remaining chapters on social applications (Part V) and those on cognition (Part III) are more speculative and metaphorical, though some of them come closer to using scientific modeling results and some even present research results (e.g., Combs, Chap. 8, this volume).

Caution: This chapter could be hazardous to your mental dynamics if attempted by the beginning reader before reading the Leibniz correspondence and Chapter 3 on basic concepts, as well as a significant portion of the remainder of the book. Some topics venture a bit into the more philosophical and mathematical than previously, and those portions can be skimmed or ignored if obscure; the gist should be evident. It was felt that some of the implications of the dynamical approach for psychology could be dealt with by such hints made necessary by the constraints which time and space requirements impose against more complete explication. Some of the interests expressed here reflect concerns among the membership of the Society for Chaos Theory in Psychology and are an attempt to put some focus on them rather than resolve them.

LANGUAGE

The issue is the extent to which there can be established an evolving, dynamical, scientific linguistic community of sufficient magnitude to increase interdisciplinary productivity. Note the implied but untestable conjecture that such an improvement could be achieved and is desirable. To make such an attempt, some caveats upon the use of language and its abuses that occurs early in the development of a new approach might be worth noting. Trying to standardize language is impossible, and to do so is like playing the chaos cop or the fractal fascist. But we might hope for sufficient clarity and communality of usage to increase communicability without suffering loss of colorfulness of language or creativity (Goldstein, 1995). What kind of aberrations commonly occur and which cause the worst problems?

Synonyms: Multiple Terms for the Same Definition

Let us get the easy, trivial one out of the way first. When a standard concept is referenced by two or more distinct terms, usually little difficulty is caused. The most obvious example in dynamics is the synonymous use of Smale's *strange attractor* which has largely given way to the Li and Yorke-inspired *chaotic attractor*. Another, less common example is the term *dynamic equilibrium* that some mathematicians occasionally use for *attractor*. The various attractors themselves have numerous, usually careless but acceptable and clear synonyms, such as *point, limit point,* and, of course *asymptote* as synonyms for *fixed-point attractor*; and *cyclic attractor* and *limit cycle* for *periodic attractor*. These are clear and trivial when the invention of a new term or variant is both clear and catches the professional fancy, such as the terms *strange* and *chaos*.

It becomes more confusing, however, when instead of a deliberate attempt to invent a new term, there is inadvertent creation of a new term from a failure of awareness of the preexistence of basic language and concepts. There are many authors in psychology who are making for great confusion by failing to become adequately familiar with basic concepts and terminology. Even in this volume, the editors often had to beg authors to standardize terminology to be consistent with dynamics. For example, occasionally there are people reinventing the concept of a Poincaré section (whose most common synonym is *strobe section*). Thus when encountering idiosyncratic language, the reader must judge whether the language is founded on a good grasp of dynamics, is consistent with that language, and represents a good selection of variants or extension of those concepts, without violating basic dynamics concepts; or whether a shakier understanding of dynamics is obfuscated by idiosyncratic language. Examples of good usage and an enviable command of dynamics are found especially in Walter Freeman's and Ralph Abraham's chapters. We cannot pretend that all of our authors possess the same mathematical sophistication, but all have a fertility of insight and imagination that make them important contributors to the development of our discipline nonetheless. Even some of the most sophisticated, such as Guastello (an expert at catastrophe theory, a major branch of dynamics and one of the first in the United States, following the lead of Zeeman in England in applying it to psychology) and the neural net folk, whose mathematical modeling is very sophisticated, have had some animated discussions over terminology. Although the editors themselves can claim only limited competence in dynamics, they often prevailed by sheer stubbornness in shaping the language used in this book, which will explain for those who read further in the field, any discrepancies between the language of some chapters herein and other writings by some of these same authors.

Multiple Definitions for the Same Term

Much more confusing than problems caused by synonyms are the problems caused by having multiple definitions for the same term.

The Strange Case of Chaos

Many disciplines have naughty words they wish they could escape. In dynamics, the bad word is *chaos*. In neural nets it is *connection*. If a physicist can use *charm* with charm and without causing harm, why is *chaos* so treacherous (Penzance, 1880)? Its lay use as meaning "disordered" can claim only a small part of the blame, for we quickly learn that *chaos* is a mixture of order and complexity, with different degrees of each as if on a continuum, or that it can be considered as the resolution of apparent opposites, like yin/yang—that is, order and disorder are but different perspectives or different extremes of the same process. A major source of this problem derives from the fact that *chaos* is becoming too popular, a buzzword, and this popularity and proselytizing implies that it is okay to be metaphorical in a loose way, to untie the term from any precise mathematical conceptualizations or operational definitions. In doing so we become schizophrenic about the term. We feel we have to use it as a code to symbolize the accessibility of dynamics as a simple and unifying language and to tap into the current popularity of the term to get an audience for the serious ideas behind it, but we are chagrined at the misconceptions not only within lay audiences but within the profession as well. Thus even those of us who are enthusiastic proselytizers of dynamics and stress its accessibility do not want its power to be lost in an appearance of oversimplification and in misunderstanding. Somewhere there is a fine line, a bifurcation point, between simplification and oversimplification. This maturing of perspective has been stressed by several authors recently (Abraham, 1993; Barton, 1994; Basar, 1990; Pribram, Chap. 22; Townsend, 1994).

A more subtle aspect of *chaos*'s becoming a buzzword is that the term was originally coined for the chaotic attractor, thus representing but one branch of dynamics, that dealing with characterizing chaotic attractors, but is now being used in an alternative meaning as standing for the whole field of dynamics. Sometimes it is generalized even further, as exemplified by Goerner (Chap. 1) who capitalized it to stress even broader use, including not only dynamics but many additional or complementary approaches to the study of complexity.

Even within the technical realm of mathematics there is some divergence of meaning in the term *chaos,* and attempting adequate definitions can be anticipated to confound the field of mathematics for years to come. Following the majority of mathematicians, we have called any attractor that is neither a fixed-point nor a periodic attractor a chaotic attractor. Some, including mathematician Deveney (1989) and neurobiologist Paul Rapp (1993, 1995), add a requirement of sensitivity to initial conditions (the divergence in the short term of trajectories from close initial points within the attractor). There are nearly periodic attractors that exist in two dimensions (created by coupling two periodic oscillators whose frequency ratio is irrational, that is, never repeating, like π), like a toroidal winding (a bagel-like shape with trajectories that wind around its surface), for which a given trajectory never comes back exactly to a previously visited point. Nearby trajectories in such a phase portrait do not show this divergence or sensitivity to initial conditions. If this case is denied to the term *chaos,* then the usual observation holds that chaos requires at least three dimensions for continuous variables because only in three dimensions could a complex trajectory fail to cross itself, and crossing itself would place it at a point previously visited; with a stationary process, the vector at that point would be the same as before and the trajectory would be off on the same trip as before, the same vectorfield holding, and thus the trajectory would be periodic. Thus many authors, such as neurobiologist Erol Basar, create a separate category of *nearly periodic* attractors (for the two-dimensional case of the surface of toroids and Mobius strips for which sensitivity to initial conditions is not involved). The term *nearly periodic* could be further misleading in that low-dimensional attractors, for example, three-dimensional attractors such as the Rössler and the Lorenz, are close to being periodic and they do possess sensitivity to initial conditions. It could be misleading also because most times series that are not simply various types of noise such as white noise and $1/f$ noise have strong frequency components in their spectra, revealing those near periodicities. What would be nice to have is a classification of different kinds of chaos and of bifurcations among them.

Far from Equilibrium

A similar problem occurs when analogous terminology is carried over from other nonlinear approaches, and again this often occurs because of inadequate understanding of these terms. The most common example is Prigogine's *far from equilibrium.* This is not a term from dynamics, but it can easily be translated to dynamical concepts and language. There have been various uses of this phrase, which implied, (1) any departure from a fixed-point attractor, (2) a chaotic attractor, (3) going through a series of bifurcations away from a fixed-point attractor, or (4) being at or near a bifurcation point, that is at an instability, rather than at a stable attractor (remember the synonym *dynamic equilibrium* for all types of attractors: point, periodic, and chaotic). For explicitness, we suggest the language of dynamics rather than the language of equilibrium theory. The concepts of stability and bifurcation have explicit mathematical definitions using topological equivalence and epsilon equivalence (specifying a range acceptable or equivalent values).

Technical Linguistic Stretching

Another common aberration, usually trivial, is to stretch a term from dynamics to cover something outside its original mathematical meaning. Again, *Poincaré section* comes to mind, with iterative or lagged maps of neural or behavioral latencies often erroneously referred to as such (Diez Martinez, Pérez, Budelli, & Segundo, 1988). They are close cousins that reveal similar information. Again, the more basics you know, the easier it is to navigate through various usages. Except for the barest introduction in Chapter 3 on basic concepts, this book is not intended to provide a comprehensive guide to proper usage. It is more of a guide to the fertility and directions toward which people in our discipline are pushing.

Truth and language are themselves interactive components, parts of a dynamic process, always fluid, ever changing, forever elusive. As Count Korzybski (1933) observed, "In the miseducation of our youth we teach them semantic rules based on static Aristotelian classifications which they must then use in dealing with a fluid dynamic universe. Such semantic habits are enough out of tune with reality to drive many people crazy."

In discussing philosophical dialogue Greeley (1991) explores the interactive hermeneutic dynamics between reality and language and goes even deeper into their relationship in noting that "it [dialogue] participates in the *creation* of reality by being the way reality is transformed."

So the yin and yang of language is that we want to have a unified approach to communication within our science, but we always have to remind ourselves of the difficulty in finding and representing truth, and of the fluidity and multiplicity in groping for it and even in creating it.

MATHEMATICS AND MODELING

When words fail us, even operationally defined words, we resort to modeling. When in the search for truth we create alternative realities, fictions, and myths we are modeling. For modeling we need rules of communicability, inductibility, deductibility, verifiability, testability, and mathematicability, and the precision that comes with them. These things fool us into thinking we can get closer to the truth. Ha! Well, sometimes they do. We do know the game is fun; it feeds a passion.

Review of Dynamical Modeling

The Nature of a Model

Remember it all starts with the vectorfield. Each point in the state space is associated with a tendency (force) to change in each dimension of the state space. Each dimension of the state space is invented to represent some aspect of observed or hypothesized reality. The tendency for change along each dimension for each point is summarized by a rule, usually a differential equation if the process is considered sufficiently continuous and smooth, or a difference equation for the discrete case. If the vectorfield is smooth enough, and our ingenuity great enough, the same equation works for all the points in the state space. The resolution of the tendencies to change along each of the dimensions is a resultant vector through the volume of space, whatever its dimensionality. As an example we give the set of first order differential equations of King, Barchas, and Huberman's (1984) four-dimensional model of the dopaminergic nigrostriatal system (Fig. 23.1) assumed to participate in normal and schizophrenic emotional functioning:

$$dX/dT = \delta - X - bY - gZ$$
$$dY/dT = aMX - rY$$
$$dZ/dT = tX - rZ$$
$$dM/dT = f(X) - cM$$

Lowercase letters represent constants: depolarizing excitatory inputs to the system, δ; receptor concentrations in two feedback loops, one short, within the substantia nigra, g; and one long, with the caudate, b; rates of release and equilibrium, a; degradative turnover, c; reuptake of presynaptic dopamine, r; and rates of nigral dopamine released per action potential, t. Uppercase letters represent variables: firing rate of the nigral neurons, X; postsynaptic concentration of released striatal neurons on the caudate neurons, Y; concentration of released nigral dopamine at the dendrodendritic terminal, Z; and concentration of dopamine within functional nigral stores M. The rate of synthesis of dopamine is given by the function

$f(X) = \alpha + \beta(X-\overline{X})^2$, where $\overline{X}$ is the mean of X, and α and β are constants.

The nonlinearity occurs in this last function where the rate of synthesis is minimal at the mean firing rate and is greater not only at higher rates where stores are being depleted rapidly but at slower rates as well. Such nonlinearities are responsible for both chaos and bifurcations; neither can exist without a nonlinearity in at least one of the equations of change. The interaction of system components is represented in the equations: The tendency of each variable to change depends not only on the value of that variable but on the value of at least one of the other variables; no variable is isolated from the influence of the others.

Figure 23.1: Neuroanatomical Schematic of the Striatonigral System
SN = Substantia Nigral Neuron
CD = Caudate Neuron
DA = Dopaminergic Synapse
(From Abraham, Abraham, & Shaw, 1990; courtesy Aerial Press.)

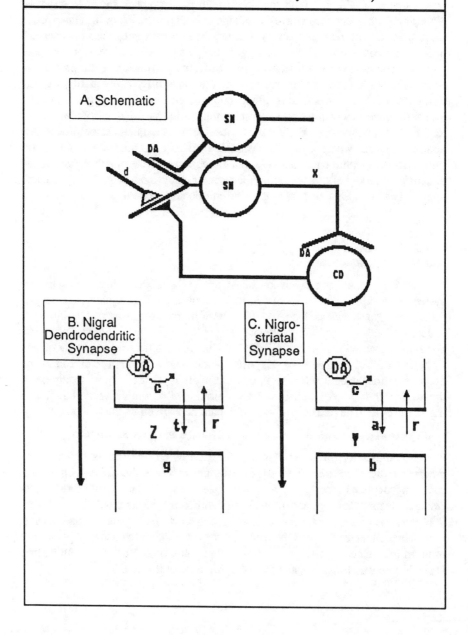

Genesis of Chaos and Bifurcations

How do you get chaos and bifurcations from such modeling? Well, you have a lot of variables pushing each other around, so it is not surprising that the result can be complex. But think of it this way. Suppose you have three clocks or three countries talking to each other. One dominates the others (a driver clock or a colonial power). No chaos, just entrainment or enslavement. The parameters that multiply the variables of influence of the strong one on the others are large; the parameters that multiply the variables of influence of the weak on the strong are small. However, if you make their mutual influence more equal, that is, increase the influence of the weaker clocks upon the stronger, or infuse political independence, money, and arms into weak nations, or weaken the domination of the colonial power, then you get more complex time keeping among the clocks, and a chaotic global economy or political system. It is like a teeter-totter with the fulcrum near the middle; it wiggles, and the kids wiggle, but it stays near the center. You get this condition by adjusting the magnitude of the parameters in the equations for the relative strength of each variable on the rate of change in another variable. In a human family system, you can have dominating members, democracy, and other intermediate flavors of complex interaction.

In the dopaminergic system of King et al. (1984), they found a composite control parameter, k, a function of several parameters of synthesis, availability, and effectiveness $[k = f(\alpha,\beta,a,b,c,r)]$, which when balanced against another control parameter, the strength of the excitatory inputs to the system (δ) was critical. Intermediate values of the latter combined with high values of the former resulted in chaos (Fig. 23.2).

Similarly, any bifurcation, not just the excitation of chaos, represents a critical value at the bifurcation point of a control parameter, where the relative importance of a variable takes a sudden change in the effectiveness of its influence when the parameter is changed). For the King system, going from a fixed-point attractor to a period 2 attractor occurs at lower values of k than those for bifurcations from period 2 to period 4, which were lower than those for excitations of chaos. Our own explorations of their system revealed a catastrophic (fold) bifurcation on the rate of release and equilibrium parameter, a (Fig. 23.3).

Concepts of chaos and bifurcations have enormous implications for psychology. Having the concept of chaos means we can now model more complex phenomena and thus relax our attempts to isolate variables from "extraneous" influences. Having the concept of bifurcation means we can find communalities among many phenomena that previously had no apparent connection and for which we had to invent different theories. Thus a major benefit is parsimony; instead of having separate disparate linear models for different stable regions (with their attractors) separated by bifurcation points, we may be able to find a unifying set of differential or difference equations that account for all and possibly for many other different phenomena that we thought were qualitatively different.

Figure 23.2: Bifurcation Diagram
δ = depolarizing inputs to system
k = measure of synthesis, effectiveness, and availability of dopamine.
s = a parameter of dopaminergic efficiency at the synapse; it influences k.
Period 1 = fixed point attractor.
Period 2, 4 = periodic attractors visiting 2 and 4 values respectively.
Chaotic = chaotic attractor.
MES = region of multiple attractors.
(From King, Barchas, & Huberman, 1984; Courtesy Roy King.)

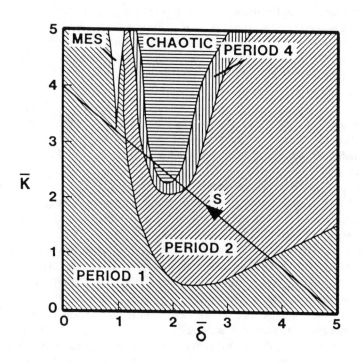

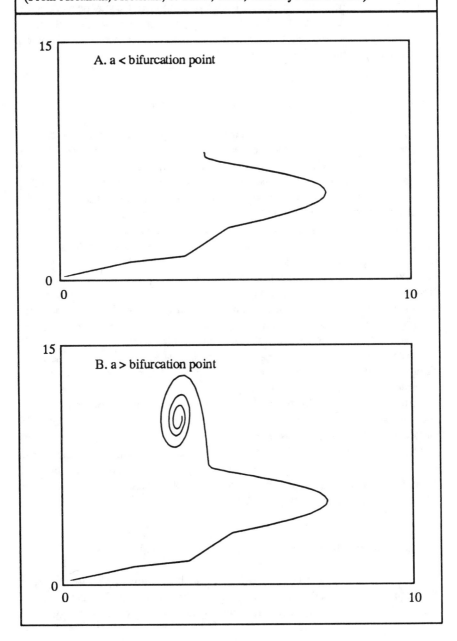

Figure 23.3: Response Diagram (Equivalent)
Change in the 4D trajectory (shadowed in 2D; M vs. X) as a function of the
control parameter, a.
(From Abraham, Abraham, & Shaw, 1990; courtesy Aerial Press.)

Part of the attractiveness of dynamics is that in this quest for parsimony we can have our complexity but we can account for much of the action with fewer variables than we thought might have been required for that apparent complexity with which we were confronted. However, sometimes we think we can get dimensional reduction to very few variates (Basar, 1990) when, indeed, we may be pushing too far (Abraham, 1993; Rössler & Hudson, 1990). Parsimony is worthy when it is a reasonable reflection of nature, not when it is a forced construction distorting our understanding of nature. Easier said than done.

Simulation, Experimental Dynamics, and Visual Geometry

The mathematical discipline of dynamics is largely experimental. There is less emphasis on analytical techniques of theorems and proofs. Instead, various equation sets are designed and then set in motion and explored with computer simulation to discover the dynamic properties we have mentioned, such as finding bifurcation points and separatrices, as well as exploring chaos and sensitivity to initial conditions. This experimental dynamics is the mathematical version of what we scientists do in empirical research. It is their explorations that have led to the computer tools we now have for our modeling and analysis, and to the visual displays that give us a quicker intuitive (and qualitative and quantitative) grasp of data and theory than did the laborious manipulation of equation sets. This computer simulation also means that we can now handle larger sets of interactive variables, making our models more realistic in handling the complexity of our subject matter. Less and less do we have to make a pretense at laboratory isolation of variables that are nearly impossible to isolate, balance, or randomize away.

There is a caution needed here, and that is that some of the techniques of simulation (computer algorithms for integrating the differential equations) are more accurate than others; some can give erroneous results. For example, the Euler integration technique has been known to yield trajectories that are not topologically equivalent to the correct ones for the prey-predator model. Thus each has to be calibrated carefully with a few mathematical objects similar to the ones you wish to explore, and their null-hypothetical counterparts. Some give erroneous results, either false positive results (Type I error) or blindness to nonlinear aspects within data, in the presence of noise or color in the noise (Type II error) (Preissl & Aertsen, 1993; Rapp, 1993, 1995).

Experimental Design and Analysis and Fine Tuning the Model

When most of us first became enthralled with dynamics as providing a real paradigm shift in psychology (a movement basically dating to Zeeman's work of the mid-1970's; but the influence of general systems theory on psychology can be seen in the major theoretical approaches of Lewin and other Gestaltists, Hull and other behaviorists, and Allport and Gibson and other cognitivists, especially, from the 1930s to the 1960s), we felt it was radically different from the experimentally reductionist approaches exemplified in most laboratory research, but that it could revolutionize research and synthesize the reductionist analytic approaches with the holistic, field observational approach. With the first blush of romance between psychology and dynamics now behind us, we can see better the communality with those traditional approaches, though we still feel a rush that dynamics represents a real liberalization for psychology, especially in fusing the accessibility and mathematical sophistication of the dynamical approach.

Functional Relationships; Characterizing Data Dynamically

The operational approach maintains that the search for relevant variables to study can be made on empirical grounds without models of hypothetical variables. It is a respectable scientific strategy. One searches for functional relationships between multivariate measures or between independent and dependent variables. What has dynamics to contribute to this approach? Plenty. In fact, the majority of applications so far in psychology are mostly of this sort, even though they often imply hidden dynamics underlying the complex behavior of data that are observed. The techniques used are simple and straightforward, but a very compelling start to getting psychology involved in the dynamics revolution.

First are the graphic techniques: plotting trajectories, various features of trajectories, and phase portraits. The information in a plotted trajectory is no different than that in a conventional graph of a time series. But the visual insights may be a bit more advantageous or provide an additional perspective (Combs, Chap. 8). Additional techniques, such as Poincaré sections (Metcalf & Allen, Chap. 5; Smith, Chap. 4), attractor reconstructions, and recurrence plots (Sabelli et al., Chap. 7) provide other visual pattern recognition techniques. Pickover (1990) has stressed the importance of presentation or pattern recognition tricks in data presentation, especially in "lateral thinking"–driven research. By displaying two identical axes in their three-dimensional recurrence plots, Sabelli et al. are able to dramatically characterize the dynamics of both stability and change; two dimensions rather than three would have been sufficient to convey the information. I discovered another example of the efficiency of visual trajectories when I looked at some trajectories of the motion of a foot raised in the air while standing on one leg, a test of sobriety used by the police. The trajectory immediately made obvious some smaller-amplitude chaotic oscillations resulting from bilateral instability. Subsequent analysis of power cospectra and coherence spectra supported this contention, but these required more effort to produce and evaluate and would have been much more difficult to evaluate without the graphical reconstruction of the actual motion. These analyses showed that some subjects could constrain the trajectory to a smaller space when inebriated (thus deceiving the police and the experimenter), but again the trajectories revealed that the control was gained at the expense of loss of coordination within certain aspects of the motion (again supported by the other analyses, and of course, they also have their own spectral graphics).

In addition to visualizing more detailed aspects of the motion within a set of data, dynamics provides a variety of measurements about the behavior of an attractor. Liapounov exponents and characteristic exponents and multipliers (complex numbers found as eigenvalues from matrix algebra) are used to characterize rates of approach and spiraling of trajectories about fixed-point and periodic attractors. Their extension to low-dimensional chaotic attractors gives some idea of the complexity and balance of convergent and divergent forces within a chaotic attractor. Another more common measure of the complexity of a data set is the fractal dimension; over thirty definitions exist. Fractal dimension can be made a principal independent or dependent variable in some psychological research (Basar, 1990; Burlingame et al., Chap. 6; Gentry, Chap. 10; Gregson, 1992).

The existence and definability of a fractal dimension has often been used to infer that a chaotic process is involved in a measured time series (or in a spatial variable). That inference transcends the use now under consideration, that of descriptive statistics, and is quite limited in terms of trying to define dimensionality to any underlying process. As a dependent variable, when its value shifts, it may be an indicator that some kind of bifurcation may have taken place. As one measure on either independent or dependent variables, it may be a discriminator of some independent (control) variable. Examples abound, such as Burlingame et al.'s different stages of a group therapeutic process; also, such as EEG during different sleep or arousal stages or under different conditions of research or health (Basar, 1990; Pritchard & Duke, 1992a). It is a good measure of complexity of a data set, when used consistently with the same analysis parameters on similar data. A great deal of exploration is required in any new research setting to determine the best analysis parameters (Basar, 1990; Rapp, 1993, 1995).

There are two varieties of this approach: the single variate and the multivariate. This distinction appears trivial at first glance. At the descriptive level, it pretty much is so except for the methodological analytic techniques used. At a deeper level it leads us to theoretical considerations. We conclude this descriptive section with this methodological distinction before proceeding to theoretical considerations.

The multivariate is actually the simpler of the two. The dimensions of the state space are the measures of the study. A trajectory or a family of trajectories representing a phase portrait is the result. If it is an observational study, then one just examines the character of the trajectory (and its characteristic features such as its fractal dimension) and evidence of its changing dramatically over time (checking it for stationarity and bifurcations). If there is an independent variable, one checks to see if the trajectory's or portrait's features are different, confirming the adequacy of the independent variable as a control parameter. You can concentrate on individual trajectories, or you can play with group data, usually running inferential statistics on the descriptive measures on the trajectories. Only a few studies have used multivariate descriptive trajectories to depict a dynamical process. The alcoholic foot just mentioned and a few multiple-trace EEG studies (Freeman, 1990; Babloyantz, 1990) are examples. Some studies have reduced multiple variables to a single variable (Burlingame et al., Chap. 6; Callahan & Sashin, 1987; Combs, Chap. 8; Hannah, 1990), though some loss of potential information is suffered in so doing.

Most studies using dynamically driven analyses report trajectories for one variable and one individual at a time, along with some of its descriptive statistics (the usual ones such as mean and variance, dynamical measures such as Liapounov exponents, and sometimes power and related spectra (Metcalf & Allen, Chap. 5; Sabelli et al., Chap. 7), and the drunken foot above; and even canonical pattern recognition (Abraham et al., 1973; Sabelli et al., Chap. 7).

A one-dimensional state space makes visualization of the trajectory for a single variate and examination of its properties difficult, so usually it is iteratively turned into a multidimensional space. In physics the motion of a body is usually depicted by a phase portrait or trajectory of its position versus its velocity. (*Phase space* refers to a state space comprised of position and velocity and higher derivatives of the motion of a body; some have generalized this term to all state spaces comprised of a variable and its derivatives; some have even generalized it to stand for *state space*.) A conservative pendulum (no forces other than gravity) has periodic trajectories (no attractors though; a phase portrait called a center; which is very unstable), a dissipative pendulum (with friction) has trajectories spiraling inward to a fixed-point attractor; it comes to rest. There is a variation on this technique that similarly reveals rate-of-change information. (Rate-of-change information may be obtained on any trajectory by coding it with equal time interval markings, so that distance along the trajectory is inversely proportional to velocity. But this is seldom done in practice, even though it is clear with two- and three-dimensional state spaces.) The variation is to plot the value of each point in the time series as a function of that time series at a fixed interval of time preceding it (called the lag or τ). This will produce a trajectory around the 45° line (Combs, Fig. 1, Chap. 8; Metcalf & Allen, several figures, Chap. 5; Sabelli et al., Fig. 2, Chap. 7). Some exploration is important in determining the best lag; and Monte Carlo techniques are used to establish a null baseline (Abraham, 1993; Basar, 1990; Pritchard & Duke, 1992b; Sabelli et al., Chap. 7).

A third dimension can be added by plotting the series displaced by two lags, and a fourth using three lags, and so on. Usually this is done, adding dimensions until the trajectory, assumed to represent an attractor, shows no significant changes. This technique (Ruelle, 1991), often called *attractor reconstruction*, also lies at the heart of defining fractal dimension, as it is part of the iterative process of increasing the dimensions of the state space until the computation of the fractal (correlation) dimension either becomes stable or fails to be definable by failing to be asymptotic within a given number of steps (Babloyantz, 1990; Burlingame et al., Chap. 6).

Thus there are a number of graphic and numerical techniques that can be brought to bear on single or multiple time series collected simultaneously that are motivated by dynamics. Their implementation on computers makes their visual examination, with rotation and zooming (magnification, amplification) much more facile and efficient. Two-dimensional snapshots (Combs, Fig. 1, Chap. 8; Metcalf & Allen, many figures, Chap. 5; Sabelli et al., Fig. 2, Chap. 7) depend on the length of the trajectory plotted for their clarity; they do not compare with the animated and magnification features of real-time computer explorations. You need a dynamical computer program to play this game.

But the case of attractor reconstruction with a single variable raises an interesting issue that transcends the descriptive use of dynamics. Why is the single time series messy, chaotic? What makes it so? Its very complexity suggests hidden processes that must contribute to it.

Theory and Model Testing

We have stated at the outset that dynamics is a metamodeling strategy for studying the mutual interaction of many factors or variables. We can stick an electrode into the brain (Abraham et al., 1973; Babloyantz, 1990; Basar, 1990; Freeman, 1987, 1990; Preissl & Aertsen, 1993); Pritchard & Duke, 1992a, 1992b; Rapp, 1993, 1995), a matrix measure into a group therapy (Burlingame et al., Chap. 6), an EKG electrode on a mental patient (Sabelli et al., Chap. 7), a self-report scale on a person's mood (Combs, Chap. 8; Hannah, 1990), a rate-of-response measure on a rat (Metcalf & Allen, Chap. 5) or other measures of learned and social behavior (Levine & Leven, Chap. 15; Smith, Chap. 4), and a measure of linguistic accuracy on real or virtual language (Prueitt, Chap. 17). We can examine mental, evolutionary, and immunological change (Combs, Chap. 8; Gilgen, Chap. 9; Goerner, Chap. 1; Goertzel, Chap. 12), apply various measures on the interaction of individuals and society (Part V), or examine creativity as revealed in literature, art, philosophy, and therapy (Mosca, Chap. 13) or word learning (Smith, Chap. 4), or even on the field of psychology itself (Tryon, Chap. 18). In all cases we are likely to get a messy signal. It is clear that this is so often not because there is a single unitary endogenous chaotic process (though that is often possible) but because there are several processes mutually influencing one another, with none completely dominating the others, and all having some partial influence on some of the others. That is what we wish to model.

Techniques of attractor reconstruction and dimensional estimation try to ask the question: If we have but one measure, what do we learn about the several processes contributing to the measured variable? How many are there, and how strong is their influence on the measured variable and on each other? The answer is often not a heck of a lot, but at least it may provide some clues. The dimensionality at best places a lower limit on the number of processes involved. Estimates of EEG dimensionality from several authors (Babloyantz, 1990; Basar, 1990; Freeman, 1987, 1990; Pritchard & Duke, 1992a, 1992b; Rapp, 1993, 1995) yield fractal dimensions that are definable in about three-fourths of the cases, and vary from about two to fifteen, with lower dimensionality in diseases such as epilepsy and Alzheimer's and with higher dimensionality representing complex mental activity. That would suggest that normally at least fifteen primary processes interact to produce EEG with the large percentage of undefinable cases suggesting many more that simply exhaust even our computer patience in attempts to discover how many. Such bifurcations among attractors of varying complexity suggest that despite the apparent complexity of the brain, for much functioning it is lower-dimensional than its appearance might suggest. Hubler (1992) explains this tendency toward lower dimensionality as the sharing of an influence on several control parameters in a complex dynamical system, a feature sought for turbulent physical systems (Lorenz, 1963; Ruelle, 1991).

Examination of an attractor might often suggest the nature of the dynamical system if its appearance is similar to that of known mathematical objects. For example, I have suggested that many psychological phenomena often display bilobed attractors (normal-abnormal, manic-depressive, etc.), possibly making them mathematical cousins of either the Lorenz attractor or the buckling column, but I was careful to further suggest that there could be differences that might be found in nature from those in the toolboxes found on mathematicians' shelves. Another example, from the basic concepts chapter herein, is the prey-predator model which can be employed for neural, behavioral, and family systems. Similarly, well-known models such as the Van der Pol oscillators or Brusselators (another common mathematical oscillator) can be used to model both individual and social approach-avoidance conflict, and the logistic equation has been used to model motivation and other psychological constructs. Even more mature models are found where knowledge of the dynamics of the system can generate, along with competent imagination of the modeler, the equations of the variables of the system, as in the King model above, and the work on the olfactory system in learning and perception by Freeman (1987), and by many examples in neural nets (Freeman, Chap. 2; Part IV; Guastello et al., Chap. 19). In some ways these models are similar to those of traditional components of variance models of inferential statistics where several variables are evaluated for their contribution to the variance of a measure, and other variables whose contributions cannot be evaluated, are considered lumped as error or noise. Experimental designs are used to evaluate the contributions of the main variables and minimize and nullify the contributions of confounding and error through counterbalancing and randomization. When modeling with dynamical systems, we have each of the principal variables represented by a differential or difference equation and a dimension of the state space, each such variable is a function of itself and some combination of the other variables. These interactive variables thus produce a simultaneous set of differential equations that are solved by computer integration. In most open systems, we still cannot guess or evaluate all the variables with which any given variable may be coupled, but as in the components-of-variance model of traditional inferential design and analysis, we hope to specify as many of the strong couplings as we can. Then we too may lump the remaining, many numerous ones, into a noise term. Such noise terms often behave like linear processes, and so if the unaccounted many but weak contributions are great, the process can be dominated by linearity. Similarly, when a process is stationary (the control parameter is constant and bifurcations are not occurring), many attractors are well behaved (their attractors are point and periodic, not chaotic) and can be represented by linear dynamical systems, as are found in many neural net models and in the Gaborian perceptual-imaging algorithms of Pribram (1991).

Typically, testing nonlinear dynamical models consists of visually comparing the trajectories or phase portraits of the models to those generated by experiment, whether from multidimensional times series or from attractor reconstructions from single time series. One of the best programs showing closeness of an observed trajectory to that of a hypothetical one is that of Freeman (1987, 1990). There are very few research programs that generate or test several different alternative theories to see which best fits the data. This has been done within neural net theory and stochastic resonance theory (stochastic resonance and simulated annealing, previously mentioned, look at the usefulness of noise in assisting bifurcations and signal following, often with linear models winning out over nonlinear), but usually these have been done with a predicted future time, rather than by following the time course of the process in detail as emphasized by dynamics through its focus on trajectories and phase portraits (Chialvo & Apkarian, 1993; Levine, 1991).

So you have two trains of thought. One, that a single measure reflects the behavior of all the hypothetical or underlying processes involved (see also references to Gershenfeld; Gullimen; & Packard in Sabelli et al., Chap. 7) and can thus represent a higher-dimensional system; and the other, that higher-dimensional processes can often be understood or modeled by lower-dimensional processes (Hubler, 1992; Ruelle, 1991). In between the twain shall meet. With a cwash, maybe? We are confronted with the usual hypothetical deductive problem that our measured variables are usually but poor relatives of the real processes underneath whose nature eludes us.

When there are many interactive factors in open systems, can we make critical tests of our theories? Long have we known that you cannot prove theories. It was felt that you could disprove some. But given enough parameters, you could fit a curve to any set of data points. If you could do that with any number of theories, then you could not discriminate between theories. In fact, you always had an infinite set of theories that might be applicable to any phenomena. You could describe an elephant; add the time variable and you could make it wag its tail, we used to quote.

Oreskes, Shrader-Frechette, and Belitz (1994) have again raised this skepticism within the context of dynamical numerical models. They point out that the rules of deductive logic to establish truth and falseness to propositions are applicable only to the closed systems of logical structures in symbolic logic and mathematics (and Gödel put even that possibility in doubt); all real systems are open systems, and their completeness unknown. This incompleteness comes not only from not knowing all the variables that might be involved but from the inability to specify the values of all the control "input" parameters. (Within dynamical investigations, when known and controlled, some of these control parameters can become independent variables.) This problem is exacerbated in field and naturalistic study. Seldom can we control or estimate the eight parameters of King's nigrostriatal anatomical-biochemical-electrophysiological system; pharmacological manipulation and estimation of a few of them can be done. Oreskes et al. point out that subcomponents of a complex dynamical system can be tested or evaluated in one situation, and those conditions may not hold in the situation in which the whole complex system is being observed or tested, so that a failure to verify a theory (to fit data to the theory) cannot be attributed to any particular subcomponent. As they put it "There is often no simple way to know whether the principal hypothesis or some auxiliary hypothesis is at fault." Furthermore, more often than not one fiddles with the theory until it fits, which is easy to do with multivariate, multiparametric theories, rather than reject it.

In addition, there is the *nonuniqueness* problem. There may be no way to critically test which of two or more theories can more adequately explain the data, yet the theories may be mutually exclusive. They cannot all be true, but there may be no empirical way to distinguish among them (Duhem, 1906/1953). Getting a match between observation and theory, as with the Freeman olfactory result, does not constitute verification. It is very satisfying to those of us pursuing dynamics to have such a success, and obtaining such a success is a major triumph. It helps to convince us we are on a viable tack. There are examples, of course, when fiddling with a theory finally wears out, or when it becomes superior with one theory displacing another, though usually the theory's survival requires one "to invoke extraevidential considerations like symmetry, simplicity, and elegance, or personal, political, or metaphysical preferences." In their very eloquent Footnote 26 (many of their footnotes contain some of their best arguments and summaries), Oreskes et al. further point out that Carnap (1935, 1336-1937/1953) and the logical positivists who tried to establish rules of meaning and testability for a unified science concluded that verification was impossible.

For dynamics, the face validity of modeling the interaction of several factors over time seems like such an obviously appropriate tactic that when coupled with the universality of the visual intuition provided by trajectories and phase portraits, it seems to point to an inevitable hegemony of a scientific future evolving from this position. These propositions were evident to René Thom and Chris Zeeman, two of the proponents most responsible for the explosive bifurcation to the current popularity of dynamics for science and psychology. Thom stressed the visual intuition; Zeeman stressed the importance of experimental evidence (we dare no longer to say verification). In practice, developing models and testing them is nonetheless proving very difficult, and time will tell how successful it will be for psychology (Barton, 1994; Townsend, 1994), but there is every reason for optimism (Abraham's Second Prognostiplatitude).

Predictability

There are various claims that chaotic processes are unpredictable. It might be better to say that there are limits to predictability. These derive from limits to resolution in deterministic systems and from probabilistic features of stochastic systems.

Deterministic Systems

The ordinary differential equations of King are deterministic. If you plug in exact values for X, Y, Z, and M, you get an exact result; only one trajectory is generated from any such given set of initial values. The state of the system at any given point in time is perfectly predictable, given rules of calculus in which infinite duration and resolution hold. However, in the real world, and in the variety of calculus that does not hold for strict infinite duration and resolution (achieved by the use of epsilon equivalence classes when approaching limits), a vector of exact starting conditions is not possible. Rather, a cloud of starting values around those numbers (epsilon in calculus, error of measurement in science, rounding in computation), no matter how small, is included in those numbers. Thus in a chaotic attractor for which *sensitivity to initial conditions* holds, the situation is like that shown in Fig. 3.2, B herein. The many trajectories within the region of the starting point eventually diverge to occupy the whole attractor. Many have stated that thus, with a chaotic attractor, prediction is impossible. That is an overstatement of our state of ignorance, for conditional probability statements can be made specifying that the trajectory will be in the attractor or will occupy a certain region in the attractor, and so forth. Although we cannot say exactly when or where a trajectory will be, the dynamics tells you an awful lot. All the trajectories are obeying the same, smooth vectorfield. This is what led to my correlative contention, *insensitivity to initial conditions*: All trajectories in a chaotic attractor look pretty much the same and give the same clues to the vectorfield and thus are to a certain extent equivalent. Since all trajectories visit every region in the attractor, eventually this must be the case.

Stochastic Systems

Besides that indeterminate caveat on deterministic dynamical systems are other variants of dynamics that introduce stochastic features. One we have already seen:

that a noise component be introduced to cover factors that influence a process but are too obscure, too numerous, or too inconsequential to incorporate as separate variables in the model of the system. Good computer programs for modeling dynamical systems allow evaluation of models with various amounts and types of noise introduced (Schaeffer, Truty, & Fulmer, 1988). There is the intermediate case, where a variable in the system is a stochastic (random) variable. That is, any given opportunity for its expression is governed by probability (a probability density function, probabilities associated with each possible value). Thus in any differential equation where the rate of change of a variable is a function of a number of variables, if at least one of those variables is a random variable, the dynamical system is stochastic.

Discrete Systems and Symbolic Dynamics

Stochastic systems are often discrete systems. That is, they have random variables that may have but few values associated with some variable or even have categorical (nominal) variables. In these cases the mathematics of sequential conditional probabilities (especially Markov processes) and information theory are often applied (Paulus, Geyer, Gold, & Mandell, 1990; Shaw, 1984).

For variables considered discrete rather than continuous, the resulting trajectories are discontinuous rather than continuous. They are graphed as iterative maps, that is, as points rather than lines. For such systems, you can get chaos in one dimension, as with the logistic equation; you do not need the usual minimum of three dimensions for chaos and sensitivity to initial conditions (or two for the nearly periodic torus). Why is that? Simply, in jumping discretely from one point to another as the trajectory evolves, crossing a previous part of the trajectory can be accomplished without landing exactly on a point previously visited and thus thrown into periodicity by its and successive vectors. The system is represented by difference equations rather than differential equations, with a discrete rather than continuous version of the calculus. The trajectory or phase portrait is called an iterative map because the difference equation is a rule of iteration. For example, the logistic equation is $x_{n+1} = \lambda x_n(1-x_n)$. One can consider the iterative map a Poincaré section of the trajectory of a continuous system whose dimensionality is one greater than that of the map. As such, the map loses information about the sequential production of the points in the map. In those studies that have used an analogous procedure for mapping latencies, such as neuronal spike latencies or interspike intervals, the loss of such information is small, evident in other features of the map, and recoverable (Diez Martinez et al., 1988). Undoubtedly most studies in the future will find some way to better graphically summarize these sequential properties. The first return map (Metcalf & Allen, Figs. 1D & 4, Chap. 5) is a good first step in that direction.

SIMILE & METAPHOR

In applied psychology it is common to use ideas borrowed from theoretically oriented research and modeling without a complete specification of the relationship between the original research situation and the applied situation, or without confirmation through applied research (Mosca for psychotherapy and literary analysis; Torre for educational psychology, for example). We do this as a matter of course, and it has proved very useful. This has become especially true of dynamics, where the concepts are appropriate to the complexity of the applied setting such as in psychotherapy and psychosocial organizations. Such metaphoric application need not always be as explicit as to involve exact numerical models and equations, or even sketched versions of response diagrams or network diagrams. (*Simile* is a better term than *metaphor* because the analogy is usually explicitly referenced but *metaphor* is the more often used term.) What could be more compelling than to discuss chaos and bifurcations for states of consciousness (Combs, Chap. 8) or for lifestyle and life space (R. Abraham, Chap. 11; Gilgen, Chap. 9)? There is the beginning of attempts at applied research in dynamics (Part II; Freeman, Chap. 2; Gentry, Chap. 10; Thelen in Goertzel, Chap. 12; Guastello, Chap. 19; Leven & Levine, Chap. 16; Levine & Leven, Chap. 15).

We can expect more applied research to be generated by dynamical thinking, but in the meantime it is hoped that the metaphoric use of dynamical concepts is inspired by a good foundation in the fundamentals of dynamics in order to generate more explicit models and tests of their applicability. When we say, "So and so's mind shut like a door," we have a pretty good idea of what a shutting door is. This suggestion is motivated by the hope for more cross-fertilization between theorists, researchers, and applied domains of psychology, such cross-disciplinary discourse being one of the main benefits of developing a language for unification/diversity. Those in more theoretical areas have much to contribute to practical matters as well (Part IV; Guastello et al., Chap. 19). Further, the metaphoric and the theoretic approaches are not so very different, as we saw that verification of theories was impossible. So scientific models too are fictions, myths. The difference is that the theoretic answers to the logical positivists demands of empiric reference or meaning, whereas the applied areas can enjoy some relaxation of such demands and some looseness of operational definition and allowance of subjective considerations.

OTHER ISSUES IN PSYCHOLOGY

There are a few issues that have received a lot of attention recently in the field of psychology to which dynamics may contribute. Here are some very brief comments on a few germane ones.

Indeterminism and Free Will

Indeterminacies at the quantum level, by dint of sensitivity to initial conditions and influence via hierarchical networking through parallel and serial paths on control parameters, can get amplified to indeterminacies at psychological and social levels. But one need not be committed to a model of indeterminacy to observe that behavior and cognition operate that way. They operate that way whether or not we live in a deterministic or nondeterministic world. That is, cognitive motion involves choice. Within the dynamical framework, some cognitive processes are equivalent (in some transformed sense) to developing self-organizatonally a response diagram of a dynamical scheme or network diagram of a complex dynamical system. Choice can take one of two forms. Cognitively, one can reset the initial conditions, especially for jumping from one basin to another, as in choosing a new goal (attractor). Or one can navigate in the control space, along control parameters, changing the phase portrait, its attractors and basins, until choices and lifestyles are established that seem to offer improvements. Even beyond this navigation within learned cognitive systems, the imagination can extrapolate new conceptions of the space and novel features of the system (in which the Sabelli et al.'s, Chap. 7, concepts of unity, dialectic struggle among paradoxical opposition, and the "cocreation" of higher dimensionality play a major role, though the higher dimensionality and the novel features can be considered as having a latent presence all the time; it just takes evolution of the universe and the mind to explore and discover them).

Since choices are made in a matrix of, at best, partial and incomplete representations of these cognitive maps, and since the indeterminacy of predicting the future within chaotic attractors is involved, and since bifurcations involve traversing regions of instability, the more significant a life choice is, the more courage it may require. These dynamical approaches to choice are consistent with the teleoponsive (Lewin, 1951; Loye, 1995; Rychlak, 1991) and soft deterministic (Sappington, 1990) approaches and quite similar to other dynamical approaches, such as that of intentional ecological psychology (Kugler, Shaw, Vincente, & Kinsella-Shaw, 1990).

The Humanist Mission of Psychology

Psychology has two basic missions. One is the better understanding of behavior, especially human behavior and cognition. The second is to apply that knowledge to the improvement of the human condition. Nurturing individuals' abilities to fulfill their potential, and societies' to optimize conditions for fulfilling human potential, is implied. This involves a sensitivity and compassion within our field and a fostering of concepts of sensitivity and compassion in society and in individuals. These are part and parcel of the fulfillment of the human condition (Combs, 1992). Dynamics can contribute to this fulfillment by being able to handle the complexity of issues relating to the interaction of individuals and society, and the interaction of a science and society (Part V).

Unification and Diversity

We have already expressed the idea that there is hope that the language of dynamics, especially the visual-topological varieties, and the metamodeling strategy of dynamics, is accessible to as well as applicable to all science, and to all applied science, including psychology. And that as such, it should assist inter- and intradisciplinary communicability, thus enabling a better balance of unification and diversity. The fractal dimensionality of the field of psychology has waxed and waned with the chaotic history of psychology (Bevan, 1991; Gilgen, 1987; Staats, 1991). Diversity and unity are important for productivity and excitement in any field, and dynamics is going to assist in both, and in the evolution of a healthy balance and of a medium-dimensional attractive psychology that will make the field a useful and fun place to be. I'm going to enjoy riding this trajectory.

It might be worth considering what one of the principal architects of the *International Encyclopedia of Unified Science* (1938), Otto Neurath, had to say about the balance of creativity and communicability:

> New ideas of scientific importance start mostly with vague and sometimes queer explanations; they become clearer and clearer, but the theories which follow will stand in time before the door with all their new vagueness and queerness. Niels Bohr expressed this historically and pedagogically essential fact in his paradoxical manner: the law of complementarity is valid also for fruitfulness and clearness of scientific theories. Must one fear by this to encourage vague speculations? No! Persons who are interested in unscientific speculation will undertake it under all circumstances. But it is useful to avoid dogmatism and bumptiousness in scientism and empirical panlogism. One can love exactness and nevertheless consciously tolerate a certain amount of vagueness. (p. 21)

REFERENCES

Abraham, F. D. (1993). Chaos in brain function. *World Futures, 37,* 41–58.

Abraham, F. D., Bryant, H., Mettler, M., Bergerson, B., Moore, F., Maderdrut, J., Gardiner, M., Walter, D., & Jennrich, R. (1973). Spectrum and discriminant analyses reveal remote rather than local sources for hypothalamic EEG: Could waves affect unit activity? *Brain Research, 49,* 349–366.

Babloyantz, A. (1990). Estimation of correlation dimensions from single and multichannel recordings—A critical view. In E. Basar (Ed.), *Chaos in brain function* (pp. 83–91). Berlin: Springer-Verlag.

Barton, S. (1994). Chaos, self-organization, and psychology. *American Psychologist, 49,* 5–14.

Basar, E. (Ed.). (1990). *Chaos in brain function.* Berlin: Springer-Verlag.

Bevan, W. (1991). A tour inside the onion. *American Psychologist, 46*, 475–483.

Callahan, J., & Sashin, J. (1987). Models of affect response and anorexia nervosa. In S. H. Koslow (Eds.), *Perspectives in biological dynamics and theoretical medicine. Annals of the New York Academy of Science* (Vol. 504, 241–259).

Carnap, R. (1935). Les concepts psychologiques et les concepts physiques, sont-ils foncièrement différents? *Revue de Synthèse, 10*.

Carnap, R. (1936; 1937). Testability and meaning. *Philosophy of Science, 3; 4*. Reprinted in H. Feigl & M. Brodbeck (Eds.). (1953). *Readings in the philosophy of science*. New York: Appleton-Century-Crofts.

Chialvo, D. R., & Apkarian, A. V. (1993). Modulated noisy biological dynamics: Three examples. *Journal of Statistical Physics, 70*, 375–391.

Combs, A. (Ed.). (1992). *Cooperation*. Philadelphia: Gordon & Breach.

Deveney, R. L. (1989). *An introduction to chaotic dynamical systems* (2nd ed.). New York: Addison-Wesley.

Diez Martinez, O., Pérez, P., Budelli, R., & Segundo, J. P. (1988). Locking, intermittency, and bifurcations in a periodically driven pacemaker neuron: Poincaré maps and biological implications. *Biological Cybernetics, 60*, 49–58.

Duhem, P. (1906/1953). *La theorie physique: Son objet et sa structure. Aim and structure of physical theory*. (P. P. Wiener, Trans.). Princeton: Princeton University Press.

Freeman, W. J. (1987). Simulation of chaotic EEG patterns with a dynamic model of the olfactory system. *Biological Cybernetics, 56*, 139–150.

Freeman, W. J. (1990). Analysis of strange attractors in EEGs with kinesthetic experience and 4-D computer graphics. In E. Basar (Ed.), *Chaos in brain function* (pp. 153–161). Berlin: Springer-Verlag.

Gilgen, A. R. (1987). The psychological level of organization in nature and interdependencies among major psychological concepts. In A. W. Staats & L. P. Mos (Eds.), *Annals of theoretical psychology* (Vol 5). New York: Plenum Press.

Goldstein, J. (1995). The tower of babel in nonlinear dynamics: Towards the clarification of terms. In R. Robertson & A. Combs (Eds.), *A chaos psychology reader*. Hillsdale: Erlbaum.

Greeley, L. (1991). *Philosophical spacing: Key to the nonlinear complex dynamics of the attentional system of the cognitive learning process in the philosophical dialectical method*. Unpublished dissertation, Harvard University.

Gregson, R. A. M. (1992). *n-Dimensional nonlinear psychophysics*. Hillsdale: Erlbaum.

Hannah, T. (1990). Mood: Chaotic attractor reconstruction. In F. D. Abraham, R. H. Abraham, & C. D. Shaw, *A visual introduction to dynamical systems theory for psychology* (Part III, Fig. 11b, p. 37). Santa Cruz: Aerial Press.

Hubler, A. (1992). Modeling and control of complex systems: Paradigms and applications. In L. Lam (Ed.), *Modeling complex systems*. New York: Springer.

King, R., Barchas, J. D., & Huberman, B. A. (1984). Chaotic behavior in dopamine neurodynamics. *Proceeding of the National Academy of Sciences of the United States of America, Neurobiology, 81*, 1244–1247.

Korzybski, A. (1933). *Science and sanity*. Lancaster: Science.

Kugler, P. N., Shaw, R. E., Vincente, K. J., & Kinsella-Shaw, J. (1990). Inquiry into intentional systems I: Issues in ecological physics. *Psychological Research, 52*, 98–121.

Levine, D. (1991). *Introduction to neural and cognitive modeling*. Hillsdale: Erlbaum.

Lewin, K. (1951). *Field theory in social science*. New York: Harper & Row.

Lorenz, E. N. (1963). Deterministic nonperiodic flow. *Journal of the Atomospheric Sciences, 20*, 130-141.

Loye, D. (1995). How predictable is the future? Chaos theory and the psychology of prediction. In R. Robertson & A. Combs (Eds.), *A chaos psychology reader*. Hillsdale: Erlbaum.

MacCorquodale, K., & Meehl, P. E. (1948). Hypothetical constructs and intervening variables. *Psychological Review, 55*, 95-107.

Marx, M. H. (1951). *Psychological theory*. New York: Macmillan.

Neurath, O. (1938). Unified science as encyclopedic integration. In O. Neurath, R. Carnap, & C. Morris (Eds.), *International encyclopedia of unified science* (pp. 1–27). Chicago: University of Chicago Press.

Oreskes, N., Shrader-Frechette, K., & Belitz, K. (1994). Verification, validation, and confirmation of numerical models in the earth sciences. *Science, 263*, 641–646.

Paulus, M. P., Geyer, M. A., Gold, L. H., & Mandell, A. J. (1990). Application of entropy measures derived from the ergodic theory of dynamical systems to rat locomotor behavior. *Proceedings of the National Academy of Science USA, 87*, 723–727.

Penzance, P. O. (1880). Understanding equations both simple and quadratical. In M-G. Stanley (Ed.), *Gilbert space*. London: Opéra Comique.

Pickover, C. A. (1990). *Computers, pattern, chaos and beauty. Graphics from an unseen world*. New York: St. Martin's Press.

Preissl, H., & Aertsen, A. (1993). Reconstruction and characterisation of neuronal dynamics: How attractive is Chaos? In A. Aertsen & V. Braitenberg (Eds.), *Information processing in the Cortex: Experiments and theory* (pp. 285–297). Berlin: Springer-Verlag.

Pribram, K. H. (1991). *Brain and perception: Holonomy and structure in figural processing*. Hillsdale: Erlbaum.

Pritchard, W. S., & Duke, D. W. (1992a). Measuring chaos in the brain: A tutorial review of nonlinear dynamical EEG analysis. *International Journal of Neuroscience, 65*, 31–80.

Pritchard, W. S., & Duke, D. W. (1992b). *Linearity versus nonlinearity in brain dynamics: Application of the surrogate-data test to EEG data*. Unpublished manuscript.

Rapp, P. (1993). Chaos in the neurosciences: Cautionary tales from the frontier. *Biologist, 40*, 89–94.

Rapp, P. (1995). Is there any evidence of chaos in the central nervous system? In R. Robertson & A. Combs (Eds.), *A chaos psychology reader*. Hillsdale: Erlbaum.

Rössler, O. E., & Hudson, J. L. (1990). Self-similarity in hyperchaotic data. In E. Basar (Ed.), *Chaos in brain function* (pp. 74–82). Berlin: Springer-Verlag.

Ruelle, D. (1991). *Chance and chaos*. Princeton: Princeton University Press.

Rychlak, J. F. (1991). Some theoretical and methodological questions concerning Harcum's proposed resolution of the free will issue. *Journal of Mind and Behavior, 12*, 135–150.

Sappington, A. A. (1990). Recent psychological approaches to the free will versus determinism issue. *Psychological Bulletin, 108*, 19–29.

Schaeffer, W. M., Truty, G. L., & Fulmer, S. L. (1988). *Dynamical software*. Tuscon: Dynamical Systems.

Shaw, R. S. (1984). *The dripping faucet as a model chaotic system*. Santa Cruz: Aerial Press.

Staats, A. W. (1991). Unified positivism and unification psychology. *American Psychologist, 46*, 899–912.

Townsend, P. (1994). A visual approach to nonlinear dynamics: Just cartoons or a serious pedagogical device? *American Journal of Psychology, 107*, 117–155.

Select Bibliography

KEY

* indicates most basic references
* indicates excellent demonstration software
+ indicates software with data analysis capabilities.
  Both types of software provide excellent manuals and introduction to dynamics; they provide the best way to learn dynamics.

REFERENCES

* Abraham, F. D., Abraham, R. H., & Shaw, C. D. (1990). *A visual introduction to dynamical systems theory for psychology*. Santa Cruz: Aerial Press.
* Abraham, R. H., & Shaw, C. D. (1992). *Dynamics, the geometry of behavior* (2nd ed.). Reading: Addison-Wesley.

Abraham, R. H. (1994). *Chaos, Gaia, Eros*. San Francisco: Harper.

Allport, F. H. (1957). *Theories of perception and the concept of structure*. New York: Wiley

Bartlett, F. C. (1932). *Remembering: An experimental and social study*. Cambridge: Cambridge University Press.

* Barton, S. (1994). Chaos, self-organization, and psychology. *American Psychologist, 9,* 5–14.

Basar, E. (Ed.). (1990). *Chaos in brain function*. Berlin: Springer-Verlag.

Bateson, G. H. (1972). *Steps to an ecology of mind*. New York: Ballantine.

Bateson, G. H. (1979). *Mind and nature: A necessary unity*. New York: Dutton.

Bevan, W. (1991). A tour inside the onion. *American Psychologist, 46,* 475–483.

Bohm, D. (1994). Soma-significance: A new notion of the relationship between the physical and the mental. *Psychoscience, 1,* 6–27.

Callahan, J., & Sashin, J. (1990). Predictive models in psychoanalysis. *Behavioral Science, 35,* 60–76.

Carpenter, G. A., & Grossberg, S. (1987). A massively parallel architecture for a self-organizing neural pattern recognition machine. *Computer Vision, Graphics, and Image Processing, 37,* 54–115.

Casti, J. L. (1992). *Reality rules: I; Picturing the world in mathematics —the fundamentals.* New York: John Wiley & Sons.

Chialvo, D. R., & Apkarian, A. V. (1993). Modulated noisy biological dynamics: Three examples. *Journal of Statistical Physics, 70,* 375–391.

Crutchfield, J. P., Farmer, J. D., Packard, N. H., & Shaw, R. S. (1986). Chaos. *Scientific American, 255,* 46–57.

Degn, H., Holden, A. V., & Olsen, L. F. (Eds.). (1987). *Chaos in biological systems.* New York: Plenum Press.

Deveney, R. L. (1989). *An introduction to chaotic dynamical systems* (2nd ed.). New York: Addison-Wesley.

Dewey, J. (1896). The reflex arc concept in psychology. *Psychological Review, 2,* 13–32.

Elkaïm, M., Goldbeter, A., & Goldbeter-Merinfeld, E. (1987). Analysis of the dynamics of a family system in terms of bifurcations. *Journal of Social and Biological Structures, 10,* 21–36.

Fischer, P., & Smith, W. R. (Eds.). (1985). *Chaos, fractals, and dynamics.* New York: Dekker.

Fogel, A. (1993). *Developing through relationships: Origins of communication, self, and culture.* New York: Harvester Wheatsheaf.

Freeman, W. J. (1975). *Mass action in the nervous system.* New York: Academic Press.

* Freeman, W. J. (1991, February). The physiology of perception. *Scientific American, 264,* 78–85.

* Freeman, W. J. (1995). *Societies of brains: A neuroscience of love and hate.* Hillsdale: Erlbaum.

Frey, P. W., & Sears, R. J. (1978). Model of conditioning incorporating the Rescorla-Wagner associative axiom, a dynamic attention process, and a catastrophe rule. *Psychological Review, 85,* 321–340.

Gentry, T., & Wakefield, J. (1991). Methods for measuring spatial cognition. In D. M. Mark & A. U. Frank (Eds.), *Proceedings: NATO Advanced Study Institute on the cognitive and linguistic aspects of geographic space* (pp. 185–217). Dordrecht: Kluwer Academic.

Gilgen, A. R. (1987). The psychological level of organization in nature and interdependencies among major psychological concepts. In A. W. Staats & L. P. Mos (Eds.), *Annals of theoretical psychology* (Vol. 5). New York: Plenum Press.

Glass, L., & Mackey, M. C. (1988). *From clocks to chaos: The rhythms of life.* Princeton: Princeton University Press.

Goerner, S. J. (1994). *Chaos and the evolving ecological universe: A study in the science and human implications of a new world hypothesis.* New York: Gordon & Breach.

Goertzel, B. (1994). *Chaotic logic: Language, mind and reality from the perspective of complex systems science.* New York: Plenum Press.

Goldstein, J. (1993). Beyond Lewin's force-field: A new model for organizational change interventions. In F. Massarik (Ed.), *Advances in Organization Development* (Vol. 2, pp. 72–78). Norwood: Ablex Press.

Gregson, R. A. M. (1992). *n-Dimensional nonlinear psychophysics.* Hillsdale: Erlbaum.

Grossberg, S., & Schmajuk, N. A. (1989). Neural dynamics of adaptive timing and temporal discrimination during associative learning. *Neural Networks, 2,* 79–102.

Guastello, S. J. (1992). Clash of the paradigms: A critique of an examination of the polynomial regression technique for evaluating catastrophe theory hypotheses. *Psychological Bulletin, 111*, 375–379.

Guess, D., & Sailor, W. (1993). Chaos theory and the study of human behavior: Implications for special education and developmental disabilities. *Journal of Special Education, 27*, 16–34.

Haken, H. (1977). *Synergetics: An introduction.* Heidelberg: Springer-Verlag.

Hanson, S. J., & Timberlake, W. (1983). Regulation during challenge: A general model of learned performance under schedule constraint. *Psychological Review, 90*, 261–282.

Harris-Warrick, R. M., Marder, E., Selverston, A. I., & Moulins, M. (Eds.). (1992). *Dynamic biological networks.* Cambridge: MIT Press.

Holden, A. V. (Ed.). (1986). *Chaos.* Manchester: Manchester University Press.

Hopfield, J. J. (1982). Neural networks and physical systems with emergent collective computational abilities. *Proceedings of the National Academy of Science, 79*, 2554–2558.

* Hubler, A. (1992). Modeling and control of complex systems: Paradigms and applications. In L. Lam (Ed.), *Modeling complex systems.* New York: Springer.

Kelso, J. A. S., Ding, M., & Schöner, G. (1992). Dynamic pattern formation: A primer. In J. E. Mittenthal & A. B. Baskin (Eds.), *Principles of organization in organisms. Proceedings of the Santa Fe Institute Studies in the Sciences of Complexity* (Vol. 13). New York: Addison-Wesley.

Kelso, J. A. S., Mandell, A. J., & Shlesinger, M. F. (Eds.). (1988). *Dynamic patterns in complex systems.* Singapore: World Scientific.

* Killeen, P. R. (1992). Mechanics of the animate. *Journal of the Experimental Analysis of Behavior, 57*, 429–463.

Kohonen, T. (1988). *Self-organization and associative memory.* New York: Springer-Verlag.

* Koslow, S. H., Mandell, A. J., & Shlesinger, M. F. (Eds.). (1987). *Perspectives in biological dynamics and theoretical medicine. Annals of the New York Academy of Science* (Vol. 504). New York: New York Academy of Sciences.

* Kugler, P. N., Shaw, R. E., Vincente, K. J., & Kinsella-Shaw, J. (1990). Inquiry into intentional systems I: Issues in ecological physics. *Psychological Research, 52*, 98–121.

Kugler, P. N., & Turvey, M. T. (1987). *Information, natural law and the self-assembly of rhythmic movement.* Hillsdale: Erlbaum.

* Levine, D. (1991). *Introduction to neural and cognitive modeling.* Hillsdale: Erlbaum.

Levine, D. S., & Leven, S. J. (Eds.). (1992). *Motivation, emotion, and goal direction in neural networks.* Hillsdale: Erlbaum.

* Levine, R., & Fitzgerald, H. E. (Eds.). (1992). *Analysis of dynamic psychological systems* (Vols. 1 & 2). New York: Plenum Press.

Lewin, K. (1951). *Field theory in social science.* New York: Harper & Row.

Lewin, R. (1992). *Complexity: Life at the edge of chaos.* New York: Macmillan.

Loye, D., & Eisler, R. (1987). Chaos and transformation: Implications of nonequilibrium theory for social science and society. *Behavioral Science, 32*, 53–65.

Mandelbrot, B. B. (1975/1977). *Les objets fractals: Forme, hasard et dimension.* Paris: Flammarion. *Fractals: Form, chance, and dimension.* San Francisco: W. H. Freeman.

Marr, M. J. (1992). Behavior dynamics: One perspective. *Journal of the Experimental Analysis of Behavior, 57*, 249–266.

Marx, M. H. (Ed.). (1951). *Psychological theory.* New York: Macmillan.

Maturana, H., & Varela, F. (1987). *The tree of knowledge*. Boston: Shambhala.

Mosca, F. (1994). *The unbearable wrongness of being*. Thornwood: Options for Living Press.

Mosekilde, E., Larssen, E., & Sterman, J. (1991). Coping with complexity: Chaos in human decision making behavior. In J. Casti & A. Karlqvist (Eds.), *Beyond belief: Randomness, prediction, and explanation in science* (pp. 199–299). Boca Raton: CRC.

Mpitsos, G. J. (1989/1990). Chaos in brain function and the problem of nonstationarity: A commentary. In E. Basar & T. H. Bullock (Eds.), *Brain dynamics*. Berlin: Springer-Verlag. And in E. Basar (Ed.), *Chaos in brain function*. Berlin: Springer-Verlag.

Neurath, O. (1938). Unified science as encyclopedic integration. In O. Neurath, R. Carnap, & C. Morris (Eds.), *International encyclopedia of unified science* (Vol. 1, Part 1). Chicago: University of Chicago Press.

Nicolis, G., & Prigogine, I. (1989). *Exploring complexity*. New York: W. H. Freeman.

Oreskes, N., Shrader-Frechette, K., & Belitz, K. (1994). Verification, validation, and confirmation of numerical models in the earth sciences. *Science, 263*, 641–646.

Packard, N. H., Crutchfield, J. P., Farmer, J. D., & Shaw, R. S. (1980). Geometry from a time series. *Physical Review Letters, 45*, 712–716.

Penrose, R. (1989). *The emporor's new mind: Concerning computers, minds, and the laws of physics*. Oxford: Oxford.

Peterson, I. (1993). *Newton's clock: Chaos in the solar system*. New York: Freeman.

Poincaré, H. (1899). *Les méthodes nouvelles de la mécanique céleste* (Vols. 1–3). Paris: Gauthier-Villars. Also in D. L. Goroff (Ed., Trans.), 1993. *New methods of celestial mechanics*. New York: American Institute of Physics.

Pribram, K. H. (1991). *Brain and perception*. Hillsdale: Erlbaum.

Pribram, K. H. (Ed.). (1993). *Rethinking neural networks: Quantum fields and biological data*. Hillsdale: Erlbaum.

* Prigogine, I., & Stengers, I. (1984). *Order out of chaos*. New York: Bantam Books.

Pritchard, W. S., & Duke, D. W. (1992). Measuring chaos in the brain: A tutorial review of nonlinear dynamical EEG analysis. *International Journal of Neuroscience, 65*, 31–80.

Quine, W. V. O. (1969). Natural kinds. In *Ontological relativity and other essays* (pp. 114–138). New York: Columbia University Press.

* Rapp, P. (1995). Is there any evidence of chaos in the central nervous system? In R. Robertson & A. Combs (Eds.), *A chaos psychology reader*. Hillsdale: Erlbaum.

Rashevsky, N. (1960). *Mathematical biophysics* (Vols. 1 & 2). New York: Dover.

Reidbord S. P., & Redington, D. J. (1992). Psychophysiological processes during insight-oriented therapy: Further investigations into nonlinear psychodynamics. *Journal of Nervous and Mental Diseases, 180*, 649–657.

* Rosen, R. (1970). *Dynamical system theory in biology*. New York: Wiley Interscience.

Rosen, R. (1985). *Anticipatory systems, philosophical, mathematical and methodological foundations*. New York: Pergamon Press.

Rössler, O. (1987). Chaos in coupled optimizers. In S. H. Koslow, A. J. Mandell, & M. F. Shlesinger (Eds.), *Perspectives in biological dynamics and theoretical medicine. Annals of the New York Academy of Science* (Vol. 504, pp. 229–240). New York: New York Academy of Sciences.

Ruelle, D. (1991). *Chance and chaos*. Princeton: Princeton.

Sabelli, H. C. (1989). *Union of opposites. A comprehensive theory of natural and human processes*. Lawrenceville: Brunswick.

+ Schaeffer, W. M., Truty, G. L., & Fulmer, S. L. (1988). *Dynamical software*. Tucson: Dynamical Systems.

Schneider, W. (1987). Connectionism: Is it a paradigm shift for psychology? *Behavior Research Methods, Instruments, & Computers, 19*, 73–83.

Schroeder, M. (1991). *Fractals, chaos, power laws: Minutes from an infinite paradise*. New York: Freeman.

Schwalbe, M. L. (1991). The autogenesis of the self. *Journal for the Theory of Social Behavior, 21*, 269–295.

Shaw, R. S. (1984). *The dripping faucet as a model chaotic system*. Santa Cruz: Aerial Press.

Skarda, C. A., & Freeman, W. J. (1987). How brains make chaos in order to make sense of the world. *Behavioral and brain sciences, 10*, 161–195.

Smith, L. B., & Thelen, E. (Eds.). (1993). *A dynamic systems approach to development: Applications*. Cambridge: MIT Press.

* Sprott, J. C., & Rowlands, G. (1990). *Chaos demonstrations*. Raleigh: The Academic Software Library; New York: American Institute of Physics.

+ Sprott, J., & Rowlands, G. (1992). *Chaos Data Analyzer*. New York: American Physics Society; New York: American Institute of Physics.

Staats, A. W. (1983). *Psychology's crisis of disunity: Philosophy and method for a unified science*. New York: Praeger Publishers.

Staats, A. W. (1991). Unified positivism and unification psychology. *American Psychologist, 46*, 899–912.

* Stewart, I. (1989). *Does God play dice? The mathematics of chaos*. Cambridge: Basil Blackwell.

* Thelen, E., & Smith, L. B. (Eds.). (1994). *A dynamic systems account of the development of action and cognition*. Cambridge: MIT Press.

* Thom, R. (1972/1975). *Stabilité structurelle et morphogenèse. Structural stability and morphogenesis* (H. Fowler, Trans.). Reading: Benjamin.

* Thompson, J. M. T., & Stewart, H. B. (1986). *Nonlinear dynamics and chaos*. Chichester: Wiley.

* Townsend, P. (1994). Chaos theory: A brief tutorial and discussion. In A. F. Healy, S. M. Dosslyn, & R. M. Shiffrin (Eds.), *From learning theory to connectionist theory: Essays in honor of William K. Estes* (Vol. 1, pp. 65–96). Hillsdale: Erlbaum.

* Townsend, P. (1994). A visual approach to nonlinear dynamics: Just cartoons or a serious pedagogical device? *American Journal of Psychology, 107*, 117–155.

Tryon, W. W. (1990). Why paradigmatic behaviorism should be retitled psychological behaviorism. *The Behavior Therapist, 13*, 127–128.

Turvey, M. T. (1990). Coordination. *American Psychologist, 5*, 938–953.

Vallacher, R. R., & Nowak, A. (Eds). (1994). *Dynamical systems in social psychology*. San Diego: Academic.

Vicenzi, A. E. (1994). Chaos theory and some nursing considerations. *Nursing Science Quarterly, 7*, 36–42.

Waldrop, M. (1992). *Complexity: The emerging science at the edge of order and chaos*. New York: Simon & Schuster.

Weiner, N. (1948). *Cybernetics or control and communication in the animal and the machine*. New York: Wiley.

Westheimer, G. (1991). Visual discrimination of fractal borders. *Proceedings of the Royal Society, London B, 243*, 215–219.

Winfree, A. T. (1987). *The timing of biological clocks*. New York: Scientific American/ W. H. Freeman.

Yates, F. E. (Ed.). (1987). *Self-organizing systems*. New York: Plenum Press.

* Yorke, J. A. (1990). *Dynamics, an Interactive Program*. College Park: Institute for Physical Science & Technology, University of Maryland. Also: New York: Springer-Verlag.

* Zeeman, E. C. (1977). *Catastrophe theory and its applications*. Reading: Addison-Wesley.

Name Index

Subject Index

About the Contributors

FREDERICK DAVID ABRAHAM

Fred's main academic post was at UCLA (with a lab at the Brain Research Institute), with briefer posts at San Diego State College, UC Irvine, and UVM. He also did brief research stints at the Friday Harbor Laboratory and the Salk Institute. He has published research in animal learning, concept formation, and the neurophysiology of motivation, learning, and ethological behavior. He then learned some dynamics from his brother and guru, Ralph. His book, *A Visual Introduction to Dynamical Systems Theory for Psychology* (with Ralph Abraham & Christopher Shaw, 1990), was the first textbook on dynamics and chaos for Psychology. He has retired to beautiful Vermont, where life's joys include telemarking and canoeing the hills and lakes near his home, and traveling with his talented wife, Precy, a professional singer, lecturing while she is on concert tours in such wondrous places as Beijing, Bangkok, Manila, Zurich, New York, and Lynchburg.

RALPH H. ABRAHAM

Ralph is a Professor of Mathematics at the University of California at Santa Cruz. He taught at Berkeley, Columbia, and Princeton before moving to Santa Cruz in 1968. He has held visiting positions in Amsterdam, Paris, Warwick, Barcelona, Basel, Florence, and Siena. He is the author of *Foundations of Mechanics* (with J. E. Marsden, 1982), *Transversal Mappings and Flows* (with J. Robbin, 1967), *Manifolds, Tensor Analysis, and Applications* (with J. E. Marsden and T. Ratiu, 1980), *Dynamics, the Geometry of Behavior* (with C. D. Shaw, 1992), *Trialogues on the Edge of the West* (with Terence McKenna and Rupert Sheldrake,

1992), *Chaos, Gaia, Eros* (1994), and *The Web Empowerment Book* (with F. Jas and W. Russell, 1994). He has been active on the research frontier of dynamics in mathematics since 1960, and in applications and experiments since 1973. In 1975, he founded the Visual Mathematics Project at the University of California at Santa Cruz.

JOSEPH D. ALLEN

Joseph is Professor and Head of the Psychology Department at the University of Georgia. His publications include over seventy articles in the areas of operant analysis, adjunctive behavior, physiology of learning, behavioral medicine, psychophysiology, and laboratory instrumentation, as well as two computer tutorial books in statistical methods. He entered the world of chaos in 1990.

KARL R. BARNUM

Karl is a recent graduate of electrical engineering from Brigham Young University. As technical adviser, he has co-authored many articles applying chaos theory to group psychotherapy interaction. His research interests include mathematical/statistical analysis methods and design techniques for database systems including accumulation, storage, and manipulation of research data.

GARY M. BURLINGAME

Gary is an Associate Professor of Psychology at Brigham Young University. His research interests include group psychotherapy, psychometrics, and research design issues. He recently co-edited the *Handbook of Group Psychotherapy: An Empirical and Clinical Synthesis* (1994), and has authored numerous papers exploring time-limited group psychotherapy.

LINNEA CARLSON-SABELLI

Linnea is known for her pioneering work applying process theory to nursing, to the development of action methods in nursing and education, and to sociodynamics in interpersonal relationships. Her doctoral dissertation, "Measuring Co-existing Opposites," led to the discovery of a mathematical connection between the process theory principle of the union of opposites and catastrophe models. Currently she is co-investigator in a collaborative study exploring the mind/body connection— how emotions and cardiac activity reciprocally affect one another.

ALLAN COMBS

Allan is a neuropsychologist and systems theorist at the University of North Carolina at Asheville and at the Saybrook Institute in San Francisco. He is co-founder of The Society for Chaos Theory in Psychology and the Life Sciences, and a member of The General Evolution Research Group. He has written and lectured extensively on chaos theory in psychology. His books are *Synchronicity: Science, Myth, and the Trickster* (with Mark Holland, 1990); *Cognitive Maps in Biology and Culture* (with V. Csanyi, Ervin Laszlo, and Robert Artigiani, 1995); *The Radiance of Being: Chaos, Evolution, and Consciousness* (1995); *Cooperation: Beyond the Age of Competition* (editor, 1992); and *A Chaos Psychology Reader* (editor with Robin Robertson, in press).

KEVIN J. DOOLEY

Kevin is Associate Professor of Mechanical Engineering at the University of Minnesota. He has research interests in quality management, statistical process control, complexity, and organizational behavior. He has worked with companies such as Honeywell, 3M, and Ford, and published in journals such as *Journal of Operations Management, International Journal of Production Research, Journal of Engineering for Industry*, and *Human Systems Management*. He is currently on the executive board of the Chaos Network and assisting with the implementation of quality improvement at the University of Minnesota.

WALTER J. FREEMAN

Walter is a Professor of Neurobiology at the University of California at Berkeley. He received the A. E. Bennett Award of the Society of Biological Psychiatry (1964), the Guggenheim Award (1966), the Titulaire de la Chaire Solvay, University of Brussels (1974), and the MERIT Award from NIMH (1990). He is current President of the International Neural Network Society. His research interests lie in mathematical modeling of nonlinear neurodynamics, based on his experimental measurements of brain activity in behaving animals, and the application of these models in biology, neurology, psychiatry, philosophy, and industry.

ADDIE FUHRIMAN

Addie is currently Dean of Graduate Studies and a Professor in the Department of Psychology at Brigham Young University. Her research interests are focused on therapeutic processes and interaction in psychotherapy groups. She has authored numerous papers on group therapy process and outcome, and recently co-edited *Handbook of Group Psychotherapy: An Empirical and Clinical Synthesis* (1994).

THOMAS A. GENTRY

Tom is a Professor of Psychology and member of the multidisciplinary Cognitive Studies faculty at California State University, Stanislaus. As project coordinator for the CSUS Center for Telecommunications Courses, he is currently developing instructional and research programs that utilize the Internet for distributed learning communities.

ALBERT R. GILGEN

Al is Professor of Psychology at the University of Northern Iowa, where he served as Head of the Department from 1973 until 1993. He was a Fulbright Exchange Lecturer at University College Galway in Ireland in 1971–72 and is a Fellow of both the American Psychological Association and the American Psychological Society. His publications include *Contemporary Scientific Psychology* (edited, 1970); *American Psychology since World War II: A Profile of the Discipline* (1982); and *International Handbook of Psychology* (co-edited with his wife, Carol, 1987). He is currently working on two books (*Soviet and American Psychology during World War II*, and *Post-Soviet Perspectives on Russian Psychology*) with his wife and two Russian psychologists, Vera Koltsova and Yuri Oleinik, both associated with the Institute of Psychology, Russian Academy of Sciences.

SALLY J. GOERNER

Sally is the Director of the Triangle Center for the Study of Complex Systems, past president of the Society of Chaos Theory in Psychology and the Life Sciences, and a member of both the European Academy of Evolution Research and The General Evolution Research Group. Her career includes fifteen years in computer research and development with companies such as Bell Northern Research Labs and McDonnell Douglas Corporation, consulting in organizational development, and private practice in psychotherapy. She is author of *Chaos and the Evolving Ecological Universe* (1994) as well as fourteen articles in areas ranging from the role of thermodynamics in evolution to Chaos' role in deepening ecological thinking. Her specialty is making Chaos and Complexity accessible to lay audiences and showing their connection to evolution and a deep ecology.

BEN GOERTZEL

Ben is a Lecturer in Computer Science at Waikato University in Hamilton, New Zealand. Although a mathematician, he has become more interested in using mathematics to explore ideas in psychology, philosophy, and artificial intelligence than in mathematics for its own sake. His long-term goals are extremely modest, including the design and construction of an intelligent computer and the achievement of digital immortality. In his spare time he composes electronic music, writes science fiction, rereads Dostoevsky, plays with his sons Zarathustra and Zebulon and his beautiful wife Gwen, and fights wild kiwis for survival. His publications include *The Structure of Intelligence* (1993), *The Evolving Mind* (1993), and *Chaotic Logic* (1994). He is currently working on two further books, one on genetic algorithms and nonlinear dynamics, and the other an e-mail philosophical trialogue with S. J. Goerner and A. Montuori.

JEFFREY A. GOLDSTEIN

Jeffrey is Professor of Organizational Behavior at Adelphi University, having previously taught at Rutgers University and Temple University. His publications include *The Unshackled Organization, Facing the Challenge of Unpredictability through Spontaneous Reorganization* (1994); *Brainwaves: Tools for a Diverse Workplace* (1994); and many articles. He is President of the Society for Chaos Theory in Psychology and the Life Sciences for 1994–1995.

STEPHEN J. GUASTELLO

Steve is Associate Professor of Industrial/Organizational Psychology and Human Factors Engineering at Marquette University, where he has taught since 1983. He is the author of over fifty articles and book chapters, many of which pertain to nonlinear dynamics in work settings. He was one of the first in the United States to do research on psychological applications of catastrophe theory. He is also a consultant to industry on organizational development, occupational safety, person-machine system design, and psychological testing issues. He is currently completing a book, *Chaos, Catastrophe, and Human Affairs: Applications of Nonlinear Dynamics to Work, Organizations, and Society.*

SAMUEL J. LEVEN

Sam has been Director since 1989 of For A New Social Science, a private research foundation based in Coral Springs, Florida. He is co-editor of *Motivation, Emotion, and Goal Direction in Neural Networks* (with Daniel S. Levine, 1992). A part of his current research is the Microfoundations Project, whose aim is to develop neural network models of individual choice in economic behavior, including the role of affect. Another part, which is related, deals with neural network modeling of the neurochemistry of depression.

DANIEL S. LEVINE

Dan is Associate Professor of Mathematics at the University of Texas at Arlington. His publications include a textbook, *Introduction to Neural and Cognitive Modeling* (1991), and two edited volumes, *Motivation, Emotion, and Goal Direction in Neural Networks* (with Samuel J. Leven, 1992), and *Neural Networks for Knowledge Representation and Inference* (with Manuel Aparicio, 1994). He is on the editorial board of the journal *Neural Networks* and is Chair of the Special Interest Group on Mental Function and Dysfunction of the International Neural Network Society. His current research is in the area of neural network modeling of higher cognitive and affective function, including decision making and the effects of frontal lobe damage.

JOSEPH V. MESSER

Joseph is Professor of Medicine at Rush Medical College, and Senior Attending Physician and former Director of the Section of Cardiology at Rush-Presbyterian St. Luke's Medical Center in Chicago. In addition, he is Director of the Interinstitutional Cardiovascular Center of the American Heart Association of Metropolitan Chicago. He engages in the practice of Cardiology as a member of Associates in Cardiology of Chicago. He is a fellow in many medical colleges and associations, in which he takes a very active role.

BRIAN R. METCALF

Brian is a doctoral student in the Biopsychology Program at the University of Georgia. The data contained in the chapter by Metcalf and Allen are based on his master's thesis. His current interest is in exploring the applications of chaos theory to the analysis of human psychophysiology.

FRANK MOSCA

Frank has held positions as a Professor of Russian Intellectual History and Literature at New York University in the sixties and seventies. Since then, through both formal training and psychotherapeutic practice, he has become an expert in alternative states of mind and hypnosis. Recently using chaos theory and a Socratic-like system of self understanding called the Option Method, he has devoted himself to scholarship and lecturing on them. Fluent in Russian, he has recently been invited to lecture on his views of human happiness in St. Petersburg, Russia. His recent publications include: "Hypnosis and Pain Control: A Quantum Perspective" in *Innovations in Pain Management* (1993); "Psychology of Freedom through Chaos: Reflections in Literature" (*Social Dynamicist*, 3(1), 1992, 1–4), *The Unbearable Wrongness of Being* (1994), and *Joywords: An Invitation to Happiness Through an Introduction to the Option Method* (1994).

PATRICIA L. MURPHY

Patricia is a graduate student at the University of Vermont with a dual concentration in Social Psychology and the History of Psychology. Her chapter in this volume originated as a prolonged discussion between the authors during a seminar on the History of Psychology, and it owes much to the instructor, Robert Lawson, and the other students, especially Carolyn Whitney-Hockman, Larry Rudiger, and Cody Brooks, for both the intensity of their intellectual curiosity and their dedication to issues of human rights. Pat recently returned from Finland, where she was conducting research while on a Fulbright Scholarship.

MINU K. PATEL

Minu is currently Assistant Professor in the College of Nursing and Biostatistician at the Research Resources Center. He has headed the section of Bio-statistics Facility in the Graduate College at the University of Illinois at Chicago since 1972. Prior to this appointment, he served as Biostatistician at Presbyterian St. Luke's Hospital (Rush University), and as Industrial Statistician at Imperial Chemical Industries (UK). In 1994 he was Visiting Professor while on sabbatical in the Department of Statistics at Bombay and Poona Universities in India. He is on the Advisory Editorial Board of *Pediatric Cardiology* and has authored more than thirty articles. His interests are in teaching statistics, conducting time series analyses, mathematically simulating statistical models, and developing computer software.

KARL H. PRIBRAM

Karl initially specialized in neurological surgery and behavioral psychotherapy, but has spent the past four decades in brain/behavior research, which he pursued first at the Yerkes Laboratories of Primate Biology, then at Yale University, and then for thirty years at Stanford University, where he received a lifetime research career award from the National Institute of Health. Upon becoming Emeritus at Stanford, he accepted the position of James P. and Anna King Distinguished Professor at Radford University, where he is supported by the Commonwealth of Virginia's Eminent Scholar Program. He is author of *Plans and the Structure of Behavior* (with George Miller and Eugene Galanter, 1960); *Freud's 'Project' Reassessed* (with Merton Gill, 1976); *Languages of the Brain* (1971); and *Brain and Perception* (1991). He has edited four Penguin volumes on *Brain and Behavior* (1954/1969); a volume of papers by Konrad Lorenz, Wilder Penfield, Holger Hyden and Horace Magoun on the *Biology of Learning* (1969); *Biology of Memory* (with Donald Broadbent, 1970); *Psychophysiology of the Front Lobes* (with Alexander R. Luria, 1973); *Central Processing of Sensory Input*; and four volumes on *The Hippocampus* (with Robert Isaacson, 1975).

PAUL S. PRUEITT

Paul is an Associate at JWK International Corporation, with main offices in the Washington D.C. area. He is leading a team of programmers in the development of an electronically mediated knowledge domain. From 1990 to 1993 he was Research Assistant Professor of Physics at Georgetown University, where he co-directed, with Professor Edward J. Finn, the Neural Network Research Facility (NNRF). In 1992, he received a National Science Foundation award supporting his work on an ecological psychology foundation to computer interfaces. His publications have been in the area of mathematical models of immune networks, neural network models of prefrontal lobe function, non-local knowledge representation, and dissipative systems models of consciousness.

HECTOR C. SABELLI

Hector is a psychiatrist and Professor of Pharmacology at Rush University. Prior to this appointment, he was Professor and Director of the Institute of Pharmacology of the University of Litoral, Argentina, and Professor and Chairman of Pharmacology at the Chicago Medical School. He has received awards in Biological Psychiatry, Neuropharmacology, Psychodrama, and Cybernetics. He has authored numerous articles published in such journals as *Nature, Science, Archives of Internal*

Medicine, American Journal of Psychiatry, and written four books, including *Union of Opposites* (1989). Argentinian born, Hector combines the interests of his parents, Antonio, a physician and philosopher, and his mother, Elena, a physiologist and pharmacist, in his pursuit of physiology as an experimentalist, a clinician, and theorist. Hector writes a weekly column on Clinical Philosophy for Chicago's Hispanic newspaper *La Raza.* His bilingual play, *María* (1992), applies his process theory to issues of social progress; it includes an introduction by Carlos Torre.

LINDA B. SMITH

Linda is Professor of Psychology and Cognitive Science at Indiana University. She has co-edited two recent books on dynamics systems approaches in psychology with Esther Thelen: *A Dynamic Systems Approach to Development* (1994) and *A Dynamic Systems Approach to the Development of Action and Cognition* (1993).

CARLOS ANTONIO TORRE

Carlos is presently a Professor at the School of Education of the City University of New York's Queens College, a member of the New Haven Board of Education, and a Fellow at Yale University, where he served for seven years (until 1991) as Assistant Dean of the College and a member of the Psychology faculty. Prior to this appointment, he was a Professor of Social Work at Northeastern Illinois University and spent a year as a Visiting Professor at the University of Puerto Rico (concurrent with his Yale appointment). He has received several awards for his work in educational psychology, including the "Medal of the Academician" of the Academy of Arts and Sciences of Puerto Rico (to which he was elected in 1987) and the Society for Chaos Theory in Psychology and the Life Sciences' first award for "humanitarian, pioneering contributions." He has several publications on dynamics and the triadic nature of the mind, including a chapter ("Chaos, Creativity, and Innovation: Toward a Dynamical Model of Problem Solving") in R. Robertson and A. Combs' forthcoming *A Chaos Psychology Reader,* and an authored volume, *El Proyecto Cayey: Una Investigación Sobre la Calidad del Pensamiento* (a study on the quality of thinking of freshmen at the University of Puerto Rico's Cayey University College, 1989).

WARREN W. TRYON

Warren is Professor of Psychology at Fordham University. A clinical psychologist, his interest in connectionist neural networks is primarily motivated by his belief that they offer an elegant solution to the mind-body problem and other philosophical schisms that have so long divided psychologists. His publications include three books: an edited volume, *Behavioral Assessment in Behavioral Medicine* (1985); a co-edited book, *Ethics in Applied Developmental Psychology* (with Celia Fisher, 1990); and an authored work, *Activity Measurement in Psychology and Medicine* (1991).

KAREN WALTHALL

Karen is a Holter monitor technician with Associates in Cardiology at Rush-Presbyterian St. Lukes Medical Center. She also coordinates the pacemaker clinic for the practice. She is presently assisting Dr. Sabelli in developing a technique to determine the states of biological systems by using heart-rate variability.

JOSEPH P. ZBILUT

Joseph is Associate Professor of Molecular Biophysics and Physiology at Rush Medical College in Chicago and Research Associate for the Section of Cardiology of VA Hines Hospital in Hines, Illinois. His research is focused on physiological nonlinear dynamics, and he has written chapters for *Nonlinearity in Biology and Medicine* (1988), *Advanced Methods in Physiological System Modeling Vol. 2* (1989), and *Rhythms in Physiological Systems* (1991). Currently he is working on a model of chaos affected by noise at singular points. Preliminary findings, presented at a conference sponsored by the Los Alamos Center for Nonlinear Studies and the Santa Fe Institute, will appear in *Fluctuations and Order: The New Synthesis*, a volume edited by M. Millonas.

ISBN 0-313-28961-1

90000>

EAN

9 780313 289613

HARDCOVER BAR CODE

4152